God's Profound and Mysterious Providence

AS REVEALED IN THE GENEALOGY OF JESUS CHRIST FROM THE TIME OF DAVID TO THE EXILE IN BABYLON

Rev. Abraham Park D.Min., D.D.

PERIPLUS EDITIONS
Singapore • Hong Kong • Indonesia

Published by Periplus Editions (HK) Ltd.

www.periplus.com

Copyright © 2011 Periplus Editions (HK) Ltd.
First Korean edition published by Huisun in 2010. www.pyungkang.com

Photographs © 2011 Hanan Isachar /www.isachar-photography.com

Scripture quotations taken from the New American Standard Bible⁎, Copyright © 1960, 1962, 1963, 1968, 1971, 1972, 1973, 1975, 1977, 1995 by The Lockman Foundation.

ISBN 978-0-7946-0717-3

Distributed by:
North America, Latin America & Europe
Tuttle Publishing
364 Innovation Drive, North Clarendon,
VT 05759-9436 U.S.A.
Tel: 1 (802) 773-8930; Fax: 1 (802) 773-6993
info@tuttlepublishing.com
www.tuttlepublishing.com

Asia Pacific
Berkeley Books Pte. Ltd.
61 Tai Seng Avenue #02-12, Singapore 534167
Tel: (65) 6280-1330; Fax: (65) 6280-6290
inquiries@periplus.com.sg
www.periplus.com

Japan
Tuttle Publishing
Yaekari Building, 3rd Floor, 5-4-12 Osaki,
Shinagawa-ku, Tokyo 141-0032
Tel: (81) 3 5437 0171; Fax: (81) 3 5437 0755
sales@tuttle.co.jp
www.tuttle.co.jp

Indonesia
PT Java Books Indonesia
Jl. Rawa Gelam IV No. 9
Kawasan Industri Pulogadung, Jakarta 13930
Tel: (62) 21 4682-1088; Fax: (62) 21 461-0206
crm@periplus.co.id
www.periplus.co.id

Printed in Singapore

14 13 12 11   10 9 8 7 6 5 4 3 2 1   1109MP

Contents

* As inserts facing inside front cover

List of Abbreviations

Bible Versions

ESV	English Standard Version
KJV	King James Version
NASB	New American Standard Bible
NIV	New International Version
NKJV	New King James Version
NLT	New Living Translation

Foreword

Recently, I received a mail from a pastor that I admire, Rev. Kang-Ro Lee (former moderator of the Reformed Presbyterian Church of Korea). It was a book about the genealogy of Jesus Christ, a common theme about which too many people have written. I did not even open the book and stuck it in a corner of my bookshelf.

Later, I was talking with my old acquaintance and he started to share with me about Rev. Abraham Park's books. Because I had no knowledge of Rev. Park nor had I read his books, I began to be curious about everything he was saying. He said that he had read a newspaper article, which motivated him to go buy and read his books. He is now waiting for the publication of the fourth book in the series.

Then, he urged me, the Old Testament scholar, to read those books. So, I took out his book and read it. In reading the book, I tried to understand the book from the perspective of the author, Rev. Park, who is a minister, and forego the various theories and perspectives proposed by contemporary theologians.

What struck me when I started reading the introduction was his testimony about spending years in a cave on Mt. Jiri in order to study and understand the Word of God. There, he read the Bible and every time he had a realization, he wrote it down on arrowroot leaves, which he bound together with bush-clover stems. These notes later became the sources for his books. I was touched by the fact that there still is a pastor in Korea who reveres and searches through the Word of God today because many Korean pastors these days do not research the Bible, even know how to study the Bible, deeply meditate upon the Word, nor have the zeal to wrestle with the Holy Scriptures for clearer understanding. Setting aside the content of the book, I believe that Rev. Park's sincere and earnest zeal for studying God's Word sets an excellent example for our young pastors today.

First of all, the fact that Rev. Park chose to study about Jesus Christ, who is the essential core of the Bible, and His genealogy in his biblical research itself makes a statement about his books—that they are not of the ordinary. The genealogy of Jesus Christ in Matthew 1:1-17 starts with Abraham, continues through David, and is divided into three periods of

14 generations. Rev. Park chose to analyze each period of the genealogy and use the combined analysis to grasp the flow of redemptive history. The book in review is an exposition of the second period of the genealogy spanning from David to the deportation to Babylon. I was quite amazed that someone who is not a trained scholar of the Bible could so tenaciously and incessantly research a single topic to produce such a vast volume of literature. Rev. Park has dug a very deep well for his entire life. Ultimately, he has poured out his doctrinal and theological beliefs, his faith and spirit, and his fervent zeal into this series of books. I believe the term epic masterpiece has been reserved for exactly such volumes.

In actuality, Rev. Park did not merely dig a deep well. He not only had depth but breadth as well. Under the rubric of the administration of redemptive history, he combined the various pieces of theology and history scattered throughout the Bible and presented a complete picture. He has brought together the stories about the individuals that comprise the genealogy of Jesus Christ in a most vivid and fascinating way. He is a natural storyteller. He does not monotonously narrate events according to their chronology, but structures the stories of the individuals in the style of expository sermon by putting appropriate titles for each section, making it possible to get a general picture of the whole just by looking at those titles and subtitles. The messages that the author conveys through the lives of the individual personages penetrate the reader's heart like an arrow. His writing style is elegant, savory, and charismatic, entrancing the reader until the last page. I think that this is one of the prominent features of this book. In fact, I teach my students that we preachers need to be good storytellers; however, it is difficult to preach on the historical books of the Bible although there are many great subject matters about which we can preach. In light of this, Rev. Park presents to us younger pastors a new model for teaching and preaching the historical books.

Moreover, the "excursus" charts and diagrams about the chronology of the kings are distinctive. They are clearly organized for laypersons, seminary students, ministers and anyone as useful reference tools to study the books of Samuel, Kings and Chronicles.

Our Lord Jesus Christ is profoundly great and magnanimous that it is not an easy task to come to a complete understanding and knowledge of Him. Many have wandered down countless paths seeking for the proper knowledge of the Lord, but not many have succeeded. We follow the path that our forefathers of faith have discovered to believe and follow Jesus Christ. Rev. Park has found Christ through this path called "genealogy." He has pioneered a new route to reach the summit, who is Christ, and he has written these books to be our guide. I believe that this route that Rev. Park discovered is one of the definite shortcuts for all Christians to reach Christ. Therefore, I recommend this book to all who love Christ and desire to know Him. I also strongly recommend that we ministers, who are to lead the way toward Christ, especially read this book and have it handy in our libraries as reference.

Dr. Seock-Tae Sohn
President Emeritus, Reformed Theological Seminary of Korea
President, Korea Evangelical Society of Old Testament Studies
Chairman of the Board, Evangelical Students Fellowship

Introduction

The Old and New Testaments, the Word of God, reveal the "administration of the mystery" (Eph 3:9) which had been hidden for ages in God. This administration is the blueprint of the redemptive history which had been planned before the ages for the salvation of mankind. The history of redemption is the history of God's administration after the fall to save His chosen people in Jesus Christ (Eph 1:4-5). At the center of the "administration" is our Lord Jesus Christ, who is the mystery of God and the hope of glory (Col 1:27; 2:2). This mystery had been hidden from the past ages and generations, but now it has been manifested to His saints (Col 1:26), and in Him are hidden all the treasures of wisdom and knowledge (Col 2:3).

This is why the Bible looks to Jesus Christ, testifies of Jesus Christ, and is fulfilled only through Jesus Christ. John 5:39 states, "It is these that testify about Me," and Luke 24:27 also states "He explained to them the things concerning Himself in all the Scriptures" (Luke 24:44).

The genealogy of Jesus Christ (Matt 1:1-17) is the most concise synopsis of Jesus Christ, who is the central figure in all 66 books of the Bible, and is thus the focal point of the redemptive administration. Therefore, without understanding the genealogy of Jesus Christ one cannot know Jesus Christ fully and can miss the overarching thread of meaning in God's grand history of redemption that begins in the book of Genesis and is fulfilled in the book of Revelation.

The third and fourth books in the History of Redemption series examine Jesus Christ's genealogy. The third book mainly discusses the first period of Jesus Christ's genealogy which encompasses the history from Abraham to David. This book, the fourth book, mainly discusses the history that pertains to the second period of Jesus Christ's genealogy. In particular, the third book revealed that most of the 430-year period of slavery in Egypt that spans from Ram to Amminadab was omitted and that approximately 300 years of the period of Judges that spans from Salmon to Boaz was omitted as well. Much encouragement poured forth on the above findings that this was a novel insight unprecedented in the history of Christianity. All of this is due to the grace given to this unworthy servant who is lesser than the scum of this earth; therefore I give all the glory to the living God in heartfelt thanksgiving.

When I began my ministry, my knowledge of the Word of God was so shallow that I went into a cave in Mount Jiri. During the three years and six months I was there I did nothing but pray and read the Bible. As I delved into reading only the Bible, I gained so much understanding through the powerful illumination of the Holy Spirit. I would record in writing every time I was enlightened. There were times I lacked paper and so I would write on the arrowroot leaves and skewer them onto bush clover stems. Later, when I obtained manuscript paper I would organize my writings and copy them onto the paper. Through such repetition, by the time I came down the mountain I had a stack of manuscripts that were as tall as my height. Even now when I look at those manuscripts, my eyes well up with tears with gratitude for the great grace of God. Each and every letter that was written on the large arrowroot leaves was trans-ferred onto manuscript paper; and when those began to deteriorate, the writing would be transferred again to notebooks. Through such countless repetitions the History of Redemption series is at last published. Truly I can only give thanks.

This book is not a theological analysis, an exegetical commentary, or an expository outline. With the heart of the shepherd who cherishes a single soul more than the whole world (Matt 16:26; 18:14), I have put together the living and active Word of God which I have preached from the pulpit of Pyungkang Cheil Church while daily praying on my knees. Through the help of God, if something was deemed profitable for the congregation members, I would not hesitate to share the Word day and night without rest (Acts 20:20, 27, 31). I poured all my heart and strength into fully revealing through the Old and New Testaments the redemptive history and Jesus Christ, who is the administration of the mystery hidden therein. In order to proclaim solely the Word of the living God, I embraced this manuscript and underwent spiritual battles through many sleepless nights. I examined each and every verse in great detail as if I were counting every downy hair on a body. On a larger scale, I also put forth all my strength in viewing those verses from a redemptive historical perspective so the context would not be lost.

My earnest desire is that through the History of Redemption series all my brethren would understand God's administration of the mystery, so that they could mature to the fullness of Christ (Eph 4:13-15; Heb

5:12-14; 6:1-2) and stand firm in the faith (Rom 1:11; 4:20; 1 Cor 1:6, 8; 2 Cor 1:21; 1 Pet 5:10). That is because this is the consistent theme of the Bible and the calling for this generation. Apostle Paul proclaimed, "But thanks be to God, who gives us the victory through our LORD Jesus Christ. Therefore, my beloved brethren, be steadfast, immovable, always abounding in the work of the LORD, knowing that your toil is not in vain in the LORD" (1 Cor 15:57-58). Second Samuel 23:5 states, ". . . For He has . . . ordered in all things, and secured," and Romans 16:25-27 states, "Now to Him who is able to establish you . . . to the only wise God." I earnestly hope that this book would aid in further establishing the faith of the saints not only in the churches of Korea but all churches throughout the world.

By all means, it is not my desire that this book would become my personal work. I sincerely pray and hope that every person reads and understands this book would become its author.

Above all, I give my most sincere thanks to God's benevolent helping hand which has allowed the History of Redemption series to be published through the dedication, ceaseless prayers, and hard work of the congregation of Pyungkang Cheil Church. Additionally, I pour out my heart of gratitude to my fellow workers who have dedicated themselves without fame or recognition, to soften up my old-fashioned expressions to fit contemporary literary styles, as well as to schematize the complicated and vast material I had organized into charts for an easier understanding.

I earnestly hope that in the remainder of our lives we would always exalt Christ alone in our bodies (Phil 1:20) and that this book would be used greatly in fully revealing the administration of the mystery which had been hidden for ages in God (Eph 3:9).

朴 润 植
Abraham Park

Rev. Abraham Park
October 3, 2009
Servant of Jesus Christ,
On the sojourner's path to heaven

עת לכל בר דעת דרך המסעות ארבעים שנה במדבר יהודה וחצב ואורך של ארץ הקדושה מנהר ב

עמלק

מדבר צין והוא קדש

ים המלח

עתר
מקדה

עיר כרמל

שבט

מדבר סיני

קדשברנע

מדבר פארן

מדבר שור

שבט
שמעון

שבט

ארץ פלשתם

ארך גשן

אלכסנדרי

לוח המסעות במדבר
אשר על פי ה׳ יסעו ועל פי החנו

טו׳ רחמה	רט׳ חרהדגד	א׳ רעמסס
טז׳ רמןפרץ	ל׳ ייבתה	ב׳ סכת
יז׳ לבנה	לא׳ עברנה	ג׳ אתם
יח׳ רסת	לב׳ עציןגבר	ד׳ פיהחירת
יט׳ קהלתה	לג׳ מדברצין	ה׳ מרה
ך׳ הרספר	לד׳ הרההר	ו׳ אילם
כא׳ חרדה	לה׳ צלמנה	ז׳ ים סוף
כב׳ מקהלת	לו׳ פונן	ח׳ מדברסין
כג׳ החרת	לז׳ אבת	ט׳ רפקה
כד׳ תרח	לח׳ דיבןגר	יו׳ אלוש
כה׳ מחקה	לט׳ עלמן דבל׳	יא׳ רפידם
כו׳ חשמנה	מ׳ הרי עברים	יב׳ מדברסיני
כז׳ מסרות	מא׳ ערבתמואב	יג׳ קברתהתאו
כח׳ בני יעקן		יד׳ חצרת

PART ONE

The Eternal Covenant and the Providence of God

CHAPTER 1

God's Administration of Redemption

The themes that run throughout the entire 66 books of the Bible are the absolute sovereignty and providence of God the Creator and salvation and restoration of fallen mankind. The means and basis of this salvation is the redemption through the cross of Jesus Christ.

In order to save the sinner and restore the entire created order, God has indwelt in time and space with sinful mankind. This history of God's indwelling and the operation of His providence within the natural world is called "redemptive history."

The administration of redemptive history corresponds to the structural framework of a building and to the spine of the human body. Therefore, studying and examining the administration of redemptive history is a most crucial work. Just as one needs to be at the top of a high mountain to get a picturesque panorama of nature, one needs to penetrate through the entire Bible using a redemptive-historical perspective to get a clear understanding of its meaning without diverting from the Divine Author's will.

The word *redemption* in "the history of redemption" means recovery of ownership by paying the price (Matt 20:28) or liberation and release of a slave or prisoner who was in shackles (Rom 3:24). Before we were redeemed through Jesus Christ, we were "imprisoned" under sin as one awaiting execution in a completely dark and sealed off prison cell (συγκλείω, *synkleiō*; Gal 3:22). Moreover, we were spiritually "held captive" due to sin and our every move was under surveillance (φρουρέω, *phroureō* ; Gal 3:23). Under such a cruel penal state, our tragic, hopeless lives were merely progressing toward the day of death which had already been set. It was the redemption of the cross of Jesus Christ which had at once set free the humankind who were living under the shadow of this inevitable death (Rom 8:1-2).

God had sent His one and only Son, Jesus Christ, who was without sin and blemish, in the likeness of sinful flesh to condemn sin by dying on the cross, thereby bearing our sins in His body (Rom 8:3; 1 Pet 2:24). Therefore, we have been redeemed and our sins have been atoned for by His precious blood (Eph 1:7; 1 Pet 1:18-19).

The precious blood of the First Coming Christ was the "ransom" money paid out to redeem us from sin and death (Exod 30:11-16; 1 Tim 2:6, Ref Num 3:44-51; 1 Cor 6:20; 7:23) and this redemption which He purchased with His blood (Acts 20:28; 1 Cor 6:20, 7:23) was achieved completely at once (Heb 7:27; 9:12-14). Jesus Christ carried the cross and bore the sins of this world to become the Lamb of atonement as was administration decreed before the ages (John 1:29; 1 Cor 5:7). Moreover, it is said to be a "ransom for many" (Matt 20:28; Mark 10:45; Rom 5:15; 1 Tim 2:6; Heb 2:9-10; 9:28) signifying that the ransom paid out by Jesus Christ is a universal grace effective for all who have been predestined for salvation (Acts 13:48; Gal 3:13-14; 1 Tim 2:6; Titus 2:14) and is effectual for all time through eternity (Heb 9:12; 10:12). This redemptive history, which unfolds with Jesus Christ at its core, progresses and is accomplished according to God's administration of redemption.

1. The administration of redemption

"God's administration of redemption" is God's work of management according to His will that He has predestined from before the ages and specifically planned for the salvation of His chosen people. In Greek, the word *administration* is οἰκονομία (*oikonomia*), which is a combination of the words οἶκος (*oikos* – home) and νέμω (*nemō*- to parcel out, to assign, to manage, to administer). Together, the word signifies "systematic planning of an activity or work," "governing of the heavens and the earth," and "abilities born out of experience, and skills."

God's administration is the driving force that leads this universe and the history of mankind, and it provides us with the certain goal toward which the past, present and future of our history is headed. God's redemptive history does not happen accidentally nor is it derived incidentally from the situation at hand. It is achieved according to God's administration as decreed before the ages (Isa 43:12-13; 46:10; Eph 3:9).

Administration as it appears in the Bible can be classified into two types. The first type signifies the plan and management of someone in authority (Eph 1:9; 3:2, 9). The second refers to the duty and the stewardship of someone under authority (Luke 16:2-4; 1 Cor 9:17; Gal 4:2;

Col 1:25). Ultimately, "administration" refers to the order and operation of all creation as they follow the Creator's plan of redemption. It also refers to God's administration and management of His time. And for us, His creatures, it signifies the stewardship which has been entrusted to us.

2. The types of administration in the Bible

The Apostle Paul has proclaimed five types of God's administration of redemption.

(1) Administration of God which is by faith

First Timothy 1:4 states, "nor to pay attention to myths and endless genealogies, which give rise to mere speculation rather than furthering the administration of God which is by faith." Here, we see the phrase, "the administration of God which is by faith."

The subject of the administration is God. There is no place for man's administration; there can only be God's administration because the creature cannot manage or take care of the entire universe. Moreover, God's administration is in faith; this administration cannot be realized or comprehended outside of faith. Only by faith can we understand, witness, and follow God's administration.

(2) Stewardship of God's grace

Ephesians 3:2 states, "If indeed you have heard of the stewardship of God's grace which was given to me for you." Here, "stewardship of God's grace" indicates that the Apostle Paul was able to become a minister of the gospel solely due to God's grace (Eph 3:7). Furthermore, it also means that it was only through grace that Paul was able to know the mystery of Christ (Eph 3:2-4). And finally, it refers to the fact that even Gentiles have become the objects of salvation through God's grace (Eph 3:6).

Therefore, the Apostle Paul is testifying that God had bestowed grace on him so that he may know God's administration of salvation, that he may participate in the ministry of His plan, and that he may be able to manage the duty given to him (Eph 3:8). How can we, who are like the refuse of all things (1 Cor 4:13), consider and survey the grand administration of the most high and great God? We can only know the administration of God through grace (1 Cor 15:10), and by that grace which has been prepared before the ages, we are saved (Eph 2:8).

(3) Administration of the mystery

Ephesians 3:8-9 states, "To me, the very least of all saints, this grace was given, to preach to the Gentiles the unfathomable riches of Christ, and to bring to light what is the administration of the mystery which for ages has been hidden in God who created all things."

This passage indicates that God's administration is a hidden mystery. And it has been hidden since "the past ages and generations" (Col 1:26), "for ages" (Eph 3:9), and "before the ages" (1 Cor 2:7). Moreover, this mystery has been "hidden in God"; therefore, no man can fathom that which would remain veiled in mystery unless God reveals it.

The phrase, *bring to light* in Ephesians 3:9 is φωτίζω (*phōtizō*) in Greek, which means "to brighten up," "to shine," and "to illuminate." Therefore, God's redemptive-historical administration of mystery cannot be fathomed by the wisdom of man, but only when it is opened up through the illumination of the Holy Spirit, can we clearly comprehend it (Ps 119:18, 130).

(4) "Administration suitable to the fullness of the times"

Ephesians 1:9-10 says, "He made known to us the mystery of His will, according to His kind intention which He purposed in Him with a view to an administration suitable to the fullness of the times, that is, the summing up of all things in Christ, things in the heavens and things on the earth."

Here the word *times* in Greek is καιρός (*kairos*) which signifies "a set time," "a decisive epoch," or "an opportune time when a special event takes place" and a certain goal is achieved within God's redemptive history. This is stating the fact that the administration of God, which has been hidden in mystery, will not be revealed unless that decisive time has been reached. The mystery of God is Jesus Christ (Col 2:2). The "administration suitable to the fullness of the times" has been achieved in the first coming of Jesus Christ (Mark 1:15) and will be consummated in the Second Advent. Ephesians 1:10 expresses this as the "summing up of all things in Jesus Christ," signifying the consummation of the "administration suitable to the fullness of the times" at Jesus' Second Coming when God restores all creation in the universe.

(5) "Stewardship from God bestowed on me"

Colossians 1:25 says, "Of this church I was made a minister according to the stewardship from God bestowed on me for your benefit, so that I might fully carry out the preaching of the word of God." Also Ephesians 3:2 speaks of the "stewardship of God's grace which was given to me." God has given to the Apostle Paul the "administration of God," the "stewardship of God's grace," the "administration of mystery," and the "administration suitable to the fullness of the times." God gave His administrations to Paul, so that the Word of God may be fulfilled through him (Col 1:25). Therefore, the Apostle Paul became a minister of the church not by his own will but only according to the administration of God. And because Paul had understood this, was he able to rejoice in his sufferings for the saints, fill up in his body the remaining afflictions of Christ for the church, and strive with all his energy according to the workings of God in him (Col 1:24-25, 29).

The redemptive-historical administration of God which has been hidden for ages and generations is now revealed through the Apostle Paul to His saints (Col 1:25-26). It is the ministry of the church to make known the hidden mystery of God. The Bible states in Ephesians 3:10 that the "manifold wisdom of God" is made known through the church. Therefore, the church must make known and proclaim to the world the One who is the mystery of God and our glorious hope, the Lord Jesus Christ (Col 1:27; 2:2).

All the saints and churches on earth are the glorious ministers of "the administration of God which is by faith," "stewardship of God's grace," "administration of the mystery," "administration suitable to the fullness of the times," and the "stewardship from God bestowed on" each of us. The reason we breathe and make our living is for the calling to reveal God's administration of mystery. The Apostle Paul, who was called "to bring to light what is the administration of mystery" (Eph 3:9), hoped that the Word of God may be fulfilled through his ministry (Col 1:24-25). Therefore, the Apostle Paul always worked fervently and willingly with the "zeal of God" according to His desires (2 Cor 11:2). Even in afflictions confronting death (2 Cor 1:8-10), Paul fulfilled his lifelong calling as an apostle to boldly proclaim the mystery of the Gospel (Eph 6:19). The Apostle's earnest expectation in all his life was that only Jesus Christ may be exalted through him whether he lives or dies (Phil 1:20). Like the Apostle Paul, we, who have been called as ministers of the Gospel, must also fathom God's administration of mystery, and fulfill the duty of proclaiming the Gospel according to the stewardship bestowed on each of us until the four corners of the earth are filled with the Word of God (Rom 15:19).

CHAPTER 2

The Eternal Covenant and Providence

God had historically established Eden in the east and stationed Adam there (Gen 2:8). Then, God told him, "but from the tree of the knowledge of good and evil you shall not eat, for in the day that you eat from it you will surely die" (Gen 2:17). However, Eve had eaten of the forbidden fruit from the tree of the knowledge of good and evil and gave some to her husband Adam, resulting in the Fall (Gen 3:6).

History of redemption, which outlines the salvation of fallen mankind, progressed according to God's administration. Since God's covenants are the links connecting redemptive history, one can say that the history of redemption is linked by a series of covenants.

The core of redemptive history is the covenant about the Messiah and its fulfillment. The core and final revelation of that covenant is Jesus Christ. Therefore, history of redemption is a "covenantal history." Moreover, covenantal history is the history of the immutable Word of God because covenants are established by God's Word, and God, the host of the covenants, is the Word (John 1:1). Our Lord Jesus Christ is the Word who became flesh and dwelt among us and He is the consummate flower of redemptive history (John 1:14). The Word is different from secular truths. There is no salvation in ideologies, philosophies, scholarly learning, other religions and other secular truths. Salvation comes only through the one who came as the Incarnate Word, Jesus Christ (John 14:6, Acts 4:12).

Moreover, the *Word* accompanies redemptive history and this *Word* is the principal agent which leads the entire history of redemption. Where the *Word* flourishes, where the *Word* is moving mightily, that is where the redemptive work of God will take place (Ref Acts 4:4; 6:7; 12:24; 17:11-12; 19:20; Col 1:5-6).

At each generation of redemptive history, God had renewed His covenants. The first revelation of the covenant was glimpsed in the promise of the Seed of the woman in Genesis 3:15 after which the covenant of God had progressed and developed through the Noahic covenant (Gen 6:18; 9:8-17), the Abrahamic covenant (Gen 12:1-3, 7; 13:14-18; 15:12-21; 17:9-14; 18:10; 22:15-18), the Sinai covenant (Exod 20:22 to 23:33; 24:7), the Davidic covenant (2 Sam 7:12-16; 1 Chr 17:11-14), and the new covenant in Jeremiah (Jer 31:31-34). God will fulfill the covenant of life and peace (Mal 2:5) and the covenant of peace (Isa 54:10; Num 25:12-13) to those who remember and hold on to the aforementioned covenants.

These covenants are not only valid in their own generations but they are effective eternally. Therefore, the covenants of God are the driving forces that lead redemptive history to its consummation and are the basis for the specific redemptive activities called the providence of God. What are the distinctive characteristics of these covenants which are effective until the end of the ages?

1. It is a sovereign covenant.

Fallen mankind (Ps 14:3; Jer 17:9; Rom 3:10) is in no way qualified to establish a covenant with God. Nonetheless, God who is greater than all (John 10:29), in order to accomplish the great plan to save His elect, unilaterally established His covenant with us.[1] Thus, the covenant is the result of God's sovereign grace and in them are contained the immutable guarantee that He will accomplish His eternal purpose at all cost.

The Bible expresses the sovereign covenant in the following ways.

(1) "My covenant"

The Bible says in Exodus 6:5, "I have remembered My covenant" and in Joshua 7:11 that Israel has "transgressed My covenant." Likewise, many verses in the Bible refer to the covenants as "My covenant" (Lev 26:15; 1 Kgs 11:11; Ps 89:28; Isa 54:10; 56:4, 6; 59:21; Jer 33:21; Mal 2:4, 5).

Genesis 6:18 says, "I establish My covenant with you." Leviticus 26:42 says, "I will remember My covenant with Jacob, and I will remember also My covenant with Isaac, and My covenant with Abraham as well." There are many more places in the Bible which speak of "My covenant" (Gen 9:9, 15; 17:2, 4, 7, 9-10, 13-14, 19, 21; Exod 19:5; Deut 31:20; Ps 50:16; 89:34; 132:12; Jer 31:32; 34:18; Ezek 16:62; 17:19; 44:7; Hos 8:1; Rom 11:27; Heb 8:9).

(2) "Your covenant"

The psalmist, as he was praying for a swift rescue of crisis-ridden Israel, pleaded, "we have not dealt falsely with Your covenant" (Ps 44:17). The prophet Jeremiah in interceding for the rebellious people of Judah entreated, "Remember and do not annul Your covenant with us" (Jer 14:21). The expression "Your covenant" also appears in Deuteronomy 33:9 and 1 Kings 19:10, 14.

(3) "The covenant of God (the LORD)"

Second Chronicles 34:32 states that the inhabitants of Jerusalem obeyed the "covenant of God" in order to recover their faith during King Josiah's time. And there are many more verses in the Bible which speak of the "covenant of God" (Lev 2:13; Ps 78:10; Prov 2:17) or the "covenant of the LORD" (Deut 29:12; Josh 7:15; 1 Kgs 8:21; Jer 22:9).

All of these expressions about the covenant teach us that the host of the covenants is God and all the covenants were established through God's sovereign grace.

2. It is an eternal covenant.

The eternal covenant that God has established is an immutable covenant which remains steadfast through time. The covenants that God has ratified with people are not only valid in their own time but will remain effective through eternity. The covenant remains valid until the content of its promise has been fully accomplished.

Genesis 9:16 says, "When the bow is in the cloud, then I will look upon it, to remember the everlasting covenant between God and every living creature of all flesh that is on the earth." Here, the word "everlasting" in Hebrew is עוֹלָם ('ôlām), which signifies "eternity" in the sense perpetual time and perfection.

God had established an eternal covenant with Abraham (Gen 17:7, 13, 19) as well as with the Israelites of the exodus (Exod 31:16; Lev 24:8; 1 Chr 16:17).

The God of peace had brought Jesus Christ back from the dead through the "blood of the eternal covenant" (Heb 13:20). The world will be judged in the end time because it has broken the everlasting covenant (Isa 24:5) whereas the people of God will be restored to life because God has established the everlasting covenant (Isa 55:3; Ezek 16:60; 37:26). In the last days, God will establish the covenant of peace to be an everlasting covenant (Ezek 34:25; 37:26).

This everlasting covenant is described in Psalm 105:8 as "The word which He commanded to a thousand generations." Here, "thousand generations" is אֶלֶף דּוֹר (*'elep dôr*) in Hebrew and does not denote a literal 1,000 generations but is an expression symbolizing eternity (Exod 20:6; Deut 7:9). Therefore, the phrase, "The word which He commanded to a thousand generations," means that God's covenant is eternal. In Psalm 105:10, it is expressed as "Then He confirmed it to Jacob for a statute, to Israel as an everlasting covenant."

What blessings will the covenantal people enjoy when the everlasting covenant is fulfilled?

First, we will be ordered and secured in all things.

Second Samuel 23:5 states, "Truly is not my house so with God? For He has made an everlasting covenant with me, ordered in all things, and secured; for all my salvation and all my desire, will He not indeed make it grow?" This shows us that through the covenant, all things will work together for good and that we will prosper in all respects (Rom 8:28; 3 John 1:2), ultimately to achieve perfect salvation.

Second, we will be joined to God.

Jeremiah 50:5 states, "Come, let us join ourselves to the Lord in an everlasting covenant that will never be forgotten" (ESV). This is a blessing where God never leaves our sides but takes care of us until the end. It is also a blessing where God enables us to fear Him and to never leave him (Jer 32:40). Consequently, God will become our God and we will become His own people (Jer 31:33).

3. It is a covenant of God's oath.

God's covenants are eternally effective because they are covenants of His oath.

When God established His covenant with Abraham, Isaac, and Jacob, He swore it as an oath (Gen 22:16-18; 24:7; 26:3; 50:24; Exod 6:8; 32:13; Num 11:12; Deut 1:8, 35; 4:31; 6:10, 18-19, 23; 7:8, 12-13; 8:1, 18; 9:5; 10:11; 11:9, 21; 13:17; 19:8; 26:3, 15; 28:11; 29:13; 30:20; 31:7, 20; Josh 1:6; 5:6; 21:43-44; Judg 2:1; Neh 9:15; Jer 11:5; 16:15;

32:22; Ezek 20:28, 42; 47:14; Mic 7:20). When he ratified the covenant through Moses at the Plains of Moab, He also did it with an oath (Deut 29:12). Also, when God made the covenant with David, it was done with an oath (Ps 89:3-4, 34-35, 49; 132:11). Psalm 89 repeatedly states, "Once I have sworn" (Ps 89:35) and "Which you swore to David" (Ps 89:49).[2]

The verb *to swear* in Hebrew is שָׁבַע (*šābaʿ*), which originally means to "promise by repeating seven times," signifying a promise which must be kept. Therefore, an oath is a solemn declaration of the necessity of keeping a promise. If a human oath is important, then God's is all the more so. In man's case, a change of circumstance or presence of other factors can always bring about a change of the human heart. However, what God has sworn by oath will never be altered or annulled (Ps 110:4), but without fail, it will be accomplished as promised. As night and day cannot be switched, God's covenant can never be broken (Jer 33:20-21).

That is why Psalm 132:11 states, "The Lord swore to David a sure oath from which he will not turn back" (ESV). What God has faithfully sworn can never be repealed no matter how Satan may try to interfere; His administration of redemptive history will surely be accomplished. Therefore, the saints who hold onto God's covenants will triumph under any kind of tribulation, distress, persecution, famine, nakedness, peril or sword (Rom 8:35-39). This is so because God will certainly not forget the covenants He has sworn by oath (Deut 4:31), but will keep them (Deut 7:12), firmly establish them (Ps 89:28), and not violate them (Ps 89:34), and perpetually fulfill them(Deut 8:18; Ps 105:9-10; Jer 11:5).

4. It is a covenant that God remembers.

God has said that He will surely keep the covenants He has made with our forefathers (Ps 105:8; 106:45; 111:5; Jer 14:21; Ezek 16:60; Luke 1:72). In Genesis 9:15-16, God says, "I will remember My covenant … remember the everlasting covenant." In Leviticus 26:45, He also states, "But I will remember for them the covenant with their ancestors, whom I brought out of the land of Egypt in the sight of the nations, that I might be their God. I am the Lord."

What does it mean that God will remember?
First, it means that He will never forget the covenant.

The verb *to remember* in Hebrew is זָכַר (*zākar*) which means "to mark" or "mention," so as to not forget. In Psalm 74:22-23, the words *remember* and *forget not* are used synonymously in comparison to one another.

Why did God not completely destroy the southern kingdom of Judah but allow them to return from the Babylonian captivity even though the kings of Judah have transgressed against Him? It is because God remembered His covenant with David. Second Chronicles 21:7 states, "Yet the LORD was not willing to destroy the house of David because of the covenant which He had made with David, and since He had promised to give a lamp to him and his sons forever."

Therefore, God will carry out the covenants and bestow lovingkindness upon those who remember and keep the covenants to a thousand generations (Deut 7:9). Moreover, His mercy will be from everlasting to everlasting (Ps 103:17-18), and He will answer with lovingkindness and truth (Ps 25:10). However, He does not care for those who do not remember the covenant (Lev 26:14-20; Heb 8:9). In Leviticus 26:18, the Bible states that those who break the covenant will be punished seven times more for their sins.

Second, it means that God will be merciful.

Luke 1:72 says, "To show mercy toward our fathers, And to remember His holy covenant." Here, remembering the covenant and showing mercy are used synonymously and in Luke 1:71, the term *salvation* is also used to mean the same thing.

God saved the Israelites from 430 years of slavery in Egypt because He remembered His covenant and had mercy on them. Exodus 2:24-25 says, "So God heard their groaning; and God remembered His covenant with Abraham, Isaac, and Jacob. God saw the sons of Israel, and God took notice of them" (Exod 6:5-7). In the last days, God will also save us completely from the hands of Satan because He remembers His covenant.

Ultimately, all covenants are God's grace. First, it is God's grace that established the covenants. The Bible says in Isaiah 55:3, "And I will make an everlasting covenant with you, according to the faithful mercies shown to David." Next, God bestows His grace because of the covenants He has established (2 Kgs 13:23). Moreover, God's grace is given in the process of His keeping the covenants (1 Kgs 8:23; 2 Chr 6:14). Therefore, the beginning, the process and the end of the covenants are all through the God's grace.

In order to become His covenantal people, we must humbly seek God's grace. The great gift of grace which Christ brings at His return will be given to such people (1 Pet 1:13; Jas 4:6).

CHAPTER 3

God's Providence and Everlasting Lovingkindness

God's administration proceeds through the covenants. The covenants are important links and the means of accomplishing redemptive history. God performs specific activities within redemptive history to fulfill His covenants once and for all. And these activities are His "providence."

The dictionary defines *providence* as the "principle which governs the natural world," or "God's will or grace which governs all things in the world."

In Hebrew it is רָאָה (*rā'â*), which means "to prepare beforehand" (Gen 22:8), and in Greek it is πρόνοια (*pronoia*), which is a combination of the words πρό (*pro*, "before") and νοέω (*noeo*, "to think"). This word literally denotes "foresight" which gradually developed to mean "providence."

Providence is God's continued exercise of authority over all things in order to achieve their appointed end—the fulfillment of all things according to God's plan. In other words, providence is God's concrete activity which He performs in order to achieve the goal of redemption. It indicates God's active and sovereign intervention in all things that take place in this world until His plan to save the sinner is fulfilled.

1. The method and sphere of God's providence

Broadly, there are three methods through which God's providence bestows benefits to mankind and the entire universe. *Preservation* is God's caring and maintenance of His creation through His Word of authority (Neh 9:6; Acts 17:28; Col 1:17; Heb 1:3). *Concurrence* is the divine activity in which God sovereignly controls and moves the thoughts and actions of men in order to realize His will (Rom 8:28; Phil 2:13). *Government* is God's rule of all creation to fully accomplish the salvation of the elect (Ps 103:19; 145:13).

The sphere of providence transcends time and space, and there is nowhere within creation where its effect is not felt. All humans (Ps 31:15; 139:16), every ethnicity and nation (Deut 32:8; Acts 17:26), every star in outer space (Isa 40:26; Ps 147:3), the sun and the atmosphere and all natural phenomena and climate conditions that take place within (Job 37:6, 10-12; Ps 147:15-19), the creatures that dwell on earth including the birds of the air down to the most insignificant microbe and even the most minute of places are all included in the sphere of God's providence. Not even a sparrow will fall to the ground apart from God (Matt 10:29). Therefore, things that may seem trivial and incidental and even occurrences that may immediately seem contradictory are all, in a mysterious way, under the sphere of God's providence.

Moreover, God sovereignly controls not only past history and present events but even the things that will take place in the future (Dan 2:21; Acts 17:26). It may have seemed outwardly that the kings of southern Judah and northern Israel were ruling; but in the background, it was God's providence at work.

God's redemptive providence, predestined for the salvation of His elect, is perfect and flawless, grounded in His administration of salvation (Deut 32:4). It will not be altered in mid-course for there is no being in heaven or on earth that can thwart God's decree and God will surely accomplish all His desired end (Rom 8:35-39).

> **Psalm 33:11** The counsel of the LORD stands forever, the plans of His heart from generation to generation.

2. God's lovingkindness that governs the universe, history, and mankind

In this world, the universe exists spatially whereas history spans temporally, and these two are converged and condensed in the "life of an individual." Psalm 136, starting with the account of the creation of the universe in Genesis, goes on to recall the redemption of the chosen people in the events of the exodus and the conquering of Canaan under Joshua. The psalm even reminisces about the grace of God in saving the individual from his low estate. And in doing so, the psalmist inserts the refrain of thanksgiving, "His lovingkindness is everlasting," in all 26 verses of the psalm. It is especially meaningful that the psalmist has praised the grace of God in three thematic sections dealing with the universe (Ps 136:1-9), history (Ps 136:10-22), and the individual life (Ps 136:23-26).

(1) God's everlasting lovingkindness which governs the entire universe

The author of Psalm 136 has witnessed God's lovingkindness which fills the universe. *Lovingkindness* speaks of God's love and mercy toward the sinner. The word indicates the "benevolent and affectionate heart" of someone who is higher in status directed toward someone in a lower status (Gen 19:19; Rom 11:22). Psalm 136 speaks of God as the "God of gods" (v. 2), "LORD of lords" (v. 3), "Him who alone does great wonders" (v. 4), "Him who made the heavens with skill" (v. 5), "Him who spread out the earth above the waters" (v. 6), and "Him who made…the sun to rule by day" and "the moon and stars to rule by night" (vv. 7, 8, 9).

Even today, the sun, the moon and the stars are orbiting in perfect alignment according to God's will. The perfect harmony of the entire created order is an expression of God's eternal wisdom, power and lovingkindness toward humankind.

The entire universe and all that is in it was created by God out of nothing (*ex nihilo*) in six days through His Word of power. As we gaze by faith upon this created order, we must realize that creation has lost its truth, goodness, and beauty due to the transgression and Fall of mankind (Gen 3:17; Rom 8:22). Through the infinite variety that is present in nature, we must be able to perceive that all creation is God's immutable "sign of lovingkindness" toward mankind (Rom 1:20; Ps 19:1-4). The benevolent will of God, who loves all humans, is clearly seen in the entire created order (Rom 1:20).

We must be able to see in creation God's existence, glory, power, love, wisdom, truth, and redemption of mankind; like creation, thanksgiving and praise must not leave our lips even for a moment (Eph 5:19; Col 3:16).

"Give thanks to the LORD, for He is good, for His lovingkindness is everlasting." (Ps 136:1)

(2) God's everlasting lovingkindness which controls the history of mankind

The universe is unfathomably vast that it may actually be too difficult to connect each presence of God's lovingkindness manifested in it to the individual. On the other hand, His lovingkindness that is present in human history is able to arouse a more abundant thanksgiving.

Psalm 136:10-22 refer to God as Him "who smote the Egyptians in their firstborn" (v. 10), "who brought Israel out from their midst . . . with a strong hand and an outstretched arm" (v. 11-12), "who led His people through the wilderness" (v. 16), "who smote great kings" (v. 17), who "slew mighty kings" like "Sihon, king of the Amorites" and "Og, king of Bashan" (vv. 18, 19, 20), who "gave their land as a heritage" (v. 21), and who gave "even a heritage to Israel His servant" (v. 22).

This is a historical account that applies not only to the Israelites. It points to God's great and compassionate work, that which was predestined before the ages to send the Seed of woman (Gen 3:15) for the redemption of all mankind living under sin. World history does not meaninglessly flow any which way. Even now, history is forcefully advancing toward its appointed goal, driven by God's fervent love and zeal to complete the salvation of His elect (2 Kgs 19:31; Isa 9:7; 37:32).

"Give thanks to the LORD, for He is good, for His lovingkindness is everlasting."

(3) God's everlasting lovingkindness which governs the life of the individual

The great God who governs the entire universe and history also governs the life of each individual. How can we express in words all of the grace that we, as individuals, have received throughout our lifetime according to God's providence? The psalmist exhorts us to give thanks to God in Psalm 136, "who remembered us in our low estate" (v. 23), who "rescued us from our adversaries" (v. 24), and "who gives food to all flesh" (v. 25). At the least, we have sustained our flesh through the consumption of food; therefore, we cannot say that God's everlasting lovingkindess is insignificant. We, who have come forth naked from our mother's wombs, have been living fully clothed, in comfort and health. Can this be by any other means than by God's lovingkindness and grace? Even if we forget the physical blessings we have enjoyed, the fact that we have received the blessing of redemption through Jesus Christ is reason enough to praise our God eternally. The prophet Habakkuk, who came to realize this by faith, confessed, "Yet I will rejoice in the LORD; I will take joy in the God of my salvation" (Hab 3:18, ESV).

"Give thanks to the Lord, for He is good, for His lovingkindness is everlasting."

Our God is the God of the entire universe; He is greater than all (John 10:29). As we think about the operation of the vast universe, the flow of the history of mankind, and the unfolding of each of our individual lives, what kind of confession are we making? A human being is a powerless existence who cannot create, govern, or control anything; and yet, are we not denying the existence of the great sovereign God and ignoring His providence? Peace does not, even for a moment, reside with the wicked for he is proud and devoid of thanks (Isa 48:22; 57:21). His life is full of grumbling, dissatisfaction, fruitless labor, and anguish. A true saint must recognize God's eternally immutable providence and lovingkindness which fill the universe, history and our lives. And this will lead us to thank and praise our Lord without ceasing.

עת לכל בר דעת דרך המסעות ארבעים שנה במדבר 'והרוחב והאורך של אדמן הקדושה מנהר במ

עמלק

מדבר צין והוא הקדש

ים המלח

מדבר סני

מדבר פארן

מדבר שור

ערץ פלשתים

שבט שמעון

שבט

באר שבע

עיר כרמל

לוח המסעות במדבר
אשר על פיהיסעוועל פיהיחנו

טז" רתמה	א" רעמסס
טז" רמןפרץ	ב" סכת
יז" לבנה	ג" אתם
יח" רסה	ד" פיהחירת
יט" קהלתה	ה" מרה
כ" הרשפר	ו" אילם
כא" חרדה	ז" ים סוף
כב" מקהלת	ח" מדברסין
כג" תחת	ט" דפקה
כד" תרה	יו" אלוש
כה" מתקה	יא" רפידם
כו" חשמנה	יב" מדברסיני
כז" מסרות	יג" קברתהתאוה
	יד" חצרת

אלכסנדרי

PART TWO

The Genealogy of Jesus Christ: The History of the Second Period

Excursus 3

The 42 Generations in the Genealogy of Jesus Christ at a Glance

Matt 1:17 Therefore all the generations from Abraham to David are fourteen generations; and from David to the deportation to Babylon fourteen generations; and from the deportation to Babylon to the time of Christ fourteen generations.

Πᾶσαι οὖν αἱ γενεαὶ ἀπὸ Ἀβραὰμ ἕως Δαυὶδ γενεαὶ δεκατέσσαρες, καὶ ἀπὸ Δαυὶδ ἕως τῆς μετοικεσίας Βαβυλῶνος γενεαὶ δεκατέσσαρες, καὶ ἀπὸ τῆς μετοικεσίας Βαβ υλῶνος ἕως τοῦ Χριστοῦ γενεαὶ δεκατέσσαρες.

	The First Period (1,163 years)	
	THE GENEALOGY IN MATTHEW 1 (14 GENERATIONS FROM ABRAHAM TO DAVID)	THE GENEALOGY IN LUKE 3 (14 GENERATIONS OF THE CORRESPONDING TIME PERIOD)
Period of the patriarchs	1 **Abraham** / אַבְרָהָם / Ἀβραάμ (Matt 1:2; 1 Chr 1:27, 34)	1 **Abraham** / Ἀβραάμ (Luke 3:34)
	2 **Isaac** / יִצְחָק / Ἰσαάκ (Matt 1:2; 1 Chr 1:28, 34)	2 **Isaac** / Ἰσαάκ (Luke 3:34)
	3 **Jacob** / יַעֲקֹב / Ἰακώβ (Matt 1:2; 1 Chr 1:34; 2:1)	3 **Jacob** / Ἰακώβ (Luke 3:34)
	4 **Judah** / יְהוּדָה / Ἰούδας (Matt 1:2-3; 1 Chr 2:1)	4 **Judah** / Ἰούδας (Luke 3:33)
	By Tamar (Matt 1:3)	
Period in Egypt	5 **Perez** / פֶּרֶץ / Φαρές (Matt 1:3; 1 Chr 2:4; Ruth 4:18)	5 **Perez** / Φαρές (Luke 3:33)
	6 **Hezron** / חֶצְרוֹן / Ἑσρώμ (Matt 1:3; 1 Chr 2:5; Ruth 4:18-19)	6 **Hezron** / Ἑσρώμ (Luke 3:33)
	7 **Ram** / רָם / Ἀράμ (Matt 1:3-4; 1 Chr 2:9-10; Ruth 4:19)	7 **Ram** / Ἀράμ (Luke 3:33)
	8 **Amminadab** / עַמִּינָדָב / Ἀμιναδάβ (Matt 1:4; 1 Chr 2:10; Ruth 4:19-20)	8 **Amminadab** / Ἀμιναδάβ (Luke 3:33)
Period of the wilderness journey and the conquest of Canaan	9 **Nahshon** / נַחְשׁוֹן / Ναασσών (Matt 1:4; 1 Chr 2:10-11; Ruth 4:20)	9 **Nahshon** / Ναασσών (Luke 3:32)
	10 **Salmon** / שַׂלְמוֹן / Σαλμών (Matt 1:4-5; 1 Chr 2:11; Ruth 4:20-21)	10 **Salmon** / Σαλμών (Luke 3:32)
	By Rahab (Matt 1:5)	
Period of the judges	11 **Boaz** / בֹּעַז / Βοός (Matt 1:5; 1 Chr 2:11-12; Ruth 4:21)	11 **Boaz** / Βοός (Luke 3:32)
	By Ruth (Matt 1:5)	
	12 **Obed** / עוֹבֵד / Ὠβήδ (Matt 1:5; 1 Chr 2:12; Ruth 4:21-22)	12 **Obed** / Ὠβήδ (Luke 3:32)
	13 **Jesse** / יִשַׁי / Ἰεσσαί (Matt 1:5-6; 1 Chr 2:12-13; Ruth 4:22)	13 **Jesse** / Ἰεσσαι (Luke 3:32)
Period of the United Monarchy	14 **David** / מֶלֶךְ דָּוִד / Δαβίδ Βασιλεύς (Matt 1:6; 1 Chr 2:15; Ruth 4:22)	14 **David** / Δαβίδ Βασιλεύς (Luke 3:31)

*The first and the second periods of the genealogy are distinguished by the two different periods of David's reign—7 years and 6 months in Hebron and 33 years in Jerusalem (2 Sam 5:4-5; 1 Chr 3:4; 29:27; 1 Kgs 2:11).

The Second Period (406 years)		
THE GENEALOGY IN MATTHEW 1 (14 GENERATIONS OF KINGS FROM DAVID TO THE DEPORTATION TO BABYLON)		**THE GENEALOGY IN LUKE 3** (14 GENERATIONS OF THE CORRESPONDING TIME PERIOD)

Period of the United Monarchy	1	**David** / דָּוִד / Δαβίδ (Matt 1:6; 1 Chr 2:15; Ruth 4:22)	
	By the wife of Uriah (Matt 1:6)		
	2	**Solomon** / שְׁלֹמֹה / Σολομών (Matt 1:6-7; 1 Chr 3:5)	15 **Nathan** / Ναθάν (Luke 3:31)
Period of the Divided Monarchy	3	**Rehoboam** / רְחַבְעָם / 'Ροβοάμ (Matt 1:7; 1 Chr 3:10)	16 **Mattatha** / Ματταθά (Luke 3:31)
	4	**Abijah** / אֲבִיָּה / 'Αβιά (Matt 1:7; 1 Chr 3:10)	17 **Menna** / Μεννά (Luke 3:31)
	5	**Asa** / אָסָא / 'Ασά (Matt 1:7-8; 1 Chr 3:10)	18 **Melea** / Μελεᾶ (Luke 3:31)
	6	**Jehoshaphat** / יְהוֹשָׁפָט / 'Ιωσαφάτ (Matt 1:8; 1 Chr 3:10)	19 **Eliakim** / 'Ελιακείμ (Luke 3:30)
	7	**Joram** / יוֹרָם / 'Ιωράμ (Matt 1:8; 1 Chr 3:11)	20 **Jonam** / 'Ιωνάν (Luke 3:30)
	Kings omitted from the genealogy		
		Ahaziah / אֲחַזְיָה (1 Chr 3:11) **Athaliah** / עֲתַלְיָה (2 Kgs 11:1-3; 2 Chr 22:12) **Joash** / יוֹאָשׁ (1 Chr 3:11) **Amaziah** / אֲמַצְיָה (1 Chr 3:12)	21 **Joseph** / 'Ιωσήφ (Luke 3:30) 22 **Judah** / 'Ιούδας (Luke 3:30)
	8	**Uzziah (Azariah)** / עֻזִּיָּה / 'Οζίας (Matt 1:8-9; 1 Chr 3:12)	23 **Simeon** / Συμεών (Luke 3:30)
			24 **Levi** / Λευί (Luke 3:29)
	9	**Jotham** / יוֹתָם / 'Ιωθάμ (Matt 1:9; 1 Chr 3:12)	25 **Matthat** / Ματθάτ (Luke 3:29)
	10	**Ahaz** / אָחָז / 'Αχάζ (Matt 1:9; 1 Chr 3:13)	
	11	**Hezekiah** / חִזְקִיָּה / 'Εζεκίας (Matt 1:9-10; 1 Chr 3:13)	26 **Jorim** / 'Ιωρείμ (Luke 3:29)
	12	**Manasseh** / מְנַשֶּׁה / Μανασσῆς (Matt 1:10; 1 Chr 3:13)	27 **Eliezer** / 'Ελιέζερ (Luke 3:29)
	13	**Amon** / אָמוֹן / 'Αμώς (Matt 1:10; 1 Chr 3:14)	28 **Joshua** / 'Ιησοῦς (Luke 3:29)
	14	**Josiah** / יֹאשִׁיָּה / 'Ιωσίας (Matt 1:10-11; 1 Chr 3:14)	29 **Er** / Ἤρ (Luke 3:28)
	Kings omitted from the genealogy		
		Jehoahaz (Shallum) / יְהוֹאָחָז (2 Kgs 23:31; 1 Chr 3:15; 2 Chr 36:1-2) **Jehoiakim (Eliakim)** / יְהוֹיָקִים (2 Kgs 23:34, 36; 1 Chr 3:15; 2 Chr 36:4)	30 **Elmadam** / 'Ελμωδάμ (Luke 3:28)

* There may be slight variations in the chronological placement of each generation because it is impossible to figure out the definite years of the 41 figures from after Nathan (Mattatha to Jesus in the Lukan genealogy) since they are mostly people whose deeds are not recorded in the Bible.

The Third Period (593 years)		
	THE GENEALOGY IN MATTHEW 1 (14 GENERATIONS FROM THE DEPORTATION TO BABYLON TO JESUS CHRIST)	THE GENEALOGY IN LUKE 3 (14 GENERATIONS OF THE CORRESPONDING TIME PERIOD)
Period of the Babylonian captivity	1 Jeconiah (Jehoiachin) / יְכָנְיָה / Ἰεχονίας (Matt 1:11-12; 1 Chr 3:16)	31 Cosam / Κωσάμ (Luke 3:28)
	King omitted from the genealogy Zedekiah (Mattaniah) / צִדְקִיָּה (2 Kgs 24:18; 1 Chr 3:16)	
	2 Shealtiel / שְׁאַלְתִּיאֵל / Σαλαθιήλ (Matt 1:12; 1 Chr 3:17)	32 Addi / Ἀδδί (Luke 3:28)
Period of reconstructing the temple and the walls	3 Zerubbabel / זְרֻבָּבֶל / Ζοροβαβέλ (Matt 1:12-13; 1 Chr 3:19)	33 Melchi / Μελχί (Luke 3:28)
	→ Hananiah (1 Chr 3:21)	34 Neri / Νηρί (Luke 3:27)
	→ Shecaniah (1 Chr 3:22)	35 Shealtiel / Σαλαθιήλ (Luke 3:27)
	→ Shemaiah (1 Chr 3:22)	36 Zerubbabel / Ζοροβαβέλ (Luke 3:27)
	→ Neariah (1 Chr 3:23)	37 Rhesa / Ῥησά (Luke 3:27)
	→ Elioenai (1 Chr 3:24)	38 Joanan / Ἰωαννά (Luke 3:27)
The inter-testamental period	4 Abihud / אֲבִיהוּד / Ἀβιούδ (Matt 1:13)	39 Joda / Ἰωδά (Luke 3:26)
		40 Josech / Ἰωσήχ (Luke 3:26)
	5 Eliakim / אֶלְיָקִים / Ἐλιακείμ (Matt 1:13)	41 Semein / Σεμεΐ (Luke 3:26)
		42 Mattathias / Ματταθίας (Luke 3:26)
	6 Azor / עַזּוּר / Ἀζώρ (Matt 1:13-14)	43 Maath / Μάαθ (Luke 3:26)
		44 Naggai / Ναγγαί (Luke 3:25)
	7 Zadok / צָדוֹק / Σαδώκ (Matt 1:14)	45 Hesli / Ἐσλί (Luke 3:25)
		46 Nahum / Ναούμ (Luke 3:25)
	8 Achim / יוֹקִים / Ἀχείμ (Matt 1:14)	47 Amos / Ἀμώς (Luke 3:25)
	9 Eliud / אֱלִיהוּד / Ἐλιούδ (Matt 1:14-15)	48 Mattathias / Ματταθίας (Luke 3:25)
		49 Joseph / Ἰωσήφ (Luke 3:24)
	10 Eleazar / אֶלְעָזָר / Ἐλεάζαρ (Matt 1:15)	50 Jannai / Ἰανά (Luke 3:24)
		51 Melchi / Μελχί (Luke 3:24)
	11 Matthan / מַתָּן / Ματθάν (Matt 1:15)	52 Levi / Λευί (Luke 3:24)
		53 Matthat / Ματθάτ (Luke 3:24)
	12 Jacob / יַעֲקֹב / Ἰακώβ (Matt 1:15-16)	54 Eli / Ἠλί (Luke 3:23)
	Mary's husband 13 Joseph / יוֹסֵף / Ἰωσήφ (Matt 1:16)	55 Joseph / Ἰωσήφ (Luke 3:23)
	By Mary 14 Jesus / יֵשׁוּעַ / Ἰησοῦς (Matt 1:16)	56 Jesus / Ἰησοῦς (Luke 3:23)

* The time span of the third period from the time of the deportation to Babylon until the inter-testament period is estimated.

* This chart uses the New American Standard Bible (NASB) for names and verses in English.

CHAPTER 4

The General History and Characteristics of the Second Period in the Genealogy

1. The general history of the second period in the genealogy

(1) Scope of history

In *The Unquenchable Lamp of the Covenant*, the third book in the History of Redemption series, we undertook an in-depth study of the first period of Jesus' genealogy. The first period encompassed the history from Abraham to David's reign in Hebron. That study concentrated on 1,163 years of history from Abraham's birth in 2166 BC until the end of David's reign in Hebron in 1003 BC. Moreover, this period includes the lives of Abraham, Isaac and Jacob, the 430 years of Israel's slavery in Egypt, 40 years of the wilderness journey and their eventual entrance into Canaan. The study also examined the conquering of Canaan, the era of the Judges, the reign of Saul (the first king of the United Monarchy), and King David's life.

This fourth book in the History of Redemption series will be dealing with the second period of Jesus Christ's genealogy. The second period of the genealogy records the history from the time David ended his reign in Hebron and started his reign in Jerusalem in 1003 BC until the deportation to Babylon. Matthew 1:11-12 specifically mentions Jeconiah (Jehoiachin) before and after the deportation to Babylon; therefore, the second deportation to Babylon (597 BC) when Jeconiah was taken into captivity becomes the event that ends the second period of the genealogy of Jesus Christ.[3] The second period of the genealogy, then, encompasses approximately 406 years of history from 1003 BC to 597 BC.

	First period	Second period	Third period
Scope of History	From Abraham to David (2166-1003 BC)	From David to deportation to Babylon (1003-597 BC)	From deportation to Babylon to Jesus Christ (597-4 BC)

(2) Historical content

David spent 10 years running from Saul. Then he was enthroned as the king of Judah in Hebron in 1010 BC (2 Sam 2:3-4, 11) where he reigned for seven years and six months. Finally, he was anointed as king over the united kingdom of Israel in 1003 BC (2 Sam 5:1-5; 1 Chr 11:1-3). This is the beginning of the second period of Jesus Christ's genealogy.

The second period of Jesus Christ's genealogy introduces a total of 14 individuals. It includes David and Solomon from the United Monarchy and King Rehoboam down to King Josiah, dealing mostly with kings of Judah in the Divided Monarchy.

David reigned 33 years after becoming king in Jerusalem, where he brought in the Ark of God (2 Sam 6:12-19; 1 Chr 15:25-29), thereby proclaiming that the sovereign who rules Israel is not he but God Almighty. After this, David had in mind the desire to build a temple for the Lord, and God established the Davidic covenant through the prophet Nathan in response to David's desire (2 Sam 7:1-17; 1 Chr 17:1-15).

Through the Davidic covenant, God declared that the one who will construct the Temple of God is not David but Solomon who will come forth from David (2 Sam 7:12-13; 1 Chr 17:11-12). Accordingly, Solomon succeeded David's throne and completed the construction of the Temple, using the materials David had prepared in utter devotion (1 Chr 22:1-19). The construction of the Temple was truly an amazing work accomplished within God's administration of redemption.

However, after the Temple was completed and the kingdom became strengthened, Solomon's corruption began as he took on many foreign wives and concubines (1 Kgs 11:1-3). These women caused Solomon's heart to turn away from God and serve other gods (1 Kgs 11:3-4, 9). At this, the Lord was infuriated and gave multiple warnings, but Solomon did not repent (1 Kgs 11:9-11). Ultimately, due to Solomon's transgressions, the kingdom was divided into two after Solomon's death. Solomon's sin became a direct cause in the division of the kingdom.

Jeroboam gathered together the 10 tribes of the north to establish the northern kingdom of Israel and the remaining two tribes became the southern kingdom of Judah. The second period of the genealogy of Jesus Christ unfolds around the kings of southern Judah starting with Rehoboam and continuing on to King Josiah.

2. The characteristics of the second period in the genealogy

The second period of Jesus Christ's genealogy contains some distinctive characteristics and they are as follows:

First, it contrasts the faith of the Gentiles against the depravity of the Jews.

The 14 generations of the second period of the genealogy starts off with the words, "David was the father of Solomon by Bathsheba who had been the wife of Uriah." Uriah was a Hittite and the only Gentile male to appear in the second group of 14 generations (2 Sam 11:3, 6, 17, 21, 24). He was not even aware that his wife had been taken by the king and was faithful to the kingdom up to the moment of his solitary death on the battlefield. On the other hand, the king of Judah, David, committed adultery with Uriah's wife, Bathsheba.

The second group of 14 generations starts out with a reference to a Gentile, namely Uriah the Hittite, making it apparent that the genealogy of Jesus Christ puts greater significance on faith rather than blood lineage. Moreover, this also testifies to the fact that God is not only the God of the Jews but also of the Gentiles (Rom 1:14-16; 3:22; 10:11-13; 1 Cor 1:24; 12:13; Gal 3:28; Ref Acts 10:9-16, 28-38; Eph 2:11-19).

Second, it shows us that even the corruption of the many generations of kings could not cut off the path to usher in Jesus Christ.

After the time of David and Solomon, the history of Israel went into rapid decline; however, the promise regarding Jesus Christ continued without interruption even under such circumstances. God ceaselessly continued to carry out the promise to usher in the Messiah through the Davidic royal lineage in spite of the rebellion of the kings.

In their 208-year history, the 19 kings of the northern kingdom of Israel went through nine dynasty changes within a repetitive cycle of treason and insurrection. Eventually in 722 BC, they were destroyed by the Assyrians. However, the 20 kings of Judah sustained the single dynasty of David. This was achieved through God's administration of redemptive history in which He was paving the path for the coming of the Messiah as a descendant of David.

In order to prevent the coming of Jesus Christ, Satan had mobilized any and all means to lead the many generations of kings into a path of unbelief, corruption, idolatry and rebellion. The result of all of these sins is God's disciplining of His people through the "deportation to Babylon" (Matt 1:11).

The southern kingdom of Judah had sustained its history for 344 years from 930 BC until 586 BC when it was destroyed by Nebuchadnezzar of Babylon. The southern kingdom of Judah was destroyed because they disregarded God's Word and did not heed the warnings of the prophets but walked the path of rebellion and idolatry (2 Chr 36:14-16). Judah's "deportation to Babylon" signifies the collapse of the Davidic dynasty. Consequently, it seemed as though Satan had triumphed and God's administration of redemptive history had come to a halt. However, God allowed His people to return from Babylonian captivity after 70 years, thereby clearly affirming that the mighty flow of the administration of redemptive history that God has promised cannot be stopped by any attempt thrown out by the powers of darkness.

Through the history of the southern kingdom of Judah, God is teaching us that He governs all history, judges disobedience and transgressions, and bestows blessings for faithful obedience and trust. Even through Judah's constant rebellion, God continued His administration of redemptive history, so that the path of the Messiah, who comes as the "Seed of woman" and the "Son of David," may not be cut off. God patiently endured the iniquities of Judah whose history was able to proceed because of His boundless love and long-suffering.

CHAPTER 5

The Basis for the Calculation of the Regnal Chronology in the Second Period of the Genealogy

It is a very important task to properly sort out the chronology of Biblical events, so to reveal the relationship between historical events and the Word of God. Biblical chronology is redemptive-historical time that contains the record of events through which God reveals Himself to mankind. The chronology of the kings of Israel is such a history because it is not only a history of the kingdom of Israel, but it is a redemptive history (*historia salutis*) in which the covenant of God has been fulfilled.

Fourteen kings are listed in the second period of the genealogy of Jesus Christ. It spans the time period starting with kings David and Solomon in the United Monarchy through the entire Divided Monarchy.

We must thoroughly investigate the chronology of the kings. Moses earnestly desired that the second generation of the wilderness journey would be a people of faith who continually obey the Word of God. When their entrance into Canaan was imminent, Moses pleaded to them the words of Deuteronomy 32:7, "Remember the days of old, consider the years of all generations." Here the word *consider* in Hebrew is בִּין (*bîn*), which means "to discern." In order to discern the years of all generations in the Bible, we must first accurately calculate them.

1. The importance of studying the chronology

It is absolutely crucial that we conduct a systematic study of the chronology of the Bible. The reason for this importance is as follows:

First, an accurate study of the chronologies uncovers the bare truth of the historical facts.

No matter how many great works God may have performed through time in history, if human beings do not know the precise chronology of these events or are uncertain about the chronological order of events, then one of the following things could take place. First, the facts of the history could be distorted or placed out of order. Second, historical accounts can be misconstrued as fiction. Third, historical facts could disappear all together. Through our study of the chronologies, we can comprehend the context and the situation of the times as they were. Moreover, their truth, value and vitality can be distinctly displayed by clearly illuminating the historical facts.

Second, an accurate study of the chronologies reveals God's mysterious and profound providence.

God's providence was not achieved apart from history; it was worked out within the flow of history itself. Therefore, a lack of an accurate chronology causes that history to be easily overlooked, and we will be unable to give due notice to what lies beneath that history. Consequently, we will be unable to comprehend the providence of God hidden within the chronology of history. God's mysterious and profound providence can be revealed in full measure and in full clarity only when the reckoning of the chronology is accurate.

Third, an accurate study of the chronologies reveals God's administration of redemptive history in full vitality.

As soon as the regnal chronologies and the detailed order of events therein are revealed, we can discover in them God's mysterious and profound providence which may have been thoughtlessly overlooked in the past. We will then be able to get an understanding of these events as if they were unfolding before our very eyes. Furthermore, when these historical facts are put into their chronological context, the layers of time will be peeled back and God's administration of redemptive history which was hidden in each of the generations will dynamically and completely come to life. Then, God's mysterious and profound providence manifested in each generation will not remain as a mere incident of the past, but transcend different periods of time and unfold as God's majestic administration of redemptive history for our present salvation and the salvation of our future descendants.

2. The basis for the calculation of regnal chronology

Until now, we have read many times the list of regnal years, kings' ages, and the synchronisms with other kingdoms which routinely appear at the beginning or end of the accounts about the reigns of kings. However, we have either overlooked or simply misunderstood them and committed the grave error of not discovering God's amazing providence of redemption contained in these regnal data.

In order to calculate the regnal years of the kings of the second period in the genealogy, we need to thoroughly investigate the biblical evidences and methods of calculating the regnal years of all the kings that have reigned in both the southern kingdom of Judah and the northern kingdom of Israel. Of course, it is certainly not an easy task to reckon the regnal years of kings. To be sure, we will at times encounter various problems in this endeavor. However, the Bible provides the clues needed to get a clear grasp of the chronology. The chronology of the kings in the Bible is inerrant and complete. Therefore, we should not cursorily peruse the detailed regnal chronology of each of the kings; rather, we should inspect them thoroughly and exhaustively (Isa 34:16). By doing so, we will be able to see the order of the seemingly complicated chronology of all of the kings from the beginning to the end.

The regnal chronology of the kings of Judah and Israel can be established based on the following principles.

First, each king's years of reign are accurately listed.
The Bible records the number of regnal years for all 20 kings of Judah and 19 kings of Israel without exception. However, the number of regnal years may at times include regencies (or joint reigns) or indicate sole reigns only. For example, the 25 years of Jehoshaphat's reign includes regency of his son Jehoram (1 Kgs 22:42). However, the 8 years of Jehoram's reign (2 Kgs 8:17; 2 Chr 21:5, 20) indicates his sole reign and does not include his 7-year regency with his father Jehoshaphat. In the case of Hezekiah also, his 15-year joint reign with his father Ahaz is not included in his regnal years. It only indicates the 29 years of his sole reign (2 Kgs 18:2; 2 Chr 29:1).

Second, each king's accession year is listed in comparison with the counterpart kingdom's regnal year.

For example, Abijam (Abijah) of the southern kingdom acceded to the throne in the 18th year of the Jeroboam's reign in the northern kingdom (1 Kgs 15:1; 2 Chr 13:1). Also, Asa of the southern kingdom became king in Jeroboam's 20th year of reign in the northern kingdom (1 Kgs 15:9). Moreover, King Nadab of the northern kingdom of Israel acceded to the throne in the second regnal year of Asa in the southern kingdom (1 Kgs 15:25) whereas Baasha of the north took the throne in Asa's third regnal year in the southern kingdom (1 Kgs 15:28, 33).

Third, in the case of the southern kingdom of Judah, the king's age at accession is recorded.

In the northern kingdom of Israel, there is no mention of the king's age at accession; however, in the south, with the exception of Abijam and Asa, every king's age at accession is listed. This enables us to calculate the king's age at death by adding his age at accession with the years of his reign. Furthermore, we can figure out the father's age at the birth of his son by subtracting the age of the king's son at accession from the king's age at death. It is recorded, "Manasseh was twelve years old when he became king, and he reigned fifty-five years in Jerusalem" (2 Kgs 21:1, 2 Chr 33:1). The Bible also says, "Amon was twenty-two years old when he became king, and he reigned two years in Jerusalem" (2 Kgs 21:19). Manasseh became king at age 12 and reigned for 55 years which means that he died at age 66. Thus, subtracting his son Amon's age at accession (22) from Manasseh's age at death (66) results in Manasseh's age at the birth of his son (66 − 22 = 44).

Fourth, the regnal years are clearly indicated for important events.

For example, 1 Kings 6:1 states, ". . . in the fourth year of Solomon's reign over Israel, in the month of Ziv which is the second month, that he began to build the house of the LORD." Also 2 Chronicles 34:8 tells us that King Josiah "in the eighteenth year of his reign : . . purged the land and the house." And lastly, 2 Chronicles 35:19 says, "In the eighteenth year of Josiah's reign this Passover was celebrated."

3. The three understandings required in the calculation of regnal chronology

The regnal chronologies of the southern and northern kingdoms are each based on their respective "chronicles of the kings."

The "Chronicles of the kings" is a brief account or record of the generations of the past. The chronicles of the kings are based on historical facts of the times and therefore they testify to the historicity of the regnal chronologies of the southern and northern kingdoms. For example, there are the chronicles of King David (1 Chr 27:24), the book of the acts of Solomon (1 Kgs 11:41), and Book of the Chronicles (Neh 12:23) which records about the patriarchs of the Levites after the return from exile. The accounts of the kings of Israel are recorded in the "Book of the Chronicles of the Kings of Israel" (1 Kgs 14:19; 15:31; 16:5, 14, 20; 22:39; 2 Kgs 1:18; 10:34; 13:8, 12; 14:15, 28; 15:11, 15, 21, 26, 31) and the account of the kings of Judah are recorded in the "Book of the Chronicles of the Kings of Judah" (1 Kgs 14:29; 15:7, 23; 22:45; 2 Kgs 8:23; 12:19; 14:18; 15:6, 36; 16:19; 20:20; 21:17, 25; 23:28; 24:5).

The respective "chronicles of the kings" of Judah and Israel each records the regnal years using different reckoning methods. Therefore, in order to properly understand the regnal chronologies of the kings, we must bear in mind and harmonize the following three points.

First, we must understand the accession year and non-accession year dating methods.
This understanding helps us to recognize whether the regnal years were counted from the year that the king acceded to the throne or from the year after his accession year.

Second, we must understand the months of Nisan and Tishri.
This deals with the problem of when (what month) the regnal year started in Judah and in Israel.

Third, we must understand regencies and joint reigns.
This will help us understand whether the kingdom was ruled by a king or by a regent or jointly at a certain period in time.

(1) Understanding the accession year and non-accession year dating methods

Israel counted the year of reign from the very year that the king acceded to the throne. This kind of reckoning where the "accession year" is not considered separately from regnal years is called the "non-accession year dating method." This method counts the year of accession, which coincides with the predecessor's last year of reign, as the first regnal year.

In contrast, Judah considered the "accession year" separately from regnal years. So the year of accession was not counted as a year of reign, but the first regnal year started on the first day of the first month of the year following the accession. This is called the "accession year dating method." For example, if King 'A' became king in the year 2008, year 2009 would be his first regnal year according to the accession year dating method. However, according to the non-accession year dating method, 2008 would be his first regnal year even if his reign started in December, and 2009 would automatically become his second regnal year. According to the accession year dating method, the last year of the preceding king's reign becomes the succeeding king's "accession year," and the succeeding king's first regnal year cannot start until the year of the preceding king's death is completely over.

In order to aid our understanding of these dating methods, we will now look at two examples, one from the Chronicles of the Kings of Judah and the other from the Chronicles of the Kings of Israel.

> **1 Kings 15:9** So in the twentieth year of Jeroboam the king of Israel, Asa began to reign as king of Judah.

This account is from the Chronicles of the Kings of Judah (1 Kgs 15:23) and thus the accession year dating method would apply. And accordingly, it states that Asa's accession year coincides with the twentieth year of Jeroboam's reign. However, if we look at this from Israel's perspective using the non-accession year dating method, Asa's year of accession would actually coincide with Jeroboam's 21st regnal year.

Next, we will take a look at 1 Kings 15:25, which is taken from the Chronicles of the Kings of Israel (1 Kgs 15:31) where the non-accession year dating method was used.

> **1 Kings 15:25** Now Nadab the son of Jeroboam became king over Israel in the second year of Asa king of Judah.

This account, following the non-accession year dating method, records that Nadab's year of accession coincides with Asa's second regnal year. However, Nadab's year of accession is actually Asa's first regnal year according to Judah's perspective using the accession year dating method.

As such, Israel, following the non-accession year dating method, will always have one more regnal year than Judah, which used the accession year dating method. One more thing that we must bear in mind is that both Judah and Israel apply their own method even when referring to the other's regnal years. Therefore, as mentioned above, the "twentieth year of Jeroboam" in 1 Kings 15:9 is according to the accession year method of Judah and "the second year of Asa" in 1 Kings 15:25 is following the non-accession year method of Israel. However, both Judah and Israel did not continuously adhere to the accession year and non-accession year dating methods respectively; both changed their methods in the midst of their histories depending on their diplomatic situations.

① **Regnal chronology reckoning method used by Judah**
The southern kingdom of Judah used the accession year dating method from the first king Rehoboam until the fourth king Jehoshaphat.[4] However, during Jehoshaphat's time, Judah entered into an alliance by marriage with the northern kingdom of Israel (2 Chr 18:1) and started using the non-accession year dating method due to Israel's influence. It started with Jehoram (fifth king) whose reign was greatly influenced by his wife Athaliah, daughter of Ahab the king of Israel. Then Athaliah's son Ahaziah (sixth king), Athaliah herself (seventh king) and Joash (eighth king) all used the non-accession year dating method.[5]

For example, during Ahaziah's time in the southern kingdom of Judah, we find evidence that shows the adoption of a new dating method. In some instances, it is recorded that Ahaziah began to reign in the 11th year of Joram the son of Ahab (2 Kgs 9:29) following the accession year dating method, whereas it is recorded elsewhere that Ahaziah began his reign in the 12th year of Joram's reign (2 Kgs 8:25). The Bible states that Jehoram and his son Ahaziah, who instituted the use of the non-accession year dating method, had walked in the way of the "house of Ahab" of Israel (2 Kgs 8:18, 27).

The southern kingdom of Judah, which had been using the non-accession year dating method due to Athaliah's influence, returned to the accession year dating method during King Amaziah's reign. The

Bible does not provide a clear answer as to why they returned to the accession year dating method during Amaziah's time. However, we can conjecture that the accession year dating method was first reinstituted by Azariah (Uzziah) who had completely broken away from Athaliah's influence; and since he was a coregent with his father Amaziah, he probably had his father's regnal years recorded according to the accession year dating method.

In summary, the southern kingdom of Judah used the accession year dating method from the first king Rehoboam until the fourth king Jehoshaphat. They started using the non-accession year dating method from Jehoram, the fifth king until the eighth king, Joash. However, from the reign of Amaziah, the ninth king, until their destruction, Judah returned to using the accession year dating method.

② **Regnal chronology reckoning method used by Israel**
The northern kingdom of Israel, in distinction from Judah, used the non-accession year dating method from the onset of the Divided Monarchy with the reign of Jeroboam. Then from the time of King Joash, they reverted to using the accession year dating method. The reason for this is that Israel had maintained friendly relations with Judah since this time, thus following Judah in adopting the accession year dating method.

Around this time, the kings who ruled Israel and Judah were both named Joash (8th king of the southern kingdom, 12th king of the northern kingdom). This also reveals that the two kingdoms had established friendly relations at this time.

Also, Amaziah of Judah, in order to attack Edom, hired 100,000 valiant warriors from Joash of Israel for 100 talents of silver (2 Chr 25:6-10). The fact that Judah received military aid from Israel is proof that their relationship was amicable.

Furthermore, Israel had used the non-accession year dating method from their first king Jeroboam until Jehoahaz, the 11th king.[6] However, from Joash (12th king) until the last king Hoshea (19th king), they followed Judah in using the accession year dating method. The evidence supporting this is the fact that the total regnal years of king Joash of Israel (797a – 781 BC) was recorded not as 17 years but as 16 years according to the accession year dating method (2 Kgs 13:10).

If we reckon the regnal chronology using the "accession year" and "non-accession year" dating methods that we have examined until now, the respective regnal chronologies of both kingdoms will certainly form a perfect harmony.

✻ Organized for the first time in history

(2) The month of Nisan (Abib — Exod 13:4; 23:15) and the month of Tishri (Ethanim — 1 Kgs 8:2)

Another important factor in reckoning regnal chronology is determining which month began the regnal year of Israel and Judah. For example, Solomon's temple began its construction in the month of Ziv (April – May) in the fourth year of his reign and was completed in the month of Bul (October – November) of Solomon's 11th regnal year (1 Kgs 6:1, 37-38; 2 Chr 3:1-2; see Excursus 5). Calculating the duration of the temple construction using these dates has different results depending on when the regnal year started. *The calculation on the basis of a Nisan-to-Nisan regnal year results in eight years (approx. 7 years and 6 months) as duration for the temple construction. However, the calculation based on a Tishri-to-Tishri regnal year comes out to seven years (approx. 6 years and 6 months) in constructing the temple.* This is because the month of Ziv can actually belong to a different regnal year depending on whether one uses the Nisan-to-Nisan year or the Tishri-to-Tishri year. That is a one-year difference. Furthermore, the fact that 1 Kings 6:38 records the construction period of the temple as being "seven years" proves to us that Judah had already adopted the Tishri-to-Tishri standard at the time of Solomon.[7]

King Josiah, in the 18th year of his reign, started to repair the temple as well as institute an extensive religious reformation (2 Kgs 22:3). After finishing all of his works, Josiah observed the Passover in the month of Nisan in his 18th regnal year (2 Kgs 23:23). Seeing that all the works including temple renovation (2 Kgs 22:3-7), discovery of the Book of the Law (2 Kgs 22:8-20), resolution to comply with the stipulations of the covenant (2 Kgs 23:1-3), wide-scale destruction of idols (2 Kgs 23:4-20), and many other works had been accomplished all by the month of Nisan in Josiah's 18th year indicates that Judah must certainly have been using the Tishri-to-Tishri regnal year (Ref Neh 1:1; 2:1).[8] But in contrast, the northern kingdom of Israel used Nisan, the month of the Passover feast, as the first month of their regnal year.

There is no direct mention in the Bible that the northern kingdom of Israel used the Nisan-to-Nisan scheme, in which the year begins with the month of Nisan (1st month), to reckon the regnal years of a king. However, we can conclude that Israel used the Nisan-to-Nisan scheme by examining their regnal years and synchronism data. King Jeroboam of the northern kingdom opted not to use the Tishri-to-Tishri scheme, which was used by the southern kingdom of Judah by considering the 7th month as the beginning of the year, in reckoning the regnal years of kings. It was perhaps because King Jeroboam of Israel wanted to oppose Judah and to be completely distinguished from them that he adopted the more traditional and widely used Nisan-to-Nisan scheme.

For further clarification, please refer to the following chart that compares the accession years and regnal periods of Judah and Israel. It is evident in the chart that Israel's time is six months ahead of Judah's time. At times, the regnal years of Israel can precede that of Judah by up to one year. Therefore, please take note that this book indicates the regnal years according to the respective methods of either the southern kingdom of Judah or the northern kingdom of Israel. See Excursuses 1 and 2

Regnal Years	931 BC		930 BC		929 BC		928 BC	
Western Calendar	Nisan	Tishri	Nisan	Tishri	Nisan	Tishri	Nisan	Tishri
Judah Southern Kingdom		a	b	a	b	a	b	
		Rehoboam's Accession year		Rehoboam's 1st regnal year		Rehoboam's 2nd regnal year		
Israel Northern Kingdom	a	b	a	b	a	b		
	Jeroboam's 1st regnal year		Jeroboam's 2nd regnal year		Jeroboam's 3rd regnal year			

Southern Kingdom of Judah
- Regnal year cycles from the month of Tishri (9th–10th month) to Tishri of next year
- Rehoboam's regnal years were reckoned according to the accession-year method.
- **A:** 6 months from Tishri to Nisan as the first half of a regnal year
- **B:** 6 months from Nisan to the following Tishri as the second half of a regnal year

Northern Kingdom of Israel

- Regnal year cycles from the month of Nisan (3rd–4th month) to Nisan of next year
- Jeroboam's regnal years were reckoned according to the non-accession-year method.
- **A:** 6 months from Nisan to Tishri as the first half of a regnal year
- **B:** 6 months from Tishri to the following Nisan as the second half of a regnal year

---

(3) Understanding regencies and joint reigns

Depending on the historical circumstances, there were, at times, two kings reigning jointly or as regents in Judah or Israel. A regent is "someone who is selected to rule on behalf of the king who is unable to reign due to extenuating circumstances such as his young age or an illness." A joint reign is a situation where two or more kings are reigning jointly.

There were more regencies and coregencies in Judah than in Israel. There was even an instance in Judah when three kings—Uzziah, Jotham and Ahaz—reigned together for about five years from 743 BC to 739 BC. See Excursus 1 Therefore, if the regnal years of the contemporaneous kings of Judah and Israel are tallied up, Judah's total will be much greater than that of Israel because Judah has many more overlapping regnal years.

For example, adding up the regnal years from Amaziah (ninth king) to Manasseh (14th king) of Judah results in a total of 197 years (29+52+16+16+29+55); however, the actual total duration of reign for these six kings is 154 years. There is a difference of 43 years (197 – 154). Moreover, we can conclude that the 43 years is the total duration of overlapping reigns due to coregencies.

We must also bear in mind that coregencies were not acknowledged sometimes, and the first year of reign was calculated from the beginning of the king's sole reign. For example, the northern kingdom of Israel indicated that the reign of Azariah, king of Judah, started on the 27th year of Jeroboam (2 Kgs 15:1). Israel had disregarded Azariah's coregency with his father Amaziah and reckoned his regnal years from when his sole reign started.

Who are the actual kings that had coregencies and how long were those overlapping periods? In all, there are seven coregencies in Judah and three in Israel. See Excursus 1 and 2 For our purposes, the periods of coregencies and sole reigns, besides the official regnal years listed in the

Bible, were reckoned using the inclusive system—that is, the first and last years of reign were included in the calculations.

① **Coregencies in the southern kingdom of Judah**

(a) In the 39th year of Asa, the king of Judah, when his foot disease was very serious, his son Jehoshaphat reigned with him for three years (1 Kgs 15:23; 22:41-42; 2 Chr 16:12-13). Jehoshaphat's three years of coregency were included in his official reign of 25 years (1 Kgs 22:42).

(b) Jehoshaphat, the king of Judah, took his son Jehoram as coregent when he had allied with Ahab of Israel to attack the kingdom of Aram. Jehoram was coregent for seven years (1 Kgs 22:2-29). Second Kings 8:16 states, "when Jehoshaphat was king of Judah, Jehoram son of Jehoshaphat began his reign as king of Judah" (NIV). Moreover, the Bible states the accession year of Jehoram of Israel as being the "second year of Jehoram" of Judah (2 Kgs 1:17) as well as the "eighteenth year of Jehoshaphat" (2 Kgs 3:1). This also is evidence that Jehoshaphat and his son Jehoram reigned jointly. However, Jehoram's seven-year coregency was not included in his official regnal period of eight years (2 Kgs 8:17; 2 Chr 21:5, 20). This was probably because Jehoshaphat's influence in the coregency overshadowed that of Jehoram.

(c) When Amaziah was defeated in his battle against Joash of Israel and was taken prisoner, his son Uzziah (Azariah) reigned in his place for 25 years (2 Kgs 14:2, 8-14; 15:1-2; 2 Chr 25:17-25; 26:1-3). Here, the 25 years of regency were included in Uzziah's official regnal period of 52 years (2 Kgs 15:2; 2 Chr 26:3).

(d) When Uzziah (Azariah) got leprosy, his son Jotham reigned in his place for 12 years (750 BC – 739 BC; 2 Kgs 15:5-7; 2 Chr 26:16-23). This regency period can be calculated based on the synchronism in Jotham's regnal data which states that he became king "in the second year of Pekah" (2 Kgs 15:32).

(e) Jotham had a 13-year coregency with his son Ahaz (2 Kgs 15:32-38; 743-731 BC). The coregency of Jotham and Ahaz can be calculated based on the synchronism in the regnal data which states that Hoshea became king in Israel (2 Kgs 17:1) "in the twelfth year of Ahaz" (731 BC). It seems that Jotham had ended his official reign of 16 years (2 Kgs 15:33; 2 Chr 27:1, 8) and handed the throne over to his son. However, he remained alive and reigned jointly with his son until his death in 731 BC (Ref 2 Kgs 15:30). Meanwhile, Ahaz's official regnal data excludes his co-regency with Jotham and indicates 16 years of his sole reign only (2 Kgs 16:2; 2 Chr 28:1).

(f) Ahaz reigned jointly with his son Hezekiah for 15 years (729b – 715 BC; 2 Kgs 16:1-2; 18:1, 9-10). This period of coregency is included in Ahaz's 16 years of reign, but is not included in Hezekiah's official regnal data.

(g) After Hezekiah became ill unto death, he received a 15-year extension of his life (2 Kgs 20:1-6). Six years into his extended life (44 years old), Hezekiah installs his young son Manasseh (12 years old) as coregent. They ruled jointly for 11 years. This co-regency is included in Manasseh's 55 years of reign (2 Kgs 21:1; 2 Chr 33:1).

② **Coregencies in the northern kingdom of Israel**

(a) King Omri's 12 years of reign includes the five years when the kingdom was divided into two parts, with Tibni ruling half of the nation in Tirzah. It also includes Omri's sole reign of eight years (1 Kgs 16:21-23).

(b) Jehoash of Israel, in preparing for the worst case scenario, installed his son Jeroboam II as a coregent before setting out to battle against Amaziah of Judah. They were coregents for thirteen years until 781 BC (2 Kgs 13:10-13; Ref 2 Kgs 14:8-23; 2 Chr 25:17-25). The 13-year coregency was included in the 41 regnal years of Jeroboam II (2 Kgs 14:23).

(c) Menahem and Pekah reigned simultaneously from two different regions. Pekah ruled in Gilead for 20 years (2 Kgs 15:27). During the first half of that reign, Menahem had a rival reign in Samaria for about 10 years. Pekahiah succeeded Menahem and reigned in Samaria for about two years (2 Kgs 15:17, 23, 27).

It is important to note that when the term of the regency is included in the official regnal years, the beginning of that regency is not deemed an "accession year" but is reckoned as the "first regnal year."[9] For example, the 41 regnal years of Jeroboam II of Israel was reckoned from the first year of his regency. This is also the case in the reigns of Jehoshaphat,

Jotham and Manasseh of Judah. One exception is the reign of Azariah. Although he had acceded to the throne as a regent, his year of accession is reckoned as an "accession year" because his father, Amaziah, had been taken prisoner and the throne had been vacant.

When all of the aforementioned principles of reckoning are applied, regnal chronology, which may have seemed like a hopelessly complicated entanglement of facts, will actually turn out to be a harmonized interplay of historical events that are accurately and precisely arrayed in their proper order. Although thousands of years have passed, the chronology that is recorded in the Bible is absolutely inerrant. We cannot but exclaim in awe at how such a seemingly jumbled chronology will actually turn out to prove that God's Word is absolutely inerrant and precise.

There is not a jot or tittle in the Bible that is without meaning (1 Cor 14:10). All Scripture is infallible and in good order, being the inspired Word of the living God. In particular, the chronologies that are recorded in 1 & 2 Kings and 1 & 2 Chronicles are in pairs and are recorded logically with precision. When we clearly comprehend the chronology of the generations of kings, the history that is contained in the letters and words will transcend the temporal gap and come alive as a vivid panorama. That is when we will be able to understand God's profound and mysterious providence which He desired to accomplish through each of the kings. And that is when we will be able to grasp the depth and breadth of God's administration of redemption.

The Comparison of the Regnal Years of the Kings of Israel and Judah

Reference Verses	Evaluation	Duration & years of reign	Judah (South)	Year
1 Kgs 11:43-12:24; 14:21-31; 2 Chr 9:31-12:16	Wicked	17 yrs. (930–913b)	Rehoboam	930
1 Kgs 15:1-8; 2 Chr 13:1-22	Wicked	3 yrs. (913b–910)	Abijam	913b
1 Kgs 15:9-24; 2 Chr 14:1-16:14	Good	41 yrs. (910–869)	Asa	910
1 Kgs 22:1-50; 2 Chr 17:1-21:1	Good	25 yrs. (871–847)	Jehoshaphat	871
2 Kgs 8:16-24; 2 Chr 21:1-20	Wicked	8 yrs. (847–840)	Jehoram	847
2 Kgs 8:24-9:29; 2 Chr 22:1-9	Wicked	1 yr. (840)	Ahaziah	840
2 Kgs 11:1-21; 2 Chr 22:10-23:21	Extremely wicked	6 yrs. (840–835b)	Athaliah	840
2 Kgs 11:21-12:21; 2 Chr 24:1-27	Good → Wicked	40 yrs. (835b–796b)	Joash	835b
2 Kgs 14:1-22; 2 Chr 25:1-28	Good → Wicked	29 yrs. (796b–767)	Amaziah	796b
2 Kgs 14:21; 15:1-7; 2 Chr 26:1-23	Good → Wicked	52 yrs. (791–739)	Azariah	791
2 Kgs 15:32-38; 2 Chr 27:1-9	Good	16 yrs. (750–735)	Jotham	750
2 Kgs 16:1-20; 2 Chr 28:1-27	Extremely wicked	16 yrs. (731–715)	Ahaz	731
2 Kgs 18:1-20:21; 2 Chr 29:1-32:33	Good	29 yrs. (715–686)	Hezekiah	715
2 Kgs 21:1-18; 2 Chr 33:1-20	Extremely wicked (Repented in the end)	55 yrs. (696–642)	Manasseh	696
2 Kgs 1:19-26; 2 Chr 33:21-25	Wicked	2 yrs. (642–640)	Amon	642
2 Kgs 22:1-23:30; 2 Chr 34:1-35:27	Good	31 yrs. (640–609b)	Josiah	640
2 Kgs 23:31-34; 2 Chr 36:1-4	Wicked	3 mos. (609b–608)	Jehoahaz	609b
2 Kgs 23:34-24:7; 2 Chr 36:5-8	Wicked	11 yrs. (608–597)	Jehoiakim	608
2 Kgs 24:8-17; 25:27-30; 2 Chr 36:9-10	Wicked	3 mos. 10 days (597)	Jehoiachin	597
2 Kgs 24:18-25:26; 2 Chr 36:11-21	Wicked	11 yrs. (597–586)	Zedekiah	597

Monarchy	Regnal years & periods	Reference Verse
Saul	40 yrs. (1050–1010)	1 Sam 13:1; Acts 13:21
David	40 yrs. (1010–970)	2 Sam 5:4; 1 Kgs 2:11
Solomon	40 yrs. (970–930)	1 Kgs 11:42; 2 Chr 9:30

* The royal lineage of David and Solomon continues down to Rehoboam in the southern kingdom of Judah.

Year	Israel (North)	Duration & years of reign	Evaluation	Reference Verses
930	Jeroboam	22 yrs. (930–909)	Extremely wicked	1 Kgs 11:26-14:20; 2 Chr 9:31-10:19; 13:1-20
909	Nadab	2 yrs. (909–908)	Wicked	1 Kgs 15:25-32
908	Baasha	24 yrs. (908–885)	Wicked	1 Kgs 15:28, 33-16:7; 2 Chr 16:1-6
885	Elah	2 yrs. (885–884)	Wicked	1 Kgs 16:6-14
884	Zimri	7 days. (884)	Wicked	1 Kgs 16:8-20
884	Tibni	5 yrs. (884–880)	Wicked	1 Kgs 16:21-22
884	Omri	12 yrs. (884–873)	Extremely wicked	1 Kgs 16:15-28
873	Ahab	22 yrs. (873–852a)	Extremely wicked	1 Kgs 16:28-22:40; 2 Chr 18:1-34
852a	Ahaziah	2 yrs. (852a–851a)	Extremely wicked	1 Kgs 22:40, 51-53; 2 Kgs 1:1-18; 2 Chr 20:35-37
851a	Joram	12 yrs. (851a–840)	Wicked	2 Kgs 1:17; 3:1-9:29; 2 Chr 22:1-9
840	Jehu	28 yrs. (840–813)	Wicked	2 Kgs 9:1-10:36; 2 Chr 22:5-7
813	Jehoahaz	17 yrs. (813–797a)	Wicked	2 Kgs 13:1-9; 2 Chr 25:25
797a	Joash	16 yrs. (797a–781)	Wicked	2 Kgs 13:9-25; 14:8-16; 2 Chr 25:17-25
793	Jeroboam II	41 yrs. (793–753)	Wicked	2 Kgs 14:16-29
753	Zechariah	6 mos. (753–752a/752)	Wicked	2 Kgs 14:29; 15:8-12
752	Shallum	1 mo. (752)	Wicked	2 Kgs 15:10-15
752	Menahem	10 yrs. (752–741)	Wicked	2 Kgs 15:14-22
741	Pekahiah	2 yrs. (741–739)	Wicked	2 Kgs 15:22-26
739	Pekah	20 yrs. (752–732/731)	Wicked	2 Kgs 15:25-31; 2 Chr 28:5-8
731	Hoshea	9 yrs. (731–722)	Wicked	2 Kgs 15:30; 17:1-41; 18:9-12

a: specifies 6-month period between Nisan and Tishri in a regnal year of the northern kingdom [e.g., ooo[a]]
b: specifies 6-month period between Nisan and Tishri in a regnal year of the southern kingdom [e.g., ooo[b]]

* All of the years on this chart are BC and follow the chronology reckoning methods of the southern kingdom of Judah and the northern kingdom of Israel.
* Total regnal years of every king are based on the Biblical record, and there may be slight differences in the regnal periods.

The Biblical Calendar

Religious calendar	Name (Babylonian)	Etymological meaning
1st month	**Nisan** (Neh 2:1; Esth 3:7) *Abib (Exod 13:4; 23:15; 34:18; Deut 16:1; Neh 2:1; Ezra 3:7)	The Hebrew word for *Nisan* is נִיסָן (*nîsān*), which means "their flight," and the Hebraic form of Babylonian word *Abib* is אָבִיב (*'ābîb*), which means "fresh, young barley ears."
2nd month	**Iyyar** *Ziv (1 Kgs 6:1, 37)	The Hebrew word for *Iyyar* is אִיָּר (*'îyār*), which means "open." The Hebraic form of Babylonian word *Ziv* is זִו (*ziw*), which means "brightness" or "flower." (Nickname: month of flowers)
3rd month	**Sivan** (Esth 8:9)	The Hebrew word for *Sivan* is סִרְוָן (*sirwān*), which means "their covering."
4th month	**Tammuz**	The Hebrew word for *Tammuz* is תַּמּוּז (*tammûz*), which means "sprout of life."
5th month	**Av**	The Hebrew word for *Ab* is אָב (*'āb*), which means "father." It also means "reed," but rarely used.
6th month	**Elul** (Neh 6:15)	The Hebrew word for *Elul* is אֱלוּל (*'ĕlûl*), which means "nothingness" or "trivial."
7th month	**Tishri** *Ethanim (1 Kgs 8:2)	The Hebrew word for *Tishri* is תִּשְׁרִי (*tišrî*), which means "first" or "offering." The Hebraic form of Babylonian word *Ethanim* is אֵיתָנִים (*'êtānîm*), which means "enduring" (Nickname: a month of enduring river).
8th month	**Marcheshvan** *Bul (1 Kgs 6:38)	The Hebrew word for *Marcheshvan* is מַרְחֶשְׁוָן (*marḥešwān*), which means "the eighth month." The Hebraic form of Babylonian word *Bul* is בּוּל (*bûl*), which means "increase" or "produce" (Nickname: a month of rainfall).
9th month	**Kislev** (Neh 1:1; Zech 7:1)	The Hebrew word for *Kislev* is כִּסְלֵו (*kislēw*), which means "his confidence."
10th month	**Tebeth** (Esth 2:16)	The Hebrew word for *Tebeth* is טֵבֵת (*ṭēbēt*), which means "goodness."
11th month	**Shebat** (Zech 1:7)	The Hebrew word for *Shebat* is שְׁבָט (*šĕbāṭ*), which means "a rod," "small branch," or "offspring."
12th month	**Adar** (Esth 3:7; Ezra 6:15) Ref Esth 3:13; 8:12; 9:1, 15, 17, 19, 21	The Hebrew word for *Adar* is אֲדָר (*'ădār*), which means "glorious" or "brilliant."

The asterisk (*) indicates the Canaanite names. All of the names on this chart mainly follow the spellings of the New American Standard Bible (NASB).

The modern civil calendar of Israel starts with Tishri as the first month of the year.

Solar calendar	Feasts	Rainfall	Climate & farming conditions
3rd–4th months	Passover (Exod 12:18; Lev 23:4) Feast of Unleavened Bread (Lev 23:6-8) Feast of First Fruits (Lev 23:10-11)	Latter rain	Barley harvest begins (Ref Ruth 1:22; 2 Sam 21:9; Josh 3:15)
4th–5th months		Dry season	Change of seasons; barley harvest
5th–6th months	Feast of Weeks; Pentecost (Lev 23:15-21)	Dry season	Wheat harvest; fruition of early figs; vineyard trimming
6th–7th months		Dry season	Very hot and dry season (scorching winds); heavy fall of morning dew; grapes ripen
7th–8th month		Dry season	Olive fruits ripen
8th–9th months		Dry season	Heat wave persists; Summer figs and dates ripen.
9th–10th months	Feast of trumpet (Lev 23:24; Num 29:1) The Day of Atonement (Lev 16:29-31; 23:27) Feast of booths (Lev 23:34-36) Holy convocation (Lev 23:36; Num 29:35)	Early rain	Plowing the fields; Pomegranates ripen.
10th–11th months		Rainy season	Heavy rainfall; time of cultivation (barley and wheat)
11th–12th months	Feast of Dedication (25th day; John 10:22) – Feast to commemorate the day when the Maccabeus family recovered the Temple of Jerusalem from Antiochus Epiphanes and cleansed the temple	Rainy season	Winter begins (heavy rainfall); Winter figs ripen.
12th–1st months		Rainy season	The coldest climate; heaviest rainfall (of hail, snow, rain); snowfall on high mountains and blossom in fields
1st–2nd months		Rainy season	Warmer climate; almond blossoms
2nd–3rd months	Feast of Purim (14-15th; Esth 9:17-21)	Rainy season	Frequent thunder and hail; flax stripped; harvest of tangerines

A calendar dates one year with the months, days, feasts, and the events within that year. A major purpose of a calendar is to facilitate daily lives by preserving a time record in respect to seasonal changes and regular cycles. That is why the calendar is based on the climate and farming. However, the calendars in the Bible bear a greater purpose and that is to promote godly lives that serve God in thanksgiving by remembering His creation of the heavens and earth and redemptive work for mankind's salvation. The years, months and days in the calendar came into existence after God said, "let them [lights] be for signs and for seasons and for days and years" (Gen 1:14).

The first month of a new year in the Bible begins with Nisan because God commanded Moses and Aaron after the Exodus, "This month shall be the beginning of months for you; it is to be the first month of the year to you," and the "first month" here is the month of Nisan (Exod 12:1-2). Ever since they received this command, the Israelite continued to use the month of Abib (Nisan) as the first month of the year (Ref Exod 12:18; 13:3-4; 23:15; 34:18; 2 Sam 11:1; 1 Kgs 8:2; 20:22; 1 Chr 20:1; Neh 1:1; 2:1; Esth 3:7).

While the twelve months of the Jewish calendar are named by ordinal numbers in the Bible (Ref 1 Kgs 6:1; 2 Kgs 25:1, 3, 8, 25, 27; 2 Chr 3:2, etc.), each of the months actually has its own proper name. Each of the months was originally called by their Canaanite appellations but after the Babylonian exile they were referred to by their new Babylonian names. Some Canaanite names for months that appear in the Bible are Abib, Ziv, Ethanim and Bul.

The psalmist in Psalm 90:12 prayed, saying, "So teach us to number our days, that we may present to You a heart of wisdom." Precise reckoning of chronology based on accurate historical facts becomes the basis upon which God's mysterious and profound providence is revealed.

PART THREE

The Genealogy of Jesus Christ: Individuals in the Second Period

An Overview of the 42 Generations in the Second Period

– 14 Generations from David to the Deportation to Babylon

People	History
1st Generation **David** דָּוִד Δαβίδ Beloved, friend ——— Good king	➤ **Period of Reign** 40 years (age 30-70, 1010-970 BC) – 7 years and 6 months in Hebron, 33 years in Jerusalem (2 Sam 5:4-5; 1 Kgs 2:11; 1 Chr 3:4-5; 29:27) ① Among the three periods in the Matthean genealogy, David concludes the first period as well as starts the second period. Thus, David is the only individual to be counted twice in the genealogy (Matt 1:17). David is being focused on as the central figure that concluded one period and opened a new one. ② The second period of the genealogy of Matthew begins with, "… David was the father of Solomon by Bathsheba who had been the wife of Uriah" (Matt 1:6). ③ David took Bathsheba as his wife (2 Sam 11) after his reign in Hebron and during the first half of his reign in Jerusalem (2 Sam 5:13-14; 1 Chr 3:4-5). ④ After David took the wife of Uriah, the prophet Nathan prophesied, "The sword shall never depart from your house" (2 Sam 12:10). Just as he prophesied, later on the southern kingdom of Judah completely collapsed and the royal line was cut off as the nation was deported to Babylon.
2nd Generation **Solomon** שְׁלֹמֹה Σολομών Peaceful ——— Good king	➤ **Period of Reign** 40 years (970–930 BC) (1 Kgs 11:42; 2 Chr 9:30) ① The third king of the United Monarchy (1 Kgs 1:38-11:43; 1 Chr 29:20 – 2 Chr 9:31), he is the second individual in the second period of Jesus' genealogy (Matt 1:6-7; 1 Chr 3:5, 10). His father was David and his mother was Bathsheba (the daughter of Ammiel, 2 Sam 12:24; 1 Chr 3:5). ② He was a good king (1 Kgs 3:3), but in the second half of his reign he took Gentile concubines and he was not wholly devoted to the Lord as his wives turned his heart after other gods (1 Kgs 11:3-4). ③ Solomon secured the greatest territory and riches in the history of Israel (1 Kgs 4:21; 2 Chr 9:26). ④ The construction of the temple of Solomon began during the 480th year after the Exodus, in the 4th year of Solomon's reign, in the month of Ziv and was completed in the month of Bul of the 11th year (1 Kgs 6:37-38; 2 Chr 3:2).

People	History
3rd Generation **Rehoboam** רְחַבְעָם Ῥοβοάμ The one who enlarges his people ——— Wicked king	➤ **Period of Reign** 17 years (age 41–58, 930–913ᵇ BC) (1 Kgs 14:21; 2 Chr 12:13) ① The first king of the southern kingdom of Judah (1 Kgs 12:1-24; 14:21-31; 2 Chr 10:1 – 12:16), he is the third individual in the second period of Jesus' genealogy (Matt 1:7; 1 Chr 3:10). His father was Solomon and his mother was Naamah the Ammonitess (1 Kgs 11:43; 14:21, 31). ② As an evil king, he committed detestable acts such as building high places, idols, and Asherim on every high hill and beneath every tree, as well as keeping male prostitutes in the land (1 Kgs 14:22-24). ③ Although the northern and southern division of the kingdom was the result of Solomon's sin (1 Kgs 11:9-13, 26-40), Rehoboam became the actual cause for the division to historically occur when he ignored the instructions of the elders and oppressed the people (1 Kgs 12:1-5). As a result, the ten tribes of the northern kingdom of Israel betrayed the house of David and established Jeroboam as king (1 Kgs 12:16-20; 2 Chr 10:16-19). ④ King Shishak of Egypt attacked Jerusalem when Rejoboam forsook the law of the Lord (2 Chr 12:1). At this time, Rehoboam listened to the warnings of the prophet Shemaiah and humbled himself. As a result, God saved the people from the hands of Shishak and his wrath was not poured out on Jerusalem (2 Chr 12:1-12).
4th Generation **Abijah** אֲבִיָּה Ἀβιά The Lord is my father **(Abijam)** אֲבִיָּם Ἀβιου The father of the sea ——— Wicked king	➤ **Period of Reign** 3 years (913ᵇ–910 BC) (1 Kgs 15:1-2; 2 Chr 13:1-2) ① The second king of the southern kingdom of Judah (1 Kgs 15:1-8; 2 Chr 13:1-22), he is the fourth individual in the second period of Jesus' genealogy (Matt 1:7; 1 Kgs 3:10). His father was Rehoboam and his mother was Maacah (the daughter of Abishalom—1 Kgs 15:2, also known as the daughter of Absalom—2 Chr 11:20-22) who was also known as Micaiah (the daughter of Uriel of Gibeah) (2 Chr 13:2). ② As an evil king, he committed all of the same sins his father Rehoboam committed, and being nothing like David his heart was not wholly committed to the Lord (1 Kgs 15:3). ③ The reason that their army of 400,000 was victorious over the northern kingdom of Israel (500,000 men of Israel fell slain, 2 Chr 13:17) who had twice their military force (800,000) was the result of Abijah having conviction (2 Chr 13:4-12) that "the rule over Israel [was given] forever to David and his sons by a covenant of salt (2 Chr 13:5)" and humbly placing his trust in "the God of their fathers" (2 Chr 13:18). ④ Although Jeroboam of the northern kingdom of Israel died without being able to recover his strength, Abijah of the southern kingdom of Judah became increasingly powerful and became the father of 22 sons and 16 daughters through his 14 wives (2 Chr 13:20-21).

People	History
5th Generation **Asa** אָסָא 'Ασά Healer/healing Good king	➤ **Period of Reign** 41 years (910–869 BC) (1 Kgs 15:9-10; 2 Chr 14:1) ① The third king of the southern kingdom of Judah (1 Kgs 15:9-24; 2 Chr 14:1 – 16:14), he is the fifth individual in the second period of Jesus' genealogy (Matt 1:7-8; 1 Chr 3:10). His father was Abijah and his mother is recorded as Maacah (the daughter of Abishalom and Absalom) (1 Kgs 15:8, 10; 2 Chr 14:1). The reason that the name is the same as Abijah's mother is because Maacah was the grandmother of King Asa but she also played the role of mother to him. Asa even deposed "Maacah" from being queen mother after she worshipped Asherah (1 Kgs 15:13). ② As a good king, Asa lived righteously and was wholly devoted to the Lord all his days (1 Kgs 15:11, 14). He drove out the male cult prostitutes, removed all the idols his fathers had made, and took down all of the high places (1 Kgs 15:12-15; 2 Chr 14:3-5). ③ Asa placed his trust in God and as a result he was greatly victorious in the battle against Zerah the Cushite (Ethiopian) who had an army of a million men and 300 chariots (2 Chr 14:9-15). ④ The war with the northern kingdom of Israel never ceased (1 Kgs 15:16). When Asa was attacked by the northern kingdom of Israel (Baasha) he was rebuked by Hanani the seer for relying on Ben-hadad the king of Aram. However, rather than repenting, Asa put Hanani in prison (2 Chr 16:1-10). As a result, Asa came down with a severe foot disease in his 39th regnal year. For two years Asa did not seek the Lord, but physicians instead and ended up dying in his 41st regnal year (1 Kgs 15:23-24; 2 Chr 16:12-14).
6th Generation **Jehoshaphat** יְהוֹשָׁפָט 'Ιωσαφάτ The Lord judges Good king	➤ **Period of Reign** 25 years (age 35–59, 871–847 BC) (1 Kgs 22:41-42) ① The fourth king of the southern kingdom of Judah (1 Kgs 22:41-50; 2 Chr 17:1 – 20:37), he is the sixth individual in the second period of Jesus' genealogy (Matt 1:8; 1 Chr 3:10). His father was Asa and his mother was Azubah (the daughter of Shilhi—1 Kgs 22:42; 2 Chr 20:31). He had six sons (Azariah, Jehiel, Zechariah, Azaryahu, Michael and Shephatiah) in addition to Jehoram (2 Chr 21:2-3). ② As a very good king, he walked in the way of David's earlier days (2 Chr 17:3) and the way of his father Asa, and he was upright before the Lord (1 Kgs 2:43; 2 Chr 20:32-33). He removed the Gentile altars and Asherim from Judah (2 Chr 17:6). ③ At the time Jehoshaphat had great riches and honor, his greatest mistake was when he allied with Ahab through marriage (2 Chr 18:1). Though the marriage of his son Jehoram with Athaliah, the daughter of the northern kingdom's King Ahab, may have brought about immediate peace (1 Kgs 22:44) with the northern kingdom of Israel, but later the entire southern kingdom of Judah became like the house of Ahab in being a hothouse of worshipping Baal (2 Chr 21:6, 13). The reason that God did not destroy the nation despite everything was because of the covenant that God established with David in which He promised to give a lamp to him always (2 Kgs 8:19; 2 Chr 21:7).

People	History
7th Generation **Jehoram** יְהוֹרָם Ἰωράμ **(Joram)** יוֹרָם Ἰωράμ The Lord is exalted, the Lord is honorable ——— Wicked king	➤ **Period of Reign** 8 years (age 32–39, 847–840 BC) (2 Kgs 8:16-17; 2 Chr 21:1, 5, 20) ① The fifth king of the southern kingdom of Judah (2 Kgs 8:16-24; 2 Chr 21:1-20), he is the seventh individual in the second period of Jesus' genealogy (Matt 1:8; 1 Chr 3:11). His father was Jehoshaphat (2 Kgs 8:16; 2 Chr 21:1) and there is no mention of his mother. ② He became an evil king because of his ungodly marriage with Ahab's daughter Athaliah (2 Kgs 8:18; 2 Chr 21:6). Instigated by his father-in-law Ahab, mother-in-law Jezebel, and wife Athaliah, Jehoram erected high places, and lured the people to play the harlot in worshiping Baal (2 Chr 21:11). After acceding to the throne and gaining power he killed his six innocent brothers with the sword (2 Chr 21:2-4). ③ Edom and Libnah had been under the southern kingdom of Judah but as Jehoram forsook the God of the forefathers they rose up and revolted (2 Kgs 8:20-22; 2 Chr 21:8-10). ④ According to the prophecy of the prophet Elijah (2 Chr 21:12-15), Jehoram was attacked by the Philistines and Arabs who carried off all the goods found in the king's palace, along with his sons and wives. Only his youngest son Jehoahaz (Ahaziah) was left and Jehoram was inflicted with an incurable disease of the bowels. At the end of two years, his bowels spilled out and he passed away to no one's regret (2 Chr 21:16-20).
8th Generation **Uzziah** עֻזִּיָּה Ὀζίας The Lord is my strength **(Azariah)** עֲזַרְיָה Ἀζαρίας The Lord has helped ——— Good king that became wicked	➤ **Period of Reign** 52 years (age 16–68, 791–739 BC; 2 Kgs 14:21; 15:1-2; 2 Chr 26:1-3) ① The tenth king of the southern kingdom of Judah (2 Kgs 15:1-7; 2 Chr 26:1-23), he is the eighth individual in the second period of Jesus' genealogy (Matt 1:8-9; 1 Chr 3:12). His father was Amaziah, his mother was Jecoliah (also known as Jechiliah of Jerusalem—2 Kgs 15:1-2; 2 Chr 26:1-3), and he loved the soil (2 Chr 26:10). ② As a good king, he did right in the sight of the Lord (2 Kgs 15:3; 2 Chr 26:4-5). Uzziah continued to seek God in the days of Zechariah, who had the understandings of the vision of God; and as long as he sought the Lord, God prospered him (2 Chr 26:5). However, Uzziah did not take down the high places (2 Kgs 15:4). ③ Since the time of Solomon, Uzziah was most powerful as his influence extended to the border of Egypt (2 Chr 26:6-8), his kingdom was solid as he established great military strength (2 Chr 26:9-15), and his fame spread afar. This was because he was marvelously helped (2 Chr 26:15^b). ④ He became arrogant in his latter years as he became powerful (2 Chr 26:16) and attempted to enter the temple of God to burn incense on the altar of incense. Azariah the priest and eighty priests of the Lord entered after him and dissuaded him but in his stubbornness Uzziah became enraged. At that moment, leprosy broke out on his forehead (2 Chr 26:16-19) and until the day of his death he lived in a separate house as a leper (2 Kgs 15:5; 2 Chr 26:20-21).

People	History
9th Generation **Jotham** יוֹתָם Ἰωαθάμ The Lord is perfect ——— Good king	➤ **Period of Reign** 16 years (age 25–40, 750–735 BC) (2 Kgs 15:32-33; 2 Chr 27:1, 8) ① The 11th king of the southern kingdom of Judah (2 Kgs 15:32-38; 2 Chr 27:1-9), he is the ninth individual in the second period of Jesus' genealogy (Matt 1:9; 1 Chr 3:12). His father was Uzziah and his mother was Jerusha (the daughter of Zadok—2 Kgs 15:32-33; 2 Chr 27:1). When his father Uzziah became a leper Jotham watched over the king's house judging the people of the land (2 Chr 26:21). ② As a good king, he did what was right in the sight of the Lord according to all that his father Uzziah had done (2 Kgs 15:34; 2 Chr 27:2). He built the upper gate of the temple of the Lord (2 Kgs 15:35b; 2 Chr 27:3ᵃ) and he became mighty because he ordered his ways before the Lord (2 Chr 27:6). ③ He devoted his heart and soul to strengthening the national defense in building military fortifications (the wall of Ophel, cities in the hill country of Judah, and fortresses and towers on the wooded hills— 2 Chr 27:3-4). ④ As a result of strengthening the national defense, he was victorious in the battle against the king of the Ammonites and he received from the Ammonites 100 talents of silver, 10,000 kors of wheat, and 10,000 kors of barley until the third year of his reign (2 Chr 27:5).
10th Generation **Ahaz** אָחָז Ἀχάζ He has grasped ——— Wicked king	➤ **Period of Reign** 16 years (age 24–40, 731–715 BC) (2 Kgs 16:1-2; 2 Chr 28:1) Ahaz entered a formal joint reign with Jotham in 735 BC, in "the seventeenth year of Pekah" (2 Kgs 16:1) of the northern kingdom of Israel. Ahaz was 20 years old at this time (2 Kgs 16:2). ① The 12th king of the southern kingdom of Judah (2 Kgs 16:1-20; 2 Chr 28:1-27), he is the tenth individual in the second period of Jesus' genealogy (Matt 1:9; 1 Chr 3:13). His father was Jotham (2 Kgs 16:1; 2 Chr 27:9) and there is no record regarding his mother. ② As an evil king, he did not do right in the sight of the Lord, but he walked in the ways of the kings of Israel in making molten images for the Baals (2 Chr 28:1-2). Furthermore, he committed the deeds of "abominations" in burning his sons in fire according to the abominations of the Gentile nations (2 Chr 28:3). ③ When he forsook the God of his forefathers, a great number of captives were taken when he was attacked by Rezin the king of Aram, 120,000 soldiers of the southern kingdom of Judah were killed in one day by Pekah the king of the northern kingdom, and 200,000 were taken captive but returned after the urging of the prophet Oded (2 Chr 28:5-15). Furthermore, during the invasion of the Edomites and Philistines, Ahaz relied on Assyria once again who not only failed to block the enemy attacks but instead afflicted (aggrieved) Ahaz (2 Chr 28:16-21). In this way, the more hardships Ahaz endured the more he sinned. He built an altar according to the pattern of the altar at Damascus and gave offerings to foreign gods, he desecrated the utensils of the temple, closed the doors of the temple of God, and built altars for himself in

People	History

every corner of Jerusalem. Ahaz provoked wrath of the Lord by committing foolish acts such as building high places for other gods in every city of Judah (2 Kgs 16:10-18; 2 Chr 28:22-25).

④ When Ahaz was facing severe hardships through the attacks of Rezin the king of Aram and Pekah the king of the northern kingdom of Israel, the prophet Isaiah gave the sign of hope proclaiming, "Behold, a virgin will be with child and bear a son, and she will call His name Immanuel" (Isa 7:14). In doing so, Isaiah planted within Ahaz's heart the conviction of salvation. In this way, Ahaz was wicked but God remembered the covenant He had made with David and gave an even surer sign of Immanuel.

11th Generation

Hezekiah

חִזְקִיָּה

Ἐζεκίας

The Lord is my strength, the Lord is strong

———

Good king

> **Period of Reign**

29 years (age 25–54, 715–686 BC; 2 Kgs 18:1-2; 2 Chr 29:1)

① The 13th king of the southern kingdom of Judah (2 Kgs 18:1 – 20:21; 2 Chr 29:1 – 32:33), he is the 11th individual in the second period of Jesus' genealogy (Matt 1:9-10; 1 Chr 3:13). His father was Ahaz and his mother was Abi (Abijah) the daughter of Zechariah (2 Kgs 18:1-2; 2 Chr 29:1).

② He was a good king and there were none like him among all the kings of Judah (2 Kgs 18:5). He walked in the ways of David and he did right in the sight of the Lord (2 Kgs 18:3; 2 Chr 29:2). He broke in pieces the bronze serpent that Moses had made and it was called Nehushtan, and he removed the high places (2 Kgs 18:4). He consecrated the temple of God (2 Chr 29:3-11) and a magnificent Passover was kept with all of Israel in which there was great joy in Jerusalem that was unparalleled since the days of Solomon (2 Chr 30:1-27).

③ Hezekiah became ill and was at the verge of death when his life was extended 15 years (Isa 38:1-8; 2 Kgs 20:1-11). However, he became proud and while he failed to repay the kindness of the Lord, Hezekiah revealed the contents of his storehouses to the envoy of Marduk-Baladon king of Babylon. Hezekiah was showing off as if to say that the wealth of the prosperous nation was the fruit of his might and endeavors. He received the proclamation that the southern kingdom of Judah would be punished and collapse under Babylon as a result of his sins (2 Kgs 20:12-18; 2 Chr 32:24-25). However, Hezekiah repented of his prideful heart and as a result the wrath of the Lord was not incurred during Hezekiah's lifetime (2 Kgs 20:19; 2 Chr 32:26).

④ In 722 BC the northern kingdom of Israel completely fell to Shalmaneser king of Assyria, and afterwards Sennacherib king of Assyria attacked to capture the cities of Judah as well (2 Kgs 18:13-37; 2 Chr 32:1-19). At that moment Hezekiah took the enemy's letter filled with slander and malice, he went up to the temple of the Lord, spread the letter before the Lord, and prayed to God (2 Kgs 19:14-19; Isa 37:14-20). The prophet Isaiah prayed with Hezekiah as well (2 Chr 32:20). As a result of their combined prayers, they reaped a miraculous victory when the angel of the Lord went out and had made corpses of the 185,000 soldiers the next morning (2 Kgs 19:35; 2 Chr 32:21-22; Isa 37:36).

People	History
12th Generation **Manasseh** מְנַשֶּׁה Μανασσῆς To forget, causing to forget ——— Extremely wicked king (Repented in his latter years)	➤ **Period of Reign** 55 years (age 12–66, 696–642 BC; 2 Kgs 21:1; 2 Chr 33:1) ① The 14th king of the southern kingdom of Judah (2 Kgs 21:1-18; 2 Chr 33:1-20), he is the 12th individual in the second period of Jesus' genealogy (Matt 1: 10; 1 Chr 3:13). His father was Hezekiah and his mother was Hephzibah (2 Kgs 21:1). ② As a very evil king, he did not follow the example of his father Hezekiah but the abominable acts of the Gentiles. Manasseh rebuilt the high places his father Hezekiah had destroyed and worshiped idols. Even worse, he built idol altars in the two courts of the holy temple of the Lord and committed other evil deeds which provoked God's anger to burst (2 Kgs 21:2-9; 2 Chr 33:2-9). Furthermore, Manasseh shed so much innocent blood that he filled Jerusalem from end to end (2 Kgs 21:16; 24:4). ③ As a very wicked king, his wicked deeds had reached its climax and were the decisive cause for the destruction of the southern kingdom of Judah (2 Kgs 23:26; 24:2-4; Jer 15:4). Due to "all the provocations with which Manasseh had provoked Him" the Lord did not turn from "the fierceness of His great wrath" (2 Kgs 23:26). ④ In the latter years of Manasseh's reign (648 BC according to the Assyrian epitaph), he encountered much misery as he was chained and dragged away to Babylon. However, he greatly repented and was restored back to his throne. It was then that he knew that the Lord is God (2 Chr 33:10-13). Although Manasseh was a malicious king, he repented and eradicated the foreign gods and the image from the temple of the Lord. He also destroyed the idol altars in Jerusalem (2 Chr 33:14-17). As a result of his thorough repentance, he was recorded in the covenantal genealogy as one continuing the holy line of the Messiah (Matt 1:10).
13th Generation **Amon** אָמוֹן Ἀμών Trustworthy, faithful, skillful ——— Wicked king	➤ **Period of Reign** 2 years (age 22–24, 642–640 BC; 2 Kgs 21:19; 2 Chr 33:21) ① The 15th king of the southern kingdom of Judah (2 Kgs 21:19-26; 2 Chr 33:21-25), he is the 13th individual in the second period of Jesus' genealogy (Matt 1:10; 1 Chr 3:14). His father was Manasseh and his mother was Meshullemeth (the daughter of Haruz of Jotbah—2 Kgs 21:19). ② As an evil king, he did evil in the sight of the Lord as his father Manasseh had done and forsook the God of his fathers (2 Kgs 21:20-22). Moreover, Amon sacrificed to all the carved images which his father Manasseh had made (2 Chr 33:22) and by not humbling himself before the Lord he fell further into sin (2 Chr 33:23). ③ Amon died pitifully in his own palace when his servants conspired against him (2 Kgs 21:23; 2 Chr 33:24). The people killed those who had conspired against King Amon and placed his son Josiah as king (2 Kgs 21:24; 2 Chr 33:25).

People	History
14th Generation **Josiah** יֹאשִׁיָּה Ἰωσίας The Lord supports, the Lord encourages ——— Good king	➤ **Period of Reign** 31 years (age 8–39, 640—609[b] BC; 2 Kgs 22:1; 2 Chr 34:1) ① The 16th king of the southern kingdom of Judah (2 Kgs 22:1 – 23:30; 2 Chr 34:1 – 35:27), he is the 14th individual in the second period of Jesus' genealogy (Matt 1:10-11; 1 Chr 3:14). His father was Amon and his mother was Jedidah (the daughter of Adaiah of Bozkath—2 Kgs 22:1). ② As a very good king, from his youth he sought the God of his father David (2 Chr 34:3), he did right in the sight of the Lord, walked in the way of David, and did not turn aside to the right or left (2 Kgs 22:2; 2 Chr 34:2). The phrase "do not turn to the right or the left" was among Moses' teachings of the correct conduct of a king (Deut 17:18-20). Josiah was the only king that was commended for keeping this teaching. Furthermore, there was no king like him who had followed "according to all the law of Moses" (2 Kgs 23:25). ③ Josiah acceded to the throne at the age of 8; at 16 years of age he began to seek the Lord (2 Chr 34:3); at 20 years of age (12th year of reign) he demolished the idols in Jerusalem (2 Chr 34:3-4); and at 26 years of age (18th year of reign) he began to repair the temple of the Lord (2 Kgs 22:3-6; 2 Chr 34:8), carried out a religious reformation (2 Kgs 23:1-20) based upon the book of the law (2 Kgs 22:8) that Hilkiah the high priest found, and celebrated the Passover on a grand scale (2 Kgs 23:21-23; 2 Chr 35:1-19). While carrying out the religious reformation, according to the prophecy of an unknown prophet 280 years before (1 Kgs 13:2), Josiah ground to dust and burned the altar at Bethel and the high place which Jeroboam had made (2 Kgs 23:15-16). ④ Josiah died in the battle against Neco (Pharaoh Neco) the pharaoh of Egypt (2 Kgs 23:29-30; 2 Chr 35:20-25). The Bible states the reason for Josiah's death as, "nor did he listen to the words of Neco from the mouth of God" (2 Chr 35:22). Josiah was like the final lamp of the southern kingdom of Judah which was beginning to decline and the people greatly mourned his death (Ref Zech 12:11). The prophet Jeremiah made a song of lamentation for him (2 Chr 35:25). After the death of Josiah, the fate of the country suddenly began to weaken and was on the path to the fall of the nation.

CHAPTER 6

The First Generation: David

David / Δαβίδ, Δαυίδ / דָּוִד
Beloved, friend

- The second king of the United Monarchy (2 Sam 2:4; 5:3)
- The first king in the second period of Jesus' genealogy

Matthew 1:6 Jesse was the father of **David** the king. **David** was the father of Solomon by Bathsheba who had been the wife of Uriah.

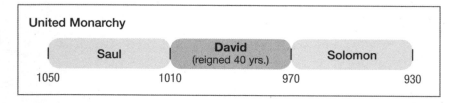

United Monarchy

Saul	David (reigned 40 yrs.)	Solomon
1050	1010	970	930

Background
Father: Jesse
Mother: A godly woman who served God (Ps 86:16; 116:16)
Sons: Solomon (Matt 1:6; Luke 3:32; Ruth 4:17) plus 19 others[10]

Characteristics
David reigned for 40 years (1010 BC – 970 BC; 2 Sam 5:4-5; 1 Kgs 2:11; 1 Chr 3:4). He reigned in Hebron for seven years and six months and had six sons there (2 Sam 3:2-5; 1 Chr 3:1-4). Then he reigned in Jerusalem for 33 years and had 13 sons there (2 Sam 5:13-16; 1 Chr 3:4-9; 14:3-7). He also had a son named "Jerimoth" (2 Chr 11:18).[11]

In Hebrew, the name David is דָּוִד (*dāwid*), and in Greek it is Δαβίδ (*Dabid*). דָּוִד (*dāwid*) in Hebrew means "beloved," "a loved one," "friend," or "lover" and is related to the root word דּוֹד (*dōwd*), which means "to boil" and "to love."

David is the individual who concludes the first 14 generations of Jesus' genealogy while beginning the second set of 14 generations. The second grouping of 14 generations in Jesus' genealogy starts out with the words, "And David was the father of Solomon by the wife of Uriah" (Matt 1:6, ESV).

1. David became the father of Solomon by the wife of Uriah.

In Matthew 1:6 it is stated, "David the king begat Solomon of her that had been the wife of Urias" (King James Version). The King James Version accurately reflects the original Greek by choosing to translate this verse by omitting the name of Bathsheba and simply referring to her as "her that had been the wife of Uriah." What would be the reason for this?

First, the genealogy is emphasizing that the faithfulness of Uriah, rather than Bathsheba, deserves to be included in the genealogy of Jesus Christ.
After committing adultery with Bathsheba, David called her husband, Uriah, back from the battlefield in order to try to get him to sleep with his wife. However, Uriah did not even go home or sleep with his wife because he was mindful of his fellow soldiers and subordinates who were still fighting in the battlefield (2 Sam 11:9-13). The law also states that one should keep away from every evil thing in time of war (Deut 23:9). So David sent Uriah to his death by putting him in the frontlines of battle where the fighting was the fiercest. Uriah died a heroic death while fighting for his country (2 Sam 11:14-17).

Second, the genealogy is emphasizing David's iniquity.
When the kingdom was engaged in a fierce battle against Ammon, David took his subordinate's wife and committed adultery with her. Then, David acted like an evil king by sending her husband into the frontlines of battle, intending to kill him (2 Sam 11:17, 24). However, Uriah was a righteous servant who was faithful even to such a malicious king. Jesus' genealogy underscores the righteousness of Uriah and the iniquity of David by contrasting them to one another.

Third, the genealogy is emphasizing God's forgiveness and grace.
Although David committed a grievous sin, he repented to the point of drenching his couch with tears after being reprimanded by Nathan the

prophet (Ps 6:6; 51:1-2, 9-14). However, the first child born to David and Bathsheba died. David pleaded for this child by fasting for seven days (2 Sam 12:15-23).

When David was greatly indignant about his own sin and repented thoroughly, God forgave him and allowed his son Solomon to become the channel of blessing through which Jesus Christ may come. This incident actually recalls to mind the passage in Romans which says, "where sin increased, grace abounded all the more" (Rom 5:20).

2. David was greatly loved by God.

Just as his name means "beloved," David was greatly loved by God during his lifetime. God anointed a mere shepherd boy as the king of a nation (2 Sam 16:11-13). For over ten years when David was running from Saul, who sought to kill him, God protected him to the end. Because God loved David, He established a covenant with him and promised to build the temple through his descendant and to establish the throne of his kingdom forever (2 Sam 7:12-16).

Though David committed adultery with Bathsheba and killed Uriah in order to conceal his sin, God forgave him when David repented thoroughly (2 Sam 12:13). Also, when David—barefoot and in tears—was chased out of Jerusalem by Absalom, God blessed him by restoring him to his throne. In his latter years, when David revealed his pride by calling for a census to show off his achievements, God relented from his wrath and curtailed the plague upon David's burnt and peace offerings at Araunah's threshing floor (2 Sam 24:25). Truly, David had experienced God's boundless mercy and love throughout his lifetime. David continuously received the great love of God during his perilous lifetime because he repented of his sins with great contrition (Ps 6:6; 51:9-14).

True repentance means to distance oneself from sin while always trying to come closer to the good. It is a complete about-face—turning away from a self-centered life to a God-centered and Word-centered life. True repentance involves intellectual recognition of, emotional contrition for, and volitional renunciation of sin. Furthermore, it also involves loving God and pursuing righteousness. We are confronted with difficulties in our lives because we have not been able to take care of the concealed sins in our hearts (Job 4:7).

Like David, we must grieve over our sins, shed tears of contrition, and repent in all sincerity. When we repent like this, God will come to us with His unchanging love; and not only will He restore us to our original station, but He will also bless us so that our lives will be richer and fuller than before (Ps 34:18; 51:17).

CHAPTER 7

The Second Generation: Solomon

Solomon / Σολομών / שְׁלֹמֹה
Peaceful

- The third king of the United Monarchy (1 Kgs 1:38-11:43; 1 Chr 29:20-2 Chr 9:31)
- The second individual in the second period of Jesus' genealogy

Matthew 1:6 David was the father of **Solomon** by Bathsheba who had been the wife of Uriah.

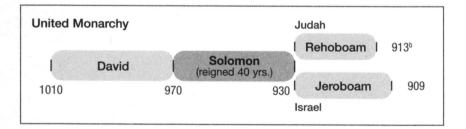

Background
Father: David (Tribe of Judah)
Mother: Bath-shua (Bathsheba) daughter of Ammiel (2 Sam 12:24; 1 Chr 3:5)

Duration of reign
Solomon reigned for 40 years (970 – 930 BC; 1 Kgs 11:42; 2 Chr 9:30).
After Solomon's death, Jeroboam seceded with ten tribes, dividing the kingdom into the southern kingdom of Judah and the northern kingdom of Israel.

Evaluation – For the most part, a good king (1 Kgs 3:3, 6; 2 Chr 8:14)
In the latter half of his reign, his many foreign wives led Solomon to follow after other gods. Solomon's heart was not wholly devoted to God as the heart of David his father had been (1 Kgs 11:4).

In Hebrew, Solomon is שְׁלֹמֹה (šĕlōmō), which means "peaceful." The word שְׁלֹמֹה is derived from the word שָׁלוֹם (šālōwm), which means "peace," "quiet," "tranquility" and "prosperity." The name signifies a "man of peace" and it is a name that God had given to him before he was even born (1 Chr 22:9a). The time of Solomon's reign was actually the most peaceful time in Israel's history. This was, in fact, a fulfillment of God's words which He had spoken before Solomon's birth (1 Chr 22:9b).

When Bathsheba gave birth to Solomon, God Himself gave the name יְדִידְיָה (yĕdîdĕyāh) through Nathan the prophet. The name means "beloved of Jehovah" (2 Sam 12:24-25), and it expresses God's immense love for Solomon. It also indicates that God has already considered Solomon for the throne after David. Solomon is actually the fourth son of David and Bathsheba, after Shimea, Shobab, and Nathan (1 Chr 3:5). However, 2 Samuel 12:24 records the account as if Solomon were born directly following Bathsheba's firstborn who had died. It was recorded this way to suggest that Solomon is the son to succeed David's throne as well as his covenant (2 Sam 12:15, 24-25).

1. Solomon firmly established the kingdom after David's death.

First Kings 2:12 states, "And Solomon sat on the throne of David his father, and his kingdom was firmly established" (2 Chr 1:1). Here the word *established* in Hebrew is in the passive form of the waw consecutive of the verb כּוּן (kûn), which means "to set up," "to be stable," and "to be established." It means that God firmly secured Solomon's royal authority as soon as he took the throne. The Davidic covenant was the basis of this divine action for God had promised in 2 Samuel 7:12, "I will raise up your descendant after you, who will come forth from you, and I will establish his kingdom." And indeed, God had firmly established Solomon's kingly authority according to that promise.

Solomon had to take a few necessary measures to firmly establish the kingdom.

First, Solomon killed Adonijah.

Adonijah was the fourth son born to David in Hebron; his mother was Haggith (2 Sam 3:4). Solomon killed his brother Adonijah as soon as he took the throne (1 Kgs 2:25). When Adonijah plotted an insurrection to succeed the throne of David, Solomon spared his life. However, Adonijah brought death upon himself by asking to marry Abishag, the servant girl who had taken care of King David (1 Kgs 2:13-21). Adonijah had shown his hidden ulterior motive to usurp the throne when he requested to marry the Shunammite maidservant who had ministered to David in his latter years (1 Kgs 1:1-4). Therefore, Adonijah was killed because he challenged God's will by persistently pursuing his royal ambitions.

When Adonijah plotted the coup d'etat, Solomon said, "If he is a worthy man, not one of his hairs will fall to the ground; but if wickedness is found in him, he will die" (1 Kgs 1:52). Solomon generously offered Adonijah a way to live despite his treasonous act—just give up all ambitions for royal power (1 Kgs 1:51-53). However, Adonijah did evil again by rekindling his desires for power by requesting to take Abishag as wife. As soon as he heard this, Solomon sent Benaiah son of Jehoiada to strike him down (1 Kgs 2:25). This incident indicates to us that whoever goes against the will of God will be destroyed (Ps 107:10-11).

Second, Solomon banished Abiathar the priest.

Abiathar the priest supported Adonijah when he attempted to usurp the throne (1 Kgs 1:7). In the past, Abiathar participated in carrying the Ark of God into Jerusalem (1 Chr 15:11-15). Moreover, he was a priest anointed by God and was faithful to David during his trials (2 Sam 15:24). Therefore, he was not killed but exiled to Anathoth (1 Kgs 2:26-27).

This event took place in accordance with the Word of God. In the past, God had declared that He would destroy Eli's clan (1 Sam 2:27-36), and Abiathar was a descendant of Eli (1 Kgs 2:27, Ref 1 Chr 24:3-6). Furthermore, the event is a fulfillment of God's Word which had proclaimed that the descendants of Eleazar would be priests forever. At the plains of Moab just prior to the entrance into Canaan, Phinehas, the son of Eleazar, took a spear and pierced through the bodies of the adulterous man and woman (Zimri and Cozbi, respectively). At this, God declared,

"Behold, I give him My covenant of peace; and it shall be for him and his descendants after him, a covenant of a perpetual priesthood" (Num 25:6-13).

Despite such a declaration by God, Zadok the descendant of Eleazar, the third son of Aaron, and Ahimelech the descendant of Ithamar, the fourth son of Aaron, served concurrently as high priests during David's reign (1 Chr 24:1-3). However, as Solomon stripped Abiathar, the son of Ahimelech, of his priesthood, the descendants of Eleazar were finally able to become the sole clan to serve as high priests. Unfortunately, the high priesthood, which was carried out by the Zadokite clan of the descendants of Eleazar, was suspended in 171 BC by the oppressive reign of Antiochus Epiphanes. Therefore, we can conclude that the prophecy of a perpetual priesthood for the line of Eleazar (Num 25:13) is a foreshadowing of the eternal priesthood of Jesus Christ who atoned for the sins of all humankind (Heb 6:20).

Abiathar was the son of Ahimelech the priest who had helped David at the beginning of his life of refuge. When Saul killed Ahimelech along with 85 other priests, Abiathar barely escaped alive and took refuge with David (1 Sam 22:20). Afterwards, when David became king, Abiathar became high priest along with Zadok (2 Sam 15:24; 1 Chr 15:11). He also aided David and stayed with him in Jerusalem even through the tumultuous times during Absalom's rebellion (2 Sam 15:35-36). However, in the end, Abiathar took part in the insurrection to enthrone Adonijah as king. This was not David's intention, and this would be the event that leads to the tragic conclusion of Abiathar's career as high priest—divestiture. One erroneous decision brought down a lifetime of commendable achievements and reputation. Overnight, Abiathar lost everything and his latter years would become a pitiful byword.

Third, Solomon killed Joab and Shimei.

When Joab, who had tried to enthrone Adonijah, heard that Abiathar had been deposed of his priestly duty, he fled to the tent of the Lord and took hold of the horns of the altar (1 Kgs 2:28). Joab recalled that Adonijah had previously held on to the horns of the altar to save his life (1 Kgs 1:50-53). However, Solomon had ordered Benaiah to kill Joab even if it was inside the house of God (1 Kgs 2:34). Solomon had done this based on the law of God which states that a man who kills intentionally shall be taken even from God's altar to be put to death (Exod 21:12-14;

Ref Deut 19:11-13). Solomon was also obeying David's deathbed instructions (1 Kgs 2:5-6).

Shimei was the one who had cursed and thrown stones at David and his servants as they were fleeing from Absalom's revolt (2 Sam 16:5-8). However, when Absalom's attempted coup had failed, Shimei—ever the opportunist—had come before David, who was about to cross the Jordan, to beg for forgiveness (2 Sam 19:16-23). Since Shimei's hometown of Bahurim was just on the other side of the brook Kidron (1 Kgs 2:8), Solomon wanted to restrict his activities by forbidding him from leaving Jerusalem. Solomon had warned that the moment he stepped across brook Kidron and out of Jerusalem, he would be put to death (1 Kgs 2:36-38).

Three years later, however, Shimei had broken his promise with Solomon by leaving Jerusalem to go to Gath to find his two servants who had taken refuge with Achish son of Maacah, king of Gath. Solomon immediately punished Shimei, who had disobeyed the order to never leave Jerusalem (1 Kgs 2:39-46). Shimei's punishment was, in fact, a fulfillment of David's dying wish (1 Kgs 2:8-9). Although Shimei was a heinous sinner, his life had been spared, and yet his gratitude for such a favor had been lightly dismissed. Moreover, he had hastily disregarded Solomon's orders. These factors contributed to his death.

With Shimei's death, most of the major foes of the kingdom had been eliminated; Solomon's kingdom was firmly established and flourishing daily (1 Kgs 2:46). Solomon had firmly established the kingdom of Israel by upholding David's final wishes to eliminate the individuals who were impediments to the will of God. In order for God's will to be firmly established and flourishing, we must first eliminate the evil which displeases God (Prov 25:5; 2 Chr 7:14; Jer 4:14; 26:3; Ezek 18:27; 33:19; Jas 1:21).

As his internal enemies had been defeated and the domestic political situation was stable, Solomon forged diplomatic relations with Egypt and married the Pharaoh's daughter to signalize their alliance (1 Kgs 3:1). Later, Solomon would even build a house for the Pharaoh's daughter (1 Kgs 9:24; 1 Chr 8:11). Through this marriage of convenience, Solomon was able to avoid confrontations with Egypt and accumulate much wealth through trade (1 Kgs 10:28-29). This may have been a necessary maneuver within the dynamics of international politics, but it was inappropriate to use the sacred institution of marriage for political means. Most importantly, this went against the Word of God (Deut 7:3-4; 17:17).

2. Solomon established the most powerful kingdom by ruling with wisdom.

Solomon had built the most powerful kingdom in the history of Israel.

First, the kingdom had secured the largest territorial area during Solomon's reign.

Solomon ruled "over all the kings from the Euphrates River even to the land of the Philistines, and as far as the border of Egypt" (2 Chr 9:26; 1 Kgs 4:21). Since he ruled over the kingdoms of this area, they all served Solomon and brought tribute to him.

Solomon was able to secure such a large territory because he had a powerful military behind him. Solomon had 12,000 horsemen, 1,400 chariots and 4,000 stalls for horses and chariots (2 Chr 9:25; 1 Kgs 4:26; 10:26).[12] However, this goes against Deuteronomy 17:16 which states, "Moreover, he [the king] shall not multiply horses for himself, nor shall he cause the people to return to Egypt to multiply horses." This was an ominous foreboding of the future downfall of Solomon's kingdom, despite the current splendor and wealth.

Second, the kingdom enjoyed the greatest prosperity during Solomon's reign.

In 1 Kings 4:20 the Bible states, "Judah and Israel were as numerous as the sand that is on the seashore in abundance; they were eating and drinking and rejoicing." Solomon's daily provision consisted of "thirty kors of fine flour and sixty kors of meal, ten fat oxen, twenty pasture-fed oxen, a hundred sheep besides deer, gazelles , roebucks, and fattened fowl" (1 Kgs 4:22-23).

One בֹּר (kōr) equals about one homer (10 ephahs, approximately 230 kg). That means 30 kors of fine flour and 60 kors of meal would be approximately 20,700 kg, which can feed around 14,000 people. The amount of meat in his daily provision is enough to feed an individual portion of 600 grams to about 14,000 people as well. Just these figures alone give us a rough idea of the prosperity of Solomon's palace and the scale of grandeur the kingdom had reached under Solomon. Second Chronicles 1:15 states, "The king made silver and gold as plentiful in Jerusalem as stones, and he made cedars as plentiful as sycamores in the lowland."

The amount of gold that came in to Solomon annually was 666 talents (1 Kgs 10:14). This reflects the amount of tax, in the weight of gold, which was collected per annum. Since one talent of gold is 34 kg in weight, 666 talents of gold would amount to 22,644 kg—an enormous weight by any standard.

Moreover, the throne upon which Solomon sat was the very symbol of opulence during his time. Solomon had made a great throne of ivory and had covered it with gold (1 Kgs 10:18). The throne had a round top in its rear and six steps leading up to it. It had an armrest on each side and next to each armrest stood a lion. There were also 12 lions, one on each side of every step leading up to the throne. No other kingdom had a throne like this (1 Kgs 10:19-20).

All of Solomon's drinking vessels were of gold, and even the vessels in the house of the forest of Lebanon were also of gold (1 Kgs 10:21). This kind of wealth and prosperity that Solomon enjoyed was a direct fulfillment of 2 Chronicles 1:12, where God declared, "Wisdom and knowledge have been granted to you. And I will give you riches and wealth and honor, such as none of the kings who were before you has possessed nor those who will come after you."

Third, the kingdom enjoyed the greatest peace during the reign of Solomon.

The Bible in 1 Kings 4:25 states, "So Judah and Israel lived in safety, every man under his vine and his fig tree, from Dan even to Beersheba, all the days of Solomon." Here the word *safety* in Hebrew is בֶּטַח (*beṭaḥ*), which means "safety," "security," "feeling of assurance." Also the expression "under his fig tree" is referring to the comfortable shade that the tree provides. The fig tree has an abundance of branches and broad leaves to provide a splendid refuge where one can rest and meditate (John 1:48). Therefore, the phrase "lived in safety . . . under his vine and his fig tree" is a metaphorical expression referring to the peace that is in the kingdom and the joy abounding in the family. Ultimately, the expression indicates that the kingdom enjoyed peace and prosperity in the days of Solomon due to God's blessings (Mic 4:4).

Such peace and prosperity in the days of Solomon was another fulfillment of God's Words to David in 1 Chronicles 22:9 which states, "Behold, a son will be born to you, who shall be a man of rest; and I will give him rest from all his enemies on every side; for his name shall be Solomon, and I will give peace and quiet to Israel in his days." Indeed, it was confessed through Solomon's lips during the dedication of the temple that God was the One who had given Israel rest (peace; 1 Kgs

8:56). Unfortunately, the kingdom would be split in two not long after this event, and perfect peace would not be achieved (1 Kgs 12).

The unprecedented peace granted during the days of Solomon is actually pointing forward to the perfect peace that will be achieved when the Prince of Peace, Jesus Christ (Isa 9:6), comes to reign (Zech 3:10). In the time of peace that Jesus Christ brings, there will be no night (Rev 21:25), no more curses (Rev 22:3), and there will no longer be any death, mourning or pain (Rev 21:4).

Fourth, people from many nations came to hear the wisdom of Solomon.
Solomon's wisdom surpassed the wisdoms of all the sons of the east and the sons of Egypt (1 Kgs 4:30). First Kings 4:31 states that Solomon was wiser than "Ethan the Ezrahite (אֶזְרָחִי, *'ezrāḥî*), Heman, Calcol and Darda, the sons of Mahol." These four brilliant men, who were well renowned for their wisdom, were part of the clan of Zerah (זֶרַח: rising, shining) according to 2 Chronicles 2:6.[13] Ethan (אֵיתָן: permanent, durable) was a descendant of Merari (1 Chr 6:44; 15:17) and is known to be the author of Psalm 89 (Heading: "A Maskil of Ethan the Ezrahite"). Heman (הֵימָן: faithful) was a Korathite (1 Chr 6:33; Ps 88:1). Heman, just like Ethan, was a singer of hymns (1 Chr 15:16-17, 19; 25:1), "the king's seer in the words of God" (1 Chr 25:5, KJV) and the author of Psalm 88 (Heading: "A Maskil of Heman the Ezrahite"). Calcol (כַּלְכֹּל: sustaining) and Darda (דַּרְדַּע: pearl of knowledge; also "Dara") were wise men on equal footing with Ethan and Heman. As such, Solomon was wiser than the sages of his generation.

Through the wisdom God had bestowed, Solomon spoke 3,000 proverbs and composed 1,005 songs (1 Kgs 4:32). Regrettably, many of these proverbs and songs have not been passed down to the later generations; but a portion of them are recorded for us in the Old Testament books of Proverbs and Song of Songs. Also, there are two Psalms by Solomon (Ps 72; 127) and the entire book of Ecclesiastes was written by him as well. Furthermore, Solomon had breadth and depth of knowledge regarding animals and plants (1 Kgs 4:33). There were many kings on earth who had heard about the wisdom of Solomon and had come to him to hear his wise sayings (1 Kgs 4:34; 10:23-25).

The Queen of Sheba had also come to test Solomon with many difficult questions, and Solomon answered all of her questions (1 Kgs 10:1-3). First Kings 10:3 comments, "nothing was hidden from the king which he did not explain to her." Here, the word *hidden* in Hebrew is עָלַם ('ālam), which means "to conceal" and "to be hidden," and it signifies that Solomon was able to unveil the answer to all of the questions posed at him.

The Queen of Sheba initially did not believe the reports regarding Solomon which she had heard back in her country. However, after her visit to Jerusalem, she exclaimed that the stories she had heard about Solomon were not even half of the truth (1 Kgs 10:6-7; 2 Chr 9:5-6). It was not just his wisdom that impressed her. When the Queen of Sheba had seen the buildings he had built, the food on his table, the seating of his officials, the array of the servants and their attires, and the stairway that led up to the temple of the Lord—the Bible states that "there was no more spirit in her" (1 Kgs 10:5). The phrase, "there was no more spirit in her," was translated as "there was no more breath in her" in the ESV and "she was overwhelmed" in the NIV. She saw with her own eyes the things which she had heard from afar, and she confirmed that the truth exceeded the stories by bounds! It was the moment of ecstatic enchantment for her! Hence, the Queen of Sheba commented on the blessedness of the servants who continually stand before Solomon and hear his wisdom. Then she blessed the Lord, the God of Solomon who had bestowed such wisdom upon the king (1 Kgs 10:8-9; 2 Chr 9:7-8). Finally, the Queen of Sheba, who had been deeply moved by the wisdom she witnessed, gave the king 120 talents of gold and great amounts of spices and precious jewels. Never before had such an event taken place (1 Kgs 10:10; 2 Chr 9:9).

How was Solomon able to forge such a powerful and prosperous kingdom?

Politically speaking, the 21st Dynasty of Egypt had waned in power to its weakest point, and Assyria was also in a debilitated state. It is conceivable that such geopolitical conditions played a role in Israel's ascendancy. But in actuality, the more fundamental reason was that God had granted Solomon wisdom, discernment and breadth of mind. The Bible states in 1 Kings 4:29-30, "Now God gave Solomon wisdom and very great discernment and breadth of mind, like the sand that is on the seashore. Solomon's wisdom surpassed the wisdom of all the sons of the east and all the wisdom of Egypt." Also, 1 Kings 10:23-24 comments, "So King Solomon became greater than all the kings of the earth in riches and in wisdom. All the earth was seeking the presence of Solomon, to hear his wisdom which God had put in his heart."

Solomon's wisdom reminds us of Jesus Christ, who is the very wisdom of God (1 Cor 1:24, 30). Jesus was, as He himself testified, someone "greater than Solomon" (Matt 12:42; Luke 11:31). Jesus lamented over the evil generation who only sought signs and yet was unable to recognize the Son of Man who is the source of all wisdom. He bemoaned over them saying that the Queen of the South will rise up with that generation at the judgment and condemn it (Matt 12:38-42; Luke 11:29-31).

Those who receive the wisdom of God will excel above and beyond anyone else on earth. Proverbs 3:15-16 states, "She [wisdom] is more precious than jewels; and nothing you desire compares with her. Long life is in her right hand; in her left hand are riches and honor." Wisdom is paramount. If you prize wisdom, she will exalt you (Prov 4:7-8).

Why did God bestow such an amazing blessing of wisdom to Solomon? When Solomon finished offering a thousand burnt offerings, God said, "Ask what you wish me to give you" (1 Kgs 3:4-5; 2 Chr 1:7). This is when Solomon sought wisdom. Solomon said in 1 Kings 3:9, "So give Your servant an understanding heart to judge Your people, to discern between good and evil. For who is able to judge this great people of Yours?" This was pleasing in the sight of the Lord (1 Kgs 3:10; 2 Chr 1:11-12).

God responded by saying, "I have also given you what you have not asked, both riches and honor, so that there will not be any among the kings like you all your days" (1 Kgs 3:13). God will certainly grant wisdom to those who recognize their shortcomings and seek after wisdom (Jas 1:5). Solomon teaches us through his prayer that our first and foremost need is not riches and honor but the wisdom of God. It is this author's earnest hope and prayer that Solomon's "blessing of wisdom" will be the blessing that is bestowed upon the saints of God who trust and follow the source of true wisdom, our Lord Jesus Christ.

3. Solomon built the temple of the Lord.

Solomon completed the temple which David had prepared for but could not finish. The construction of the temple was started in the month of Ziv in Solomon's fourth regnal year and finished in the month of Bul in his 11th regnal year (1 Kgs 6:1, 37-38; 2 Chr 3:2).

(1) A few distinctive features about the construction of Solomon's temple

First, Solomon's temple is founded upon David's God-centered faith (1 Chr 22; 28; 29:1-19).

Most kings will concentrate on building their own palaces when the kingdom is enjoying peace. When King David had defeated all his enemies and was enjoying rest on every side, he had a holy desire to think of God first and to build a house for Him (2 Sam 7:1-3). It was a desire to unite the entire kingdom with God's temple at the center. As such, David's desire to build the temple was solely motivated for God and by his desire to seek God (1 Chr 29:1b, 3). The purpose of the construction of the temple was also entirely for the glory of God. That is why he says that it is "for the Name of the LORD my God" (1 Chr 22:7; NIV), "for the service for the house of God" (1 Chr 29:7), "for the house of my God" (1 Chr 29:2-3), and "for Your holy name" (1 Chr 29:16).

Accordingly, David, along with the entire kingdom, poured all of their strength into preparing the necessary materials for Solomon to build the temple of God. They voluntarily and cheerfully gave even of their own personal properties (1 Chr 29:3-8). David praised the Lord before the entire congregation by confessing to God that "Yours, O LORD, is everything that is in the heavens and earth" (1 Chr 29:11). He went on saying, "Yours is the dominion" (1 Chr 29:11, NASB), "both riches and honor come from You" (1 Chr 29:12), "You are the head and ruler over all" (1 Chr 29:11, 12), and "in Your hand lies the power to make great and to strengthen everyone" (1 Chr 29:12). He also admitted that "Everything comes from you, and we have given you only what comes from your hand" (1 Chr 29:14, NIV). His confession that everything comes from God and all belong to Him (1 Chr 29:16) is the epitome of a God-centered life of faith. David and the people of Israel who prepared the materials for the temple of God looked forward to the completion of the temple in Solomon's time and were overcome with joy and thankfulness (1 Chr 29:9, 17).

Solomon's temple could not have been completed if it were not for David's God-centered faith. Although David knew that his hands could not build the temple for he had shed much blood on the battlefield (1 Kgs 5:3; 1 Chr 22:8; 28:3), in his utter devotion, David prepared all the necessary conditions for the construction of the temple which was to be accomplished by Solomon. David even commanded the leaders of

Israel to "set your heart and your soul" to help Solomon build the temple of God (1 Chr 22:17-19). Furthermore, King David even took a census of the Levites 30 years old and older and found them to be 38,000 in number. He then divided and allocated to them the work that was to be done inside the temple once it was completed (1 Chr 23:3-6). Then David implored Solomon to pour his heart into building the temple as God had commanded. He wholeheartedly encouraged his son, "Be strong and courageous, do not fear nor be dismayed . . . Of the gold, the silver and the bronze and the iron there is no limit. Arise and work, and may the LORD be with you" (1 Chr 22:13-16; Ref 1 Chr 28:9-10, 20-21).

Finally, David entrusted to God his son Solomon, who was to take up the critical task of building the temple. He pleaded earnestly, "and give to my son Solomon a perfect heart to keep Your commandments, Your testimonies and Your statutes, and to do them all, and to build the temple, for which I have made provision" (1 Chr 29:19).

Second, Solomon's Temple was constructed on Mount Moriah in Jerusalem (790 meters above sea level; 2 Chr 3:1).

This was the place of faith where Abraham offered up Isaac as a sacrifice (Gen 22:1-19). This was also the place called the "threshing floor of Araunah the Jebusite" which David purchased with a penitent heart so that he may offer an atoning sacrifice to God for his transgression which he committed when he took a census (2 Sam 24:18-25; 1 Chr 21:18-30). David said of this place, "This is the house of the LORD God, and this is the altar of burnt offering for Israel" (1 Chr 22:1). These events teach us that temple construction is founded upon faith and repentance.

Third, the plans for Solomon's Temple were given to David by God Himself (1 Chr 28:11-19).

The Bible tells us in 1 Chronicles 28:19, "'All this,' said David, 'the LORD made me understand in writing by His hand upon me, all the details of this pattern.'" Also in 1 Chronicles 28:12 it speaks of, "the pattern of all that he had by the spirit" (KJV). Here the word "pattern" is תַּבְנִית (*tabnît*) in Hebrew which means "plan."

The details of the plan which God Himself had made known are as follows:

① The porch of the temple, storehouses, upper rooms, inner rooms, and the room for the mercy seat (1 Chr 28:11)

② The courts of the house of the Lord, all the surrounding rooms, the storehouses of the house of God and the storehouses of the dedicated things (1 Chr 28:12)

③ All the utensils of service in the house of the Lord, the weight of gold and silver used for the gold and silver utensils (1 Chr 28:13-14)

④ The weight of gold and silver used for the golden lampstands and their golden lamps as well as for the silver lampstands and their silver lamps (1 Chr 28:15)

In 2 Chronicles 4:7, reference is only made to the ten golden lampstands, which were placed in the temple, and there is no mention of any silver lampstands. It is presumed that the silver lampstands were used elsewhere within the temple.

⑤ The weight of gold to be used for the tables of the bread of the Presence and the weight of silver used for the silver tables (1 Chr 28:16)

⑥ The weight of pure gold used for the forks (fleshhooks – KJV), basins, and cups (small vessels for storing spices – KJV) and the weight of the golden bowls and silver bowls (1 Chr 28:17)

⑦ The weight of refined gold to be used for the altar of incense, and the weight of gold for the pattern of the chariot of the cherubim (1 Chr 28:18; KJV)

David explained in detail to Solomon his son all the plans of the interior of the temple down to even the weights of gold and silver to be used (1 Chr 28:11-13). Not only that, David prepared all the necessary materials needed to finish the temple according to the plan God had showed him. His preparation was thorough, making provisions for even the minute details such as the nails for the doors and the gates and the clamps (1 Chr 22:2-19).

If it were not for David's meticulous preparation, it would have been impossible for Solomon to complete the construction of the temple. The Bible testifies in 1 Kings 6:38, "the house was finished throughout all its parts and according to all its plans." Thus, 2 Chronicles 8:16 states, "So the house of the Lord was perfected" (KJV).

The size of the temple, its plans, all the vessels in the temple and the rites of worship to be performed within were all done according to the Word of God. And this was also the case when Noah's ark or Moses' Tabernacle was built. God told Noah the materials to be used, the size of the ark and even the details of the plan such as the placement of the window (Gen 6:14-16); and Noah did according to all that God had commanded in the plans (Gen 6:22; 7:5). God transmitted to Moses the details of the plans for the tabernacle (Heb 8:5) and told him, "According to all that I am going to show you, as the pattern of the tabernacle and the pattern of all its furniture, just so you shall construct it" (Exod 25:9), "after the pattern for them, which was shown to you on the mountain" (Exod 25:40), "Then you shall erect the tabernacle according to its plan which you have been shown in the mountain" (Exod 26:30). Moses merely did what the LORD had commanded him (Exod 40:16, 19, 21, 23, 25, 27, 29, 32).

The history of redemption—from its inception, development and down to its conclusion—is completely a work of God. He does not discuss or consult with human beings for this work. The power that drives redemptive history is entirely the grace and blessing of God which seeks to save the sinner who is bound for death.

Fourth, a total of 183,850 people were mobilized for the construction of the temple.

Forced laborers taken from the Israelites were 30,000 (1 Kgs 5:13), and of the Gentile forced laborers, 70,000 were transporters and 80,000 were hewers of stone in the mountains (1 Kgs 5:15; 2 Chr 2:17-18). Also, there were 3,300 chief deputies (1 Kgs 5:16) and 550 chief officers (1 Kgs 9:23) who were to oversee the work and rule over the people doing the work for the temple.

While 1 Kings records that there were 3,300 chief deputies (1 Kgs 5:16) and 550 chief officers (1 Kgs 9:23), 2 Chronicles states that the numbers were 3,600 (2 Chr 2:2) and 250 (2 Chr 8:10) respectively. Both accounts agree on the total number of overseers at 3,850. The record of 1 Kings listed the overseers according to rank as 3,300 and 550; however, 2 Chronicles classified the overseers according to ethnicity: 3,600 Gentile overseers and 250 Israelite overseers. Therefore, we can deduce that out of the 550 higher ranking officers, 250 were Israelites while 300 were Gentiles. The total number of the work force including the laborers as well as the overseers is 183,850. Of this number, 153,600 are Gentiles (2 Chr 2:17-18), which indicates there were more Gentiles than the Israelites.

The historic Temple of Solomon was completed in about six years and six months without any flaws because these numerous workers had been mobilized in complete devotion to God (1 Kgs 6:37-38; 2 Chr 8:16). The number "183,850" represents all, without exception, who participated in the construction of the temple which was carried out according to God's administration of redemption. Likewise, God does not forget an inkling of the work we have done within redemptive history. He remembers and records them all and will repay us according to each of our deeds (Matt 16:27; 1 Cor 3:8; Rev 2:23; 20:12; 22:12).

The participation of Gentiles in the building of Solomon's Temple illustrates how Jews and Gentiles will both participate in the construction of the kingdom of God in Christ Jesus (Eph 3:6). The Gospel of Jesus Christ transcends all distinctions in ethnicity, gender and social position; whether Greek or Jew, there is no discrimination in the salvation of Jesus Christ (1 Cor 1:24; 12:13; Gal 3:28; Col 3:11).

Fifth, the cedar used in the construction of the temple was transported by sea from Tyre.

The cedar and cypress timber were cut down in the mountains of Lebanon and transported to the shores of Phoenicia. Then from there, they were made into huge rafts to be taken by sea to the place Solomon had designated, which was Joppa (1 Kgs 5:8-9; 2 Chr 2:16). Then from Joppa, the timbers were transported by land to Jerusalem which is about 56 km away. Joppa, the closest port city from Jerusalem, was a naturally formed sea port with boulders serving as breakwaters. King Hiram gladly cooperated with Solomon and performed the arduous task of having to transport the timber by sea from Lebanon to Joppa, then over the rough and rugged terrain from Joppa to Jerusalem.

Since Israel does not have an abundance of forest areas, the timber needed to build the temple was not available domestically. Appropriately, Hiram (Huram) king of Tyre, who had always loved David, sent his servants to Solomon, and this served as the opportune moment for Solomon. Hiram greatly rejoiced at hearing Solomon's request and sent all the necessary cedar and cypress timbers (1 Kgs 5:1-10). In return, Solomon gave Hiram 20,000 kors of wheat as food for his household and 20 kors of beaten oil every year (1 Kgs 5:11). Not only that, Solomon also paid wages to Hiram's servants, the woodsmen; he gave them 20,000 kors of crushed wheat, 20,000 kors of barley, 20,000 baths of wine and 20,000 baths of oil (2 Chr 2:10). There was peace between Solomon and Hiram and they even made a covenant with each other (1 Kgs 5:12). These two

Dan – Jeroboam made two golden calves and set one in Bethel and the other in Dan in order to prevent the Israelites from going to Jerusalem to worship God (1 Kgs 12:25-29).

Beersheba – Beersheba means "seven wells" or "the well of the oath" and was located at the southernmost part of Judah (Judg 20:1; 1 Kgs 4:25).

Megiddo – Megiddo was one of the cities that King Solomon
built as a key military site (1 Kgs 9:15, 19).

Megiddo – King Josiah was killed in a battle against Pharaoh Neco king of Egypt which took place here (2 Kgs 23:29-30; 2 Chr 35:20-24).

Samaria – Omri bought the hill of Samaria from Shemer for two talents of silver and built a city on it after he became king over Israel (1 Kgs 16:23-24).

Hazor – King Solomon built this city as a key military site (1 Kgs 9:15, 19).
In the days of King Pekah, Tiglath-pileser king of Assyria came and captured this city (2 Kgs 15:29).

religiously incompatible, rival kingdoms were able to cooperate because God granted special providence so that the temple may be constructed.

Sixth, no sound was heard during the construction of the temple (1 Kgs 6:7).

When the temple was being built, Solomon commanded that the stones be prepared to their exact sizes at the quarry so that they only needed to be fitted into place at the temple. There were 80,000 stone-cutters in the mountains (1 Kgs 5:15). In order to build God's house, Solomon's builders, Hiram's builders and the Gebalites cut the stones and prepared them (1 Kgs 5:18). As a result, there was neither hammer nor axe nor any iron tool heard in the house while it was being built.

> **1 Kings 6:7** The house, while it was being built, was built of stone prepared at the quarry, and there was neither hammer nor axe nor any iron tool heard in the house while it was being built.

The temple is the place of God's presence. He has chosen to put His name there (1 Kgs 9:3; 2 Chr 6:6, 20; 33:4). His eyes, ears and heart are in the temple perpetually (1 Kgs 8:29; 9:3; 2 Chr 7:15-16). The temple is the place of reconciliation between God and mankind; therefore, unnecessary noises of men should not be heard there.

That is why the church must be ringing with the sounds of preaching, prayer and praises only (Isa 56:7). The church must be moved with the sound of God and not by the sounds of men. It must abound with the Word of God.

(2) The structure of Solomon's Temple

The plans of Solomon's temple were given by God Himself (1 Chr 28:12, 19), and the temple was finished according to those plans (1 Kgs 6:37-38). The structure of Solomon's temple was similar to that of the Tabernacle. This tells us that Solomon's temple was to continue the spiritual tradition of Moses' Tabernacle.

Solomon's temple was founded upon huge stones (1 Kgs 5:17; 7:9). If the foundation stones of Solomon's temple were of the same size as the foundation stones of the royal palace, the stones' standard size was likely to be 10 cubits (approx. 5 yd.) by 8 cubits (approx. 4 yd.; 1 Kgs 7:10). According to 1 Kings 5:17, great (גָּדוֹל, *gādôl*: great) and costly (יָקָר, *yāqār*: rare) stones were quarried and hewn and laid as the foundation. In light of redemptive history, these stones and the foundation of the temple signify Jesus Christ (Isa 28:16; Matt 16:18; 1 Cor 3:11; 10:4).

① **The outer structure of the temple**
First, the temple was 60 cubits in length, 20 cubits in width, and 30 cubits in height (1 Kgs 6:2).

Since one cubit is approximately 18 inches, the length of the temple was about 30 yards, the width was about 10 yards and the height was about 15 yards.

Second, there was a porch in the front of the temple (1 Kgs 6:3).

The porch was an annex to the main building and served as the main entrance and sitting room. The length of the porch was 20 cubits (approx. 10 yd.); it protruded out 10 cubits (approx. 5 yd.) from the front of the building.

Third, there were windows with artistic frames and side chambers in three stories (1 Kgs 6:4-5).

The windows were fixtures used to let in light and air. Solomon also built side chambers of three stories along the walls of the house around both the nave and the inner sanctuary. The lower story was 5 cubits (approx. 2.5 yd.) wide, the middle was 6 cubits (approx. 3 yd.) wide and the top was 7 cubits wide (approx. 3.5 yd.; 1 Kgs 6:6). The entrance to the middle floor was on the right side of the temple and there was a winding staircase that went from the lower story to the middle and to the third (1 Kgs 6:8). These chambers along the walls were the priests' rooms, where they would eat the most holy offerings and store them also (Ezek 42:13). As mentioned above, while the structural frame of the temple was being built, there was neither hammer, nor axe, nor any iron tool heard in the house for the stones were dressed and cut perfectly according to measurements at the quarry so there was no need to use the tools again (1 Kgs 6:7; Ref Exod 20:25; Deut 27:5).

When the exterior of the temple was finished, the Word of God came upon Solomon. In 1 Kings 6:12-13 God said, "Concerning this house which you are building, if you will walk in My statutes and execute My ordinances and keep all My commandments by walking in them, then I will carry out My word with you which I spoke to David your father.

I will dwell among the sons of Israel, and will not forsake My people Israel." With the interior construction still remaining, God was reaffirming to Solomon the purpose of building His temple which was to enable the people to obey the Word of God completely.

② **The inner structure of the temple**
First, the inner walls of the temple were overlaid with cedar boards which were then overlaid with gold (1 Kgs 6:14-22).

While the outer walls were made of stone, the inner walls were covered with cedar boards so that the stones would not show through, and then they were all overlaid with gold. That is why the Bible says, "all was cedar, there was no stone seen" (1 Kgs 6:18) and it goes on to say, "He overlaid the whole house with gold, until all the house was finished. Also the whole altar which was by the inner sanctuary he overlaid with gold" (1 Kgs 6:22).

The reason the interior of the temple was completely overlaid with gold was so that the inside of the temple could be brightly lit with the light coming from the lampstand of pure gold. This is indicating that Jesus Christ is the only light for the Church (John 1:4-5; 8:12; 9:5; Rev 2:1).

Second, the room for the holy of holies was prepared.
The holy of holies was a place that the high priest could only enter one day a year to offer the sin offering. The measurements for the holy of holies were 20 cubits (approx. 10 yd.) in length, width and height (1 Kgs 6:20). The Ark of the Covenant was placed inside the holy of holies (1 Kgs 6:19), and they made two cherubim of olive wood which were each 10 cubits high (approx. 5 yd.) on the Ark of the Covenant. One wing of the cherubim was 5 cubits long, thus it was 10 cubits from one end of the wing to the other end. The two cherubim were standing with wings spread out so that the wing of one cherub was touching one wall and the wing of the other was touching the other wall (1 Kgs 6:23-27). Therefore, the entire holy of holies was spanned by the wings of the cherubim. The cherubim were also overlaid with gold (1 Kgs 6:28). Since the number *10* symbolizes "fullness" and "completeness," the size of the cherubim bespeaks the presence and the filling of the holiness of God within. The amount of gold used to overlay the interior of the holy of holies was 600 talents (approx. 20,400 kg; 2 Chr 3:8).

Third, there were doors for the inner sanctuary (holy of holies) and the nave (temple).

The door for the entrance to the inner sanctuary was made of olive wood (1 Kgs 6:31) while the door for the entrance to the nave was made of cypress wood (1 Kgs 6:33-34). The door for the nave was made of cypress wood, which is lighter, because this entrance was to be used frequently, whereas the door for the inner sanctuary was made with the heavier olive wood to prevent any warps or bends.

A veil was placed between the inner sanctuary (holy of holies) and the nave (temple). The veil was made of violet, purple, crimson, and fine linen and embroidered with cherubim (2 Chr 3:14). It was to be hung on clasps of gold so that they can be open and shut side to side.

There was also an inner court, which was called the "court of the priests" (2 Chr 4:9). The walls of the inner court was made of three rows of well-hewn stones and a row of thick cedar beams (1 Kgs 6:36). The word *row* in Hebrew is טוּר (*ṭûr*), which indicates a layer of individual physical things arranged in a straight line or piled on top of one another.[14]

Fourth, engravings of cherubim, palm trees and open flowers were carved into the walls all around the inner sanctuary and the nave (1 Kgs 6:29).

Cherubim, palm trees and open flowers were also carved into the doors (1 Kgs 6:32, 35). The cherubim symbolizes holiness (Isa 6:1-3; Ref Ezek 10), the palm tree symbolizes great joy and victory (John 12:13), and the open flower symbolizes beauty and life overflowing with vitality.

Fifth, there were ten lampstands and ten tables for the bread of the Presence inside the temple (1 Kgs 7:48-49; 2 Chr 4:7-8).

In the description of Moses' Tabernacle, the Bible gives a detailed explanation about the lampstand and the table for the bread of the Presence; however, in describing the temple of Solomon, a detailed description about the lampstand and the table for the showbread (bread of the Presence) are not provided. This is because Solomon's temple was modeled after Moses' Tabernacle. The main difference is that there was only one lampstand and one table for the bread in the Tabernacle while there were ten of each in Solomon's temple. They were placed five to the right and five to the left of the inner sanctuary (1 Kgs 7:49; 2 Chr 4:7).

The table for the bread of the Presence was made of gold (1 Kgs 7:48), and since they seem to have been positioned near the lampstands, it is possible to conjecture that they were placed right in front of the lamp-stands. Twelve showbreads were placed on each table, thus a total of 120 showbreads were inside the temple of Solomon.

The lampstand symbolizes Jesus Christ, the light of the world, who came to brighten the world that has been darkened by sin (John 1:4; 8:12; 9:5; 12:35, 46). The bread also points to Jesus Christ who is the bread of life that has come down from heaven (John 6:35, 48, 50-51).

In Moses' Tabernacle, there were one each of the basin, lampstand and the table for the showbread; but in Solomon's temple, there were ten of each (2 Chr 4:6-8). The number *ten* is the number of fullness and completeness. Thus, the number indicates how the work of salvation that was limited to the nation of Israel will now expand throughout the universe and to the nations through the work of Jesus Christ. Moreover, it is also an indication that this work will be fully realized and consummated through God's administration of redemption.

③ **Making of the utensils of the temple**
After the construction of the temple was finished, Solomon ordered two pillars of bronze to be made and placed in front of the nave of the temple (1 Kgs 7:13-22). He also had the sea of cast metal (1 Kgs 7:23-26), ten stands of bronze and ten basins (1 Kgs 7:27-39) made along with the pails, the shovels and the bowls (1 Kgs 7:40-45).

These were all made of bronze by Hiram (Huram) of Tyre. Hiram's mother was a widow from the tribe of Naphtali and his father was a worker in bronze (1 Kgs 7:14a; Ref 2 Chr 4:16). As someone born to such parents, Hiram was filled with wisdom, understanding and skill (1 Kgs 7:14; Ref 2 Chr 2:11-13). King Solomon brought Hiram from Tyre to perform all the works for manufacturing in bronze (1 Kgs 7:13-14, 40).

First, he made the two pillars (Jachin, Boaz) of bronze in front of the nave of the temple (1 Kgs 7:21; 2 Chr 3:17).

Most of the utensils that were to furnish the temple were similar to the ones used in the tabernacle. One unique feature about the temple of Solomon was that it had two bronze pillars in front of the hall. They were 18 cubits high (approx. 9 yd.)[15] and 12 cubits (approx. 6 yd.) in circumference (1 Kgs 7:15; Jer 52:21). We can figure, then, that the diameter was about 2 yards for both pillars. They were made of molten bronze (1 Kgs 7:16), four fingers in thickness and hollow within (Jer 52:21b).

The pillar on the right was named "Jachin" and the one on the left was called "Boaz" (1 Kgs 7:21). The name *Jachin* is יָכִין (*yākîn*) in Hebrew, which means "He will establish." It teaches us that since God has established both the temple and the Davidic dynasty, both will be kept firmly established perpetually. The name *Boaz* is בֹּעַז (*bō'az*) in Hebrew, which is a combination of the word עַז (*'az*), meaning "strong" and "mighty," and the word בֹּ (*bô*), meaning "in." Combined, the name means "strength in him." This reveals to us that the One who upholds the temple with strength and empowers the house of David is the one and only God. Therefore, whenever the Israelites saw the two pillars before the temple, they were reminded of God's faithfulness and His eternal immutability.

Second, he set the sea of cast metal on the right side, toward the southeast corner of the house (1 Kgs 7:39; 2 Chr 4:10).

The sea was made of cast bronze and looked like a large basin. It was called the "sea" because it was so large that it seemed enough to hold the water of the sea within it. Its diameter was 10 cubits (approx. 5 yd.), circumference was 30 cubits (approx. 15 yd.) and its height was 5 cubits (approx. 2.5 yd.; 1 Kgs 7:23; 2 Chr 4:2). It was indeed colossal. The sea was placed in the inner court of the temple and was used by the priests and the Levites to wash themselves (2 Chr 4:6; Ref Exod 29:4; Lev 8:6). The sea was supported by 12 oxen, three facing each of the cardinal directions (north, south, east and west) and their tails were all turned inward (1 Kgs 7:25; 2 Chr 4:4). These 12 oxen represent the obedience and sacrifice of the 12 tribes of Israel (Lev 1:3; 1 Sam 6:14). The sea was able to hold 2,000 baths of water. Since one bath is equivalent to 22.71 liters, the total volume of the sea was 45,420 liters (1 Kgs 7:26b)! This enormous size exhibits to us the steadfast firmness which cannot be shaken or damaged by any external impact whatsoever.

There were lily designs engraved into the top of the pillars and the brim of the sea (1 Kgs 7:22, 26). The lily is a common wildflower found in the fields of the Palestine region. It signifies God's grace and protection (Matt 6:28; Luke 12:27-28).

Third, he made ten stands of bronze and ten basins of bronze (1 Kgs 7:27-39).

The basins were placed five on the right side of the house and five on the left side of the house (1 Kgs 7:39). The ten bronze stands were used to support the ten basins (1 Kgs 7:38, 43); the basins were used to wash the sacrificial offerings (2 Chr 4:6). The basins were also of bronze and the diameter was 4 cubits. Each basin was able to hold 40 baths (908.4 liters, 1 bath = 22.71 liters) of water (1 Kgs 7:38). The bronze stands for the basins were each 4 cubits in length and width and 3 cubits in height (1 Kgs 7:27). All ten of them were made of the same casting, with one measurement and form (1 Kgs 7:37). Each of the stands was made with bronze wheels and axles so that the water can be transported easily (1 Kgs 7:30, 32).

Fourth, he also made the pails, shovels and bowls (1 Kgs 7:40, 45).

Every utensil in the house of God was made of polished (KJV: bright) bronze (1 Kgs 7:45). The word *polished* is מְמֹרָט (*mĕmōrāṭ*) in Hebrew which is the pual (intensive passive) participial form of the word מָרַט (*māraṭ*) meaning "to polish, make smooth." This word suggests that all the utensils in the temple were buffed and polished until they were shining brightly. This is an indication of the utter devotion that went into making everything in the temple.

On the one hand, we see that the interior decorations of the temple were mostly of gold, but the utensils used outside were made of the crude and common bronze. If the gold symbolizes the inviolable purity and glory of God, then we can say that the bronze symbolizes the character of Christ who is with mankind, experiencing our sufferings and sympathizing with our weaknesses (Heb 4:15).

This is how Solomon finished making the utensils of the temple (1 Kgs 7:40). First Kings 7:48 states, "So Solomon made all the vessels that were in the house of the LORD" (ESV). Also 1 Kings 7:51 says, "Thus all the work that King Solomon performed in the house of the LORD was finished. And Solomon brought in the things dedicated by his father David, the silver and the gold and the utensils, and he put them in the treasuries of the house of the LORD."

Finally, the construction of the temple, which was started in the month of Ziv in the fourth year of Solomon's reign, was completed in the month of Bul in Solomon's eleventh regnal year (1 Kgs 6:37-38; 2 Chr 3:2). In regard to this, 1 Kings 9:25 simply comments, "So he finished the house," while 2 Chronicles 8:16 states, "Thus all the work of Solomon was carried out from the day of the foundation of the house of the LORD, and until it was finished. So the house of the LORD was completed." The word *foundation* here signifies the "foundation stone which cannot be moved," "the founding site." This is referring to the foundation that was laid at the threshing floor of Ornan the Jebusite (2 Chr 3:1-3).

The phrase "all the work...was carried out" tells us that everything related to the construction of Solomon's temple from start to finish had been prepared meticulously a long time ago. That is why all the work related to the temple was completed without any flaws.

Solomon was able to carry out all the work because God had already given David the plan for the temple (1 Chr 28:11-19). First Chronicles 28:19 states, "'All this,' said David, 'the LORD made me understand in writing by His hand upon me, all the details of this pattern.'" David prepared for the house of God with all his ability all the materials needed according to the details of the pattern that God had shown him (1 Chr 28:2). He prepared gold, silver, bronze, iron, and all kinds of precious stones in the proper weight according to their use (2 Chr 29:2). He prepared in detail, even iron to make the nails for the doors of the gates and for the clamps (1 Chr 22:3). The stones were cut and prepared at the quarry according to the details of the pattern that God had shown him.

As such, all the work was carried out from the day of the foundation of the house of the Lord until it was finished according to the details of the plan that God had shown David (2 Chr 8:16), and thus there was no discrepancy in measurements nor was there anything lacking or left over. So the temple of Solomon was completed throughout all its parts and according to all its plans (1 Kgs 6:37-38; 2 Chr 8:16). No matter how well a man makes a plan, there are many times when there are shortages or surplus of supplies. Also, there are inevitably parts of the construction that are not completely satisfactory when the builder looks at the finished result. However, all things that God plans and proceeds have no shortage or surplus in any aspect, and the result is fully satisfactory.

After the temple was completed and the Ark of the Covenant was enshrined in its rightful place, the cloud and the glory of the Lord filled the house of the Lord (1 Kgs 8:10) so that the priests could not minister within (1 Kgs 8:11). This indicates that God had acknowledged all the works of Solomon's Temple.

(3) The redemptive-historical significance of Solomon's Temple

The construction of Solomon's temple was started in the fourth year of his reign which was 966 BC. First Kings 6:1 tells us that this was "the four hundred and eightieth year after the sons of Israel came out of the land of Egypt."

The Israelites had worshiped in the Tabernacle during the 40 years of the wilderness journey after their exodus from Egypt. Then, exactly 480 years later, a permanent temple had been established in the land of Canaan. Viewed from the administration of redemptive history, this is proof positive that the land of Canaan is a possession of the Israelites. In fact, the preparation for and the process of the temple construction shows us the process through which a human being is raised up in Jesus Christ as the temple, the dwelling place of God (1 Cor 3:16; 6:19; Eph 1:23; 2:22).

What is the significance of the temple construction which Solomon had completed?

First, it signifies the fulfillment of the Davidic covenant.

God had promised David a son and He also promised that this one son will build the house of the Lord (2 Sam 7:12-13). The completion of the temple by David's son Solomon shows us the fulfillment of the Davidic covenant.

Second, it points toward the true temple which Jesus Christ will build in the future.

The name *Solomon*, which means "peace," points us toward Jesus Christ, the Prince of Peace, who brings true peace to the world (Isa 9:6; John 14:27). Just as Solomon finished the temple construction, Jesus comes to finish the true temple (John 2:19-21). Therefore, the Davidic covenant, which was initially fulfilled through Solomon, will ultimately be fulfilled by Jesus Christ when He comes to finish His temple (Rev 21:22).

Third, it shows us a temple-centered faith.

Solomon built the temple before he built his palace. He built the temple for 7 years, and he built his palace for 13 years. So he spent 20 years altogether in building the temple and his palace (1 Kgs 6:37-38; 7:1; 9:10; 2 Chr 8:1).

Moreover, the temple and the palace were built facing each another,[16] which demonstrates an intimate relationship between the two structures. This intimate positioning of the two buildings indicates that the people of Israel and their king must subject themselves solely to the reign of God.

(4) The prayer of dedication for the temple

In the month of Ethanim, the seventh month, Solomon assembled all the people of Israel and brought up the Ark of the Covenant (1 Kgs 8:1-11). When we take into consideration the time it must have taken to make the utensils of the temple, this must be the seventh month of the year following the completion of the temple (approximately 11 months from the end of construction).[17]

After the Ark of the Covenant was enshrined, Solomon confesses in his dedication address that everything had been fulfilled according to God's Word (1 Kgs 8;12-21). In 1 Kings 8:20 he says, "Now the LORD has fulfilled His word which He spoke."

Then Solomon followed with a dedicatory prayer. He stood before the altar of the Lord facing the assembly of the people of Israel and prayed with both hands lifted up toward heaven (1 Kgs 8:22-53; 2 Chr 6:12-42). Then he also knelt on his knees and prayed with both hands lifted up to heaven (2 Chr 6:13-14).

His prayer was as follows.

First, he prayed that God would keep His promises of the Davidic covenant (1 Kgs 8:23-26; 2 Chr 6:12-17). Second, he prayed that God would heed the prayers of His people (1 Kgs 8:27-30; 2 Chr 6:18-21). Third, he prayed that God would forgive when the people repented (1 Kgs 8:31-40, 46-53; 2 Chr 6:22-31). Fourth, he prayed that God would heed the prayers of the foreigner as well (1 Kgs 8:41-43; 2 Chr 6:32-33). This prayer reveals to us that Solomon's faith did not limit God only to Israel, but believed that He is the God of all mankind and universe. Fifth, Solomon prayed that God would answer when the people go out to battle and pray to God toward the temple (1 Kgs 8:44-45; 2 Chr 6:34-35). Sixth, he prayed that when the people sin and are taken captives to the land of their enemies and pray to God toward the temple from the land of their enemies, that God would forgive them, have mercy on them, listen to their supplications and heed their prayers (1 Kgs 8:46-53; 2 Chr 6:36-42).

When Solomon had finished his dedication address and prayer, fire came down from heaven and consumed the burnt offering and the sacrifices, and the glory of the Lord filled the temple. The priests could not enter the temple because it was filled with the glory of the Lord (2 Chr 7:1-2). That is when "All the sons of Israel, seeing the fire come down and the glory of the LORD upon the house, bowed down on the pavement with their faces to the ground, and they worshiped and gave praise to the

LORD, saying, 'Truly He is good, truly His lovingkindness is everlasting'" (2 Chr 7:3).

The king and the people finished the seven-day dedication of the temple (8th–14th day of the 7th month) and celebrated the Feast of Booths (15th–21st day of the 7th month) for seven days. They capped off the entire occasion with a closing ceremony (22nd day of the 7th month) to complete a massive 15-day dedication and offering event. On the 23rd day of the 7th month, the people all went back to their homes (1 Kgs 8:62-66; 2 Chr 7:4-10).

Solomon offered 22,000 oxen and 12,000 sheep as peace offerings (1 Kgs 8:63; 2 Chr 7:5). Having accepted the utmost thanksgiving (dedicatory sacrifices) offered by Solomon and the people, God responded by keeping the covenant He had established with the Israelites. He also promised that His eyes, ears, heart and Name will be at the temple perpetually (1 Kgs 9:1-3; 2 Chr 7:11-18).

Furthermore, if Solomon obeys all the commands of God and keeps His statutes and ordinances, Israel's throne will be established perpetually. However, if he disobeys to follow after other gods and worship them, then Israel will be destroyed. God declared, "even this house which I have consecrated for My name I will cast out of My sight" (1 Kgs 9:4-9; 2 Chr 7:19-22). Therefore, the welfare of Israel's future was contingent upon their obedience to God.

4. God chastised Solomon because of his transgressions in his latter years.

After Solomon finished building the temple and the palace, he built strongholds and cities at key military sites (the Millo, the wall of Jerusalem, Hazor, Megiddo, Gezer, etc.; 1 Kgs 9:15, 19). As the kingdom became wealthy and powerful, Solomon slowly began to fall into depravity. Solomon loved many Gentile women besides the daughter of Pharaoh (1 Kgs 11:1). The word *loved* in Hebrew is אָהַב ('āhab), which conveys romantic love between a man and a woman, usually connoting sexual relations. Solomon was not only achieving political and diplomatic goals in his romantic endeavors with these many women, but he was also gratifying his own sexual desires.

Although God had forbidden intermarriage with Gentiles (Exod 34:16; Deut 7:3-4), 1 Kings 11:2 states that Solomon held fast to the

Gentile women in love. Here the phrase "to hold fast" in Hebrew is דָּבַק (dābaq), which means "to cling," "to adhere," "to be joined to," thus connoting a strong obsession for or dependence upon an object or being. Therefore, the phrase indicates that Solomon had become a prisoner of his own sexual desires and was dependent upon the Gentile women. Though Solomon should have been dependent on God, he had given his heart to the Gentile women and had become dependent on them (Neh 13:26).

Solomon had 700 wives and 300 concubines, totaling 1,000 in all. Deuteronomy 17:16-17 exhorts, "He [the king] shall not multiply wives for himself, or else his heart will turn away." As a result of Solomon's disobedience to this exhortation, his many wives and concubines all brought with them foreign gods that they served. Moreover, the 1,000 wives and concubines turned the heart of the elderly king away from God and made him go after other gods (1 Kgs 11:3-4). Solomon built high places for these gods. The Bible testifies in 1 Kings 11:6-8, "Solomon did what was evil in the sight of the LORD, and did not follow the LORD fully, as David his father had done. Then Solomon built a high place for Chemosh the detestable idol of Moab, on the mountain which is east of Jerusalem, and for Molech the detestable idol of the sons of Ammon. Thus also he did for all his foreign wives, who burned incense and sacrificed to their gods."

Solomon, who had been led to sin by all of those women, wrote later in his life, "And I discovered more bitter than death the woman whose heart is snares and nets, whose hands are chains. One who is pleasing to God will escape from her, but the sinner will be captured by her" (Eccl 7:26). The New Living Translation translated it as "I discovered that a seductive woman is a trap more bitter than death. Her passion is a snare, and her soft hands are chains. Those who are pleasing to God will escape her, but sinners will be caught in her snare."

Anyone who has succeeded and stands at the peak of one's career or field is prone to be tempted and stumble. When we are successful, we must be all the more determined to obey God's Word and withstand the lures of this world.

(1) God's two warnings toward Solomon

1 Kings 11:9-10 Now the LORD was angry with Solomon because his heart was turned away from the LORD, the God of Israel, who had appeared to him twice, and had commanded him concerning this thing, that he should not go after other gods; but he did not observe what the LORD had commanded.

To which two appearances of God is the above passage alluding? First, God appeared to Solomon after he offered one thousand burnt offerings at Gibeon (1 Kgs 3:5). Next, God appeared to Solomon after he had finished building the temple and the palace (1 Kgs 9:1-2). At each of these appearances, God not only gave him the Words of blessings, but also Words of warning outlining the consequences of disobedience to God's commands. God spoke to him firmly, saying that He will cut off Israel from the land and cast out even the holy temple from His sight.

First Kings 9:6-7 warns sternly, "But if you or your sons indeed turn away from following Me, and do not keep My commandments and My statutes which I have set before you, and go and serve other gods and worship them, then I will cut off Israel from the land which I have given them, and the house which I have consecrated for My name, I will cast out of My sight so Israel will become a proverb and a byword among all peoples."

In his latter years, however, Solomon dismissed God's warning because he had been ensnared by the lust of his flesh. Therefore, God told Solomon, "I will surely tear the kingdom from you, and will give it to your servant . . . However, I will not tear away all the kingdom, but I will give one tribe to your son for the sake of My servant David and for the sake of Jerusalem which I have chosen" (1 Kgs 11:11-13). Thus it was Solomon's transgressions that caused the division of the kingdom of Israel into the northern and the southern kingdoms.

(2) God's judgment on Solomon's transgressions

After Solomon's corruption, God declared His judgment and carried it out immediately. First, He raised up Hadad the Edomite to be an adversary of Solomon (1 Kgs 11:14-22). God also raised up Rezin of Damascus (Aram) as another adversary of Solomon (1 Kgs 11:23-25).

God, then, told Jeroboam through the prophet Ahijah that he will receive ten tribes of the kingdom. Jeroboam was a man whom Solomon had appointed to oversee the forced labor of the house of Joseph after noticing the young man's industriousness (1 Kgs 11:28). First Kings 11:30-31 describes: Then Ahijah took hold of the new cloak which was on him and tore it into twelve pieces. He said to Jeroboam, "Take for yourself ten pieces; for thus says the LORD, the God of Israel, Behold, I will tear the kingdom out of the hand of Solomon and give you ten tribes."

Just as this prophecy had declared, Jeroboam took ten tribes and founded the northern kingdom of Israel upon Solomon's death while Rehoboam ruled over the two tribes of the southern kingdom of Judah.

Solomon had been thoroughly trained in the faith by his father David. However, he took on many wives and concubines who led him to commit the grave sin of accepting and worshiping their foreign gods in his latter years. The Bible continually testifies that Solomon had not walked in the ways of his father David.

> **1 Kings 11:4** . . . his heart was not wholly devoted to the LORD his God, as the heart of David his father had been.
>
> **1 Kings 11:6** Solomon did what was evil in the sight of the LORD, and did not follow the LORD fully, as David his father had done.

Through Solomon's life, we can realize that it is as important for oneself to overcome the temptations of the world and obey the Word of God as much as it is important for parents to transmit faith. Solomon had once been a wise king who had been blessed by God. The way to maintain the God-given grace is to obey and abide by the Word of God. David's final words were, "Keep the charge of the LORD your God, to walk in His ways, to keep His statutes, His commandments, His ordinances, and His testimonies, according to what is written in the Law of Moses" (1 Kgs 2:3). But apparently, Solomon had not engraved the final words of his father David deep within his heart, nor did he obey the two stern warnings that God had given him. When Solomon obeyed God's Word, the kingdom had peace just as his name signifies. However, when he followed after other gods, broke God's covenant, and disobeyed His commands, the kingdom was split in two (1 Kgs 11:9-13).

Obedience to God's Word brings peace to the nation, church and family. On the other hand, when we rashly dismiss the Word of God and disobey, the nation, church and family will be torn into pieces; and the pain of division will remain with them. Likewise, Solomon's transgression not only affected him, but it had also brought about the division and the decline of the entire kingdom. Solomon's iniquitous ways notwithstanding, God did not completely destroy the kingdom but left one tribe to be a lamp for His servant David (1 Kgs 11:36). God did this because He remembered His covenant with David (2 Sam 7:16). Moreover, this was the sovereign providence of God preparing the way for the coming of Jesus Christ who is the heart of redemptive history, so that God's plan and work of salvation may continue on.

✳ Systematically explained for the first time in the history

The Time It Took to Construct Solomon's Temple

> **1 Kings 6:37-38** In the fourth year the foundation of the house of the Lord was laid, in the month of Ziv. In the eleventh year, in the month of Bul, which is the eighth month, the house was finished throughout all its parts and according to all its plans. So he was seven years in building it.

First Kings 6:37-38 record the actual time taken in building Solomon's Temple. The construction began in the month of Ziv (the second month) in Solomon's fourth regnal year (2 Chr 3:2) and ended in the month of Bul (the eight month) in his eleventh regnal year. The total construction time is recorded as "seven years." 1 Kings 9:10 states that Solomon built both the house of the Lord and the king's house in twenty years. According to 1 Kings 7:1, Solomon took thirteen years to build his house. From comparing these two verses, it is evident that Solomon's Temple took "seven years" (20 − 13 = 7) to build.

However, when reckoned by a yearly cycle that begins with Nisan, a calendric system commonly used in those days, it may seem more correct to record the construction period as "eight years." This is because there is a total of eight years counting from Solomon's fourth regnal year when the temple's construction began, to the eleventh year when it ended (i.e., fourth regnal year[1], fifth year[2], sixth year[3], seventh year[4], eighth year[5], ninth year[6], tenth year[7], and eleventh year[8]).✳ Why then does the Bible record the actual time of building Solomon's Temple as "seven years (1 Kgs 6:38)" instead of eight?

This is because in Solomon's days regnal years were reckoned by a yearly cycle that begins with Tishri (the seventh month) instead of Nisan (the first month). Several evidences for the usage of this reckoning method are discussed in pages 55–57 of this book.

Solomon's fourth regnal year in the Tishri cycle is actually equivalent to the fifth regnal year in the Nisan cycle. This is because the Nisan cycle proceeds six months ahead of the Tishri cycle. Hence, when Solomon's regnal years are reckoned by the Tishri cycle, the time of building Solomon's Temple is "seven years," which is one year lesser than the "eight years" in the Nisan cycle. Regardless of whether the Tishri or Nisan cycle was used to reckon the regnal years, the time of building the temple was reckoned on a calendar (which began with Nisan, the first month, and ended with Adar, the twelfth month) that had been widely used at that time.✳✳ Below is a chart to assist our understanding:

Then, what is the precise time taken to build the temple? Since the construction began in the month of Ziv (the second month) in the fourth year of Solomon's reign and ended in the month of Bul (the eighth month) in his eleventh year, it is generally viewed as seven years and six months based on a simple calculation. Such views are listed below.

Views that it took seven years and six months to build Solomon's Temple

"Seven and a half years were spent in building."

R.W. Bahr, First Kings, trans. Young-chul Bae, (Lange Commentary on the Holy Scriptures, vol. 11; Seoul: Logos, 1999). 150.

....

"The time spent in this building. It was but seven years and a half from the founding to the finishing of it, v. 38. Considering the vastness and elegance of the building, and the many appurtenances to it which were necessary to fit it for use, it was soon done."

Matthew Henry, *Matthew Henry's Commentary on the Whole Bible: Complete and Unabridged in One Volume*, 1 Ki 6:15–38 (Peabody: Hendrickson, 1996).

....

"The temple construction was completed after seven years and six months in the month of Bul (the eighth month in Jewish calendar) in the eleventh year of Solomon."

Thompson II Biblical Compilation Committee, *Thompson II Biblical Commentary* (Christian Wisdom, 2008), 519.

....

"The entire construction lasted seven years. . . more precisely, it took seven and a half years."

Thomas L. Constable, *1 and 2 Chronicles*, trans. Dong-hak Moon & Myung-jun Lee (BKC, vol. 6; Seoul: Tyrannus, 1989), 54.

....

"The foundation was laid in the fourth year in the month *Ziv* (see v. 1), and it was finished in the eleventh year in the month *Bul*, i.e., the eighth month, so that it was built in seven years, or, more precisely, seven years and a half, "according to all its matters and all its due."

Carl Friedrich Keil and Franz Delitzsch, *Commentary on the Old Testament, vol. 3*, (Peabody, MA: Hendrickson, 2002), 61.

"The construction of the temple was completed in seven and a half years."

F.B. Meyer, *Meyer Commentary* (Seoul: Emmaus, 1995), 183.

"About seven years and six months were needed to complete the temple."

Paul R. House, *1, 2 Kings*, (New American Commentary, vol. 8; Nashville, Tennessee: Broadman & Holman Publishers, 1995), 129.

"The building took seven years to complete (vv. 37-38) – or more precisely, seven years and six months."

Iain W. Provan, *1 and 2 Kings*, (New International Biblical Commentary; Peabody, Massachusetts: Hendrickson Publishers, 1995), 67.

"Solomon's Temple only took seven and a half years to build."

F. W. Farrar, *The First Book of Kings*, (The Expositor's Bible; New York: A.C. Armstrong and Son, 1903), 166.

"Thus seven years and six months were consumed in this work, and this period. This is rounded off to an even seven years, the number of perfection."

Simon J. De Vries, *1 Kings*, Word Biblical Commentary, vol. 12 (Waco, Texas: Word Books, 1985), 96.

"The time spent in constructing the temple was actually seven and one-half years (see vs. 1)."

Clyde M. Miller, *First and Second Kings*, The Living Word Commentary on the Old Testament, vol. 7 (Abilene, Texas: Abilene Christian University Press, 1991), 149.

"The actual time of building was seven years and a half."

I.W. Slotki, *Kings*, (Soncino Books of the Bible; London: The Soncino Press, 1971), 46.

"More exactly, 'seven years and six months,' since Zif was the second, and Bul the eight month."

J. M. Fuller, *1 Samuel-Esther*, the Bible Commentary (Grand Rapids, Michigan: Baker Book House, 1953), 159.

"It took Solomon seven years and six months to finish the temple."

Russell H. Dilday, 1, 2 Kings, the Communicator's Commentary
(Waco, Texas: Word Publisher, 1987), 92.

"The temple took seven and a half years to build."

Norman H. Snaith, *The Interpreter's Bible*, vol. III (Nashville, Tennessee: Abingdon Press, 1954), 60.

"The house was precisely seven and a half years in building – a short period."

J. Hammond, 1 Kings, The Pulpit Commentary (Peabody, Massachusetts:
Hendrickson Publisher, 1950), 111.

"The temple took seven and a half years to complete in all its details and specifications."

Donald J. Wiseman, 1 and 2 Kings, (Tyndale Old Testament Commentaries;
Downers Grove, Illinois: Inter-Varsity Press, 1993), 111.

"A total of seven and one-half year, but that is rounded off to seven years in verse 38."

Howard F. Vos, 1, 2 Kings, (Bible Study Commentary; Grand Rapids, Michigan:
Lamplighter Books, 1989), 59.

"The temple project was completed in the eleventh year of Solomon's reign, in the month of Bul (October). This means that the temple was 7.5 years in the building, rounded off by the sacred historian to seven years."

James E. Smith, *The Books of History*, 1 Ki 6:15–35 (Joplin, Mo.: College Press, 1995).

"Seven years were spent building the temple, from the 4th year of Solomon's reign (966 b.c.; cf. comments on 6:1) to his 11th year (959 b.c.). More precisely, this was seven and one-half years. Ziv is April-May and Bul, the eighth month, is October-November."

John F. Walvoord, Roy B. Zuck and Dallas Theological Seminary, *The Bible Knowledge Commentary : An Exposition of the Scriptures*, 1 Ki 6:37–38 (Wheaton, IL: Victor Books, 1983-).

"The construction required seven and a half years (6:37-38)."

David S. Dockery, Trent C. Butler, Christopher L. Church et al., Holman Bible Handbook,
(Nashville, TN: Holman Bible Publishers, 1992), 249 .

"At length, in the autumn of the eleventh year of his reign, seven and a half years after it had been begun, the temple was completed in all its architectural magnificence and beauty."

M.G. Easton, *Easton's Bible Dictionary* (Oak Harbor, WA: Logos Research Systems, Inc., 1996).

"It took seven-and-one-half years to build Solomon's Temple. And one hundred and eighty-three thousand six hundred men worked on it."

Paul Lee Tan, *Encyclopedia of 7700 Illustrations: Signs of the Times* (Garland, TX: Bible Communications, Inc., 1996).

"The building was begun in the second month of the fourth year and completed in the eighth month of the eleventh year of Solomon's reign, comprising a period of seven and a half years, which is reckoned here in round numbers."

Robert Jamieson, A. R. Fausset, A. R. Fausset et al., *A Commentary, Critical and Explanatory, on the Old and New Testaments*, 1 Ki 6:37 (Oak Harbor, WA: Logos Research Systems, Inc., 1997).

However, the time taken to build Solomon's Temple becomes seven years and six months when reckoned by the Nisan cycle. When reckoned by Tishri cycle as it was actually used then, the building time becomes approximately six years and six months. There is one year difference between the two reckoning methods because the month of Ziv (the second month) in the fourth regnal year in the Tishri cycle is equivalent to the month of Ziv (the second month) in the fifth regnal year in the Nisan cycle.

Hence, counting from the month of Ziv in the fifth year (in the Tishri cycle, this month of Ziv is in the fourth year) to the month of Bul in the eleventh year on the Nisan cycle calendar, there are seven years (fifth[1], sixth[2], seventh[3], eighth[4], ninth[5], tenth[6], eleventh[7] regnal years). Therefore, 1 Kings 6:37-38 records the time taken to build the temple as "seven years."

Approximately 3,000 years have passed since the Solomon's Temple construction began in the year 966 B.C. It is truly by the work of God's grace and powerful illumination by the Holy Spirit that the time taken to build the temple (i.e., around six years and six months) has been elucidated for the first time since the time of its construction 3,000 years ago.

*"Reckoning the total years of an event such as in reckoning regnal years follows the inclusive reckoning method. According to this method, fractions of years were reckoned as though they were full years." [R. K. Harrison, *Introduction of the Old Testament* (Peabody, Massachusetts: Hendrickson Publishers, 2004), 182.]

Ref.— Compare Gen 17:12 and Lev 12:2-3; Gen 42:17 and Gen 42:18; 2 Kings 18:9 and 18:10; Luke 24:21 and Matt 12:40, 27:63, Mar 8:31, Act 10:40. 1 Cor 15:4.

** "In the book of Kings as well as in others, a year is reckoned starting with the month of Nisan regardless of whether the year begins in spring or fall." [R.K. Harrison, *Introduction to the Old Testament*, 182.]

Ref. – Exod 12:2, 18; 13:3-4, 23:15; 34:18; 2 Sam 11:1; 1 Kgs 8:2; 2-:22; 1 Chron 20:1; Neh 1:1; 2:1; Esth 3:7)

The months used in this book are based on the religious calendar (one year = Nisan (first month) to Adar (twelfth month)).

CHAPTER 8

The Third Generation: Rehoboam

> ## Rehoboam / ʿΡοβοάμ / רְחַבְעָם
> One who enlarges his people

— The first king of the southern kingdom of Judah (1 Kgs 11:43-12:24; 14:21-31; 2 Chr 9:31-12:16)
— The third individual in the second period of Jesus' genealogy

Matthew 1:7 Solomon was the father of Rehoboam, Rehoboam the father of Abijah, and Abijah the father of Asa.

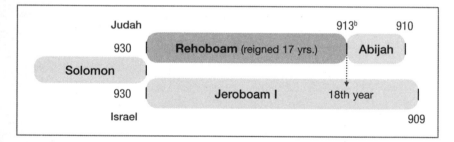

Background
Father: Solomon (1 Kgs 14:21)
Mother: Naamah (Ammonitess; 1 Kgs 14:21, 31; 2 Chr 12:13)

Duration of reign
Reigned for 17 years after acceding to the throne at 41 years of age (930 BC – 913ᵇ BC; 1 Kgs 14:21; 2 Chr 12:13)
Jeroboam acceded to the throne as the first king in the northern kingdom of Israel at this time (930 BC).

Evaluation – wicked king
He set up high places, sacred pillars and Asherim. He did all kinds of abominations like allowing male cult prostitutes in the land (1 Kgs 14:22-24).

Rehoboam is Solomon's son who had become king in his father's place after Solomon's death. The kingdom was divided into the southern kingdom of Judah and the northern kingdom of Israel during Rehoboam's reign. The name *Rehoboam* is רְחַבְעָם (*rĕḥab'ām*) in Hebrew. This is a combination of the words רָחַב (*rāḥab*), which means "to broaden," "to make wide," and "to enlarge," and the word עַם (*'am*), which means "people." Therefore, the name means "to enlarge the people."

1. Rehoboam caused the kingdom to be divided into the southern kingdom of Judah and the northern kingdom of Israel.

Although Israel enjoyed unprecedented prosperity during the reign of Solomon, the people had to suffer the yoke of backbreaking toil (1 Kgs 5:13-16) and heavy taxes (1 Kgs 10:14) due to Solomon's construction of the temple and the palace. Upon Solomon's death, the people of Israel requested that Rehoboam lighten the hard service and the heavy yoke (1 Kgs 12:4). Here the words *hard service* are קָשֶׁה (*qāše*: cruel) and עֲבֹדָה (*'ăbōdâ*: labor) in Hebrew. Thus, *hard service* denotes "cruel labor," comparable in difficulty to the days of slavery in Egypt.

Rehoboam did not heed the instructions of the elders to lighten the yoke for the people. Instead, he listened to the counsel of the young men with whom he had grown up and became oppressive to the people (1 Kgs 12:6-15). Then, the ten tribes of Israel responded by saying, "What portion do we have in David?" (1 Kgs 12:16). Thus, they rebelled against the house of David and enthroned Jeroboam as their king (1 Kgs 12:16-19; 2 Chr 10:16-19).

Although the division of the kingdom was the judgment God gave for Solomon's transgressions (1 Kgs 11:9-13, 26-40), what actually caused this tragedy to take place in history was Rehoboam's oppressive reign.

The context of Rehoboam's tyrannical reign is as follows.

First, Rehoboam ignored the instructions of the elders.

The word *elder* in Hebrew is זָקֵן (*zāqēn*), which means "someone with deep wisdom which comes from many of life's experiences, an elder." The elders that Rehoboam had disregarded were wise men who had advised Solomon regarding the affairs of the state (1 Kgs 12:6). However, by ignoring the counsel of these old men, who had accumulated much experience and wisdom during their long years in life, Rehoboam became the very person to split up the kingdom. Leviticus 19:32 exhorts, "You shall rise up before the grayheaded and honor the aged, and you shall revere your God; I am the LORD" (Ref Prov 16:31; 20:29).

Second, Rehoboam ignored the people.

Rehoboam responded with tyranny saying, "My father made your yoke heavy, but I will add to your yoke; my father disciplined you with whips, but I will discipline you with scorpions" (1 Kgs 12:14). Rehoboam should have regarded the people and the elders highly since the voice of the people often represents what is needed for the kingdom. Rehoboam did not think to consider the problems faced by the people; he dismissed the elders' advice and disregarded the opinions of the people which ultimately resulted in the division of the kingdom.

2. The kingdom of Judah was strengthened during the first three years of Rehoboam's reign.

According to 2 Chronicles 11:17, the kingdom of Judah was strengthened during the first three years of Rehoboam's reign. Here, the word *strengthened* is חָזַק (*ḥāzaq*) in Hebrew and means "to be strong," "to be resolute," and "to be firm." With the use of the piel (intensive) form of the Hebrew verb, the word comes to denote a kingdom so strong that no other kingdom can invade.

Why was the kingdom so powerful during the early years of Rehoboam's reign?

First, it was because Rehoboam obeyed.

As soon as the kingdom was divided due to Rehoboam's oppressive ways, the king summoned 180,000 soldiers to attack the northern kingdom of Israel. However, Rehoboam was told by Shemaiah the prophet that this was not God's will and immediately relented in obedience.

Second Chronicles 11:4 states, "So they listened to the words of the LORD and returned from going against Jeroboam." Here the words "listened" (וַיִּשְׁמְעוּ, *wayyišmĕʿû*) and "returned" (וַיָּשֻׁבוּ, *wayyāšubû*) are both in the waw consecutive form thus meaning that Rehoboam listened to the Words of God and obeyed immediately.

Relenting from attacking the northern kingdom of Israel was probably unacceptable for Rehoboam. If the kingdom were to be divided during his lifetime, all blame for this would be upon his head. However, Rehoboam gave up on his own thoughts and obeyed the Word of God. As a result, the kingdom was powerful during the early part of his reign.

Second, it was because of Rehoboam's construction efforts to build up the kingdom's defenses.

After obeying God and giving up on his plans to attack the northern kingdom of Israel, Rehoboam turned his attention to strengthening the kingdom's defenses. At the time, the southern kingdom of Judah had been greatly debilitated since the northern kingdom of Israel had seceded with ten tribes and only the tribes of Judah and Benjamin remained in the south.

Therefore, Rehoboam built 15 cities (Bethlehem, Etam, Tekoa, Bethzur, Shoco, Adullam, Gath, Mareshah, Ziph, Adoraim, Lachish, Azekah, Zorah, Aijalon, Hebron) in the frontiers to defend against foreign invasions (2 Chr 11:5-10). These were all fortified cities (2 Chr 11:10b); and seeing that most of them were in the south and the west, they were most likely built with the powerful kingdoms of Egypt and Philistia in mind.

In 2 Chronicles 11:5, the word *defense* is מָצוֹר (*māṣôwr*) in Hebrew, which signifies a fortification with an impregnable rampart. Rehoboam built these 15 fortresses and strengthened them greatly by stationing captains in them with stores of food, oil and wine along with shields and spears (2 Chr 11:11-12). Second Chronicles 11:11 testifies that Rehoboam "also strengthened the fortresses." Here the words *also strengthened* is just one Hebrew word, חָזַק (*ḥāzaq*) in the piel (intensive) form, and is used again in 2 Chronicles 11:17. In other words, Rehoboam strengthened the kingdom by building fortresses strong enough to prevent other nations from invading. A nation's defenses are not strengthened automatically. A nation's defenses are strengthened when people put their faith and trust in God and pour their efforts into building up the defense system.

Third, it was because godly sons of the northern kingdom of Israel moved southward (2 Chr 11:13-17).

Second Chronicles 11:13 states, "Moreover, the priests and the Levites who were in all Israel stood with him from all their districts." Here the phrase *stood with him* is in the hithpael (reflexive) form of the verb, יָצַב (*yāṣab*). When this verb is used in the reflexive form, it means "to station oneself," "take one's stand," "stand," "present oneself," and "stand with someone."[18] In other words, godly sons of Israel actively and voluntarily returned to Rehoboam and stationed themselves in their rightful positions to take up their respective duties. This was a great source of strength for Rehoboam.

They returned south like this because Jeroboam in Israel had set up golden calves at Bethel and Dan and forced the people to worship them and many other idols. Moreover, he had non-Levites lead the sacrifices (1 Kgs 12:25-33; 2 Chr 11:13-15). At that time even many of the laity followed the Levites down to Jerusalem. These were people "who set their hearts on seeking the LORD God of Israel" (2 Chr 11:16). The New Living Translation expresses this as "those who sincerely wanted to worship the LORD." These people emigrated southward because they sincerely sought God and desired to worship Him freely. In reality, they had risked their lives to flee so that they may find true worship. Rehoboam, who had been influenced by such godly people, was strengthened for three years. When there is an abundance of godly people in a nation, their influence grows, and the nation is strengthened by the help of such people (2 Chr 11:17).

3. The treasures in the temple of the Lord and of the royal palace were taken away because of Rehoboam's pride.

As the kingdom became established and strong, Rehoboam became proud. Rehoboam had forgotten the fact that it was entirely through God's grace that the kingdom became powerful. How did Rehoboam's pride show through?

First, he forsook the Word of God.

Second Chronicles 12:1 states, "When the kingdom of Rehoboam was established and strong, he and all Israel with him forsook the law of the LORD." A haughty person is one who forsakes the Word of God.

When the king forsakes the Word of God, the people are bound to follow his example and do the same. When the pastor forsakes the Word of God, the congregation is bound to follow his example. God told Joshua, "This book of the law shall not depart from your mouth, but you shall meditate on it day and night, so that you may be careful to do according to all that is written in it; for then you will make your way prosperous, and then you will have success" (Josh 1:8).

Second, he set up high places, sacred pillars and Asherim.

Those who forsake the Word of God are ultimately bound to forsake God Himself and commit idolatry. First Kings 14:22-24 states, "Judah did evil in the sight of the Lord, and they provoked Him to jealousy more than all that their fathers had done, with the sins which they committed. For they also built for themselves high places and sacred pillars and Asherim on every high hill and beneath every luxuriant tree. There were also male cult prostitutes in the land. They did according to all the abominations of the nations which the LORD dispossessed before the sons of Israel."

It was even more iniquitous that their idolatry was linked to sexual depravity. The Asherah (singular form of Asherim) was the image of a female goddess who was known to grant an abundant harvest of agriculture. There were temple prostitutes at the shrines of the idol and they would perform lewd sexual acts publicly during the goddess worship. "Male cult prostitutes" (1 Kgs 14:24) were also involved in the sacrifices and offerings to the foreign idols. These all go to show how extremely depraved and fallen Judah had become (Ref Lev 19:29; Deut 23:17; 1 Kgs 15:12; 22:46; Job 36:14).

The reason Rehoboam had become so haughty was due to his profligate life of marriage. Rehoboam had 18 wives and 60 concubines, totaling 78 women in all (2 Chr 11:21). Rehoboam had three sons—Jeush, Shemariah and Zaham—through Mahalath the daughter of Jerimoth the son of David (2 Chr 11:18-19); and by Maacah the daughter of Absalom, he had Abijah, Attai, Ziza and Shelomith (2 Chr 11:20). Abijah later becomes the king to succeed Rehoboam (2 Chr 11:22). Just as Solomon had fallen into idolatry because of his many wives and concubines, Rehoboam naturally became idolatrous because of his many wives and concubines. It also seems likely that his mother Naamah the Ammonitess (2 Chr 12:13) was influential in leading Rehoboam away from God and into idolatry (1 Kgs 14:21; 2 Chr 12:13).

God sent Shishak, king of Egypt, to discipline Rehoboam who had forsaken the Word of God and who initiated idol worship in Judah. In Rehoboam's fifth year of reign, Shishak came up against Jerusalem and "took away the treasures of the house of the LORD and the treasures of the king's house" and everything else including the shields of gold that Solomon had made (1 Kgs 14:25-26; 2 Chr 12:2-12). Shishak was the founder of the 22nd Dynasty in Egypt who ruled for 21 years from 945 to 924 BC. He was the king who had provided much assistance to Jeroboam when he started an uprising to secede from the then unified kingdom of Israel (1 Kgs 11:40).

God allowed King Shishak to attack Judah, so that He may discipline Rehoboam. However, God did not completely destroy the southern kingdom of Judah at this time because Rehoboam humbled himself before God when the prophet Shemaiah declared on behalf of God, "You have forsaken Me, so I also have forsaken you to Shishak" (2 Chr 12:5-7). Humbling oneself is the act of lowering one's body in reverence toward God (Jas 4:10). In the second half of 2 Chronicles 12:7 it says, "They have humbled themselves *so* I will not destroy them, but I will grant them some *measure* of deliverance, and My wrath shall not be poured out on Jerusalem by means of Shishak." Here, the expression "some measure of deliverance" means that God did rescue Judah from the hand of Egypt, but He did not save them completely. God allowed a significant amount of distress to come upon them and rescued them just in time to evade complete destruction.

Rehoboam made bronze shields in place of the plundered gold shields and committed them to the care of the commanders of the guards at the gates of the king's palace (1 Kgs 14:27). These bronze shields symbolize the decline of the southern kingdom of Judah since the days of Solomon. At the same time they demonstrate how God's grace was upholding His people even through the decline of the kingdom.

Second Chronicles 12:14 comments, "He did evil because he did not set his heart to seek the LORD." Here the word *set* is the verb כּוּן (*kûn*), which means "to establish, to be firm, to be confirmed, to set up." In its hiphil (causative) form as used in this verse, the word indicates "the state of being firmly established." Throughout his life, Rehoboam was never firmly established in his faith; he was always wavering. Therefore, he did not wholly seek God but committed iniquities. As a result, he was continuously warring against Jeroboam and the northern kingdom of Israel during his entire 17-year reign (1 Kgs 14:30; 2 Chr 12:15).

If Rehoboam had set his heart toward God alone and continually humbled himself to honor the people, then such battles would not have taken place. Therefore, we are convinced that we need humility to revere and cherish the Word of God. Furthermore, we need to be humble enough to value and honor the advice of the wise men and the people of God.

CHAPTER 9

The Fourth Generation: Abijah or Abijam

Abijah / Ἀβιά / אֲבִיָּה
The Lord is my father.

Abijam / Αβιου / אֲבִים
The father of the sea

- The second king of the southern kingdom of Judah (1 Kgs 15:1-8; 2 Chr 13:1-22)
- The fourth individual in the second period of Jesus' genealogy

Matthew 1:7 . . . Rehoboam the father of **Abijah**, and **Abijah** the father of Asa.

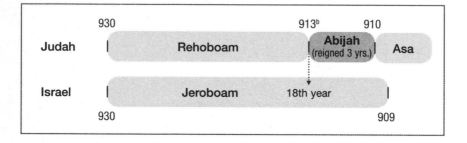

Background
Father: Rehoboam (1 Kgs 14:31; 2 Chr 12:16)
Mother: Maacah (daughter of Absalom; 1 Kgs 15:2; 2 Chr 11:20-22)
In 2 Chronicles 13:2, she is recorded as "Micaiah" (daughter of Uriel of Gibeah)

Duration of reign
Reigned for 3 years (913b – 910 BC; 1 Kgs 15:2; 2 Chr 13:2), the king's age at accession is not mentioned.
Abijah became king in the southern kingdom of Judah in the 18th year of Jeroboam's reign (1 Kgs 15:1; 2 Chr 13:1). From the perspective of the northern kingdom of Israel, who follows the non-accession year dating method, Abijah's year of accession would be Jeroboam's 19th regnal year, not his 18th.

Evaluation – wicked king
Initially, he trusted in God and was triumphant in his battle against Israel. But afterwards, he committed all the sins of his father Rehoboam, and his heart was not like the heart of David (1 Kgs 15:3).

Historical sources – Chronicles of the Kings of Judah (1 Kgs 15:7), the treatise of the prophet Iddo (2 Chr 13:22)

Abijah succeeded Rehoboam to become the second king of the southern kingdom of Judah. The name *Abijah* is אֲבִיָּה (*ăbiyyâ*) in Hebrew and is formed by combining the word אָב ('āb), meaning "father" and the word יָה (*yâ*), which is a shortened form of the word "Yahweh." Therefore, the name *Abijah* means "the LORD is my father." Abijah's other name is אֲבִיָּם (*'ăbiyyām*), which is a combination of the word אָב ('āb) for "father" and the word יָם (*yām*) for "sea." Therefore, it means "the father of the sea."

1. Abijah was not worthy to become king, but he was enthroned by the grace of God.

Abijah was the firstborn son of Rehoboam's second wife, Maacah (daughter of Absalom; 2 Chr 11:20). Abijah had three older brothers above him—Jeush, Shemariah and Zaham—who were born to Rehoboam's first wife, "Mahalath the daughter of Jerimoth the son of David" (2 Chr 11:18-19). Such circumstances notwithstanding, Rehoboam made Abijah, who was fourth in line, king before his three elder brothers (2 Chr 11:20-22). This was because Rehoboam loved Maacah the most out of his 18 wives and 60 concubines (2 Chr 11:21). Therefore, Abijah should have realized that it was through God's grace that he became king even though he was not qualified as such. Thus, he should have lived his entire life in reverence before God. However, he committed all the sins of his father Rehoboam and his heart was not wholly devoted to the Lord his God like that of his father David (1 Kgs 15:3).

2. Abijah was greatly triumphant in the war against the northern kingdom of Israel.

Just as wars never ceased between Rehoboam and Jeroboam, Judah continued to fight against Jeroboam and the northern kingdom of Israel even during Abijah's time (1 Kgs 15:6-7).

In this war, Abijah's army in Judah was numbered at 400,000 while Jeroboam in Israel had an army of 800,000 (2 Chr 13:3). The situation at the time was as follows. Previous king Rehoboam battled Shishak of

Egypt for five years only to sustain a crushing defeat (2 Chr 12:1-9). Since then, the battle with Jeroboam had continued for 12 years. Judah was overwhelmingly outnumbered, facing an 800,000 men army of Israel and what seemed to be certain defeat. However, as soon as the war started, Abijah declared to Jeroboam and the army of Israel, "O sons of Israel, do not fight against the LORD God of your fathers, for you will not succeed" (2 Chr 13:12).

Abijah was asserting that fighting against the southern kingdom of Judah was tantamount to fighting against God Himself. The southern kingdom of Judah possessed the covenant of salt by which God had promised to give the rule over Israel forever to David and his descendants (2 Chr 13:5). However, the northern kingdom of Israel had betrayed that covenant and had become a kingdom that worshiped golden calves, the very thing that God detested (2 Chr 13:6-8).

Abijah rebuked Jeroboam for betraying God by driving out the true priests and following the ways of the foreign nations by appointing priests for what are not gods (2 Chr 13:9a; Ref 1 Kgs 12:31; 13:33). Moreover, Abijah sharply criticized King Jeroboam for allowing anyone who brings a young bull and seven rams to become a priest (2 Chr 13:9b).[19] In reality, King Jeroboam had completely strayed from God's commands and was completely devoid of godliness; he had completely betrayed God (2 Chr 13:10-11).

Abijah's bold, covenant-based declaration was the driving force behind Judah's victory. Jeroboam had set an ambush and was attacking Judah from the front and rear. However, the Judahites cried out to the Lord while the priests blew their trumpets (2 Chr 13:14). Here the word *cry* in Hebrew is צָעַק (ṣā'aq), meaning "to cry out," "call," and "cry for help."[20] In this situation where they were completely outnumbered, the people of Judah anxiously cried out to God for help. The phrase, "the priests blew the trumpets," in its plural form signifies that many priests were synchronized in blowing the trumpets. The act of blowing the trumpets in time of war signalizes the call for the help of God according to the Law of Moses (Num 10:9; 31:6).

When they cried out and blew the trumpets, God routed Jeroboam and all Israel so that Judah slew 500,000 men of Israel and reaped a great victory (2 Chr 13:13-17). Second Chronicles 13:18 comments that Judah was triumphant because they trusted in the Lord their God. Those who fully trust in the Lord and firmly believe in a triumphant outcome will truly be victorious even in the face of precariously dangerous situations.

3. Abijah walked in the way of iniquity once he became powerful.

Abijah continued to grow in power after his victory in battle. Thereafter, he took for himself 14 wives and had 22 sons and 16 daughters by them (2 Chr 13:21). Once he became powerful, Abijah's heart got proud and he neglected the affairs of the kingdom. He sought after physical satisfaction by engrossing himself in the carnal pleasures of life. The more powerful he grew, the further he distanced himself from God. First Kings 15:3 comments that "He [Abijah] walked in all the sins of his father which he had committed before him; and his heart was not wholly devoted to the LORD his God, like the heart of his father David." God did not prolong the reign of Abijah, but took his life after a short three-year reign. This was the result of his many sins and idolatry before God. When Abijah relied on God, His divine powers were manifested in him so that no other power on earth could rival that of Abijah. However, he departed from God and became a foolish being who was engrossed in the hedonistic ways of the world.

4. There are two names for Abijah's mother.

Second Chronicles 13:2 records Abijah's mother as "Micaiah the daughter of Uriel." Here the name *Micaiah* (מִיכָיָהוּ) means, "who is like God,"[21] or "who is like unto Jehovah?"[22] It signifies that no one can rival God.

On the other hand, 2 Chronicles 11:20-22 and 1 Kings 15:2 record Abijah's mother as "Maacah (מַעֲכָה) the daughter of Abishalom." In the expression "daughter of Abishalom," the word for "daughter" in Hebrew is בַּת (*bat*). This word does not strictly denote a daughter only but can also mean "granddaughter." Thus, in actuality, Maacah is the granddaughter of Abishalom (אֲבִישָׁלוֹם – same as Absalom, son of David) and the daughter born by Uriel and Tamar (2 Sam 14:27; 2 Chr 13:2). It is interesting that the mother of Absalom (Abishalom) was also named "Maacah" (2 Sam 3:3; 1 Chr 3:2). This Maacah was the daughter of Talmai, king of Geshur, who married King David and gave birth to Absalom. Absalom took refuge with his maternal grandfather Talmai, king of Geshur, for three years after having killed his half-brother Amnon for raping Tamar, his sister (2 Sam 13:37-39).

The name *Maacah*, then, is the name of both Absalom's mother as well as his granddaughter.[23] *Maacah* means "oppression" or "pressure (literally, she has pressed)."[24] Maacah was loved by Rehoboam more than any other wife or concubine (2 Chr 11:21). Though she was the grandmother of King Asa, she raised him as her son (1 Kgs 15:10; 2 Chr 15:16) and wielded much power and influence until the time of King Asa. However, she was deposed by grandson King Asa because she had made a detestable image for Asherah (1 Kgs 15:13; 2 Chr 15:16).

God could have immediately destroyed the southern kingdom of Judah for all of Abijah's terrible sins. However, He relented and bestowed mercy and grace because He remembered His covenant with David (1 Kgs 15:3-4; 2 Chr 21:7). When we examine the life of Abijah, the early part of his life corresponded with the meaning of his name, "the LORD is my father"; he gained victory in battle through his God-centered faith and ruled justly. But later, he forsook God and lived as a foolish king immersed in the hedonistic ways of the world. If Abijah had sustained his initial faith, his life could have been victorious until the end.

CHAPTER 10

The Fifth Generation: Asa

Asa / ᾽Ασά / אָסָא

Healer, healing

- The third king of the southern kingdom of Judah (1 Kgs 15:9-24; 2 Chr 14:1-16:14)
- The fifth individual in the second period of Jesus' genealogy

Matthew 1:7-8 . . . Abijah the father of **Asa. Asa** was the father of Jehoshaphat . . . .

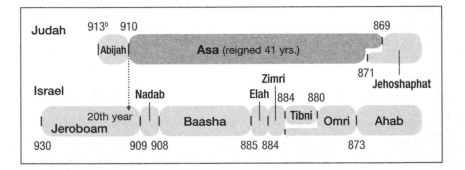

Background

Father: Abijah (Abijam) (1 Kgs 15:8; 2 Chr 14:1)
Mother: Maacah (daughter of Abishalom; 1 Kgs 15:10; 2 Chr 15:16)

Duration of reign

Reigned for 41 years (910 BC – 869 BC; 1 Kgs 15:10). The king's age at accession is not recorded.
Asa acceded to the throne in the 20th year of Jeroboam (1 Kgs 15:9). From the perspective of the northern kingdom of Israel using the non-accession year dating method, "twentieth year of Jeroboam" in which Asa took the throne is actually the twenty-first year of Jeroboam's reign.

Asa succeeded Abijah and became the third king of the southern kingdom of Judah. During his 41-year tenure as king, the northern kingdom of Israel went through seven different kings (Jeroboam, Nadab, Baasha, Elah, Zimri, Omri and Ahab). The name *Asa* in Hebrew is אָסָא (*'āsā'*), which is derived from the Chaldean word "Asa," meaning "to heal." Thus, the name means "healer."

1. There was peace during the first ten years of Asa's reign.

Second Chronicles 14:1 states, ". . . his son Asa became king in his place. The land was undisturbed for ten years during his days." Initially, Asa did good and right in the sight of the God. He removed the foreign altars and high places and tore down the sacred pillars and the Asherim (2 Chr 14:3). Asa also had the people of Judah observe the law and the commandments while removing the high places and the incense altars from all the fortified cities of Judah (2 Chr 14:4-5).

However, 1 Kings 15:14 states, "But the high places were not taken away; nevertheless the heart of Asa was wholly devoted to the LORD all his days." The "high places" that Asa had not taken away were not for worshiping idols but for worshiping the Lord God (2 Chr 33:17). Israel had two types of high places, one for idol worship (1 Kgs 14:22-23; 2 Kgs 21:3; 23:8-19; 2 Chr 20:33; 21:11; 28:4, 24-25; Jer 7:31; 19:5; 32:35; Ezek 16;16) and another for worshiping the Lord their God (2 Chr

33:17). Since there is no mention of idolatry along with the expression, "the high places were not taken away" (1 Kgs 15:14), we can conclude that the high places that Asa did not remove were not for idolatry but were "His high places" (Ref 2 Kgs 18:22; 2 Chr 32:12).

Asa was seeking God through such actions. Second Chronicles 14:7 states, ". . . because we have sought the LORD our God; we have sought Him." The word *sought* in this verse is דָּרַשׁ (*dāraš*) in Hebrew, which signifies a passionate pursuit of something. God granted peace during Asa's reign because Asa sought after Him passionately. Peace within the family and the nation is a blessing that is bestowed when we passionately seek after God. In the early part of his reign, Asa acted in line with the meaning of his name as he "healed" idolatrous Judah and ruled justly to bring peace within the kingdom.

God becomes the firm stronghold, shield and fortress to those who seek Him. The waves of tribulations, sorrow and worries can never encroach upon those who pursue God. Those who seek God receive absolute security and peace as a bird roosting in her nest.

> **2 Chronicles 14:5-7** And the kingdom was undisturbed under him . . . since the land was undisturbed, and there was no one at war with him during those years, because the Lord had given him rest. ". . . He has given us rest on every side." So they built and prospered.

2. Asa fought and triumphed against Zerah's army of a million men.

When there was peace during Asa's reign, Zerah the Ethiopian attacked Judah with an army of a million men and 300 chariots. At this time, Asa had an army of 300,000 men bearing large shields and spears and 280,000 men bearing shields and wielding bows; in all, there were 580,000 valiant men (2 Chr 14:8-9).

This was a grand-scale war that lasted for four years and mobilized all the resources of both kingdoms. It is clearly recorded in 2 Chronicles 15:10 that this was the third month of the fifteenth year of Asa's reign. Moreover, 2 Chronicles 14:10 records that Asa had peace for the first ten years of his reign. Therefore, the war against Ethiopia's army of a million lasted a long time—of about four years—starting in Asa's eleventh regnal year and ending the third month of the fifteenth regnal year.

Objectively speaking, this was a situation in which Judah could not prevail. However, Asa cried out to God, "'LORD, there is no one besides You to help *in the battle* between the powerful and those who have no strength; so help us, O LORD our God, for we trust in You, and in Your name have come against this multitude. O LORD, You are our God; let not man prevail against You'" (2 Chr 14:11).

God heeded Asa's prayer and struck the Ethiopians and defeated them, so that they fled. Asa pursued them and destroyed them, making sure that they could not recover (2 Chr 14:13). This was an awesome event in which we can realize the meaning of the phrase, "the LORD is not restrained to save by many or by few" (1 Sam 14:6). Judah reaped countless spoils from this war. After the war, Asa sacrificed to the Lord 700 oxen and 7,000 sheep from the spoils they had gathered (2 Chr 15:11).

3. Asa carried out a religious reformation.

Asa could have become proud about the great victory reaped against the Ethiopians; however, God sent to Asa the prophet Azariah to warn him as well as to encourage him to begin a new religious reformation. Azariah warned, "The LORD is with you when you are with Him. And if you seek Him, He will let you find Him; but if you forsake Him, He will forsake you" (2 Chr 15:2). Then he also declared, "But you, be strong and do not lose courage, for there is reward for your work" (2 Chr 15:7). This was an encouragement to Asa not to lose heart but to forge ahead boldly with a religious reformation.

Asa was encouraged through these words and removed the abominable idols and restored the altar of the Lord. There were some who defected to Judah from the northern kingdom of Israel when they saw that God was with Asa (2 Chr 15:9). The people assembled at Jerusalem on the third month of the fifteenth year of Asa to sacrifice to the Lord. They made a covenant to seek the Lord their God with all their heart and soul. So the Lord gave the southern kingdom of Judah rest on every side (2 Chr 15:10-15).

Furthermore, Asa removed Maacah from the position of queen mother because she had made a horrid image as an Asherah. He cut down the image, crushed and burned it at the brook Kidron (1 Kgs 15:13; 2 Chr 15:16). Maacah was, in fact, Asa's grandmother; but since Asa's mother had passed away early on, his grandmother was acting as his mother and therefore, she was called his mother.

Maacah was the wife that Rehoboam loved more than all the other wives and concubines (2 Chr 11:21-22). She was also the mother of the next king, Abijah (2 Chr 13:1-2). Moreover, she is also referred to as the mother of the succeeding king Asa (2 Chr 15:16; 1 Kgs 15:13). It seems likely that Maacah enjoyed great authority during the reigns of her husband Rehoboam and her son Abijah, which enabled her to worship idols to her heart's content. More than likely, she sustained her influence during the reign of grandson Asa and continued to serve her idols. We can surmise that Maacah enjoyed tremendous power; consequently, the negative influence that her idolatry transmitted to the kingdom was most likely very serious. King Asa was so thorough in carrying out his religious reformation that he even removed his grandmother—who was more like a mother—from her position as queen mother (1 Kgs 15:13; 2 Chr 15:16). This was because Asa's reverence for the Word of God was stronger than his personal affections for his grandmother (Ref Matt 10:36-37).

There were no wars from the time Maacah was deposed from her position until the 35th year of Asa's reign (2 Chr 15:19).[25] God's peace comes to dwell continually with a true reformation that is carried out in full obedience to the Word of God.

4. Asa relied on the kingdom of Aram during a battle.

In the 36th year of Asa's reign,[26] Baasha king of Israel went up to fight against Judah. Baasha fortified Ramah to prevent anyone from going down to Judah and to use it as a base of operations in conquering the southern kingdom of Judah. Then, Asa took all the silver and gold from the treasuries of the house of the LORD and the treasuries of the king's house and sent them to Ben-hadad the king of Aram. Asa asked the king of Aram to break his treaty with Israel and to help him attack the northern kingdom. Ben-hadad accepted the silver and gold sent by Asa and attacked the northern kingdom of Israel which made the construction work at Ramah come to a halt (1 Kgs 15:16-22; 2 Chr 16:1-6). Then Asa took the construction materials at Ramah and built Geba of Benjamin and Mizpah with them (1 Kgs 15:22; 2 Chr 16:6).

Asa relied on a foreign power and not God during a national crisis. Furthermore, he gave the treasures of the holy temple, which is God's possession, to a foreign king. These were both great acts of sin before God. Asa forgot about the grace of God who had enabled him to defeat Ethiopia's million-men army at the beginning of his royal tenure, and tried to overcome this national crisis through worldly means. Of course, through the help of the Aramean army, the immediate crisis was thwarted and Baasha's army withdrew; however, the southern kingdom of Judah was embroiled in a seemingly endless war with Aram from thence forward.

At that time, the seer Hanani rebuked, "Because you have relied on the king of Aram and have not relied on the LORD your God, therefore the army of the king of Aram has escaped out of your hand" (2 Chr 16:7). Rather than repenting, Asa became enraged at hearing these words. He imprisoned Hanani the seer and oppressed some of the people (2 Chr 16:10). King Asa had lost his humility unlike in the past when he had boldly performed a religious reformation at the encouragement of the prophet Azariah (2 Chr 15:1-7). Many days of peace and prosperity within the kingdom had instilled great pride into the king. Asa had heard the prophet's rebuke. He had heard how God moves to and fro throughout the earth, watching every movement of mankind (2 Chr 16:9). And yet, he committed the grave sin of persecuting and incarcerating the prophet. We must examine ourselves to see if we are not condemning others while unable to reform the terrible pride within.

5. Asa was severely diseased in his feet in the latter years of his reign.

Asa became severely diseased in his feet in the 39th year of his reign (1 Kgs 15:23; 2 Chr 16:12). This was God's way of giving King Asa a last chance to repent. However, Asa did not seek God to treat his disease, but he sought out skilled physicians (2 Chr 16:12). In the New Living Translation, 2 Chronicles 16:12 is translated, "In the thirty-ninth year of his reign, Asa developed a serious foot disease. Yet even with the severity of his disease, he did not seek the Lord's help but turned only to his physicians."

Asa sought out human methods to treat his disease rather than turning to God, who had given that disease. Ultimately, even in his severe pain, King Asa did not seek God, but suffered for two years. Then, he died in the third year, which was the 41st year of his reign (2 Chr 16:13-14). His son Jehoshaphat had been a co-regent for three years due to Asa's foot disease (Ref 1 Kgs 22:41-42).

"The LORD is your healer" (יְהוָה רָפֶא: *yhwh rāpā'*); God is a God who heals us (Exod 15:26). God is the ultimate physician who heals our physical, mental and spiritual diseases. Jesus can heal any and all diseases (Luke 5:17; 6:19). He has taken up all of our infirmities and diseases (Matt 8:17). However, Asa did not rely on God, the true physician in the latter years of his life, and he was unable to escape the fetters of his illness because he sought out human physicians. We must believe that God is the ultimate healer and go forth to Him. God will not turn away from those who trust and rely on Him, but He will become our physical and spiritual healer.

CHAPTER 11

The Sixth Generation: Jehoshaphat

> **Jehoshaphat / Ἰωσαφάτ / יְהוֹשָׁפָט**
> The Lord judges

— The fourth king of the southern kingdom of Judah (1 Kgs 22:1-50; 2 Chr 17:1-21:1)
— The sixth individual in the second period of Jesus' genealogy

Matthew 1:8 Asa was the father of **Jehoshaphat**, **Jehoshaphat** the father of Joram . . . .

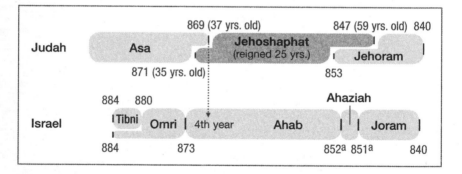

Background
Father: Asa (1 Kgs 22:41; 2 Chr 17:1)
Mother: Azubah (daughter of Shilhi; 1 Kgs 22:42; 2 Chr 20:31)

Duration of reign
Acceded the throne at age 35 and reigned for 25 years (871–847 BC; 1 Kgs 22:41-42)
Jehoshaphat took sole reign of the southern kingdom of Judah in the fourth year of Ahab in the northern kingdom of Israel (1 Kgs 22:41). From the perspective of the northern kingdom of Israel using the non-accession year dating method, the "fourth year of Ahab" is actually his fifth year. Since Jehoshaphat first sat on the throne as a coregent due to his father King Asa's foot disease, an accession year is not counted but the first year of his regency is reckoned as the first year of his reign.

Jehoshaphat succeeded his father Asa and became the fourth king of the southern kingdom of Judah. Jehoshaphat walked in the way of his father Asa and did not turn from them; he ruled with justice in the land (1 Kgs 22:43). The name *Jehoshaphat* is יְהוֹשָׁפָט (*yĕhōwšāpāṭ*) in Hebrew. It is a combination of the words יְהוָה (*yhwh*), which means "Jehovah," and the word שָׁפַט (*šāpaṭ*), which means "to judge." Therefore, the name *Jehoshaphat* means "the LORD judges."

1. Jehoshaphat had great riches and honor.

Second Chronicles 17:5 in the New International Version states, "The Lord established the kingdom under his control; and all Judah brought gifts to Jehoshaphat, so that he had great wealth and honor." Jehoshaphat was greatly blessed when he became king because the Lord was with him (2 Chr 17:3) and He "established the kingdom in his control" (2 Chr 17:5, NASB).

Then, why was God with Jehoshaphat?

First, it was because Jehoshaphat walked in the "earlier ways of his father David" (2 Chr 17:3-4, ESV).

Here, the "earlier ways of his father David" is a phrase that describes David's life at the beginning of his reign when he had feared God and lived in righteousness—the time before his sin. Jehoshaphat followed the example of David's pure faith of his earlier days and lived a righteous life in reverence to God.

Second, it was because Jehoshaphat was deeply committed to fully obeying the commands of God (2 Chr 17:4, 6).

Jehoshaphat sent out Levites throughout all the cities of Judah to teach the Word of God (2 Chr 17:8-9). But 1 Kings 22:43 states, "However, the high places were not taken away; the people still sacrificed and burnt incense on the high places." The high places mentioned in this passage are not places to worship idols (1 Kgs 14:22-23; 2 Kgs 21:3; 23:8-19; 2 Chr 20:33; 21:11; 28:4, 24-25; Jer 7:31; 19:5; 32:35; Ezek 16:16); they were for worshiping the Lord God (2 Chr 33:17; Ref 2 Kgs 18:22; 2 Chr 32:12). If Jehoshaphat had fully obeyed the command of God to worship at "the place in which the LORD your God will choose" (Deut 12:11-14) and had removed even the other high places which were scattered about throughout the kingdom, then his religious reformation would have been that much more complete.

Third, it was because Jehoshaphat had destroyed the idols.

Jehoshaphat did not seek the Baals, but removed the high places and the Asherim (2 Chr 17:3, 6). God instilled fear upon all the kingdoms surrounding Judah, so that they did not make war against Jehoshaphat. Moreover, God made the Philistines and the Arabians bring tributes to Jehoshaphat (2 Chr 17:10-11).

Fourth, it was because Jehoshaphat devoted himself to strengthening the national defense.

Jehoshaphat became more and more powerful and built fortresses and storage cities throughout Judah; he had a powerful army of 1,160,000 men (2 Chr 17:12-19). Adnah was a commander of thousands in Judah and he had 300,000 valiant warriors under him (2 Chr 17:14). Johanan (or Jehohanan) also had 280,000 men with him (2 Chr 17:15) while Amasiah son of Zichri had 200,000 valiant warriors with him (2 Chr 17:16). From the tribe of Benjamin, the valiant warrior Eliada led 200,000 men armed with bows and shields (2 Chr 17:17) while next to him Jehozabad had 180,000 men equipped for war (2 Chr 17:18). These were all valiant warriors of Judah (2 Chr 17:13).

When David conducted a census, there were 500,000 troops in Judah (2 Sam 24:9). Moreover, Abijah, the second king of the southern kingdom of Judah, had an army of 400,000 (2 Chr 13:3) while Asa the third king had 580,000 troops (2 Chr 14:8). Compared to these numbers, Jehoshaphat's army of 1,160,000 men is twice in size of the army during his father Asa's time.

Jehoshaphat had many worthy men of faith under him. Their names are Adnah (עַדְנָה: pleasure), Johanan/Jehohanan (יְהוֹחָנָן: Jehovah has graced), Amasiah (עֲמַסְיָה: whom Jehovah carries in his bosom),[27] Eliada (אֶלְיָדָע: God knows), and Jehozabad (יְהוֹזָבָד: Jehovah has endowed).[28] These were all men who served the king (2 Chr 17:19), especially Amasiah, who "willingly offered himself unto the LORD" (2 Chr 17:16, KJV). The kingdom became steadily more powerful during Jehoshaphat's reign because there were such faithful servants who did not look after their own interests, but gave up their entire lives solely for the glory and the kingdom of God.

2. Jehoshaphat allied himself with King Ahab through marriage.

When Jehoshaphat's wealth and honor were at their highest, he allied himself with Ahab by marriage (2 Chr 18:1). This is a reference to the marriage between Jehoshaphat's son Jehoram and Ahab's daughter Athaliah. By forging a marital alliance with Ahab, who had officially introduced Baal worship to the northern kingdom of Israel, Jehoshaphat had also enabled Baal worship to be introduced to Judah as well. This was Jehoshaphat's own way of dealing with Aram, whose power was widely renowned at the time, and Assyria, who was building up their power base.

A few years after the marriage alliance with Ahab, Jehoshaphat accepted Ahab's offer and participated in the war against Aram at Ramoth-gilead. At that time, 400 false prophets and Zedekiah all prophesied that they should go to war at Ramoth-gilead. However, one man, Micaiah the prophet, prophesied that Ahab will die if they go to war at Ramoth-gilead (1 Kgs 22:14-23; 2 Chr 18:4-16). The prophet Micaiah warned that God had put a deceiving spirit in the mouths of the false prophets, but Jehoshaphat and Ahab ignored the will of God that was delivered through Micaiah's warning and went to the battle at Ramoth-gilead. As a result, Ahab gets hit by a random arrow that someone shot and died in battle just as the prophecy (1 Kgs 22:29-40; 2 Chr 18:28-34). We can learn some important lessons from this event.

First, a believer must have spiritual discernment.
Spiritual discernment is a special gift which enables one to distinguish the thoughts of man or even deceptions of evil spirits, and it is closely related to the gift of prophecy (1 Cor 12:10; 1 Thes 5:19-21). In other words, spiritual discernment is the ability to distinguish whether some-

thing is from God, from man's thoughts, or from evil spirits. The gift of spiritual discernment is doubly crucial in the last days.[29]

Surprisingly, there are many ministers or leaders who have the spirit of deception like false prophets and proclaim falsehood as if it were the truth. These people have strength in numbers and their message sounds plausible enough so that without spiritual discernment, one would fall prey to them easily. First John 4:1 warns us, "Beloved, do not believe every spirit, but test the spirits to see whether they are from God, because many false prophets have gone out into the world."

Second, God sometimes utilizes deceiving spirits.

The prophet Micaiah declared in 1 Kings 22:23, "behold, the LORD has put a deceiving spirit in the mouth of all these your prophets." This teaches us that even the activities of Satan take place under permission from God. God allowed the evil spirit to work within King Saul (1 Sam 16:14), and He also allowed Satan to test Job (Job 1:6-7, 12; 2:6).

Third, human beings may play their tricks, but the Word of God will always be fulfilled.

Ahab, who had heard the prophet Micaiah's foreboding words, resorted to petty trickery like going into battle in disguise (1 Kgs 22:30). However, Ahab got struck in a joint of the armor by an arrow that was shot randomly by a certain man. He bled profusely from this wound and ultimately died (1 Kgs 22:34). The random arrow that struck Ahab was by necessary coincidence; the arrow was shot randomly but its target was certain. This teaches us that no matter how many tricks a man may play, we cannot prevent the Word of God from being fulfilled in our lives. King Ahab was able to evade the enemies' eyes, but he could not escape God's providence.

Although Jehoshaphat barely escaped alive and returned safely to Jerusalem, Jehu the son of Hanani the seer rebuked, "Should you help the wicked and love those who hate the LORD and so bring wrath on yourself from the LORD?" (2 Chr 19:2).

In this passage, God had rebuked two things. First, God rebuked Jehoshaphat for helping the wicked. Second, God reproached him for loving those who hate the Lord. Here the word *wicked* in Hebrew is רָשָׁע (*rāšā'*), which means "wicked," "criminal," or "ungodly," and is a reference to King Ahab. The phrase "those who hate" is actually just one word שֹׂנֵא (*śānē'*) in Hebrew, which is in the plural form and refers to Ahab and all those who follow him. When we are blessed with God's grace, wealth and honor, we must be careful not to allow human thoughts or personal ties to cause us to befriend people who hate the Lord (Jas 4:4).

3. After repenting, Jehoshaphat carried out a second religious reformation.

Although Asa incarcerated Hanani for rebuking him (2 Chr 16:7-10), Jehoshaphat repented after hearing the rebuke of Jehu. Then, he started another religious reformation.

First, Jehoshaphat himself went throughout the kingdom to bring the people back to the Lord their God (2 Chr 19:4).

Jehoshaphat toured the kingdom from Beersheba to the hills of Ephraim and proclaimed the message of reformation—"Return to the LORD God!" Beersheba was at the southernmost point of the kingdom of Judah while the hills of Ephraim was at the northern borders of Judah. Jehoshaphat toured the entire kingdom and reinstituted the educational policy, which had once been executed before (2 Chr 17:7-9). By so doing, he carried out his comprehensive religious reformation. Knowing that a true spiritual reformation cannot take place without the Word of God, Jehoshaphat began his religious reformation by teaching the Word of God to the people.

Second, Jehoshaphat appointed professional judges in each of the cities and commanded them to judge with the fear of the Lord (2 Chr 19:5-7).

Jehoshaphat appointed judges for each of the cities to ensure justice was given to the people of Judah. He advised the judges, "Consider what you are doing, for you do not judge for man but for the LORD who is with you when you render judgment" (2 Chr 19:6). Jehoshaphat was deeply committed to making sure that justice would be carried out in his kingdom.

Third, Jehoshaphat systematized the division and delegation of the judiciary work (2 Chr 19:8-11).

Jehoshaphat set up a central judicial court in Jerusalem. He had Amariah the chief priest render judgment on all religious matters, and Zebadiah was to judge all things pertaining to the kingdom, such as civil lawsuits between the citizens of Jerusalem (2 Chr 19:8-11).

Jehoshaphat's judicial reform was an effort to crack down on the practice of idol worship, which was spreading through the kingdom since the marriage alliance with Ahab, by probing deep into the lives of the people of Judah to purify them through the Word of God. Just as the meaning of his name suggests, Jehoshaphat had instituted a judiciary system in which God was the Supreme Judge of the land.

4. Jehoshaphat defeated the coalition forces of three nations.

After Jehoshaphat performed his second religious reformation, the coalition forces of Moab, Ammon and Mount Seir attacked Judah. This was a fulfillment of the Word of God. After his marriage alliance with Ahab, Jehoshaphat committed the sin of participating in the battle at Ramoth-gilead. Regarding this, God prophesied through the prophet Jehu, "wrath has gone out against you from the LORD" (2 Chr 19:2, NRSV). God's wrath was displayed through the attack of the coalition forces of Moab, Ammon and Mount Seir. However, Jehoshaphat reaped a great victory because the coalition forces fought against one another and killed each other, and Judah was able to collect a great spoil from the war.

What was the secret to this victory?

First, the entire kingdom fasted and prayed.
Jehoshaphat was afraid and thus proclaimed a fast throughout the kingdom and the people willingly obeyed the decree by fasting and crying out to God (2 Chr 20:3-4). All of Judah was standing before God, even the infants, children and the women (2 Chr 20:13). The wisest thing to do in times of great trials, which cannot be resolved through human abilities, is to come humbly before the Lord and cry out to Him (Ps 50:15; Jer 29:12-13).

Then, God spoke through the prophet Jahaziel the Levite saying, "The battle is not yours but God's. . . 'You *need* not fight in this *battle;* station yourselves, stand and see the salvation of the LORD on your behalf, O Judah and Jerusalem.' Do not fear or be dismayed; tomorrow go out to face them, for the LORD is with you" (2 Chr 20:15-17).

Second, they put on holy attire and sang praises in front of the armies.
Jehoshaphat selected singers and had them put on holy attires to go out before the armies to sing praises to God. They sang, "Give thanks to

the LORD, for His lovingkindness is everlasting" (2 Chr 20:21). When they began singing the praises, God set ambushes against the armies of Ammon, Moab and Mount Seir, and they were routed. The Ammonites and the Moabites rose up against the people of Mount Seir and destroyed them completely. Then, the armies of Ammon and Moab slaughtered each other to utter destruction (2 Chr 20:22-23). Just as the words, "You need not fight in this battle" (2 Chr 20:17), Jehoshaphat was triumphant without even having to fight. When the people of Judah came to the lookout of the wilderness, they saw that no one had escaped (2 Chr 20:24). So Jehoshaphat and his people went and took for themselves their spoil, including goods, garments, and valuable things. And they took three days taking the spoil because there was more than they could carry. Then on the fourth day, the people assembled at the valley of Beracah to praise God who gave them a great victory that day. The name *Beracah* is בְּרָכָה (*bĕrākâ*) in Hebrew and means, "blessing," "prosperity," and "praise of God."

The battle belongs to God. God is also the judge of the wicked ones in this world. It will also be God who controls the outcome of the spiritual battle of the end times (Rev 12:7). Therefore, we must rely on God even if we are faced with overwhelmingly great tribulations. A victorious outcome is not gained through our abilities; it is achieved by completely relying on God.

5. Jehoshaphat could not sever ties with the kings of Israel, the northern kingdom.

The kingdom enjoyed peace after the war against the coalition forces of Moab, Ammon and Mount Seir because God granted Jehoshaphat rest on all sides (2 Chr 20:30). However, Jehoshaphat renewed alliances with the kings of Israel in his latter years. God was not pleased about such alliances with the kings of Israel because every single one of them was evil.

First, Jehoshaphat made an alliance with King Ahaziah to build ships together.

The prophet Eliezer declared "Because you have allied yourself with Ahaziah, the LORD has destroyed your works," and indeed the ships were broken (2 Chr 20:35-37). Here the word *allied* in Hebrew is חָבַר (*hābar*), which means "to unite"or "to join."[30] The Bible specifically highlights such an alliance three times (2 Chr 20:35-37). Moreover, the word *destroyed* in Hebrew is פָּרַץ (*pāraṣ*), meaning "to break up" or "to break in pieces."[31] This shows us how all unions that are evil in God's sight will ultimately end in failure. After realizing that the alliance with Ahaziah was not the will of God, Jehoshaphat finally refused Ahaziah's offer to sail together in a joint voyage (1 Kgs 22:49).

Second, Jehoshaphat allied with Jehoram of Israel and participated in the war against Moab.

Moab, who had been paying 100,000 lambs and the wool of 100,000 rams in tribute to the northern kingdom of Israel, rebelled and declared its independence. Jehoram of Israel sought the help of Jehoshaphat of Judah to deal with this rebellion. Since they were linked in a marriage alliance, Jehoshaphat could not refuse and entered the battle. Seven days into the war, they ran out of water and the situation became dire. Then, Jehoshaphat asked, "Is there not a prophet of the LORD here, that we may inquire of the LORD by him?" (2 Kgs 3:11), and was able to find the man of God, Elisha. Jehoshaphat was barely able to attain a dramatic victory with the help of Elisha (2 Kgs 3:16-27).

All of these things occurred because Jehoshaphat had given his son Jehoram in marriage to Athaliah (daughter of Ahab and Jezebel), and this marriage had become a huge source of sin within the southern kingdom of Judah. During Solomon's time, it was his many marriages, of which God disapproved, that caused the division of the kingdom (1 Kgs 11:1-13). In effect, they had disobeyed the Word of God in Deuteronomy 7:3-4 which stated, "Furthermore, you shall not intermarry with them; you shall not give your daughters to their sons, nor shall you take their daughters for your sons. For they will turn your sons away from following Me to serve other gods; then the anger of the Lord will be kindled against you and He will quickly destroy you."

The people of the southern kingdom of Judah may have briefly recovered their faith due to the religious reforms instituted by Jehoshaphat. However, they suffered immensely after his death because of the extremely wicked government that resulted from the root of sin that Jehoshaphat had left behind.

We must learn from the life of Jehoshaphat that God surely judges all sins. Therefore, we must not seek any compromise with sin; armed with resolute determination, we must sever any and all ties that may lure us into sin.

CHAPTER 12

The Seventh Generation: Jehoram or Joram

> **Jehoram / ᾿Ιωράμ / יְהוֹרָם**
>
> The Lord is exalted, the Lord is honorable
>
> **Joram / ᾿Ιωράμ / יוֹרָם**

– The fifth king of the southern kingdom of Judah (2 Kgs 8:16-24; 2 Chr 21:1-20)
– The seventh individual in the second period of Jesus' genealogy

Matthew 1:8 . . . Jehoshaphat the father of **Joram**, and **Joram** the father of Uzziah.

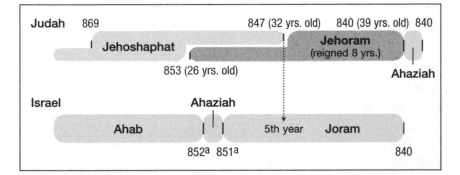

Background
Father: Jehoshaphat (2 Kgs 8:16; 2 Chr 21:1)
Mother: no record in the Bible

Duration of reign
Starting in 853 BC, Jehoram reigned jointly in a coregency with his father Jehoshaphat for seven years (Ref 2 Kgs 1:17; 3:1). Then he acceded the throne at age 32 for an eight-year sole reign (847–840 BC; 2 Kgs 8:16-17; 2 Chr 21:5, 20). Jehoram became king in the southern kingdom of Judah to reign by himself in the "fifth year of Joram" the king of Israel (2 Kgs 8:16). From Jehoram to Joash, Judah used the non-accession year dating method just like Israel.

Evaluation – wicked king (2 Kgs 8:18; 2 Chr 21:6)

Active prophets – Elijah (2 Chr 21:12)

Historical sources – Chronicles of the Kings of Judah (2 Kgs 8:23)

Jehoram, the son of Jehoshaphat, was the fifth king of the southern kingdom of Judah. Although his grandfather Asa and father Jehoshaphat were both good kings, Jehoram did not have their faith passed down to him and became a wicked king. His name is sometimes written in the short form, "Joram" (1 Chr 3:11; Matt 1:8). In Hebrew, Jehoram and Joram are the same word.

The name *Jehoram* in Hebrew is יְהוֹרָם (*yĕhōwrām*), which is a combination of the words יְהוָה (*yhwh*), which means "Jehovah," and רוּם (*rûm*), which means "to be raised" or "to be exalted." Therefore, the name *Jehoram* means "the LORD is exalted" or "the LORD is honorable."

1. Jehoram brutally murdered his innocent brothers.

Jehoshaphat handed the kingdom over to Jehoram his firstborn and to his other sons; he gave many gifts of silver, gold, precious things and fortified cities of Judah (2 Chr 21:3). However, once Jehoram had acceded the throne and secured his authority, he killed all six of his brothers along with some of the officials of Israel who had supported Jehoram's siblings (2 Chr 21:4). He did this to strengthen his royal authority; but ultimately, it was because his brothers were opposed to the idolatry committed by Jehoram and his wife. Second Chronicles 21:13 states, "You have also killed your brothers, your own family, who were better than you." The names of the brothers "who were better than" Jehoram were Azariah (the Lord has helped), Jehiel (God lives), Zechariah (the Lord remembers), Azaryahu (the Lord has helped), Michael (who is like God), and Shephatiah (the Lord has judged; 2 Chr 21:2). Although his brothers lived good lives, worthy of their names, Jehoram could not even live up to his name and walked the path of a murderer.

Had Jehoram lived a life exalting God, he would not have killed his brothers. Rather than exalting God, he foolishly exalted his regal power.

2. Jehoram walked in the ways of the house of Ahab (2 Kgs 8:18).

Jehoram's wife was Athaliah, the daughter of King Ahab of Israel. She was the granddaughter of Omri and an ungodly woman who had been indoctrinated in the idolatrous ways of Ahab and Jezebel. Her wickedness rivaled that of her mother Jezebel (2 Kgs 11:1; 2 Chr 22:10). Second Chronicles 21:6 states, "He walked in the way of the kings of Israel, just as the house of Ahab did (for Ahab's daughter was his wife), and he did evil in the sight of the LORD." The root cause of Jehoram's iniquitous ways was his wife, the daughter of Ahab. Jehoram was inculcated in the ways of his father-in-law Ahab, mother-in-law Jezebel, and wife Athaliah so that he disseminated Baal worship throughout Judah. Jehoram was ultimately unable to break free from his wife's sphere of influence.

As Jehoram showed disregard for God in his governance, God made the nations that were "under the hand" of Judah to rebel against them. Edom and Libnah revolted against Judah and broke free from the control of Jehoram (2 Kgs 8:20-22; 2 Chr 21:8-10). As a result of Jehoram's adulterous worship of idols, God stirred up the spirit of the Philistines and the Arabians to attack the southern kingdom of Judah (2 Chr 21:16-17). The Philistines had brought gifts and silver as tribute to Jehoshaphat; and the Arabians brought flocks, 7,700 rams and 7,700 male goats (2 Chr 17:11). But these same peoples were now attacking Judah during the reign of Jehoram. They had looted the royal palace of its precious things and even carried away Jehoram's sons and wives so that no one was left to him except his youngest son Jehoahaz (Ahaziah; 2 Chr 21:17). The kingdom was mired in darkness, wallowing in its wretched misery.

Jehoram's sins were gravely egregious, deserving total destruction. However, God did not destroy the southern kingdom of Judah because He had established a covenant with David to give a lamp to him and his sons forever (2 Kgs 8:19; 2 Chr 21:7).

3. Jehoram did not repent even after hearing the warning from Elijah the prophet.

Jehoram did not repent even during the continuing rebellions of Edom and Libnah. Instead, he erected many high places in the mountains of

Judah and caused the people to play the harlot by worshiping idols (2 Chr 21:11). The prophet Elijah sent a letter to Jehoram of the southern kingdom of Judah warning him of his wicked deeds. The letter outlines five major points of warning (2 Chr 21:12-15).

First, the letter accuses Jehoram of not walking in the ways of the good kings—"the ways of Jehoshaphat" and "the ways of Asa" (2 Chr 21:12). Second, it accuses him of walking in the "ways of the kings of Israel" and causing the people of Judah to play the harlot like the house of Ahab (2 Chr 21:13). Third, it accuses him of killing his brothers (all six) who were better than him (2 Chr 21:2-4, 13). Fourth, it prophesies that the Lord will strike Jehoram's people, sons, wives and all his possessions with a great calamity (2 Chr 21:2-4, 14). Fifth, it prophesies that Jehoram will be severely diseased in his bowels and will die because his bowels will come out (2 Chr 21:15).

The sad thing about all this is that Jehoram did not repent at all even after hearing such dreadful warnings. Therefore, God stirred up the spirits of the Philistines and the Arabians to attack Jehoram. They invaded the southern kingdom of Judah and took away all the possessions in the king's house, his sons, and his wives so that only his youngest son Jehoahaz (Ahaziah) was left (2 Chr 21:16-17).

Yet, the Lord did not destroy everyone even though Jehoram had done so much evil because He had made the covenant with David and promised to give a lamp to him through his sons always (2 Kgs 8:19; 2 Chr 21:7).

4. Jehoram died from a disease of the bowels.

Jehoram witnessed every word, as prophesied by Elijah the prophet, coming true. Yet, he did not repent, and thus he suffered a severe (incurable) disease of the bowels (2 Chr 21:19). In two years, his bowels had come out and he died (2 Chr 21:19).

The expression, "in the course of time, at the end of two years," in 2 Chronicles 21:19 implies that God had continued to give Jehoram chances to repent. However, Jehoram was not at all penitent and faced death in extreme pain and anguish. Second Chronicles 21:19 testifies, "He died in great pain." This expression indicates that Jehoram actually died in extreme agony, rolling around in anguish, and conveys how wretchedly dismal the final moments of his life were.

Although God had given him a chance to repent by giving him a disease of the bowels, Jehoram refused to repent even to the end and died in his sins. The consequences of such an unrepentant heart can be seen in the events after his death. Jehoram was a king of a nation, and yet his life ended in misery. It is most likely that Jehoram's death is the most wretched of all such accounts described in the Bible. Although the king of a nation had died, not one person made a fire in his honor (2 Chr 21:19). This means that not even the barest minimum display of sorrow was to be seen at the death of Jehoram. Moreover, the Bible relates, "He departed with no one's regret" (2 Chr 21:20), meaning that no one was mourning for Jehoram's death. The moment he forsook God (2 Chr 21:10), he himself was forsaken by everyone in the world. He was buried in the city of David, but not in the tombs of the kings (2 Chr 21:20). How miserable is the end of this king's life for he could not even be buried in the tombs of the kings! Exclusion from the royal tombs signifies Jehoram's exclusion from the lineage of the kings of Judah.

As saints, we should leave behind fruits of faith that can be commemorated after our passing. Moreover, we should leave resplendent marks on earth that will be pleasing to God. Those who exalt God will be exalted by God, but those who despise Him will be scorned by Him in turn (2 Sam 2:30). The moment we forsake God (2 Chr 21:10), we will be thoroughly forsaken by the world in utter humiliation (Jer 17:13).

CHAPTER 13

The Eighth Generation: Uzziah or Azariah

> **Uzziah / Ὀζίας / עֻזִּיָּה**
> The Lord is my strength
>
> **Azariah / Ἀζαρίας / עֲזַרְיָה**
> The Lord has helped

- The tenth king of the southern kingdom of Judah (2 Kgs 14:21; 15:1-7; 2 Chr 26:1-23)
- The eighth individual in the second period of Jesus' genealogy

Matthew 1:8-9 . . . Joram the father of **Uzziah. Uzziah** was the father of Jotham
. . . .

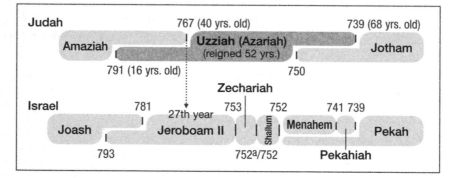

Background
Father: Amaziah (2 Kgs 15:1; 2 Chr 26:1)
Mother: Jecoliah (of Jerusalem; 2 Kgs 15:2), also known as Jechiliah (2 Chr 26:3)

Duration of reign
Became king at age 16 and reigned for 52 years (791–739 BC; 2 Kgs 14:21; 15:1-2; 2 Chr 26:1-3). When Uzziah started his sole reign in the southern kingdom of Judah, it was the 27th year of Jeroboam II of Israel (2 Kgs 15:1). Uzziah started his sole reign as Amaziah ended his reign in Judah in the year 767 BC. Since it is recorded that Zechariah of Israel acceded to the throne (753 BC) in the "thirty-eighth year of Azariah" (2 Kgs 15:8), it seems likely that Uzziah had already been reigning jointly with Amaziah since 791 BC.

Evaluation – was good but became wicked in the latter years (2 Kgs 15:3-5, 34; 2 Chr 26:4-5)

Active prophets
Zechariah (2 Chr 26:5), Isaiah (2 Chr 26:22, Isa 1:1)

Historical sources
Chronicles of the Kings of Judah (2 Kgs 15:6)
Record of the prophet Isaiah the son of Amoz (2 Chr 26:22)

Uzziah succeeded Amaziah and became the tenth king of the southern kingdom of Judah. It seems that Uzziah was his official regal name (2 Chr 26:1-4) while Azariah was his birth name (2 Kgs 14:21; 15:1; 1 Chr 3:12). The Chronicler has chosen to use the regal name of "Uzziah" because the name "Azariah" coincides with the name of a priest in the same time period (2 Chr 26:17).

The name *Uzziah* is a combination of עֹז ('ōz: strength, power) and יָה (yāh: shortened form of Yahweh) thus meaning "the LORD is my strength." The name עֲזַרְיָה ('ăzaryâ) is formed by combining עָזַר ('āzar: to help) and יָה (yāh: shortened form of Yahweh) to mean "the LORD has helped."

1. Uzziah sought the Lord and became prosperous.

Things went well for Uzziah as soon as he took the throne; therefore, he restored Eloth (2 Chr 26:2). Eloth was also known as "Elath" or "Ezion-geber" and was the northernmost city on the Gulf of Aqaba. It was an important trading center for the southern kingdom of Judah. Through this key port city, Uzziah had opened up the path to revitalize maritime trade in Judah.

Uzziah did right in the sight of the Lord just as his father Amaziah had done (2 Chr 26:4). Second Chronicles 26:5 states, "He continued to seek God in the days of Zechariah, who had understanding through the vision of God; and as long as he sought the LORD, God prospered him."

The word *vision* in this verse is in the construct from of the Hebrew word רָאָה (rā'â) and means "observing closely" or "perceiving." Therefore, *vision* signifies "revelation of God attained by watching God closely." The word *understanding* is in the hiphil participle form of the Hebrew word בִּין (bîn) and means "to cause to understand," "to give understanding," or "to teach."[32] Therefore, the phrase that is translated, "Zechariah, who had understanding through the vision of God" in the NASB actually means "Zechariah, who imparted understanding in regard to the revelation of God." This is illustrating how Zechariah was a spiritual teacher of Uzziah and instructed him in the faith. When we seek God under the tutelage of a spiritual teacher who has understanding of His Word, the result that ensues is the blessing of prosperity (2 Chr 26:4-5).

In 2 Chronicles 26:5, the word *prospered* in Hebrew is צָלַח (ṣālaḥ) and means "to rush," "to advance," and "to prosper." If God prospers us, then we are able to advance and rush forward no matter what types of obstacles may stand before us.

Uzziah was able to defeat the Philistines, the Arabians and the Meunites through the help of God. The Ammonites even gave tribute to Uzziah and his fame spread all the way to the border of Egypt (2 Chr 26:6-8).

As Uzziah's prosperity grew and his fame had spread far and wide, he strengthened domestic affairs even more. First, he built towers in Jerusalem at the Corner Gate, the Valley Gate and the corner buttress and fortified them (2 Chr 26:9). Also, he built towers in the wilderness and dug many cisterns for water storage in order to promote livestock ranching. Moreover, he had great affection for agriculture so he had many plowmen and vinedressers in the hill country and in the fertile fields cultivate the soil (2 Chr 26:10).

Uzziah had also formed an army for battle with 2,600 heads of the households. They had under them 307,500 troops who were an elite force ready to wage war with great power to help the king against the enemy (2 Chr 26:13). Uzziah had prepared for them shields, spears, helmets, body armor, bows, and sling stones (2 Chr 26:15). Furthermore, Uzziah had skilled men invent engines of war to be placed on the towers and on the corners of the walls to shoot arrows and great stones (2 Chr 26:15). As such, Uzziah had fortified the nation and the southern kingdom of Judah thrived in an unprecedented prosperity.

This statement in 2 Chronicles 26:15 sums up for us the reason for such thriving, "he was marvelously helped until he was strong." The word for "marvelously" in this statement is פָּלָא (pālā') in Hebrew and means "to separate," "to be wonderful," and "to be surpassing." In other words, Uzziah had become strong because he received help that was surpassingly marvelous for man to comprehend. When we pray, we will also receive help that is surpassingly marvelous just like "Azariah."

2. Uzziah became a leper because of his pride in the latter years of his reign.

When Uzziah became powerful, he became proud. He entered the temple of God and attempted to burn incense on the altar of incense (2 Chr 26:16). Such actions were derived from extreme greed and pride which sought to exercise not only royal authority but also priestly duties. Uzziah's attempt to usurp priestly rights was a blasphemous challenge against the absolute sovereignty of the One who instituted the priestly office.

Azariah, the priest, along with 80 other priests tried to deter Uzziah from committing the treacherous act. This was God's way of giving Uzziah another chance to rethink his action. Whatever the situation may be, when we realize that a course of action is not the will of God—even if the warning comes from the lips of a babe—we must heed such warnings and refrain from carrying through.

Uzziah was infuriated at the priests and continued his attempt to burn incense on the altar, and ultimately, leprosy broke out on his forehead. Uzziah was quickly rushed out of the temple because the Lord had smitten him with leprosy. He remained leprous until the day of his death, and he had to live in a separate house (2 Kgs 15:5; 2 Chr 26:16-23).

Amos 1:1 and Zechariah 14:5 allude to a great earthquake that took place during Uzziah's time. The historian Josephus explains that this earthquake happened in connection to the incident in which Uzziah was struck with leprosy while he personally tried to burn incense on the altar (*Antiquities*, IV. 10.4).[33] As such, a leader's haughtiness not only brings about misfortune in his/her own life, it can also bring about great disasters to the entire nation causing extreme pain and anguish to all.

Uzziah's extended reign was an opportune time in which faith could have blossomed. Due to the foolish pride of the powerful Uzziah, the faith of the entire nation had collapsed. Uzziah was not buried in the grave of his fathers but was buried near his ancestors for he was a leper (2 Chr 26:23; NRSV).

According to 2 Kings 15:3-4, Uzziah did right in the sight of the Lord; however, the high places were not removed. A partial uprightness can lead to pride. Consequently, Uzziah did not receive God's help but had all of his blessings taken away from him.

While Uzziah humbly sought the Lord, "God's strength" helped Uzziah. But when his heart was hardened and became proud, he stood in opposition to God. God generously bestows His grace to those who are humble (Prov 3:34; Jas 4:6; 1 Pet 5:5). However, He will undoubtedly cause the proud to stumble and fall (Ps 147:6). He will humiliate and scorn them (Prov 11:2; 18:12; 29:23); and ultimately, they will come to sudden destruction (Prov 29:1). From King Uzziah's life, we have been reminded anew what is more important than one's initial faith is to remain consistently unwavering in faith while maturing in personal character, learning how to live in humility (1 Cor 10:12; Eph 6:24).

CHAPTER 14

The Ninth Generation: Jotham

Jotham / Ἰωαθάμ / יוֹתָם

The Lord is perfect

- The eleventh king of the southern kingdom of Judah (2 Kgs 15:32-38; 2 Chr 27:1-9)
- The ninth individual in the second period of Jesus' genealogy

Matthew 1:9 . . . Uzziah was the father of **Jotham**, **Jotham** the father of Ahaz . . . .

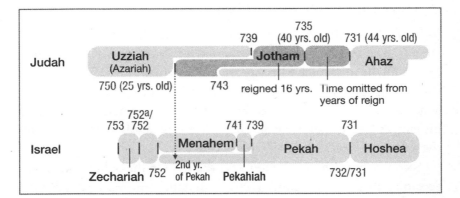

Background
Father: Uzziah (2 Kgs 15:32; 2 Chr 27:1)
Mother: Jerusha (daughter of Zadok; 2 Kgs 15:33, 2 Chr 27:1)

Duration of reign
Became king at age 25 and reigned for 16 years (750–735 BC; 2 Kgs 15:32-33; 2 Chr 27:1, 8)
Jotham became king in Judah in the "second year of Pekah" in Israel (2 Kgs 15:32). Twice, the Bible records Rezin and Pekah's alliance in order to attack Judah (2 Kgs 15:37; 16:5). This is indirect evidence that Jotham reigned jointly with his son Ahaz (735–731 BC).

Jotham succeeded Uzziah and became the eleventh king of the southern kingdom of Judah. The name Jotham (יוֹתָם, *yôtām*) is a combination of the words יְהוָה (*yhwh*), which means "Jehovah," and תָּם (*tām*), which means "perfect," "complete," and "lacking nothing in physical strength or beauty." Therefore, the name Jotham means "the LORD is perfect."

1. Cautioned by his father's wrongdoing, Jotham did not enter the temple of the Lord.

Jotham's father Uzziah had entered the temple of God, which was restricted to all but the priests, and attempted to burn incense on the altar. As a result, he was struck with leprosy and eventually died. While Uzziah suffered leprosy for 12 years, Jotham attended to the affairs of the state as a regent. During this time, Jotham witnessed the tragic conclusion of his father's life. Jotham took all this to heart; he resolved never to enter the temple of God and actually never did.

Second Chronicles 27:2 states, "He did right in the sight of the LORD, according to all that his father Uzziah had done; however he did not enter the temple of the LORD. But the people continued acting corruptly." The word *continued* in this verse is עוֹד (*'ôwd*) in Hebrew and means "repeatedly" or "continuance." Therefore, the verse is indicating that the people had been acting corruptly from before Jotham's reign until now, even while Jotham was doing right before God by not entering the temple.

Although the king was humble and upright in the sight of God, the people were still apathetic to faith and continued to follow their wicked ways. The Bible prophesies that such occurrences will take place in the last days. Revelation 22:11 says, "Let the one who does wrong, still do wrong; and the one who is filthy, still be filthy; and let the one who is righteous, still practice righteousness; and the one who is holy, still keep himself holy" (also 2 Tim 3:13).

Jotham was unexpectedly placed on the throne as a regent due to his father's leprosy; however, he never belittled or looked down upon his father. He always stayed upright before God. Moreover, Jotham only took after the good ways of his father Uzziah. That is why 2 Kings 15:34 comments, "He did what was right in the sight of the LORD; he did according to all that his father Uzziah had done." Jotham's righteous reign can be interpreted as his penitent effort to make amends for his leprous father's iniquities. Furthermore, Jotham continued all of the works that his father Uzziah had started.

Despite Jotham's relatively long reign of 16 years (if we count from 731 BC, it would be 20 years), the amount of writing dedicated to his story is quite sparse (2 Kgs 15:32-38; 2 Chr 27:1-9). Moreover, it is quite unusual that there are no shortcomings recorded about Jotham like the other kings. Such a flawless evaluation regarding Jotham is a sharp contrast compared to the severely negative evaluation about his son Ahaz.

2. Jotham devoted himself to strengthening the national defense by building up the military defense facilities.

In order to defend against the threat of the Assyrians, who were expanding their power base in the north, as well as the aggression of the northern kingdom of Israel and the kingdom of Aram, Jotham initiated a large-scale construction of military defense facilities.

> **2 Chronicles 27:3-4** He built the upper gate of the house of the Lord, and he built extensively the wall of Ophel. Moreover, he built cities in the hill country of Judah, and he built fortresses and towers on the wooded hills

First, Jotham built the upper gate of the house of the Lord (2 Kgs 15:35).

The word *upper* in Hebrew is עֶלְיוֹן (ʿelyôn) and means "highest" or "most high." Therefore, of the many gates in the house of the Lord, the "upper gate" is a reference to the gate located up high in the northern side. This was the gate used by the king to go from his royal palace to the outer courtyard of the temple of God. Jotham's construction of the gate leading to the outer courtyard of the temple reveals his deep yearning to be near the temple at all times and that he had a special zeal for such a life.

Second, Jotham did extensive work on the wall of "Ophel."

The word *Ophel* in Hebrew is עֹפֶל (*'ōpel*) and means "a mound" or "a hill." Here the term is used as a proper noun, designating a ridge of hills reaching approximately 800 meters above sea level and situated to the southeast of Jerusalem. This ridge of hills served a crucial purpose in the defense of Jerusalem because they were like "fortified strongholds." Jotham built on top of the extant walls and extended them thereby fortifying the defense facilities against foreign aggression. The Bible later records that Manasseh "encircled the Ophel . . . and made it very high" when he repented and returned to God (2 Chr 33:14).

Third, Jotham built cities in the hill country of Judah.

The word for *hill country* in Hebrew is הַר (*har*), indicating a "hill," "mountain," and "hill country" or a region of height from which one can look down on the lower plains. In the Palestine region, there are high mountain ranges extending on both sides of the Dead Sea. The hill country of Judah is located in one of these high and dangerous mountain ranges, and that is where Jotham built cities. He built the cities there because the people could quickly flee to these cities rather than the vulnerable cities of the plains in case of foreign invasions.

Fourth, Jotham built fortresses and towers on the wooded hills.

The word *fortresses* in Hebrew is בִּירָנִית (*bîrānît*), which refers to a fort where a large number of troops can be quartered. A fortress built in the wooded hills is well camouflaged and thus is perfect for mounting surprise counterattacks when enemies invade. The word *towers* is מִגְדָּל (*migdāl*) in Hebrew and such a tower was used to observe the movements of the enemies in order to prepare in advance for any invasive attacks (2 Chr 14:7; 26:9).

At the time, due to Assyrian King Tiglath-pileser III's military expeditions and expansion of his sphere of influence, many surrounding nations were feeling very threatened.[34] King Menahem of the northern kingdom of Israel had given a tribute of 1,000 talents of silver to Tiglath-pileser of Assyria—who went by "Pul" after his conquest of Babylon—at around this time also (2 Kgs 15:19-20).

In response to mounting international pressure in the region, Jotham devoted his energy into the construction work to strengthen the nation and build up its defense facilities. Furthermore, Jotham had already put his son Ahaz on the throne as a coregent (12 years old at the time, 743 BC). This shows his foresightedness as he looked beyond his time to the future in his effort to strengthen the nation's defense. It seems that all of this activity reveals Jotham's strong national consciousness as the supreme commander of the kingdom.

In light of the history of the kings, the work of building up the national defenses was a sign of the impending blessings of God. There actually was a lot of construction work that took place during the reigns of godly kings. The reigns of Rehoboam (2 Chr 11:5-12), Asa (2 Chr 14:6-7), Jehoshaphat (2 Chr 17:12-13), Uzziah (2 Chr 26:9-10) and Manasseh (after his repentance; 2 Chr 33:14)—are good examples of this.

3. The kingdom became rich and powerful when Jotham followed the way of the Lord.

As a result of Jotham's diligent efforts in building up the defenses of the kingdom, Judah was able to overcome the attack of the Ammonites without any foreign aid (2 Chr 27:5). After his victory against the Ammonites, Jotham received 100 talents of silver, 10,000 kors of wheat, and 10,000 kors of barley from Ammon for three years (2 Chr 27:5). One hundred talents of silver amounts to 3.4 tons, and 10,000 kors of wheat equals a huge amount of 2,164,680 liters. The word כֹּר (kōr) in Hebrew is a unit of measure, which is equal to approximately 18 liters.

Jotham progressively became stronger because he ordered his ways before God. Second Chronicles 27:6 states, "So Jotham became mighty because he ordered his ways before the LORD his God." The New Living Translation states this same verse as, "King Jotham became powerful because he was careful to live in obedience to the LORD his God."

"To order one's ways before God" signifies living according to the Word of God. The Word of God is the very path that we must be on (Ps 119:105). Therefore, Christians must pray as David did saying, "Make me know Your ways, O LORD; teach me Your paths" (Ps 25:4).

Jotham's great grandfather Joash, grandfather Amaziah, and father Uzziah all had something in common. All three of them started their reigns very well; however, they rebelled against God in the latter half of their reigns and concluded their lives tragically. On the other hand, Jotham did right before God from the beginning to the end of his reign and concluded his royal tenure in peace. King Jotham lived an upright life before God, but his people continued to commit evil (2 Chr 27:2). That is why God sent King Rezin of Aram and Pekah son of Remaliah to attack Judah in the latter years of Jotham's reign (2 Kgs 15:37).

The Bible records the account of the war with Rezin, king of Aram and Pekah, son of Remaliah as if it happened twice, once during Jotham's reign (2 Kgs 15:37) and once during Ahaz's reign (2 Kgs 16:5; Isa 7:1). This is because the war took place when the two kings were in coregency.

It was due to Jotham's limitations as a leader that his faith was not transmitted to the people. Second Kings 15:35 explains, "Only the high places were not taken away; the people still sacrificed and burned incense on the high places." The high places had become the breeding grounds for the sins of the people. Ultimately, by not removing the high places, Jotham could not fully accomplish his duty to lead the people to the right path.

A true leader must be able to lead the people to the right path and bring about transformation in their lives. As people of God, we must not be satisfied with a passive life of faith where only we ourselves are saved from sin. We must actively spread the Gospel to bring change to the lives of unbelievers or even Christians who have strayed from the faith, so that they may also live a proper life of faith.

CHAPTER 15

The Tenth Generation: Ahaz

> **Ahaz / Ἀχάζ / אָחָז**
> He has grasped

- The twelfth king of the southern kingdom of Judah (2 Kgs 16:1-20; 2 Chr 28:1-27)
- The tenth individual in the second period of Jesus' genealogy

Matthew 1:9 Uzziah was the father of Jotham, Jotham the father of **Ahaz**, and **Ahaz** the father of Hezekiah.

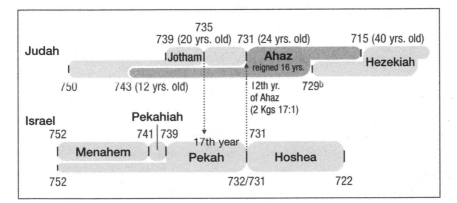

Background
Father: Jotham (2 Kgs 16:1; 2 Chr 27:9)
Mother: no record in the Bible

Duration of reign
Became king at age 20 and reigned with Jotham as a coregent; then at age 24, he started his sole reign and reigned for 16 years (731–715 BC; 2 Kgs 16:2; 2 Chr 28:1)
After ending his regency with his father Jotham, he was officially enthroned as the sole king. Therefore, we reckon his first year as the accession year (731 BC).

Ahaz acted as vice-regent under King Jotham as early as 743 BC while his grand-father King Uzziah was still alive ([Ref] 2 Kgs 17:1). Three kings—Uzziah, Jotham and Ahaz—reigned jointly for five years (743-739 BC). Then, Ahaz started his official regency in 735 BC, which was the 17th year of Pekah of the northern kingdom of Israel (2 Kgs 16:1). This was also when his father Jotham ended his official reign of 16 years.

Evaluation – wicked king (2 Kgs 16:3-4; 2 Chr 28:1-2)

Active prophets – Isaiah (Isa 1:1), Micah (Mic 1:1)

Historical sources
Chronicles of the Kings of Judah (2 Kgs 16:19)
Book of the Kings of Israel and Judah (2 Chr 28:26)

Ahaz succeeded Jotham and became the 12th king of the southern kingdom of Judah. The name *Ahaz* is derived from the Hebrew word אָחָז (*'āḥaz*) and means "to grasp," "to take hold," and "to seize."[35]

Second Kings 17:1 states, "In the twelfth year of Ahaz king of Judah, Hoshea the son of Elah became king over Israel in Samaria." When Hoshea became king in the northern kingdom of Israel, it was just after Pekah ended his 20-year reign, and in Judah, it was the 20th year of Jotham son of Uzziah (2 Kgs 15:30, 731 BC). Since Hoshea became king in the "twelfth year of Ahaz" (2 Kgs 17:1), that would mean that Ahaz became king in 743 BC.

Ahaz acceded the throne at age 20 and reigned for 16 years (2 Kgs 16:2; 2 Chr 28:1). Accordingly, when Ahaz ended his 16-year reign, he would have been 36 years old (20 + 16 = 36). Moreover, since his son Hezekiah was 25 years old when he started his sole reign (2 Kgs 18:2; 2 Chr 29:1), it would seem that Ahaz had Hezekiah when he was just 11 years old (36 − 25 = 11). However, this is an incorrect interpretation of the Bible. The solution to this error is contained in the regnal data, which states that Ahaz became king in the 17th year of Pekah of Israel (2 Kgs 16:1). The "seventeenth year of Pekah" is 735 BC. This is the year when Ahaz started his official coregency with his father Jotham. Ahaz reigned jointly with Jotham for 5 years (735–731 BC). After his coregency, he officially began his sole reign and was on the throne for 16 years. Ahaz was 20 years old when he began his coregency with his father Jotham (735 BC). When he officially took the throne as sole regent (731 BC), he was 24 years old. Therefore, when Ahaz ended his 16-year reign, he was 40 years old, and that would mean that he had Hezekiah when he was 15 years old (40 – 25 = 15).

Since Ahaz was 20 years old in 735 BC (2 Kgs 16:1-2), he had become a vice-regent (743 BC) at the age of 12. Ahaz ruled a total of 29 years from 743 to 715 BC.[36]

The breakdown of Ahaz's 29-year reign is as follows. When Jotham was still on the throne, Ahaz served as vice-regent for 9 years (743–735 BC). Then from the "seventeenth year of Pekah" of Israel (2 Kgs 16:1), Ahaz reigned jointly for five years as coregent with his father (735–731 BC). 735 BC is the year when King Jotham ended his official reign of 16 years (2 Kgs 15:33; 2 Chr 27:1, 8). The four years from 735 to 731 BC is omitted from the official regnal period of the southern kingdom of Judah because the entire kingdom was trampled underfoot by the Assyrians during this time (2 Kgs 15:29-16:20; 2 Chr 28:5-21).[37]

First, due to Aramean invasions, they lost Elath and a great multitude was taken captive to Aram (2 Kgs 16:5-6; 2 Chr 28:5). Second, due to the attacks by the northern kingdom of Israel, tremendous human casualties had been incurred such as having 120,000 killed in one single day while another 200,000 were taken as prisoners (2 Chr 28:5-8). Third, many people were taken captives after an attack by the Edomites (2 Chr 28:17). Fourth, after the Philistine invasion, they lost some cities in the lowland of Judah as well as many cities in the Negev to the Philistines (2 Chr 28:18). Fifth, the Assyrian king Tiglath-pileser, from whom Judah had sought help, did not help Judah but rather afflicted them. Ahaz took some valuables from the house of the Lord, the king's house and the house of the officials to give to the king of Assyria; however, this did not avail any benefits but they were trampled underfoot instead (2 Chr 28:20-21).

After finishing the five-year coregency, Ahaz reigned for 16 years (according to the accession year dating method; 731–715 BC). His 16-year reign, which started after Jotham's death, includes three years of Ahaz's sole reign (731–729b BC) and approximately 15 years (729b–715 BC) of joint reign with his son Hezekiah. Just as his father Jotham had done, Ahaz had his son Hezekiah sat on the throne with him (age 11 at the time; 2 Kgs 18:2; 2 Chr 29:1). The duration of Ahaz's and Hezekiah's coregency can be calculated using the regnal data in 2 Kings 18:1 which states that Hezekiah became king in the "third year of Hoshea." While father Jotham and son Hezekiah were both good kings, Ahaz was a very wicked king.

1. Ahaz followed the abominable ways of the Gentiles.

Second Chronicles 28:3 speaks about the "abominations" that Ahaz had committed. In Hebrew this word is תּוֹעֵבָה (*tōw'ēbâ*) and means "something disgusting" or "abhorrence." Through this word, we can understand that Ahaz's life was all about eating, drinking and breathing sin—enough to disgust God.

First, Ahaz walked in the ways of the kings of Israel and made molten images of Baal (2 Chr 28:2).

Second, Ahaz burned incense in the valley of Ben-hinnom, even burning his own sons as sacrifice (2 Kgs 16:3; 2 Chr 28:3).

Third, Ahaz sacrificed and burned incense on the high places, on the hills and under every green tree (2 Kgs 16:4; 2 Chr 28:4).

Ahaz and Jehoram were kings who promulgated the idolatrous ways of the Israelite kings to the people of the kingdom of Judah (2 Kgs 8:18; 16:3-4). In presenting the account of the lives of Judah's kings, the Bible clearly introduces their mothers' names. It is quite telling that the names of the mothers of Ahaz the extremely wicked king (2 Kgs 16:1-2; 2 Chr 28:1) and Jehoram the wicked king (2 Kgs 8:16-17; 2 Chr 21:1) are not mentioned.

Although Ahaz was instructed in the true faith by Jotham, he discarded the lessons of this holy education and left God to follow after idols as soon as he took the throne. The worship we give to God with our hearts enthralled by anything in the world other than God is abominable and abhorrent before God (1 Jn 2:15-17). God delights in those who are clean, honest and pure; He will be near to them. Moreover, He will not withhold any good thing from such people (Ps 84:11).

2. Ahaz did not rely on God but on the army of Assyria.

(1) Ahaz suffered much harm from the attack by the allied forces of Rezin the king of Aram and Pekah the king of Israel.

At the time, Rezin king of Aram allied with Pekah king of Israel to institute an anti-Assyrian policy in the region. However, Judah adopted a pro-Assyrian policy; and thus, Aram and Israel came together to attack Judah. Rezin king of Aram and Pekah king of Israel assembled their forces together and besieged Jerusalem when Ahaz was reigning jointly with his father King Jotham (2 Kgs 15:36-38; 16:1, 5). The Bible records that

Ahaz's heart and the heart of the people shook as the trees of the forest were shaken by the wind (Isa 7:1-2).

Outwardly, it seems as the allied forces of Aram and Israel attacked Judah for political reasons; but in reality, it was the providence of God at work, trying to awaken Ahaz to his sin when Ahaz forsook God and walked in the ways of the kings of Israel by making molten images of the Baals and followed the abominations of the Gentiles by burning his sons in fire and sacrificing and burning incense on the high places, on the hills and under every green tree (2 Kgs 16:3-6; 2 Chr 28:6).

Although Aram and Israel could not conquer Jerusalem or kill Ahaz (2 Kgs 16:5), they were able to do great damage to Judah. At this time, God gave Ahaz into the hands of the king of Aram, and Rezin king of Aram first attacked Elath and drove out the people of Judah. Then, the Arameans came and lived there (2 Kgs 16:6). Rezin defeated Judah and carried away a great number of captives to Damascus (2 Chr 28:5). God had also given Judah into the hands of the king of Israel, and Pekah the king of Israel, boiling with rage, killed 120,000 soldiers of Judah in one day. At this time, Zichri, a mighty man of Ephraim, killed Maaseiah the king's son (בֵּן, bēn: offspring), as well as Azrikam the ruler of the house and Elkanah the second to the king. Moreover, Pekah took away 200,000 men and women of Judah as captives (2 Chr 28:5-8).

However, the prophet Oded went out to meet the army that was coming back from Samaria and said to them, "Behold, because the LORD, the God of your fathers, was angry with Judah, He has delivered them into your hand, and you have slain them in a rage which has even reached heaven" (2 Chr 28:9). The expression, "a rage which has even reached heaven" demonstrates that Israel was extremely enraged and violently massacred and captured all the people of Judah they could.

Moreover, the prophet Oded declared that it is a sin to try to make the people of Judah into their slaves by saying, "Now you are proposing to subjugate for yourselves the people of Judah and Jerusalem for male and female slaves. Surely, do you not have transgressions of your own against the LORD your God?" (2 Chr 28:10). Furthermore, he commanded them, "Now therefore, listen to me and return the captives whom you captured from your brothers," and proclaimed in regard to the matter in which they tried to subjugate the many people of Judah into male and female slaves, "for the burning anger of the LORD is against you" (2 Chr 28:11).

Pricked by the harsh rebuke of the prophet Oded, the hearts of the four heads of Ephraim were greatly moved. Azariah (עֲזַרְיָה: the Lord has helped) the son of Juhanan, Berechiah (בֶּרֶכְיָה: the Lord has blessed) the son of Meshillemoth, Jehizkiah (יְחִזְקִיָּה: the Lord has strengthened) the son of Shallum, and Amasa (עֲמָשָׂא: the one with burden) the son of Hadlai arose against those who were coming from the battle to stop them (2 Chr 28:12). Saying that Israel already had sins and guilt and that making captives of their brothers in Judah would be an act of adding to their sins and guilt, they claimed, "His burning anger is against Israel" (2 Chr 28:13). It is noteworthy that there were four officers who raised their voices of righteousness in rebuking the people even in the midst of severe corruption in the northern kingdom of Israel, which was to be destroyed in the near future.

Having felt a strong prick of conscience at the authoritative rebuke and warning of the prophet Oded and the four officers, the armed men of Israel left the captives and the spoil before the officers and all the assembly (2 Chr 28:14). Then the men who were designated by name to manage the captives arose and went through the process of taking them back step by step with care. They clothed all their naked ones from the spoil for they were taken captive naked, gave them sandals for they were barefooted, fed them and gave them drink for they could not eat or even drink anything, and anointed them with oil for they were all injured and weary. They even led all their feeble ones (כָּשַׁל, kāšal: to stumble, to stagger usually from weakness or weariness) on donkeys, and brought them to Jericho, to their brothers, and returned to Samaria (2 Chr 28:15).

(2) Through the prophet Isaiah, God sternly warned not to rely on the Assyrians.

When Rezin king of Aram and Pekah king of Israel allied together to invade Judah, God spoke through the prophet Isaiah and warned them not to rely on Assyria. God also said that Judah should not despair because Aram and the northern kingdom of Israel are merely "two stubs of smoldering firebrands" (Isa 7:4). Furthermore, the two allied kingdoms had schemed to destroy the house of David and install "son of Tabeel" as king in place of Ahaz (Isa 7:5-6). However, their wicked plans never panned out and it was prophesied that the northern kingdom of Israel will be shattered within 65 years to never again form a nation (Isa 7:7-9).

To convince Ahaz of the reliability of this prophecy, Isaiah asked him to seek a sign. But when Ahaz refused to seek a sign (Isa 7:10-13), the Lord Himself provided a sign saying, "Behold, a virgin will be with child and bear a son, and she will call His name Immanuel" (Isa 7:14). Here, the name *Immanuel* symbolically affirms that God will be with the southern kingdom of Judah and take care of them even amidst extreme hardship.

(3) Ahaz ignored God's warning and sought for help from the Assyrian king.

Even after God showed him a sign, King Ahaz did not believe His Word proclaimed by Isaiah and simply dismissed it altogether. He, then, sent a messenger to Assyrian king Tiglath-pileser saying, "I am your servant (עֶבֶד, 'ebed: a slave) and your son." With such words of submission and surrender, he sent the silver and gold from the temple and the treasuries of the palace as offerings, seeking salvation from the Assyrian king (2 Kgs 16:8).

In 2 Chronicles 28, it is recorded as if King Ahaz sought help from the Assyrians after the Edomites and the Philistines attacked Judah. Second Chronicles 28:16-17 states, "At that time King Ahaz sent to the kings of Assyria for help. For again the Edomites had come and attacked Judah and carried away captives."

In this verse, the phrase "at that time" (בָּעֵת הַהִיא, bā'ēt hahî') in Hebrew is a prepositional phrase, which indicates that this was occurring at the same time as the event recorded in the verses just prior to 2 Chronicles 28:16. That very event was the invasion of the southern kingdom of Judah by Aram and the northern kingdom of Israel. In other words, King Ahaz had requested the help of the Assyrians when the coalition forces of Aram and Israel were invading Judah.

Furthermore, in 2 Chronicles 28:17, the phrase "for again" is one Hebrew word, וְעוֹד (wĕ'ôd) and means "and again." This signifies that Ahaz sought help from the Assyrians when the coalition forces of Aram and Israel invaded, and then Judah was invaded again by the Edomites.

If we were to delineate the events at the time in chronological order, the coalition forces of Aram and Israel invaded first. In response to this, Ahaz sought reinforcement from the Assyrians; however, the Edomites and the Philistines attacked the southern kingdom of Judah before the Assyrian relief arrived in Judah (2 Chr 28:16-18).

(4) **The invasion of the Edomites and Philistines was God's great providence to humble Judah, who had greatly sinned against the Lord.**

When the Assyrians heard the cry of help from Ahaz, they did not come to aid Judah right away. The Assyrians came to attack the Arameans who were returning from the invasion of Judah. They conquered Damascus, the capital of Aram, and killed Rezin their king (2 Kgs 16:7-9). Also, Tiglath-pileser king of Assyria attacked Pekah king of Israel and "captured Ijon and Abel-beth-maacah and Janoah and Kedesh and Hazor and Gilead and Galilee, all the land of Naphtali" and took them captive to Assyria (2 Kgs 15:29). Later in Israel, Hoshea made a conspiracy against Pekah, who was anti-Assyria, and became king in his place in the 20th year of Jotham (731 BC; 2 Kgs 15:30; 17:1). It is clear that the Assyrians were not coming to aid the southern kingdom of Judah but was merely using their request for help as a pretext to attack Aram and the northern kingdom of Israel in order to expand Assyrian territory.

When Judah's national power had become weakened due to the invasion of Aram and Israel, Edom—which had been a vassal state—came and attacked Judah and carried away captives (2 Chr 28:17). Judah had once defeated Edom during the time of King Amaziah (2 Chr 25:14, 19). That same Edom came and attacked (נָכָה, nākâ: be hit, be struck down) Judah and carried away captives (שָׁבָה, šābâ: take captive), and Judah had fallen into a great despair (2 Chr 28:17).

Judah suffered successive invasions. At about the time the Edomites were attacking from the southeastern side, the Philistines invaded (פָּשַׁט, pāšaṭ: to make a dash, raid) on the southwestern side. Judah lost the cities of the lowland and of the Negev to the Philistines at this time. The Philistines had taken Beth-shemesh, Aijalon, Gederoth, and Soco with its villages, Timnah with its villages, and Gimzo with its villages, and they settled there (2 Chr 28:18). Most of these cities were strategic points for national defense, and losing them altogether to the Philistines meant that their fences for protection were down.

Why did God allow the Edomites and the Philistines to attack Judah immediately after the invasion of Aram and Israel? Second Chronicles 28:19 explains, "For the LORD humbled Judah because of Ahaz king of Israel, for he had brought about a lack of restraint in Judah and was very unfaithful to the LORD."

Through the invasion of the Edomites and the Philistines, God was humbling King Ahaz and the southern kingdom of Judah. The word *humbled* in Hebrew is כָּנַע (*kāna'*) and means "to be subdued," "to bring down low," or "to bend the knee." This verb is used in the hiphil (causative) form which signifies that "God made Judah to bend her knees and humbled her." God will certainly humble, discipline and judge those who are disobedient to His Word.

(5) Assyria actually afflicted the southern kingdom of Judah.

After attacking the Arameans and the Israelites, the Assyrians arrived late in Judah. When they arrived, the Edomites and the Philistines were attacking the southern kingdom of Judah. However, rather than helping Judah, the Assyrians actually afflicted them. Second Chronicles 28:20 states, "So Tilgath-pilneser king of Assyria came against him and afflicted him instead of strengthening him." Here, the term *afflicted* is צוּר (*ṣûr*) in Hebrew and means "to besiege" or "distress." Despite having received tremendous amounts of presents from Ahaz, the king of Assyria pressured and tormented the southern kingdom of Judah rather than helping them.

Although Ahaz had received sufficient warnings from God, he did not rely on God. Likewise, we will also fall victim to our own schemes and receive greater afflictions from the thing or person upon which we rely if we do not rely on God. The worldly methods and iniquitous schemes upon which we rely instead of God will ultimately ensnare us into a tragic situation; they will become the fetters that bind us. We must only rely on God who is the fundamental solution to all of life's problems and the safest refuge in the day of trouble. Psalm 146:3-5 also say, "Do not trust in princes, in mortal man, in whom there is no salvation. His spirit departs, he returns to the earth; in that very day his thoughts perish. How blessed is he whose help is the God of Jacob, whose hope is in the LORD his God."

3. Ahaz transgressed against God even more during the time of distress.

Second Chronicles 28:22 says, "Now in the time of his distress this same King Ahaz became yet more unfaithful to the LORD." The word *distress* is צָרַר (*ṣārar*) in Hebrew, meaning "to bind," "to cause distress," and "to cramp." This word indicates that Ahaz's hardship was inexpressibly great.

Thus, *distress* is a word that displays the extreme suffering that Ahaz underwent as Judah was invaded by the coalition forces of Aram and Israel, followed by Edom and Philistia, the kingdom was trampled underfoot, and many Judahites were taken captive.

Even amidst such trouble, Ahaz did not repent; he even sacrificed to the gods of Damascus. He also gathered and desecrated the utensils of the temple and closed the doors of the house of God. Finally, Ahaz made altars for himself in every corner of Jerusalem thereby provoking the wrath of God (2 Chr 28:23-25).

To make matters worse, King Ahaz went to Damascus to meet Tiglath-pileser king of Assyria. There, he saw the altar of the Assyrian god and sent the pattern of the altar to have an exact replica made in Jerusalem. Furthermore, Ahaz sinned by offering various sacrifices on the altar and even moved the bronze altar to the north side to make room for the new altar (2 Kgs 16:14). He commanded all the people of the land to burn all kinds of offerings—including the morning burnt offering, the evening meal offering, and the burnt offering—on this replica of the Assyrian altar. He also removed "the side panels (NASB: borders)" of the stands for the basins (NASB: laver) and moved the basins. He also removed the "sea" from the bronze oxen and put it on a stone base (2 Kgs 16:17, NIV). The "sea" was especially sturdy and built in a way so that it could not be easily moved or damaged (1 Kgs 7:23-26). The fact that Ahaz moved the sea shows us how aggressive he was in his sins.

The pattern of the temple is decided by God (Exod 25:9; 26:30; 1 Chr 28:12). However, Ahaz changed the pattern of the temple as he saw fit. This was a great sin that challenged the authority of God.

Nonetheless, Urijah the priest built the altar of the Assyrian god just as Ahaz commanded and even obeyed in sacrificing on that altar (2 Kgs 16:11-16). Second Kings 16:16 says, "So Urijah the priest did according to all that King Ahaz commanded." It is the duty of the priests to offer sacrifices to God according to the Law that God had given them. However, it is deeply lamentable to know that Urijah the priest feared the wicked king that tried to abolish God's will more than he feared God and took the lead in offering sacrifices to Gentile idols.

Ahaz had thrown off the hand of God and was challenging God's authority at will—the same Ahaz had become a vice-regent at age 12; then, at age 20, started to take hold of the leadership as coregent. From then on, he reigned for 29 years until he died at the age of 40. He was not buried in the glorious tombs of the kings but became the third in the line after Jehoram (2 Chr 21:20) and Joash (2 Chr 24:25) to be buried in the city of Jerusalem. Second Chronicles 28:27 states, "So Ahaz slept with his fathers, and they buried him in the city, in Jerusalem, for they did not bring him into the tombs of the kings of Israel." For a king, this is quite humiliating before his descendants. Ahaz was forsaken by God and his people not only while he was alive but even after death. Dismal humiliation and defeat await those who continue to rebel against God by relying on worldly powers rather than God. Today, we must realize that one is happiest when God takes a hold of him/her for His use. Let us be thankful for this and be even more faithful to fulfilling our God-given duties.

CHAPTER 16

The Eleventh Generation: Hezekiah

> **Hezekiah / Ἐζεκίας / חִזְקִיָּה**
> The Lord is my strength, the Lord is strong

- The 13th king of the southern kingdom of Judah (2 Kgs 18:1-20:21; 2 Chr 29:1-32:33)
- The 11th individual in the second period of Jesus' genealogy

Matthew 1:9-10 . . . Ahaz the father of **Hezekiah**. **Hezekiah** was the father of Manasseh . . . .

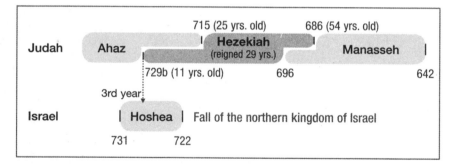

Background
Father: Ahaz (2 Kgs 18:1; 2 Chr 28:27)
Mother: Abi (Abijah) [daughter of Zechariah; 2 Kgs 18:1-2; 2 Chr 29:1]

Duration of reign
Became king at age 25 and reigned for 29 years (715-686 BC; 2 Kgs 18:2; 2 Chr 29:1). This excludes approximately 15 years of joint reign with Ahaz.
When Hezekiah started his joint reign (age 11) with his father Ahaz, it was the "third year of Hoshea" of Israel (2 Kgs 18:1). The northern kingdom of Israel was destroyed in the sixth year of Hezekiah (ninth year of Hoshea, 2 Kgs 18:9-10). Twenty two years after the destruction of the northern kingdom of Israel (14th year of Hezekiah's sole reign), King Sennacherib of Assyria invaded the southern kingdom of Judah (2 Kgs 18:13).

> **Evaluation – good king**
> Hezekiah did right in the sight of the LORD according to all that his father David had done (2 Kgs 18:3; 2 Chr 29:2). Second Chronicles 31:20 comments, "he did what was good, right and true before the LORD his God."
>
> **Active prophets** – Isaiah (Isa 1:1), Micah (Mic 1:1)
>
> **Historical sources**
> Chronicles of the Kings of Judah (2 Kgs 20:20)
> The vision of Isaiah the prophet, the son of Amoz, and the Book of the Kings of Judah and Israel (2 Chr 32:32)

Hezekiah succeeded Ahaz and became the 13th king of the southern kingdom of Judah. Hezekiah trusted in the Lord so that there was no king like him before or after his reign (2 Kgs 18:5). The Bible devotes the most amount of writing to him among all the kings of Judah and Israel combined.

The name *Hezekiah* is formed by combining the word חָזַק (*ḥāzaq*), meaning "strong" and "firm," and the word יָה (*yāh*), which is a shortened form of "Yahweh" or Jehovah. Therefore, the name means "the LORD is my strength, the LORD is strong."

1. Hezekiah boldly carried out a religious reformation.

The following are the contents of the religious reformation carried out by Hezekiah.

First, Hezekiah, in the first month of his first year, repaired the temple.

The phrase "the first year of his reign, in the first month" (2 Chr 29:3) alludes to the month of Nisan in the year 715 BC when Hezekiah started his sole reign. The doors of the temple, which were closed due to the continuous wickedness of Hezekiah's father Ahaz (2 Chr 28:24), were all opened by Hezekiah (2 Chr 29:3). He also lit the lamps of the temple which had been put out (2 Chr 29:7) and started to burn incense in the temple again. He also consecrated the Levites and removed all unclean things such as the Gentile altars from the temple (2 Chr 29:5). The work, which started on the first day of the first month, reached the porch of the Lord on the eighth day. Then they took eight more days to cleanse the inside of the temple. Thus, it took 16 days in total to cleanse the temple completely (2 Chr 29:3, 17). Also, Hezekiah prepared and consecrated all the utensils which his father King Ahaz had discarded during his sinful reign. Then, they placed them before the altar of the Lord (2 Chr 29:19).

King Hezekiah confessed that God, in His wrath, forsook Jerusalem and the kingdom of Judah, making them become an object of dread, horror, and ridicule, when the temple was defiled and the worship was ceased; and their ancestors had fallen by the sword (2 Chr 29:7-9).

Second, Hezekiah worshiped God and gave offerings of thanksgiving.
Hezekiah gave sin offerings and burnt offerings at the newly cleansed temple. Hezekiah had them bring seven bulls, seven rams, seven lambs and seven male goats to offer as a sin offering for the kingdom, the sanctuary and Judah. They also brought the male goats of the sin offering for the king and the assembly to lay their hand on them (2 Chr 29:20-24).

Laying on of the hands on one's sacrificial animal signifies the transfer of sins from the person to the animal. The animal, which sheds its blood in sacrifice, foreshadows Jesus Christ the Passover Lamb, who took up our sins and died in our place on the cross (John 1:29). The Old Testament sacrifice achieved a one time, temporary atonement, whereas Jesus Christ accomplished an eternal redemption for us (Heb 9:12; 10:12).

They also sang, blew the trumpets and played musical instruments while the burnt offering was being given (2 Chr 29:25-28). This signifies the joy of being redeemed from sin. With the sound of trumpets, the darkness within the hearts of the people, which had been full of sin and idolatry, would have dissipated as the praise of faith rang out loud and clear.

After the sin offerings and burnt offerings were given, Hezekiah ordered that sacrifices and thank offerings be brought. The assembly brought so many burnt offerings that there were not enough priests to skin the burnt offerings (2 Chr 29:31-34).

Therefore, 2 Chronicles 29:36 states, "Then Hezekiah and all the people rejoiced over what God had prepared for the people, because the thing came about suddenly." To the human perception, certain works may seem to have occurred suddenly. However, we may realize later that God had been preparing for this in the background as we notice how the work brings great joy and benefits to many people.

Third, Hezekiah had Israel and Judah keep the Passover.

The Passover is a great festival which celebrates the exodus of the Israelites from the 400-year slavery in Egypt through the power of God. Unleavened bread (bread made without yeast/leaven), roasted lamb, and bitter herbs were eaten as Passover food (Exod 12:5-11; Num 9:1-11). The Passover Lamb is a type of Jesus Christ who redeemed us from sin (1 Cor 5:7).

Hezekiah, his princes, and the assembly had conferred and decided to celebrate the Passover in the second month instead of the first because there were not enough priests who had been consecrated, and the people had not been gathered in Jerusalem (2 Chr 30:2-3).

Hezekiah sent men to all Israel and Judah and wrote letters to Ephraim and Manasseh to encourage them to come and celebrate the Passover together (2 Chr 30:1). The couriers took the letter from the king and his princes, as Hezekiah commanded, and circulated them throughout Israel from Beersheba to Dan (2 Chr 30:5-10).

Dan was located on the northern border during the time of the United Monarchy of Israel (1 Sam 3:20; 2 Sam 17:11; 24:2; 1 Kgs 4:25; 1 Chr 21:2). Hezekiah had taken advantage of the lax governance of the Assyrians, who had conquered the northern kingdom of Israel in 722 BC, to urge the people living in the northernmost part of Israel to come and celebrate the Passover.

Hezekiah believed that keeping the Passover, which had been neglected until then, was an act of returning in complete submission to God (2 Chr 30:8). Although there were many people of the northern kingdom of Israel who laughed and mocked at this effort (2 Chr 30:10), there were some from Asher, Manasseh, and Zebulun who humbled themselves and came to Jerusalem (2 Chr 30:11). Moreover, God inspired the people of Judah to give them one heart to do what the king and the princes had commanded by the Word of God (2 Chr 30:12).

After the Passover was celebrated as such, the whole assembly decided to celebrate another seven days which they did in great joy (2 Chr 30:23). This was an unprecedented celebration of the Passover feast. Hezekiah contributed 1,000 bulls and 7,000 sheep to the assembly while the princes contributed 1,000 bulls and 10,000 sheep to the assembly (2 Chr 30:24). Hezekiah and the princes had donated such a great number of bulls and sheep so that the people can enjoy the Passover feast. Furthermore, the priests who had not been consecrated during the first week of the Passover feast (2 Chr 29:34) were now consecrated. Therefore, there were a sufficient number of priests to offer sacrifices. The two-week long Passover feast proceeded without any difficulties, and there was great joy in Jerusalem. Second Chronicles 30:26-27 states, "So there was great joy in Jerusalem, because there was nothing like this in Jerusalem since the days of Solomon the son of David, king of Israel. Then the Levitical priests arose and blessed the people; and their voice was heard and their prayer came to His holy dwelling place, to heaven."

The word *joy* in this verse is שִׂמְחָה (śimḥâ) in Hebrew and means "joy," "rejoicing," "gladness," and "pleasure." True joy and gladness for the people of God can be obtained when a proper relationship with God is established through the recovery of worship.

Fourth, Hezekiah destroyed all kinds of idols.

Hezekiah broke the pillars in pieces and cut down the Asherim (2 Chr 31:1). "Pillars" refer to Canaanite idols shaped like pillars. These were objects that were worshiped in the high places. Hezekiah was the only king who obeyed the second command of the Ten Commandments as well as the command, "Take care that you do not offer your burnt offerings at any place that you see, but at the place that the LORD will choose in one of your tribes" (Deut 12:11-14, ESV). He had carried out a more thorough reformation than all of the other preceding kings. Moreover, Hezekiah broke in pieces the bronze serpent that Moses had made because the people were worshiping it like an idol. It had been called "Nehushtan," meaning "thing of brass." (2 Kgs 18:4).

Fifth, Hezekiah reestablished the offering and the tithe.

In order to provide for the priests and the Levites, Hezekiah commanded the people to bring the first fruits and the tithes of all the produce of the field (2 Chr 31:5-6). This was a perpetual statute that God commanded Moses—that the first fruits of the grain, wine and the oil may be given to the priests (Num 18:12-13) while the tithes were to be given to the Levites (Num 18:21-24).

Hezekiah had given a portion of his goods as an offering according to the law, and by so doing, he had set an example to be emulated in his religious reformation (2 Chr 31:3). The example set by the leader had aroused the obedience of the people. Furthermore, Hezekiah prepared rooms to store the offerings and put officers in charge to manage them (2 Chr 31:11-19). After preparing the rooms in the temple to store the tithes and the offerings, Hezekiah set the Levite Conaniah (כּוֹנַנְיָהוּ: Jehovah has established) in charge with his brother Shimei (שִׁמְעִי: renowned, the Lord has heard) as second in command. They also had ten overseers under their authority (2 Chr 31:11-13).

The above mentioned religious reformation of Hezekiah was good, right, and true before the Lord his God (2 Chr 31:20). Hezekiah's forceful religious reformation reminds us of Jesus Christ's cleansing of the temple (John 2:13-22).

Hezekiah was able to keep the commands of God completely because he clung to the Lord (2 Kgs 18:5-7). Here, the word *clung* is דָּבַק (*dābaq*) in Hebrew and means "to cling," "to stick," and "to stay close." The word signifies that Hezekiah had discarded all distractions and had maintained a deep relationship with God through meaningful fellowship.

As a result of the reforms, God was with Hezekiah and made him prosper wherever he went. God is with those who cling to Him and enacts reforms in obedience to His Word; He will make them prosper wherever they go (2 Kgs 18:6-7).

2. Hezekiah had his life extended 15 years on the verge of death.

King Hezekiah was rare among the kings of Judah and Israel in that he was good and righteous. He trusted in the Lord, the God of Israel, so that there was no one like him among the kings of Judah before or after him (2 Kgs 18:5). But all of a sudden, God gave Hezekiah a fatal disease. Isaiah delivered God's message saying, "Set your house in order (Give charge to your house), for you shall die and not live" (2 Kgs 20:1; 2 Chr 32:24; Isa 38:1). Chronologically, this was after Hezekiah's religious reform and before Assyria's first invasion of the southern kingdom of Judah.

When God has pronounced the sentence of death, who can stop Him? Who can overturn His Word? After Hezekiah had suffered through his illness and recovered, he expressed his grief and sorrow from before by confessing, "I am to enter the gates of Sheol . . . I will not see the LORD . . . I will look on man no more among the inhabitants of the world. Like a shepherd's tent my dwelling is pulled up . . . as a weaver I rolled up my life. . . . You make an end of me" (Isa 38:9-12). His pain and anguish from the disease was so severe that he confessed that the Lord breaks all his bones like a lion and the pain will bring an end to his life soon (Isa 38:13).

Why did God suddenly pronounce death upon Hezekiah? God desired Hezekiah—standing at the threshold of life and death—to trust and rely on Him all the more, so that He can grant him the blessing of a miraculous cure.

After receiving the sentence of death from the prophet Isaiah, Hezekiah turned his face toward the wall and prayed (2 Kgs 20:2). This act signified that Hezekiah was giving up everything in the world to concentrate wholeheartedly on relying on God through prayer. He discarded his reputation and authority as king and wept bitterly saying, "Remember now, O LORD, I beseech You, how I have walked before You in truth and with a whole heart and have done what is good in Your sight" (2 Kgs 20:3; Isa 38:3).

Hezekiah cried so much that in the *Amplified Bible*, Isaiah 38:14-15 is translated as:

> Like a twittering swallow or a crane, so do I chirp and chatter; I moan like a dove. My eyes are weary and dim with looking upward. O LORD, I am oppressed; take my side and be my security [as of a debtor being sent to prison]. But what can I say? For He has both spoken to me and He Himself has done it. I must go softly [as in solemn procession] all my years and my sleep has fled because of the bitterness of my soul.

When a person is caught in extreme despair, he is unable to speak coherently and starts to twitter like a bird in meaningless chatter. Hezekiah could not sleep as he poured out his soul in his prayer to God.

God heard Hezekiah's prayer and saw his tears (2 Kgs 20:5; Isa 38:5). Before Isaiah had gone out of the middle court, the Word of the Lord came to him (2 Kgs 20:4). God immediately cured Hezekiah of his illness by having him apply a cake of figs on the boil (2 Kgs 20:7; Isa 38:21). He also extended Hezekiah's life by 15 years (2 Kgs 20:6; Isa 38:5). Moreover, as a sign to show that God has healed Hezekiah, God made the shadow go back ten steps (2 Kgs 20:8-11; Isa 38:7-8). This was an amazing miracle of God just like the incident in Joshua 10:12-13, when the sun had stopped for almost one day.

As Hezekiah received the promise of a 15-year extension of his life from Isaiah, he also heard God promise, "I will deliver you and this city from the hand of the king of Assyria; and I will defend this city for My own sake and for My servant David's sake" (2 Kgs 20:6; Isa 38:6).

King Hezekiah became the sole monarch at age 25 and ruled 29 years until he was 54 years old (715-686 BC; 2 Kgs 18:1; 2 Chr 29:1). He received the pronouncement of death at age 39 which was the fourteenth year of his reign.

3. Hezekiah became proud after his life was extended.

After hearing that Hezekiah had been sick, Berodach-baladan, king of Babylon, sent letters and a present to Hezekiah (2 Kgs 20:12). God's intention to test Hezekiah was working behind-the-scenes of this incident. God wanted to test Hezekiah and see if he would give all glory to God for healing his illness and for all the blessings he has received thus far (2 Chr 32:31).

The New International Version translates 2 Chronicles 32:31 as, "But when envoys were sent by the rulers of Babylon to ask him about the miraculous sign that had occurred in the land, God left him to test him and to know everything that was in his heart."

However, King Hezekiah showed the messengers of Babylon all that was in the treasure house, the treasuries and even the armory. By doing this, he was subtly parading his own achievements. Second Chronicles 32:24-25 states, "In those days Hezekiah became mortally ill; and he prayed to the LORD, and the LORD spoke to him and gave him a sign. But Hezekiah gave no return for the benefit he received, because his heart was proud; therefore wrath came on him and on Judah and Jerusalem."

As a result of Hezekiah's actions, the prophet Isaiah relayed the message from God saying that all that he has shown to the Babylonians will be transferred to them (2 Kgs 20:17). This was a prophecy about the destruction of the southern kingdom of Judah at the hands of Babylon. In history, this would be fulfilled approximately 115 years later (586 BC).

After being rebuked by God, Hezekiah felt remorse and repented about his prideful ways and lack of thanksgiving. Therefore, he was told by God that the wrath would not come upon Hezekiah in his lifetime (2 Chr 32:25-26).

4. Hezekiah went to battle against Assyria twice.

(1) The first invasion by Assyria

In the 14th year of Hezekiah, King Sennacherib of Assyria invaded Judah (2 Kgs 18:13). Assyria had destroyed the northern kingdom of Israel in 722 BC, and now they were starting to attack Judah who had adopted an anti-Assyrian policy (2 Kgs 18:7). Second Kings 18:13-16 recounts Sennacherib's first invasion of Judah. At this time, Hezekiah did not entrust himself to God but evaded Assyrian aggression by paying 300 talents of silver, 30 talents of gold, and the gold overlays stripped from the doorposts to the king of Assyria as tribute. Three hundred talents of silver equals 10,200 kg, and 30 talents of gold is equivalent to 1,020 kg. More than 10 tons of silver and 1 ton of gold was paid as tribute! All of this was a consequence of not fully trusting in God.

Hezekiah had been healed of his fatal disease and received a 15-year extension of life through the grace of God. Afterwards, when the messengers of Babylon came to visit, Hezekiah showed them all that was in the palace and in the treasuries (2 Kgs 20:12-15). The storehouses of the palace were still full of treasures at this point in time. And these treasures were given out to the Assyrian king during their first invasion. Therefore, we can deduce that chronologically, the pronouncement of death given to Hezekiah came first, then Hezekiah was healed of his disease and the treasuries were shown to the Babylonian messengers. After this, God sent the Assyrians on their first invasion of Judah to discipline Hezekiah. It was at this time that all the gold and silver that was in the treasuries were taken away by the Assyrians.

(2) The second invasion by Assyria

When Assyria invaded Judah for the second time (2 Chr 32:1-2), King Hezekiah had realized his previous mistake and fully trusted in the Lord. First, Hezekiah cut off all the water supplies outside of the city to prevent the enemy from getting any water (2 Chr 32:3-4). It was at this time that Hezekiah performed the amazing construction work of stopping the waters of Gihon from flowing out of the city and diverting it underground and back into the city. According to inscriptions, this underground water canal was about 1,200 cubits long (approx. 547 meters).[38] Furthermore, Hezekiah rebuilt and raised up all the wall that was broken down and built another outside wall. He also reinforced the Millo (A rampart between the inner and outer walls of the city, made by filling the space with earth) in the City of David, made many weapons and shields, and appointed military officers to lead the armed forces (2 Chr 32:5-6).

Emboldened by faith, Hezekiah set the people at ease. Second Chronicles 32:7-8 says, "'Be strong and courageous, do not fear or be dismayed because of the king of Assyria nor because of all the horde that is with him; for the one with us is greater than the one with him. With him is only an arm of flesh, but with us is the LORD our God to help us and to fight our battles.' And the people relied on the words of Hezekiah king of Judah."

But the Assyrian king's envoy, Rabshakeh, used all kinds of wicked words to weaken the hearts of Hezekiah's servants and the people. Rabshakeh said, "Hear the word of the great king, the king of Assyria. Thus says the king, 'Do not let Hezekiah deceive you, for he will not be able to deliver you from my hand'" (2 Kgs 18:28-29). He went on to deride them by saying, "Do not listen to Hezekiah when he misleads you, saying, 'The LORD will deliver us'" (2 Kgs 18:32).

In this precarious moment of being surrounded by his enemies, Hezekiah tore his clothes, covered himself with sackcloth, and entered the house of God to pray (2 Kgs 19:1). He also had Eliakim, who was in charge of the king's household, Shebna the scribe, and the elders of the priests cover themselves in sackcloth and sent them to Isaiah the prophet to ask for his prayer (2 Kgs 19:2-4). Then, Hezekiah took the threatening letter from the king of Assyria, spread it out before the Lord, and prayed earnestly (2 Kgs 19:14-19).

When King Hezekiah tore his clothes and put on sackcloth (2 Kgs 19:1), it was an act of faith, expressing his complete dependence on God as the kingdom was confronted with a calamitous and dangerous situation that the king could not resolve on his own (2 Kgs 6:30; Esth 4:1). Through this act, the king was confessing that he was nothing before God. Moreover, it was an act of deep contrition and repentance arising from facing such extreme anguish and sorrow (Gen 37:34; 2 Sam 3:31; 1 Kgs 21:27).

As Hezekiah heard King Sennacherib insulting God, he prayed with righteous indignation, "Incline Your ear, O LORD, and hear; open Your eyes, O LORD, and see; and listen to the words of Sennacherib, which he has sent to reproach the living God. . . Now, O LORD our God, I pray, deliver us from his hand that all the kingdoms of the earth may know that You alone, O LORD, are God" (2 Kgs 19:16-19).

When the prophet Isaiah and King Hezekiah came together that day and prayed with one heart (2 Chr 32:20; Ref 2 Kgs 19:20), God sent the angel of the Lord that night and struck down 185,000 enemy troops (2 Kgs 19:35; Isa 37:36; Ref 2 Chr 32:21). King Sennacherib returned to his own land only to be killed with the sword by his own son (2 Kgs 19:37; 2 Chr 32:21; Isa 37:38) just as Isaiah had prophesied (2 Kgs 19:7; Isa 37:7). And the southern kingdom of Judah reaped a dramatic victory that day.

All of these events were God's answers to the earnest prayer of King Hezekiah of the southern kingdom of Judah. Though we may be surrounded by danger on all sides, God will send thousands upon thousands of the host of His angels to perform a miraculous salvation for us when we earnestly cling to Him in reverence and prayer (Gen 32:1-2; Ps 34:7; 68:17; 148:2; Dan 7:10).

5. Hezekiah did not fully pass down his faith to his son Manasseh.

After the second Assyrian invasion, Hezekiah's life was full of riches and honor (2 Chr 32:27), and all that he did succeeded (2 Chr 32:30). When King Hezekiah died at age 54, they buried him in the upper section of the tombs of the sons of David, and the people of Jerusalem honored him at his death (2 Chr 32:33).

While Hezekiah was a good and righteous person, he was not entirely able to transmit his faith to his son Manasseh, thereby leaving behind the embers of tragedy in the southern kingdom of Judah. Hezekiah hoped that Manasseh would succeed the throne and rule as a good king. That is why Hezekiah set Manasseh as a coregent for 11 years (696-686 BC) from age 12 to 22, so that he could be trained as a leader. The year 696 BC was six years after Hezekiah recovered from his fatal illness and received a 15-year extension on his life. It was also six years from the time he received the prophecy of Judah's destruction from Isaiah.

In consideration of all this, Hezekiah should have recognized the 15-year life extension as his opportunity to fulfill his final mission and made every effort to teach the Word of God to all the people so that they may recover a wholehearted faith. Most of all, he should have been diligent in the transmission of faith and a thorough instruction of the law to King Manasseh, who was to lead the next generation. For 11 years, Hezekiah may have instructed Manasseh about the dignity and refinements a king should possess; but in retrospect, we can deduce that his faith was not transmitted properly. Consequently, after Manasseh took the reins, the southern kingdom of Judah was sinful before God, and they started declining uncontrollably toward total destruction.

Manasseh's 55 years of long and wicked reign was a direct result of Hezekiah's failure to properly transmit his faith to his son. Regrettably, the prideful attitude that Hezekiah once possessed was entirely transmitted to Manasseh. Manasseh's wicked reign of 55 years became a decisive factor contributing to the destruction of Judah by Babylon (2 Kgs 21:11-15; 23:26-27; 24:3-4; Jer 15:4).

Hezekiah wholly relied on God for his strength as he enacted the religious reforms that brought great joy to Jerusalem. However, his faith was not properly transmitted but ended with his generation. Then for 55 years of Manasseh's wicked reign, the people of the southern kingdom of Judah once again fell into a period of great spiritual darkness.

CHAPTER 17

The Twelfth Generation: Manasseh

> **Manasseh / Μανασσῆς / מְנַשֶּׁה**
> To forget, causing to forget

- The fourteenth king of the southern kingdom of Judah (2 Kgs 21:1-18; 2 Chr 33:1-20)
- The twelfth individual in the second period of Jesus' genealogy

Matthew 1:10 Hezekiah was the father of **Manasseh**, **Manasseh** the father of Amon, and Amon the father of Josiah.

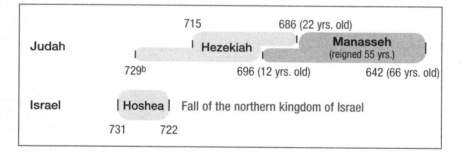

Background
Father: Hezekiah
Mother: Hephzibah (2 Kgs 21:1)

Duration of reign
Became king at age 12 and reigned for 55 years (696-642 BC; 2 Kgs 21:1; 2 Chr 33:1). After his 11-year coregency with his father King Hezekiah (696-686 BC), Manasseh had a sole reign of 45 years (686-642 BC).

Evaluation–wicked king (2 Kgs 21:2-9; 2 Chr 33:2-9) but he repented in his latter years (2 Chr 33:10-13).

Active prophet – Nahum (Nah 1:1)

Historical sources
Chronicles of the Kings of Judah (2 Kgs 21:17)
Records of the Kings of Israel (2 Chr 33:18)
Records of the Hozai (2 Chr 33:19)

Manasseh succeeded Hezekiah and became the 14th king of the southern kingdom of Judah. He had a reign of 55 years which was the longest reign out of the kings of Judah and Israel combined. The name Manasseh in Hebrew is מְנַשֶּׁה (*mĕnašše*), derived from the word נָשָׁה (*nāšâ*), which means "to forget"or "to deprive." Therefore, the name Manasseh means "to forget" or "causing to forget."

1. Manasseh was the most evil among all the kings.

Manasseh was the most evil king out of the 20 kings of Judah. He rebuilt the high places that Hezekiah had destroyed. He erected altars for Baal and even made an Asherah. He also worshiped all the host of heaven (2 Kgs 21:3, 7). Not only that, he also made human sacrifices and consulted mediums and spiritists which provoked the Lord to anger (2 Kgs 21:6; 2 Chr 33:6).

King Hezekiah must have instructed and disciplined his son during his 11-year joint reign with his son Manasseh. Unlike his father, however, Manasseh did evil in the sight of God. Although parents' faith can have positive influences upon their children, it is ultimately the willful resolve and faith of the individual child that determines whether he would be righteous before God. Therefore, the determination and faith of the individual is just as important as the parents' instruction of faith. It is quite regrettable to see Manasseh walk down a most evil path even though he was born to parents of good faith.

Manasseh's greatest transgression was building altars for idols in God's holy house (2 Kgs 21:4-5). It was an act of defiance against God for Manasseh to build altars for idols in the inner and outer courts of the temple of God.

The subjects of the kingdom were misled by Manasseh and acted even more wickedly than the other nations. The prophets risked their lives to warn them so that they may realize their sins; however, they did not heed their cries (2 Kgs 21:9-15).

2 Chronicles 33:9-10 Thus Manasseh misled Judah and the inhabitants of Jerusalem to do more evil than the nations whom the Lord destroyed before the sons of Israel. The Lord spoke to Manasseh and his people, but they paid no attention.

Moreover, Manasseh shed the blood of many innocent and godly people of Jerusalem. Second Kings 21:16 says, "Moreover, Manasseh shed very much innocent blood until he had filled Jerusalem from one end to another; besides his sin with which he made Judah sin, in doing evil in the sight of the LORD" (2 Kgs 24:4).

Manasseh killed countless numbers of people who rebuked his sinful ways. According to Jewish traditions, Manasseh is said to have killed the prophet Isaiah by sawing his body in two. In regard to Manasseh's wicked reign, God said, "Behold, I am bringing *such* calamity on Jerusalem and Judah, that whoever hears of it, both his ears will tingle" (2 Kgs 21:12). This is God's proclamation that He will bring about a horrible judgment that has been unheard of in the past (Ref 1 Sam 3:11; Jer 19:3).

Furthermore, 2 Kings 21:13 states, "I will stretch over Jerusalem the line of Samaria and the plummet of the house of Ahab, and I will wipe Jerusalem as one wipes a dish, wiping it and turning it upside down." Here, the term *line* (or measuring line – NIV, ESV) and *plummet* (or plumb line – NIV, ESV) are measuring tools used in construction. The tool used by God as a standard to measure the deeds of mankind is the Word of God. Just as God destroyed the northern kingdom of Israel for betraying His Word (2 Kgs 18:9-12), God—using the same standard of judgment—is now pronouncing a judgment of destruction to the southern kingdom of Judah for their treachery. Previously, God's righteous judgment upon the various sins and rebellious acts of the southern kingdom of Judah have been deferred because of the Davidic covenant (1 Kgs 11:12; 2 Kgs 8:19; 19:34; 2 Chr 21:7). However, Manasseh's sins provoked God to lay down His judgment and were instrumental in bringing about the destruction of the southern kingdom of Judah (2 Kgs 21:11-15; 23:26-27; 24:3-4; Jer 15:4).

Just as the meaning of his name indicates, Manasseh caused himself and the entire kingdom to forget about God's laws. He shed much innocent blood, and brought about an intensely dark spiritual state that cut off the flow of godly faith. We must understand that we will encounter a darkened spiritual state and bring upon ourselves the judgment of God when we lose sight of God's Word.

2. Manasseh repented in the latter years of his reign.

In accordance with God's prophecy of judgment, God brought the commanders of the Assyrian army to strike the southern kingdom of Judah. They also bound Manasseh with bronze chains and took him to Babylon (2 Chr 33:11). There are accounts of the Assyrian invasion of the southern kingdom of Judah in 648 BC (49th year of Manasseh' reign) in some Assyrian tablet inscriptions. The allusion to "bronze chains" is expressed with the Hebrew word נְחֹשֶׁת (nĕḥōšet), which refers to bronze chains used to bind beasts. Manasseh was bound like a beast and taken to Assyria as a captive. When Manasseh was being dragged away as a captive, he finally realized the sins of his past and repented.

In a single moment, Manasseh lost all of his honor, wealth, and power as the king of Judah. And in that tragic moment, as he was being led away as an Assyrian prisoner, Manasseh finally sought God. After suffering the humiliation and hardship as a prisoner, Manasseh put off his former sinful ways and lived a thoroughly repentant life.

Second Chronicles 33:12-13 states, "When he was in distress, he entreated the LORD his God and humbled himself greatly before the God of his fathers" (2 Chr 33:23). Here, the word *humbled* is כָּנַע (kāna') in Hebrew and means "to be brought into subjection," "to bend the knee," and "to be subdued." It signifies one's regard of oneself as being less than human, as one who is cursed. Moreover, the verse says that he "greatly" (מְאֹד, mĕ'ōd: exceedingly, greatly) humbled himself, indicating that Manasseh truly repented from the heart.

God heard Manasseh's sincere repentance and earnest entreaty. Therefore, He enabled him to return to Jerusalem and restored him to the throne. At last, Manasseh realized that the Lord is God.

> **2 Chronicles 33:13** When he prayed to Him, He was moved by his entreaty and heard his supplication, and brought him again to Jerusalem to his kingdom. Then Manasseh knew that the Lord was God.

(1) God forgives us when we repent.

Although Manasseh was a wicked king, God forgave him when he repented. As such, God's mercy and compassion are boundless. Whoever repents immediately when he is given a chance will be forgiven and will not perish, but whoever does not repent cannot avoid God's wrath and judgment (Luke 13:1-5). Since the sins of the first man Adam have spread to all mankind, whoever does not repent will perish (Job 4:7; Rom 5:12).

Looking back in our lives, have we not sinned with our lips? If we have not spoken our words in the name of our Lord, then that is a great sin before God. Matthew 12:36-37 says, "But I tell you that every careless word that people speak, they shall give an accounting for it in the day of judgment. For by your words you will be justified, and by your words you will be condemned." Also, Colossians 3:17 states, "Whatever you do in word or deed, do all in the name of the Lord Jesus, giving thanks through Him to God the Father" (Ref Eph 5:20). If there are things that you have done to manifest your own glory and not in the "name of the Lord Jesus," then you should thoroughly repent for those things. When we repent, though our sins are like scarlet, they shall be as white as snow; though they are red like crimson, they shall become white like wool (Isa 1:18).

We have hope because God forgave even a wicked king like Manasseh when he repented in times of trouble. Moreover, God took him and used him as a channel of faith that continues the holy lineage through which Jesus Christ would come. That is tremendous encouragement for us. No matter what kinds of sins we may have committed until now, I earnestly hope that we will receive the blessings of recovery and compassion from God today by thoroughly repenting of our sins (Ps 51:9-12).

(2) True repentance entails eradicating the source of sin.

After repenting, Manasseh removed the foreign gods and the idols from the temple of God; he also broke down all the altars in Jerusalem. Then, he restored the altar of the Lord and offered the peace offerings and the thanks offerings. Furthermore, he ordered the people of Judah to serve and offer sacrifices to the Lord God of Israel only (2 Chr 33:14-17). All of these acts teach us that repentance must be accompanied by volitional severance from the former way of life.

The word *repent* can be expressed as נָחַם (nāḥam, Job 42:6) or שׁוּב (šûb, Ps 7:12) in Hebrew. The word נָחַם (nāḥam) means "to regret," "to be sorry," or "to repent" and thus signifies a true repentance that comes from deep within the heart. The word שׁוּב (šûb) means "to return" and signifies leaving the place of sin and returning to one's rightful place with God. Therefore, repentance is not simply realizing one's wrongdoings and feeling terrible about it. Repentance entails a decisive act of willfully forsaking the former sinful way of life (Isa 55:7).

Even though King Manasseh had repented, the people continued to offer sacrifices at the high places. Second Chronicles 33:17 states,

"Nevertheless the people still sacrificed in the high places, although only to the LORD their God." Originally, sacrifices to God are to be offered only at the chosen place, the temple in Jerusalem (Deut 12:5, 11, 13-14, 17-18, 26). God did not permit the people to offer sacrifices to Him at the high places. Nevertheless, the people during Manasseh's time, even when offering sacrifices to God, offered it at the high places out of convenience. Ultimately, the high places became the breeding ground for the sin of idolatry and the source of transgression that led to the fall of the people of Judah.

True repentance entails complete destruction of the source of sin. If the source is not removed, then the sin will return someday. If there is a "spiritual high place" in any part of our lives, then we must completely destroy this source of sin and live a thoroughly God-centered life.

(3) The influence of sin puts down deep roots.

For 49 years, Manasseh sinned before God and then was taken captive to Assyria. Seeing that he returned from captivity not long after he was taken, it would seem that Manasseh repented before God and carried out a reformation for about six years. Six years was just too short of a time to change the hearts of the people, which had been hardened through the 49 years of idolatry. That is why, even though Manasseh had ordered the people of Judah to destroy the idols, the high places were not removed (2 Chr 33:16-17).

Moreover, Amon, who succeeded Manasseh to become the next king of Judah, did evil in the sight of the Lord. The evil he committed was sacrificing to the carved images that his father Manasseh had made (2 Chr 33:22). However, he did not repent like Manasseh but sinned even more (2 Chr 33:23). The sins committed by the father had greatly influenced the son.

Such examples in history show us clearly how deep the roots of evil really are. If the roots of sin are not completely removed, they will eventually sprout again and bear fruits of sin. Therefore, what is more important than to repent after sinning is to try our best to live a life of self-control by keeping with the Word of God, so as to avoid being swept up by the waves of sin.

When Manasseh died, he was not buried with his fathers but was in a garden in his own house, "in the garden of Uzza" (2 Kgs 21:18). Manasseh had forgotten about God's grace and spent most of his life engrossed in serving idols. Consequently, even after death, he had to suffer the humiliation of not being buried in the tombs of the kings.

When we repent, God, in His boundless love, does not remember our previous transgressions. It was this boundless love of God that bestowed upon Manasseh the blessing of being included in the genealogy of Jesus Christ. We must take to heart the example of Manasseh's life and repent of our sins in utter contrition. Better yet, let us not lose sight of God's Word before we start to sin; let us live a life of remembrance!

CHAPTER 18

The Thirteenth Generation: Amon

Amon / Ἀμών / אָמוֹן

Trustworthy, faithful, skillful

- The fifteenth king of the southern kingdom of Judah (2 Kgs 21:19-26; 2 Chr 33:21-25)
- The thirteenth individual in the second period of Jesus' genealogy

Matthew 1:10 Hezekiah was the father of Manasseh, Manasseh the father of Amon, and Amon the father of Josiah.

	715		686	642 (22 yrs. old)	640 (24 yrs. old)
Judah		Hezekiah		Manasseh	Josiah
	729ᵇ		696	**Amon** (reigned 2 yrs.)	609ᵇ
Israel	Hoshea	Fall of the northern kingdom of Israel			
	731 722				

Background
Father: Manasseh
Mother: Meshullemeth (daughter of Haruz of Jotbah; 2 Kgs 21:19)

Duration of reign
Became king at age 22 and reigned for two years (642–640 BC; 2 Kgs 21:19; 2 Chr 33:21).

Evaluation – wicked king (2 Kgs 21:20-22; 2 Chr 33:22)
He did not humble himself before the Lord but multiplied guilt (2 Chr 33:23).

Historical sources
Chronicles of the Kings of Judah (2 Kgs 21:25)

As the son of Manasseh, Amon became the 15th king of the southern kingdom of Judah. The name *Amon* (אָמוֹן, *'āmōwn*) means "faithful" or "skillful" and is derived from the Hebrew word אָמַן (*'āman*), which means "to confirm," "to be faithful," or "to believe in."

1. Amon did evil in the sight of the Lord.

Second Kings 21:20 states, "He did evil in the sight of the LORD, as Manasseh his father had done." The phrase "as Manasseh his father had done" signifies that Amon had taken after his father's unbelief, idolatry and wickedness. Of all the kings of Israel and Judah, the only person who had the expression "as . . . had done" mentioned about him was King David. This is a testimony that David was the quintessential good king who had done right in the sight of God. However, that same expression was now used for Manasseh, meaning that he was the quintessential wicked king who habitually did evil in the sight of God. In regard to Amon's deeds, the Bible comments, "For he walked in all the way that his father had walked, and served the idols that his father had served and worshiped them. So he forsook the LORD, the God of his fathers, and did not walk in the way of the LORD" (2 Kgs 21:21-22).

When Amon was 16 years old (648 BC), he watched his father Manasseh being dragged away in chains into captivity. He also observed how Manasseh repented after returning from captivity and enacted his reforms. Despite all this, he did not follow after Manasseh's faithful ways after his repentance, but only took after Manasseh's rebellious ways of the past.

2. Amon's servants conspired against him and he died a wretched death.

Second Kings 21:23 states, "The servants of Amon conspired against him and killed the king in his own house" (2 Chr 33:24). The king's house (palace) is his place of residence and thus the safest place for him. It is indeed quite ludicrous for the king to be killed in his palace by none other than his own servants. Once a person has forsaken God, whatever protective measures that he may create for himself will be useless. Psalm 127:1 states, "Unless the LORD builds the house, they labor in vain who build it; unless the LORD guards the city, the watchman keeps awake in vain."

Fortunately, the people of the land killed those who conspired against King Amon and made Josiah king in his father's place (2 Kgs 21:24). Who are these "people of the land"? These were people behind the scenes, armed with the faith in God, who earnestly desired for the Davidic dynasty to continue on without ceasing. These people stood behind Josiah, whom they made king, and lit the final torch of faith in the southern kingdom of Judah.

If Amon had humbled himself and repented, he could have become a faithful and trustworthy king in accordance with the meaning of his name. However, he did not take after Manasseh who humbled himself and repented. Rather, Amon followed in the rebellious ways of Manasseh before his repentance (2 Chr 33:22) and encountered a wretched end to his life. Even today, God earnestly desires to look after and reside with ones who serve Him in faithfulness and integrity (Ps 101:6).

CHAPTER 19

The Fourteenth Generation: Josiah

> ## Josiah / Ἰωσίας / יֹאשִׁיָּה
> The Lord supports, the Lord encourages

- The sixteenth king of the southern kingdom of Judah (2 Kgs 22:1-23:30; 2 Chr 34:1-35:27)
- The fourteenth individual in the second period of Jesus' genealogy

Matthew 1:10-11 . . . Amon the father of **Josiah**. **Josiah** became the father of Jeconiah and his brothers, at the time of the deportation to Babylon.

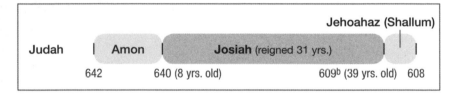

Background
Father: Amon (2 Kgs 21:26; 2 Chr 33:25)
Mother: Jedidah (daughter of Adaiah of Bozkath; 2 Kgs 22:1)

Duration of reign
Became king at age eight and reigned for 31 years (640-609b BC; 2 Kgs 22:1; 2 Chr 34:1).

Evaluation – good king (2 Kgs 22:2; 2 Chr 34:2)
He walked in all the way of his father David and did not turn aside to the right or to the left (Ref – Deut 17:18-20).

Active prophets
Prophetess Huldah (2 Kgs 22:14-20; 2 Chr 34:22-28)
Zephaniah (Zeph 1:1): testified about the judgment and salvation that is to come in the day of the LORD.
Jeremiah (2 Chr 35:25; Jer 1:2; 25:2-3; 36:1-2)

Historical sources
Chronicles of the Kings of Judah (2 Kgs 23:28)
Book of the Kings of Israel and Judah (2 Chr 35:26-27)

Josiah succeeded Amon and became the 16th king of the southern kingdom of Judah. Even though the servants of the king deposed Amon by killing him, the godly people of the land who want a continuation of the Davidic dynasty installed the eight-year-old child Josiah as the king of Judah.

The name *Josiah* (יֹאשִׁיָּה) is formed by combining the shortened form for Yahweh, which is יָה (*yāh*), and the word אֲשׁוּיָה (*'ăšûyâ*), meaning "buttress," "support," or "foundation." Thus the name means "the LORD supports," "the LORD encourages."

1. Josiah carried out the last religious reformation in Judah, the southern kingdom.

Prior to Josiah, King Hezekiah had enacted a thorough religious reform. Forty-six years after Hezekiah had been buried in the "upper section of the tombs of the sons of David" (686 BC; 2 Chr 32:33), his great-grandson Josiah became king at the young age of eight. Manasseh and Amon had nullified the righteous reforms of Hezekiah. By the time Josiah appeared on the scene, the entire kingdom was full of idols and the temple of God was desolate.

King Josiah, who had acceded to the throne at an early age, walked in the ways of David and revived the religious reforms of Hezekiah. Second Kings 22:2 states, "He did right in the sight of the LORD and walked in all the way of his father David." Historically, there were only three good kings—Jehoshaphat (2 Chr 17:3), Hezekiah (2 Kgs 18:3), and Josiah—who had received such favorable evaluations. Among the three, Josiah was the only one who received the additional comment, "nor did he turn aside to the right or to the left" (2 Kgs 22:2; 2 Chr 34:2). Taking such comments into consideration, we can be certain that he truly lived a godly life before God (2 Kgs 23:25).

Josiah became king at age eight and started to seek the Lord at age 16 (eighth year after accession; 2 Chr 34:3). Then at age 20 (12th year after accession), he started to purge Judah and Jerusalem by removing idols and exhuming the bones of idolatrous priests and burning them. Then he expanded this work out into the regions of Manasseh, Ephraim, Simeon, Naphtali, and the surrounding areas and purged the ruined cities (2 Chr 34:3-7). Moreover, at age 26 (18th year after accession), he discovered the book of the law while repairing the temple (2 Kgs 22:3-13; 2 Chr 34:8-21). King Josiah had taken six years to remove all the idols from the land before starting the repair work of the temple. Thus, the 18th year of Josiah was the climactic year in his religious reformation (2 Kgs 22:3-23:23).

The following are some distinctive characteristics of Josiah's religious reforms.

First, Josiah's religious reforms were nationwide.

The reforms started in Jerusalem (2 Kgs 23:4-7) and then were carried out throughout Judah (2 Kgs 23:8-14). The reforms were even enacted in the northern kingdom of Israel (2 Kgs 23:15-20). Conscious of his ethnic oneness with the northern kingdom, Josiah enabled Israel to recover their faith and thereby prevented the evil practices of idolatry from crossing over into the southern kingdom of Judah.

Second, Josiah's religious reforms were thorough.

The scenes of King Josiah ridding the temple and the kingdom of idols are described in very provocative terms. This reveals how thorough Josiah's reforms truly were.

For example, expressions like "burned" (2 Kgs 23:4, 6, 11, 15-16, 20), "broke down" (2 Kgs 23:7-8, 12, 15), "did away with" (2 Kgs 23:5), "ground it to dust" (2 Kgs 23:6, 12, 15), "threw its dust" (2 Kgs 23:6), "defiled" (2 Kgs 23:8, 10, 13, 16), "removed" (2 Kgs 23:19), "broke in pieces" (2 Kgs 23:14), "cut down" (2 Kgs 23:14), and "slaughtered" (2 Kgs 23:20) were used.

Josiah defiled Topheth in the valley of the son of Hinnom where people offered human sacrifices (2 Kgs 23:10). He did away with the horses and chariots that were dedicated to the sun (2 Kgs 23:11). He broke down the altars, which were on the roof in the upper chamber of Ahaz, and the altars which Manasseh had made in the two courts of the house of the Lord (2 Kgs 23:12). Josiah also defiled and abolished all the high places which were before Jerusalem on the right of the mount of destruction (2 Kgs 23:13-14). The "mount of destruction" was a name given to the peak of Mount of Olives where Solomon had built numerous high places for the idols served by his many foreign wives (1 Kgs 11:4-8). Truly, Josiah's religious reforms were thorough and reached deep into the various corners of the kingdom.

Third, Josiah's religious reforms destroyed all of the idols.

Josiah brought out of the temple all the vessels made for Baal, Asherah and for all the host of heaven and burned them. He also did away with everyone who worshiped idols and burned incense to Baal, the sun, moon, and the constellations and to all the host of heaven (2 Kgs 23:4-5). He brought the Asherah from the temple out to the brook Kidron and burned it and ground it to dust (2 Kgs 23:6). He also broke down the houses of the male cult prostitutes (2 Kgs 23:7). Also, he broke down the altar at Bethel and the high places that Jeroboam had made and burned the Asherah (2 Kgs 23:15).

"Idols" are images or forms representing false gods. Idolatry can involve the sun, moon, and stars in heaven; animals like oxen, cats, snakes and crocodiles; and handicrafts made by men or any other thing that is worshiped as a god (Acts 17:16; 1 Cor 8:5).

> **Psalm 115:4-7** Their idols are silver and gold, the work of man's hands. They have mouths, but they cannot speak; they have eyes, but they cannot see; they have ears, but they cannot hear; they have noses, but they cannot smell; they have hands, but they cannot feel; they have feet, but they cannot walk; they cannot make a sound with their throat.

The "temple" is a symbol of God's presence and reign; it is the holy place where He meets with His people (Exod 25:8, 22; 29:42-43; 30:6, 36; Lev 16:2; Num 17:4). It is also the place where God has put His name (Deut 12:11; 1 Kgs 5:3, 5; 8:16-20; 9:3; 1 Chr 22:6-7, 10, 19; 2 Chr 6:20; 7:16; 33:4), as well as His eyes and heart to be there perpetually (1 Kgs 8:29; 9:3; 2 Chr 6:40; 7:14-16).

Therefore, the house of God must not be dilapidated. It must be kept clean in order to fulfill its task of glorifying God. The temple was not regarded as simply a building but as a sublime personality to be respected that the law even commanded to "revere My sanctuary" (Lev 19:30; 26:2). As such, the worship that was performed in it was greatly cherished. Josiah understood the value of the temple through the Word of God and that is why he repaired the temple.

Fourth, Josiah's religious reforms fulfilled the prophecy uttered around 280 years ago.

Josiah was a very special king about whom a nameless prophet prophesied long ago (1 Kgs 13:1-2). When Jeroboam, the first king of the northern kingdom of Israel, burned incense on the altar at Bethel, the nameless prophet prophesied, "O altar, altar, thus says the LORD, 'Behold, a son shall be born to the house of David, Josiah by name; and on you he shall sacrifice the priests of the high places who burn incense on you, and human bones shall be burned on you'" (1 Kgs 13:2). This very prophecy was precisely fulfilled approximately 280 years later when King Josiah burned bones on the altar at Bethel (2 Chr 34:4-5). Surely, God is the sovereign ruler of history whose words are always carried out exactly as they were spoken through His lips (Num 23:19).

Having the buried bones exhumed from the graves and burned was the biggest dishonor that the dead and their descendants could receive. Through such acts, King Josiah deeply impressed upon the people why they should not commit idolatry.

2. Josiah discovered the book of the law and ratified a covenant.

Josiah, at age 26 (in the 18th year of reign), was in the midst of repairing the temple when the high priest Hilkiah discovered the book of the law as he was taking out the offering money from the house of the Lord (2 Kgs 22:3-8; 2 Chr 34:8-14). The expression "book of the law" in 2 Kings 22:8 is סֵפֶר הַתּוֹרָה (*sēper hattôrâ*) in Hebrew, which generally refers to the scroll that has the Pentateuch (Genesis, Exodus, Leviticus, Numbers, and Deuteronomy) written on it. The book of the law that Hilkiah discovered was delivered to King Josiah by Shaphan the scribe who, in turn, also read from the book in front of the king (2 Kgs 22:9-10; 2 Chr 34:15-18). When Josiah heard the words of the book, he tore his clothes and wept (2 Kgs 22:11; 2 Chr 34:19, 27).

In order to inquire about the words contained in the book of the law that was found in God's temple, Josiah sent Hilkiah, Ahikam, Achbor, Shaphan, and Asaiah to Huldah the prophetess. Huldah was the wife of Shallum, the keeper of the wardrobe, and she lived in the Second Quarter of Jerusalem (2 Kgs 22:14; 2 Chr 34:22). Huldah said that since the people of Judah forsook God and worshiped idols, the curses recorded in the book will come upon them. Moreover, she prophesied that Josiah's eyes will not see the disaster that will come upon the land, but he will be gathered to his grave in peace (2 Kgs 22:15-20; 2 Chr 34:23-28).

Josiah called and gathered all the elders of Judah and Jerusalem, and all the people, both small and great, were with him. King Josiah himself read from the book of the covenant in the hearing of the people and they agreed to abide by the covenant (2 Kgs 23:1-3; 2 Chr 34:29-31). Moreover, the king stood by the pillar and "made a covenant before the LORD to walk after the LORD, and to keep His commandments and His testimonies and His statutes with all his heart and with all his soul, to perform the words of the covenant written in this book" (2 Chr 34:31). During all the days that Josiah was alive, the land was rid of its abominations, and the people of Israel served the Lord God. The inhabitants of Jerusalem obeyed the Lord and did not stray from His covenant (2 Chr 34:32-33).

Josiah's reforms were true reforms that were supported by the Word of God. Second Kings 23:25 states, "Before him there was no king like him who turned to the LORD with all his heart and with all his soul and with all his might, according to all the law of Moses; nor did any like him arise after him."

The word *reform* means "to put or change into an improved form or condition."[39] A proper attitude toward the Word of God brings about reform (2 Tim 3:16), and God's Word is properly proclaimed through a true reform (2 Kgs 23:2). A true reformation that is based on the Word of God must also take place today.

Furthermore, Josiah celebrated a grand-scale Passover according to the Word of God (2 Chr 35:1-19). Second Kings 23:22 states, "Surely such a Passover had not been celebrated from the days of the judges who judged Israel, nor in all the days of the kings of Israel and of the kings of Judah." Also, 2 Chronicles 35:18 comments, "There had not been celebrated a Passover like it in Israel since the days of Samuel the prophet."

3. Josiah died in a battle against King Neco of Egypt.

Josiah's reign lasted just prior to the destruction of the Assyrian Empire (who had destroyed the northern kingdom of Israel) in 608 BC by the Neo-Babylonian Empire. At this time, Egypt intended to battle Babylon at Carchemish in order to aid Assyria and prevent Babylon's southern expansion. Neco king of Egypt had to pass through the Palestine region in order to get to Carchemish. At this time, Josiah, who had taken an anti-Assyrian stance, collided with Egypt in battle.

Pharaoh Neco king of Egypt sent messengers to Josiah to request amicable relations. He clearly stated his position that the enemy he is coming up to battle is not King Josiah. Pharaoh Neco stated, "Stop for your own sake from *interfering with* God who is with me, so that He will not destroy you" (2 Chr 35:21).

However, King Josiah was adamant on making war. He disguised himself to fight in the battle where he was shot with an arrow and suffered a severe injury. He eventually died upon arriving at Jerusalem. Second Chronicles 35:22 comments, "Nor did he listen to the words of Neco from the mouth of God." Through the mouth of Neco, God was warning Josiah not to fight the battle. However, Josiah did not understand that this was from God and insisted on a battle which would lead to his death (2 Kgs 23:29; 2 Chr 35:23-24).

When a word is relayed in the name of God, we should listen carefully even if that word is from the mouth of an enemy. God oversees everything that goes on in this world. Therefore, we must not lose sight of the fact that God can certainly reveal His will even through the mouths of Gentiles (Ref Ezra 1:1-3).

Josiah's death was such an unfortunate and sad event that all the people of Judah and Jerusalem mourned over it. Jeremiah even wrote a lament for Josiah, and male and female singers mournfully sang over him. Lamenting over his death became an ordinance in Israel that continues until today. Those lamenting words are also recorded in the Lamentations (2 Chr 35:24-25).

Josiah, through his religious reforms, had temporarily halted the declining spiritual state of the southern kingdom of Judah. Their spiritual degradation had sharply accelerated during the 55-year reign of Manasseh and the two-year reign of Amon during which time they committed extreme wickedness and idolatry before God. While the southern kingdom of Judah was speeding toward their destruction, God upheld them during the days of Josiah to delay their destruction. Ironically, this would also imply that the national fate of Judah would suddenly degenerate after the death of Josiah, making destruction inevitable.

The prophet Zephaniah, who was active during the time of Josiah, proclaimed the imminent judgment of God by using expressions like "I will completely remove all things" (Zeph 1:2), "I will remove . . . I will remove . . . I will cut off" (Zeph 1:3), "I will cut off" (Zeph 1:4), and "He will make a complete end, indeed a terrifying one, of all the inhabitants of the earth" (Zeph 1:18). Just as this proclamation stated, the southern kingdom of Judah would experience the tragic misfortune of having their nation destroyed and its people taken into captivity in Babylon after the time of Josiah. If God does not support the kingdom, it can no longer sustain itself and thus will crumble and perish instantly.

Conclusion: Ceaseless progression of the administration of redemptive history in the history of the southern kingdom of Judah

As the Davidic dynasty continued on in the southern kingdom of Judah, the northern kingdom of Israel underwent many dynastic changes and eventually crumbled in 722 BC. God sustained the Davidic dynasty in the southern kingdom of Judah because He remembered His covenant with David. The covenant promised, "Your house and your kingdom shall endure before Me forever; your throne shall be established forever" (2 Sam 7:16; 1 Chr 17:12-14).

In 2 Chronicles 21:7 the Bible states, "Yet the LORD was not willing to destroy the house of David because of the covenant which He had made with David, and since He had promised to give a lamp to him and his sons forever" (1 Kgs 11:36; 2 Kgs 8:19). Despite Judah's repeated rebellion, God preserved and protected them in order to keep the covenant which He had made with David. However, we must remember that this covenant is strictly conditional. In 2 Samuel 7:14 God says, "When he commits iniquity, I will correct him with the rod of men and the strokes of the sons of men." God saw that the sins of the southern kingdom of Judah had reached its fullness and had gotten to a point where they could not be undone; therefore, in order to discipline Judah, God allowed them to be taken as captives into Babylon.

Until Judah's deportation to Babylon, God had abundantly bestowed His grace and mercy by holding back his anger many times, forgiving their sins, and waiting patiently for their repentance. The Bible says regarding God's dealings with Judah, "And many times You rescued them according to Your compassion" (Neh 9:28), and "You bore with them for many years" (Neh 9:30). The Bible also mentions that God "did not make an end of them or forsake them" (Neh 9:31). From early in the morning, God had diligently sent His prophets and urged the people to repent (Jer 25:4; 26:5; 29:19; 35:15; 44:4).

However, the people of Judah mocked the prophets and disdained the Word of God (2 Chr 36:15-16). They did not obey the instructions of God or respond to His call. They stiffened their necks and acted according to the hardness of their hearts (Jer 7:13, 25-26; 11:7; 32:33; Zech 7:13). Furthermore, they did evil in the sight of God and chose to do the things in which God does not delight (Isa 65:12). They killed the prophets who admonished them to return to God and committed great blasphemies (Neh 9:26). God would no longer leave their wickedness alone. At last, He removed them from before Him and made them "a curse to all the nations of the earth" (Jer 26:6). Judah's deportation into Babylonian captivity was a means of disciplining their iniquities that had reached their fullness and could no longer be undone.

The book of 2 Chronicles concludes with the proclamation of Cyrus' edict ordering the Israelites, who were in Babylonian captivity, to return to their homeland (2 Chr 36:22-23). This shows us that the destruction of the southern kingdom of Judah was not the end. This was a powerful notification announcing that God would train and purify His people through the disciplinary means called the Babylonian captivity and bring them back.

> **2 Chronicles 36:22-23** Now in the first year of Cyrus king of Persia—in order to fulfill the word of the LORD by the mouth of Jeremiah—the LORD stirred up the spirit of Cyrus king of Persia, so that he sent a proclamation throughout his kingdom, and also put it in writing, saying, "Thus says Cyrus king of Persia, 'The LORD, the God of heaven, has given me all the kingdoms of the earth, and He has appointed me to build Him a house in Jerusalem, which is in Judah. Whoever there is among you of all His people, may the LORD his God be with him, and let him go up!' "

Through the destruction of the southern kingdom of Judah and their exile in Babylon, it seemed as if God's work of redeeming His chosen people had been halted. However, this was God's providence to destroy those who have transgressed against Him and renew redemptive history through the "remnants," who have kept their godly faith and repented in truth. God's love toward His chosen people had never been cut off. God had demanded repentance for the sins of His people by putting them through harsh discipline. Through such discipline, He had reformed them as a holy people who can take charge of God's history of redemption.

God's redemptive-historical administration had immutably progressed without interruption toward its destined goal even through the catastrophic destruction of Judah. All covenants of the Old Testament—including the covenant of the "seed of the woman" (Gen 3:15), the Abrahamic covenant (Gen 15:17), and the Davidic covenant (2 Sam 7:12-16)—were being fulfilled and continuing to proceed within the administration of redemptive history toward the ultimate fulfiller of all covenants, Jesus Christ. Even the disastrous destruction of the northern kingdom of Israel and the southern kingdom of Judah could not interrupt this process.

עמלק

מדבר צין הוא קדש

ים המלח

עתר · מקדה

עיר כרמל

שבט

קדש ברנע

מדבר סיני

מדבר פארן

מדבר שור

ארץ פלשתם

באר שבע

שמעון שבט · שבט

אשקלון

גת · ביתמועבה

אקב גשן

פתם · שדה

צין

אלכסנדרי

גישים

לוח המסעות במדבר
אשר על פי ה' יסעו ועל פי ה' יחנו

כט' הרהגדגד	טו' רתמה	א' רעמסס
ל' ימבתה	טז' רמן פרץ	ב' סכת
לא' עברנה	יז' לבנה	ג' אתם
לב' עציןגבר	יח' רסת	ד' פיהחירת
לג' מדברצין	יט' קהלתה	ה' מרה
לד' הרההר	כ' הרספר	ו' אילם
לה' צלמנה	כא' חרדה	ז' ים סוף
לו' פונן	כב' מקהלת	ח' מדבר סין
לז' אבת	כג' תחת	ט' דפקה
לח' דיבןגר	כד' תרח	י' אלוש
לט' עלמן דבלתה	כה' מתקה	יא' רפידים
מ' הרי עברים	כו' חשמנה	יב' מדברסיני
מא' ערבתמואב	כז' מסרות	יג' קברתהתאוה
	כח' בני יעקן	יד' חצרות

The History of the Kings That Were Omitted from the Second Period in the Genealogy of Jesus Christ

The genealogy of Jesus Christ in Matthew 1 is a summarized record of God's administration in the history of redemption. The genealogy encapsulates God's mysterious and profound providence, which was at work throughout the 2,162 years of vast history from the time of Abraham until Jesus Christ. However, this genealogy of Jesus Christ is not a continuous record of all the generations; many of them have been omitted from parts of the genealogy. I have explained about the generations that are omitted in the first period of the genealogy in *The Unquenchable Lamp of the Covenant*, the third book in the History of Redemption series. Many people have given praises greater than I deserve, saying that it was a splendid achievement for a pastor who is not even a theologian because no one in the world had ever explained about the missing parts of the genealogy.[40]

I would like to summarize what I had written in the seventh chapter of *The Unquenchable Lamp of the Covenant* about the omitted generations in the first period of Jesus Christ's genealogy. Then I would like to continue to discuss the omitted generations in the second period of the genealogy. The omitted parts of the first period are between Ram and Amminadab, and between Salmon and Boaz. In the second period, generations between Joram and Azariah (Uzziah) have been omitted.

CHAPTER 20

The Generations Omitted from the First Period in the Genealogy of Jesus Christ

The first period in the genealogy of Jesus Christ encompasses a period of about 1,163 years from the birth of Abraham (2166 BC) until King David's reign in Hebron (1003 BC).[41] There are two general sections where generations were omitted.

1. The Omission Between Ram and Amminadab (Matt 1:4)

Most of the 430-year period of slavery in Egypt

> **Matthew 1:4** Ram was the father of Amminadab, Amminadab the father of Nahshon, and Nahshon the father of Salmon.

In the first period of Jesus Christ's genealogy, the generations between Ram and Amminadab, which span over most of the 430 years in Egypt, were omitted. The clues for the existence of omissions are as follows.

First, Ram was Hezron's son (Matt 1:3). First Chronicles 2:9 clearly states, "Now the sons of Hezron, who were born to him were Jerahmeel, Ram and Chelubai." Thus, it is certain that Ram is Hezron's own son and there is no omitted generation in between them. Hezron's name is included in the list of the 70 people who moved to Egypt with Jacob (Gen 46:12). Therefore, Hezron and his son Ram lived during the early stage of the 430 years in Egypt.

Next, Amminadab was Nahshon's father (Num 2:3; 10:14; Matt 1:4), and Nahshon was the leader of the sons of Judah during the 40-year wilderness journey after the exodus (Num 2:3; 10:14). It is deduced that Nahshon's father Amminadab was part of the generation that came out of Egypt during the exodus, and thus lived during the last stages of the 430 years in Egypt. Another indication of Amminadab's time is the fact that his daughter Elisheba was married to Aaron the high priest (Exod 6:23).

As discussed above, Hezron and Ram lived during the first stages of the 430 years in Egypt while Amminadab and Nahshon lived during the last stages of the 430 years in Egypt. Therefore, the majority of the time spent in Egypt was omitted between Ram and Amminadab in Matthew 1.

2. The Omission Between Salmon and Boaz (Matt 1:5)

About 300 years during the period of the judges

> **Matthew 1:5** Salmon was the father of Boaz by Rahab, Boaz was the father of Obed by Ruth, and Obed the father of Jesse.

About 300 years from the time of the judges, including the conquest and settlement of Canaan, were omitted between Salmon and Boaz in the first period of Jesus Christ's genealogy. The clues for the existence of these omissions are as follows.

First, Salmon married the harlot Rahab (Matt 1:5).[42] Since Rahab was living in the city of Jericho when the Israelites entered Canaan, it can be construed that she lived during the early stages of the Canaan conquest. Consequently, Salmon, who married Rahab, is also from the same time period.

Next, Boaz lived in the latter part of the period of the judges. Boaz married Ruth and had Obed. Moreover, the Bible clearly testifies that Obed was David's grandfather—"the father of Jesse, the father of David" (Ruth 4:13-17, 21-22).

David was born in 1040 BC (Ref 2 Sam 5:4). If we reckon that an average generation is about 25 to 30 years long, then the year of Obed's birth would have taken place around 1110 to 1090 BC, which was during the time of Judge Jephthah (1104–1099 BC).[43] In Judges 11:12-26, Judge Jephthah makes an argument in his message to the Ammonite king that he does not have the right to come and claim the land that had been occupied by the Israelites for the past 300 years. It is evident from this argument that Jephthah became the judge of Israel about 300 years after the conquest of Canaan.

Now, since Salmon lived during the conquest of Canaan and Boaz lived toward the latter part of the judges' period, there must have been a gap of about 300 years between Salmon and Boaz, including a large portion of the 16-year conquest and settlement in Canaan and most of the period of the judges.

God omitted the time of the judges from Jesus' genealogy because everyone did what was right in his own eyes for there was no king in Israel (Judg 21:25). This omission confirms the fact that the time of the judges was spiritually dark and corrupt (Judg 2:7-10).

As we have seen thus far, God had omitted the time of spiritual darkness (most of the 430 years in Egypt and about 300 years from the period of the judges) from the genealogy of Jesus Christ. By so doing, God is demonstrating that the purpose of Jesus Christ's genealogy is not to record a complete list of all generations in the fleshly lineage, but to record the lineage of faith that reveals God's administration in the history of redemption.

CHAPTER 21

The Generations Omitted
from the Second Period in the
Genealogy of Jesus Christ

The second period of Jesus Christ's genealogy (Matt 1:6-11) includes the time of King David, Solomon, and the Divided Monarchy of the Northern and Southern kingdoms. The second period starts in 1003 BC with the conclusion of David's seven-year, six-month reign in Hebron and the beginning of his reign in Jerusalem (2 Sam 5:4-5; 1 Kgs 2:11; 1 Chr 3:4). The second period ends with Jeconiah being taken to Babylon during the second deportation (2 Kgs 24:8-12; 2 Chr 36:9-10) in 598 BC. Therefore, the duration of Jesus Christ's genealogy is about 405 years.

In comparison with actual history, however, Jesus Christ's genealogy is missing a few generations of kings from the southern kingdom of Judah. Although Matthew 1:8 states, "Joram was the father of Uzziah," Uzziah was actually Joram's great-great grandson (1 Chr 3:11-12).

The second period of Jesus Christ's genealogy records 14 generations from David, but there were actually 17 generations. There are three generations missing in between Joram (Jehoram) and Uzziah, namely Ahaziah, Joash, and Amaziah. Including Athaliah, who reigned for six years, a total of four kings were omitted from the genealogy.

1 Chr 3:11-12	Joram	Ahaziah (1 yr.) 2 Kgs 8:26 2 Chr 22:2	Athaliah (6 yrs.) 2 Kgs 11:3 2 Chr 22:12	Joash (40 yrs.) 2 Kgs 12:1 2 Chr 24:1	Amaziah (29 yrs.) 2 Kgs 14:2 2 Chr 25:1	Azariah (Uzziah)
Matt 1:8	Joram	──────────────── Omitted ──────────────→				Uzziah

Why is Matthew 1 missing these four kings? The purpose of the genealogy in Matthew 1 is not to record a continuous descent of the bloodline, but to show the unceasing flow of the covenant through the spiritual line of faith. The Bible explains that not all who are descended from Israel are Israel, but that there are "children of the flesh" born of the flesh and the "children of the promise" born of the Word of promise (Rom 9:6-9). The children of the promise are the true Israel, the sons of Abraham who will carry on the covenant of God.

Of the two sons of Abraham, Ishmael was 13 years older than Isaac. Nevertheless, Ishmael was "born according to the flesh," and Isaac, though he was younger, was the covenanted son born "through the promise" (Rom 9:7-9; Gal 4:22-31; cf. Gen 21:1-3). This happened "so that God's purpose according to *His* choice would stand, not because of works but because of Him who calls" (Rom 9:11). Likewise, you are not saved by fleshly or blood lineage, but "if you belong to Christ, then you are Abraham's descendants, heirs according to promise" (Gal 3:29). Since the genealogy of Jesus Christ in the Gospel of Matthew is a genealogy of people who had pure faith and carried on God's covenant within His administration of redemptive history, the generations that stood against God's will were omitted.

The four kings who were omitted from the second period of Jesus Christ's genealogy had the following common points:

First, the four kings were related to Athaliah, King Ahab's daughter.

King Ahaziah was the son of Jehoram (Joram), born through Athaliah (the daughter of King Ahab and granddaughter of Omri of the northern kingdom of Israel; 2 Kgs 8:18, 26). It was through his father Jehoshaphat's alliance that Jehoram was married to Athaliah, the daughter of Ahab of the northern kingdom of Israel (2 Chr 18:1). Jehoram walked in the way of the kings of Israel, just as the house of Ahab had done, for the daughter of Ahab became his wife (2 Kgs 8:18; 2 Chr 21:6). He was instigated by his father-in-law Ahab, mother-in-law Jezebel, and wife Athaliah, and spread Baal worship throughout Judah.

Ahaziah, the son born of wicked Jehoram and Athaliah, also followed his mother's wicked counsel. He followed the teachings that led him to disobey God and "did evil in the sight of the LORD like the house of Ahab" (2 Chr 22:2-5). After the death of King Ahaziah, Athaliah usurped the throne and destroyed every royal offspring of the house of David; however, one member, Joash, barely survived (2 Kgs 11:1-2; 2 Chr 22:10-11).

Joash became king of Judah after Athaliah, who reigned six years. Joash did what was right while the priest Jehoiada was alive, but started serving the Asherim and the idols after Jehoiada died at the age of 130

(2 Chr 24:15-19). He was influenced by officials of Judah who had worshiped idols when they were under Athaliah. Moreover, he and the officials conspired against Jehoiada's son Zechariah, who proclaimed the Word of God before the people to turn them back from the sin of idolatry, by stoning him to death in the court of the house of the Lord (2 Chr 24:20-21, cf. Matt 23:35). Thus, Joash did not remember the kindness that Jehoiada had shown him (2 Chr 24:22).

Amaziah, who succeeded Joash, did what was right according to the Word of the Lord in the beginning but later turned to idol worship (2 Chr 25:1-2, 14-16). It was quite evident that he could not completely get away from the influence of unbelief that had been passed down from Athaliah.

Second, the four kings were wicked kings who served idols.

Ahaziah walked in the way of Ahab and did evil in the sight of the Lord (2 Kgs 8:27). Athaliah worshiped Baal and set up altars (2 Kgs 11:18). Joash was godly in the beginning, but later served the Asherim and the idols (2 Chr 24:17-19). Amaziah brought the gods of the sons of Seir, set them up as his gods, bowed down before them, and burned incense to them (2 Chr 25:14).

Third, the four kings did not die of natural causes.

Ahaziah was killed by Jehu of Israel in Megiddo (2 Kgs 9:27). Athaliah was put to death at the Horse Gate of the king's house (a place where the horses enter the palace grounds) as a result of the priest Jehoiada's insurrection (2 Kgs 11:13-16; 2 Chr 23:12-15). Joash was greatly injured in battle and his own servants conspired against him and murdered him (2 Kgs 12:20-21; 2 Chr 24:25). Amaziah was also killed by his own servants (2 Kgs 14:19-20; 2 Chr 25:27-28).

When Amaziah served idols, God sent a prophet to rebuke him, but Amaziah did not repent and said to the prophet, "Have we appointed you a royal counselor? Stop!" (2 Chr 25:16a). The prophet boldly gave a final warning, "I know that God has planned to destroy you, because you have done this and have not listened to my counsel" (2 Chr 25:16b). As the prophet had warned, Amaziah was utterly defeated in battle against Joash of Israel (2 Chr 25:17-22). Amaziah, who was brimming with confidence, was captured and taken captive by the northern kingdom of Israel. Then, the Israelites tore down 400 cubits (approx. 200 yd.) of the wall of Jerusalem, stole all the gold, silver, utensils, and treasures from the house of God, and took the people as hostages (2 Kgs 14:13-14; 2 Chr 25:23-24). After ten years of disgrace under captivity, Amaziah returned and reigned with Uzziah for 15 years (2 Kgs 14:17; 2 Chr 26:1), but his servants conspired against him and killed him (2 Kgs 14:19-20).

Second Chronicles 25:27 explains that the servants began to conspire against him "from the time that Amaziah turned away from following the LORD." When they conspired against him in Jerusalem, he fled to Lachish (45 km southwest from Jerusalem). However, they sent after him to Lachish and killed him there. Then, they brought him on horses and buried him at Jerusalem in the city of David (2 Kgs 14:19-20; 2 Chr 25:27-28).

As we have seen above, God ended the lives of these four kings (Ahaziah, Athaliah, Joash, and Amaziah), who had been influenced by Athaliah to worship idols, in a most wretched way. Moreover, by omitting these four kings from the second period of Jesus' genealogy, God demonstrated His execution of judgment against the wicked ones who attempt to snuff out the lamp of the covenant. And in this way, He revealed His administration of redemptive history (2 Kgs 8:27; 2 Chr 22:3). We will now look closely into God's administration in the history of redemption by studying about the kings who were actually active in history yet omitted from the second period of Jesus Christ's genealogy.

1. Ahaziah / Ὀχοζίας / אֲחַזְיָה
The Lord has grasped, the Lord's possession

Jehoahaz / Ιωαχαζ / יְהוֹאָחָז
The Lord has grasped, the Lord sustains

- The sixth king of the southern kingdom of Judah (2 Kgs 8:24-9:29; 2 Chr 21:16-17; 22:1-9)
- He was the son of Joram (Jehoram) and was omitted from the genealogy of Jesus Christ in the Gospel of Matthew.

Matthew 1:8 ...Jehoshaphat the father of Joram, and Joram the father of Uzziah.

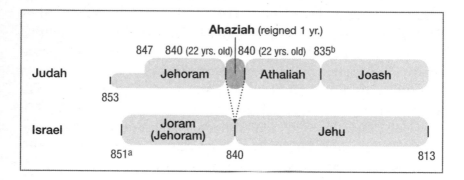

Background
Father: Jehoram (2 Kgs 8:24; 2 Chr 22:1)
Mother: Athaliah (2 Kgs 8:26; 11:1; 2 Chr 22:2)

Duration of reign
He acceded to the throne at the age of 22 and reigned one year (840 BC, 2 Kgs 8:26; 2 Chr 22:2).
Ahaziah became king of Judah in the 11th (2 Kgs 9:29) or the 12th year (2 Kgs 8:25) of King Joram of Israel.

Evaluation – wicked (2 Kgs 8:27; 2 Chr 22:3-4)

Historical sources: He is not recorded in the chronicles.

Ahaziah succeeded his father Jehoram and became the sixth king of the southern kingdom of Judah. When the Lord stirred up the spirit of the

Philistines and the Arabs to attack Jehoram, his older sons were all slain. Consequently, Ahaziah, Jehoram's youngest son, became king (2 Chr 21:16-17; 22:1). Second Chronicles 22:1 states that the inhabitants of Jerusalem made Ahaziah king. He became king at the age of 22 (2 Kgs 8:26), but 2 Chronicles 22:2 states that Ahaziah was 42 years old when he became king.[44] Ahaziah's other name is Jehoahaz (2 Chr 21:16-17). The name Jehoahaz is יְהוֹאָחָז (yĕhōw'āḥāz) in Hebrew. The name is a compound of יְהוָה (yĕhovāh), which means "Jehovah (LORD)" and אָחַז ('āḥaz), which means "to grasp," "take hold," or "take possession." Therefore, the name means "the LORD has grasped." The name *Ahaziah* in Hebrew is אֲחַזְיָה ('ăḥazyâ) and also means "the LORD has grasped" or "the LORD's possession." This name is a compound of אָחַז ('āḥaz), which means "to grasp," "take hold," or "take possession," and יָה (yāh), the contracted form of יְהוָה (yĕhovāh).

1. Ahaziah walked in the way of the house of Ahab.

Second Kings 8:27 states, "He walked in the way of the house of Ahab and did evil in the sight of the LORD, like the house of Ahab had done, because he was a son-in-law of the house of Ahab." Although Ahab's actual son-in-law was Jehoram, Ahaziah's father, the above passage is emphasizing the fact that Ahaziah was also influenced by his father Jehoram and his mother Athaliah in walking in the way of the house of Ahab and committing sin in the sight of the Lord.

Second Chronicles 22:3 also states, "He also walked in the ways of the house of Ahab, for his mother was his counselor to do wickedly." The word *counselor* is יוֹעֶצֶת (yô'aṣt), the participial form of יָעַץ (yā'aṣ), meaning "to counsel" and "to advise." It is evident that Athaliah continued to counsel and advise her son Ahaziah while he was on the throne, influencing him to worship idols and commit evil like the house of Ahab.

Ahaziah saw his father Jehoram doing evil and being smitten by the Lord as a result. He also witnessed his father dying with no one's regret as his bowels came out because he did evil (2 Chr 21:18-20). Nonetheless, Ahaziah was still influenced by his mother Athaliah to follow the way of King Ahab and Jezebel.

2. Ahaziah was killed by Jehu.

Ahaziah went with Joram the son of Ahab to war against Hazael king of Aram at Ramoth-gilead (2 Kgs 8:28-29; 2 Chr 22:5-6). Joram and Ahaziah were, respectively, uncle and nephew by relation. Joram was wounded during the war and returned to Jezreel. Then, Ahaziah went down to see Joram. At this time, Jehu, who was a captain of the northern kingdom's army (2 Kgs 9:5), killed Joram by shooting his arrow through Joram's heart (2 Kgs 9:24). Then, when Ahaziah fled, Jehu and his soldiers pursued him all the way to Megiddo and Ahaziah died there (2 Kgs 9:27). Ahaziah's death took place according to the prophecy of Elijah (1 Kgs 21:21). The final work of destroying the house of Ahab was done through Jehu (2 Kgs 9:27). Jehu was given a special task at his anointing to strike down the house of Ahab and every male person that belongs to Ahab (2 Kgs 9:1-10). Second Chronicles 22:7 explains that Ahaziah, Ahab's son-in-law, was killed by Jehu, "whom the LORD had anointed to cut off the house of Ahab."

According to 2 Kings 9:27, Ahaziah died in Megiddo, but its parallel passage, 2 Chronicles 22:9, states that it was Samaria. This is because 2 Chronicles 22:9 used the word *Samaria* to refer to the entire northern kingdom of Israel.

Ahaziah was miserably killed by an insurgent of a foreign country which he was visiting. Upon seeing his death, the people said, "He is the son of Jehoshaphat, who sought the LORD with all his heart" (2 Chr 22:9). This was an expression of regret that the true faith of Jehoshaphat, who had sought the Lord with all his heart, was not transmitted down to his grandson. The life of Ahaziah, who had died after only one year of reign, is a clear example of what happens to those whose lives are not "grasped" by God.

Like the meaning of the name Ahaziah (i.e., "the LORD's possession"), we belong to God (Lev 20:26; Zech 2:12). We are God's own possession (Ps 135:4; Mal 3:17). God protects and guides those who are His own possession. Isaiah 43:1-2 states, "...you are Mine! When you pass through the waters, I will be with you; and through the rivers, they will not overflow you. When you walk through the fire, you will not be scorched, nor will the flame burn you."

Nevertheless, Ahaziah was influenced by his evil mother Athaliah and lived wickedly. Moreover, in complete disregard for the will of God, he even went out to war in alliance with Joram (his uncle), the son of

Ahab the king of Israel. He pulled himself out of God's "grasp" and joined hands with the wicked. God caused the evil man Joram and his companion Ahaziah to fall to the ground at the same time. Psalm 147:6 states, "The LORD supports the afflicted; He brings down the wicked to the ground." The wicked, who are proud and distance themselves from God, will certainly fall to the ground. Therefore, Christians must live humbly as His own possessions whom God grasps with His right hand.

2. Athaliah / Γοθολια / עֲתַלְיָה
Whom the Lord has afflicted

— The seventh king of the southern kingdom of Judah (2 Kgs 11:1-21; 2 Chr 22:10-23:21)

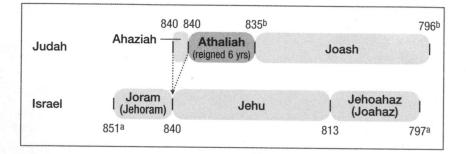

Background
Father: Ahab (2 Kgs 8:18; 2 Chr 21:6)
Mother: Jezebel, the daughter of Ethbaal king of the Sidonians (1 Kgs 16:31)

<Athaliah>
The granddaughter of Omri king of Israel
The daughter-in-law of King Jehoshaphat, the fourth king of Judah (2 Chr 18:1)
The wife of King Jehoram, the fifth king (2 Chr 21:5-6)
The mother of King Ahaziah, the sixth king (2 Kgs 8:26; 11:1; 2 Chr 22:2, 10)

Duration of reign
She reigned 6 years (840 BC – 835[b] BC, 2 Kgs 11:3-4; 2 Chr 22:12; 23:1)
Athaliah of Judah and Jehu of Israel acceded to the throne in the same year (840 BC, 2 Kgs 11:3-4; 12:1). Since the Bible does not provide a year to synchronize the beginning of Athaliah's reign with, the duration of Athaliah's reign is calculated from Joash's synchronism which is the seventh year of Jehu (2 Kgs 12:1).

Evaluation – extremely wicked (2 Kgs 11:1; 2 Chr 22:3, 10)

Historical sources: She is not recorded in the chronicles.

After the death of King Ahaziah, Athaliah took her son's place on the throne. The name *Athaliah* (עֲתַלְיָה, *ʿătalyâ*) is composed of עֲתְלִי (*ʿatlay*) and יָה (*yāh*; contracted form of "Jehovah"). עֲתְלִי (*ʿatlay*) is derived from a word that means "to press down." Thus, the name *Athaliah* means "whom the LORD has afflicted."

1. Athaliah destroyed all the royal offspring from the house of Judah.

When Ahaziah was suddenly assassinated in the northern kingdom of Israel, Athaliah was determined to utilize this vacancy in the throne of Judah to make herself king. She followed through her plan by destroying all the "royal offspring" (2 Kgs 11:1; 2 Chr 22:10). The "royal offspring" includes all of Ahaziah's sons and relatives who were eligible to succeed the royal throne. In other words, Athaliah wiped out Ahaziah's own sons, who are her own grandsons. She thought that killing those people would obliterate the royal seed from the house of Judah because during the latter years of Jehoram's reign, all of Ahaziah's brothers had been carried away by the Philistines and the Arabs who bordered the Ethiopians (2 Chr 21:11-17). All 42 sons of Ahaziah's brothers, who were remaining, were killed when God took Jehu and punished the house of King Ahab (2 Kgs 10:13-14, 2 Chr 22:8). The use of the word *offspring* (זֶרַע, *zera'*), which has a connotation of "successor" or "heir," in describing Athaliah's act of destroying the "royal offspring" indicates Athaliah's evil intention to annihilate the royal lineage of David. This was an individual's ambition, but also an evil act that interfered with God's sovereign will.

When Athaliah killed all of the royal seed and challenged God's providence, Jehoram's daughter and Ahaziah's sister, Jehoshabeath (Jehosheba), stole (גָּנַב, *gānab*: steal away, take items without permission by owner) Joash (one year old) and placed him and his nurse in the bedroom so that he would not be put to death (2 Kgs 11:2; 2 Chr 22:11). Jehoshabeath was the wife of Jehoiada the priest (2 Chr 22:11). Since then, Joash lived in hiding in the house of the Lord for six years (2 Kgs 11:3; 2 Chr 22:12). God's providence preserved David's royal lineage by hiding Joash. Athaliah, with evil ambition, attempted to destroy David's royal lineage, but she could not stop God's providence of redemption. It appeared as though the forces of Satan had prevailed for a moment, but God made it evident that His redemptive-historical administration will certainly prevail in the end.

2. Athaliah was put to death as part of Jehoiada's reformation.

After six years of Athaliah's wicked regime, Jehoiada the priest finally made a determination. He sent for the captains of hundreds of the Carites and of the guard, and brought them into the house of the Lord. He then made a covenant with them and put them under oath, and showed them Joash, the seven-year-old prince (2 Kgs 11:4; 2 Chr 23:1). How astounded and overjoyed they must have been when Jehoiada showed them Joash, whom they thought had been killed by Athaliah six years ago along with all of David's descendants! Although Joash was only a seven-year-old boy, the fact that an offspring of David was still alive must have been a great hope, consolation, and joy to those who held onto God's covenant with a seeking heart. Second Chronicles 23:1 clearly lists the names of the five captains of hundreds that were present at that time: Azariah (עֲזַרְיָה, *'ăzaryâ*: Yahweh has helped) the son of Jeroham, Ishmael (יִשְׁמָעֵאל, *yišmā'ē'l*: God hears) the son of Johanan, Azariah (עֲזַרְיָה, *'ăzaryâ*: Yahweh has helped) the son of Obed, Maaseiah (מַעֲשֵׂיָה, *ma'ăśēyâ*: work of Yahweh) the son of Adaiah, and Elishaphat (אֱלִישָׁפָט, *'ĕlîšāpāṭ*: God has judged) the son of Zichri. They went throughout Judah and gathered the Levites from all the cities of Judah and the heads of the fathers' households of Israel, and they came to Jerusalem (2 Chr 23:2).

Jehoiada the priest, who had anxiously protected David's offspring, Joash, for six long years, made a determination to start a revolution even at the risk of his own life. He said, "Behold, the king's son shall reign, as the LORD has spoken concerning the sons of David," and finally brought the last remaining descendant from David's seed to the royal throne (2 Kgs 11:4-21; 2 Chr 23:3-11). Jehoiada was a true religious leader of his time who sincerely loved the covenant and yearned for King David.

Since Jehoiada had to start a revolution without the knowledge of Athaliah, he chose a Sabbath day as the date of the insurrection. He commanded one third of the soldiers who come in on the Sabbath to keep watch at the king's house, one third at the gate Sur (or the Foundation gate), and one third at the gate behind the guards (2 Kgs 11:5-7; 2 Chr 23:4-5). The Levites surrounded the king with their weapons in their hands (2 Chr 23:7). Jehoiada stationed all the people, with their weapons in their hands, from the right side of the house to the left, by the altar and by the house, around the king (2 Chr 23:10). Then, he brought the king's son out and put the crown on him and gave him the testimony and made him king; and the people clapped their hands and said, "Long live the king!" (2 Kgs 11:12; 2 Chr 23:11)

The king stood by the pillar with the captains and the trumpeters guarding him; and all the people of the land rejoiced, blew trumpets, and singers with their musical instruments lead the praise. Then, Athaliah tore her clothes and cried, "Treason! Treason!" (2 Kgs 11:13-14; 2 Chr 23:12-13). Even though she was the one who had usurped David's throne, she cried out saying that Joash's becoming king was an act of treason and made a frantic last-ditch effort. Jehoiada gave the command to have Athaliah and whoever followed her put to death with the sword after she came out of the house of God and arrived at the entrance of the Horse Gate (gate for the horses of the royal family) of the king's house (2 Kgs 11:15-16; 2 Chr 23:14-15). When Athaliah arrived at the entrance of the Horse Gate, she was put to death by the sword of the people (2 Kgs 11:16, 20; 2 Chr 23:15, 21). All the people tore down the house of Baal and killed Mattan the priest of Baal before the altars (2 Kgs 11:18; 2 Chr 23:17).

Athaliah's evil influence held sway over Judah for 13 years (847 BC – 835b BC), during which time Jehoram reigned for eight years, Ahaziah for one year, and Athaliah herself for six years. During this period, the southern kingdom of Judah was filled with despair and darkness because of the evil influence exerted by the daughter of King Ahab. Idol worship was practiced throughout the country and brutal crimes were so rampant that innocent people lived with bated breath. From the start of her marriage, Athaliah took on the role of Satan's puppet and tried to put out the holy lamp of Judah in order to turn its history into the history of darkness. When the nation was in danger of total collapse due to Athaliah's great massacre of David's royal family , God reestablished the Davidic covenant through Jehoiada the priest (2 Kgs 11:4). Then, God enthroned Joash, David's offspring, allowing peace and new hope to come upon Judah. After Athaliah was put to death, all the people of the land rejoiced and the city was quiet (2 Kgs 11:20; 2 Chr 23:21).

Those who stand against God will eventually be afflicted by God and die a miserable death. It will be in the end time when Jesus Christ the King of all kings comes, that the devil, the false ruler of the world, and his subjects will be destroyed.

3. Joash / 'Ιωάς / יוֹאָשׁ
The Lord is mighty

— The eighth king of the southern kingdom of Judah (2 Kgs 11:21-12:21; 2 Chr 24:1-27)
— He was the grandson of Joram and son of Ahaziah. He reigned over Judah 40 years, but was omitted from the genealogy of Jesus Christ in the Gospel of Matthew.

Matthew 1:8 ...Jehoshaphat the father of Joram, and Joram the father of Uzziah.

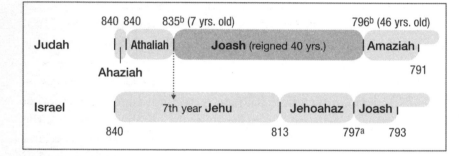

Jehoiada the priest put Athaliah to death and enthroned Joash as the eighth king of Judah. With the heart of the father, Jehoiada took two wives for Joash, and Joash became the father of sons and daughters (2 Chr 24:3). The name Joash is יוֹאָשׁ (yôʼāš) in Hebrew, a variation of יְהוֹאָשׁ (yĕhôʼāš), meaning "The LORD is mighty."

1. Joash restored the house of the Lord.

The temple of Jerusalem (the house of the Lord) had become worn down through the years since it was constructed during the time of King Solomon, and broken into during Athaliah's tyranny. The holy things that were consecrated for offering to God were even used for the Baals (2 Chr 24:7).

Thus, Joash commanded the priests to repair all damaged parts of the house of the Lord. Nevertheless, the priests did not repair the damages of the house even by the 23rd year of King Joash (2 Kgs 12:5-6). The reason was that the priests used the money offered up by the people for things other than the repair work. Therefore, King Joash banned them from taking money from people and repairing the damages of the house of the Lord (2 Kgs 12:7-8).

Then, Joash set a chest outside by the gate of the house of the Lord (2 Kgs 12:9; 2 Chr 24:8) and collected all the money which was brought into the house of the Lord. He had this money used only for repairing the house of the Lord and gave it to those who did the work of the service of the house of the Lord, (i.e., stonecutters, masons, carpenters, workers in iron and bronze, etc.), letting them purchase the material needed for repairing (2 Kgs 12:9-15; 2 Chr 24:8-12).

As a result, the repair work progressed, and they restored the house of God according to its specifications and strengthened it (2 Chr 24:13). The money left over from repairing the house of the Lord was made into utensils for the house of the Lord. All the days when Jehoiada was alive and standing by King Joash's side, burnt offerings were offered continually to the Lord (2 Chr 24:14). God must have been greatly pleased when the house of the Lord, which had been defiled ruthlessly during the tyranny of Athaliah, was beautifully repaired.

2. Joash forsook God's grace and worshiped idols.

Jehoiada the high priest reached a ripe old age of 130 and died. Although he was not a king, he was buried in the city of David among the kings (2 Chr 24:15-16). After his death, however, the officials of Judah came to the king and tempted him to worship idols, and the king served the Asherim and the idols (2 Chr 24:17-19). The officials of Judah, who led Joash to worship idols, did not do anything while Jehoiada the high priest was alive, but came and tempted Joash to idolatry after the death of Jehoiada. These were people who had taken the lead in serving idols during Athaliah's reign and revealed their unbelief once again after Jehoiada's death.

In order to have Joash realize his sins, God sent a prophet to warn him first, but Joash did not listen to the prophet. Then, Jehoiada's son Zechariah stood above the people and rebuked them saying, "Thus God has said, 'Why do you transgress the commandments of the LORD and do not prosper? Because you have forsaken the LORD, He has also forsaken you'" (2 Chr 24:20). However, the people stoned him to death in the court of the house of the Lord at the command of Joash. Even as he was dying, Zechariah prayed, "May the LORD see and avenge!" (2 Chr 24:22)

Rather than repenting, Joash killed the son of his lifesaver, who loved and cared for him. He had truly forsaken grace. Although Jehoiada rescued him from death, protected him, and eventually established him as king, leading him to live uprightly before God, Joash followed the officials in serving idols and stoned Jehoiada's son to death.

What was the end of the one who forsook grace and challenged the mighty God?

First, the Aramean army destroyed all the officials of the people and executed judgment on Joash. Second Chronicles 24:23 records, "Now it happened at the turn of the year that the army of the Arameans came up against him; and they came to Judah and Jerusalem, destroyed all the officials of the people from among the people, and sent all their spoil to the king of Damascus." The phrase *at the turn of the year* is לִתְקוּפַת הַשָּׁנָה (*litqûpat haššānâ*) in Hebrew, meaning "at the circuit (completion) of the year." Hence, God took the Aramean army and struck Judah at the end of the same year when Zechariah died. "All the officials" destroyed at that time were the officials that tempted Joash to idolatry (2 Chr 24:17). The Aramean army was much smaller than the army of Judah in number, but they were able to defeat the great army of Judah because the mighty God was using them to punish Judah.

Second Chronicles 24:24 states, "Indeed the army of the Arameans came with a small number of men; yet the LORD delivered a very great army into their hands, because they had forsaken the LORD, the God of their fathers. Thus they executed judgment on Joash." The word *judgment* used in this verse is שָׁפַט (*šepeṭ*) in Hebrew, meaning "to judge" or "to execute judgment." When Joash forgot about His grace and forsook God, He judged Joash through the army of the Arameans.

Second, Joash was severely injured, and his own servants conspired against him and murdered him. When the Aramean army captured Gath and was set to go up to Jerusalem, Joash was able to turn them around by sending all the sacred things and gold that was found among the treasuries of the house of the Lord and of the king's house to Hazael, king of Aram. Nevertheless, Joash was severely injured in this war. Soon after the war, his own servants (i.e., Jozacar the son of Shimeath and Jehozabad the son of Shomer) conspired against him and struck him to death (2 Kgs 12:17-21; 2 Chr 24:25).

The horrible death of Joash confirms the biblical truth that one reaps what he has sown. The verb *murder*, used in describing Joash's death (2 Chr 24:25), is הָרַג (*hārag*) in Hebrew, which was used to describe an act of cruelly slaughtering or striking a person to death. Interestingly, the same verb was used when Joash killed Zechariah (2 Chr 24:21). Joash's servants struck him to death in the same way that Joash stoned Zechariah to death in defiance of God and His grace.

Whatever one sows, that will he also reap (Gal 6:7). Joash was buried in the city of David, but not in the tombs of the kings (2 Chr 24:25). On the contrary, Jehoiada the priest was buried among the kings in the city of David (2 Chr 24:16a). This was because Jehoiada had done well in Israel and to God and His house (2 Chr 24:16b).

Today, we must have the works of living faith, trying to "render to the LORD for all His benefits" toward us by remembering God's grace. We must give thanks rather than stand against the mighty God by forsaking His grace (Ps 116:12; Jas 2:22). Then, we certainly will be blessed in what we do (Jas 1:25).

4. Amaziah / Αμεσσιας / אֲמַצְיָה
The Lord is mighty, the Lord has strength

– The ninth king of the southern kingdom of Judah (2 Kgs 14:1-22; 2 Chr 25:1-28)
– He was the great-grandson of Joram, grandson of Ahaziah, and son of Joash. He reigned over Judah 29 years, but was omitted from the genealogy of Jesus Christ in the Gospel of Matthew.

Matthew 1:8 ...Jehoshaphat the father of Joram, and Joram the father of Uzziah.

Background
Father: Joash (2 Kgs 14:1; 2 Chr 24:27)
Mother: Jehoaddan of Jerusalem (2 Kgs 14:2; 2 Chr 25:1)

Duration of reign
He acceded to the throne at the age of 25 and reigned for 29 years (796[b] – 767[b] BC, 2 Kgs 14:1-2; 2 Chr 25:1).
Amaziah became king of Judah in the second year of King Joash of Israel (2 Kgs 14:1).

Evaluation – good but turned wicked (2 Kgs 14:3-4; 2 Chr 25:2).
He acted right in the sight of the Lord in the beginning, yet not wholeheartedly. Later, he turned away from following the Lord (2 Chr 25:27[a]). When Amaziah began to serve idols and mocked the prophets (2 Chr 25:14-16), his servants conspired against him. While fleeing from the conspirators, Amaziah was killed wretchedly (2 Kgs 14:19-20; 2 Chr 25:27-28).

Historical sources
The Book of the Chronicles of the Kings of Judah (2 Kgs 14:18)
The Book of the Kings of Judah and Israel (2 Chr 25:26)

Amaziah succeeded Joash and became the ninth king of the southern kingdom of Judah. The name *Amaziah* is אֲמַצְיָה (*'ămaṣyâ*) in Hebrew, a compound word composed of אָמַץ (*'āmaṣ*) and יָה (*yāh*). The word אָמַץ means "to be strong," "to be brave," and "to show strength," and the word יָה (*yāh*) is the contracted form of the Lord's name "Jehovah." Thus, the name *Amaziah* means "the LORD is mighty" or "the LORD has strength." The meaning of his name is similar to his father Joash's name.

1. Amaziah lived according to God's Word at first.

After becoming king, Amaziah made sure that the kingdom was firmly in his hand and killed the servants who had slain Joash his father (2 Kgs 14:5; 2 Chr 25:3). However, he did not put their children to death (2 Kgs 14:6; 2 Chr 25:4). This was because the book of the Law of Moses stated, "Fathers shall not be put to death for sons, nor sons be put to death for fathers, but each shall be put to death for his own sin" (Deut 24:16; Ezek 18:4, 20).

Amaziah must have wanted to destroy all the families of those who conspired against his father, but he gave his effort to live according to God's Word. This was right in the sight of the Lord (2 Kgs 14:3; 2 Chr 25:2).

2. Amaziah relied on money and military power.

There is no one stronger than God in the entire world. No matter how wealthy or militarily powerful people may be, they are like leaves in the autumn wind. Rather than trusting in the mighty God, Amaziah trusted in money and military powers of the world. This was proven by his act of hiring 100,000 warriors from the northern kingdom of Israel for 100 talents of silver when he already had 300,000 choice soldiers (2 Chr 25:5-6). Since one talent of silver is 34 kg, 100 talents of silver would amount to 3.4 tons.[45]

At this time, a man of God came to Amaziah and told him to send the army of Israel back, warning him, "But if you do go, do it, be strong for the battle; yet God will bring you down before the enemy, for God has power to help and to bring down" (2 Chr 25:7-8). However, Amaziah asked, "But what shall we do?" for he had paid so much money and did not want to lose it, and the man of God answered, "The LORD has much more to give you than this" (2 Chr 25:9). Thus, in obedience, Amaziah let the troops of Israel go home (2 Chr 25:10). Then, Amaziah strengthened himself, led the army of Judah, and went to the Valley of Salt and struck down 10,000 of the sons of Seir, the Edomites (2 Chr 25:11). Then, he took Sela (the capital of Edom) by war and named it Joktheel (יָקְתְאֵל, "subdued by God"; 2 Kgs 14:7; 2 Chr 25:11). Also, the army of Judah "captured 10,000 alive and brought them to the top of the cliff and threw them down from the top of the cliff, so that they were all dashed to pieces" (2 Chr 25:12).

> **2 Chronicles 25:10-12** Then Amaziah dismissed them, the troops which came to him from Ephraim, to go home; so their anger burned against Judah and they returned home in fierce anger. Now Amaziah strengthened himself and led his people forth, and went to the Valley of Salt and struck down 10,000 of the sons of Seir. The sons of Judah also captured 10,000 alive and brought them to the top of the cliff and threw them down from the top of the cliff, so that they were all dashed to pieces.

This incident teaches us that there is a blessing of amazing victory when we obey God's Word even at the cost of a great financial loss. The army of Israel that Amaziah had hired and sent back home returned in fierce anger (2 Chr 25:10b) and raided the cities of Judah on their way back, striking down 3,000 people and plundering much spoil (2 Chr 25:13). This was a result of Amaziah's act of hiring the troops from Israel without asking God. If he had trusted God instead of money or military powers of this world, he would not have had to go through such suffering.

3. Amaziah served idols and persecuted God's prophet.

When he returned from the battle against the sons of Seir, Amaziah committed a grave sin against God for he brought their idols, set them up as his gods, bowed down before them, and burned incense to them (2 Chr 25:14). Thus, God's anger burned up against him and sent a prophet to him who rebuked him saying, "Why have you sought the gods of the people who have not delivered their own people from your hand?" (2 Chr 25:15). Rather than repenting from the rebuke, Amaziah said to the prophet, "Have we appointed you a royal counselor? Stop!" The prophet stopped with a bold proclamation, "I know that God has planned to destroy you, because you have done this and have not listened to my counsel" (2 Chr 25:16).

Although Amaziah was victorious in the battle against Seir because of God's help, he had already become proud as though the victory was a result of his own strength and yelled "Stop!" to the prophet that God sent to him. Amaziah's act of yelling at the prophet that God sent to him was no different than directly challenging God. Because of such pride, Amaziah was completely defeated in the battle against Joash, king of Israel (2 Chr 25:17-24). Truly, pride goes before destruction (Prov 16:18). God is opposed to the proud, but gives grace to the humble (Jas 4:6).

4. With boasting pride, Amaziah fought against Joash, king of Israel, and was taken captive.

In order to avenge the troops of Israel for plundering the cities of Judah, Amaziah declared war against Joash, king of Israel (2 Kgs 14:8; 2 Chr 25:17). It was truly arrogant and foolish for Amaziah to start this war in hopes of killing his own people and taking their land. Amaziah was utterly destroyed the moment he became proud. Joash of the northern kingdom of Israel had given prior warning to Amaziah who was inflated with pride and unaware of his own limits. However, Amaziah's heart had so hardened that he did not listen (2 Kgs 14:9-11a; 2 Chr 25:18-20). Joash faced Amaziah at Beth-shemesh of Judah and defeated Amaziah mercilessly, as a wild beast passing by and trampling the thorn bush (2 Kgs 14:9b, 11b-12; 2 Chr 25:18b, 21-22). Amaziah, who had gone out to war full of confidence, was defeated and taken captive by Israel. Joash tore down 400 cubits (approx. 200 yd.) of the Jerusalem wall and took all the gold, silver, and utensils from the house of God. He also took the people as hostages (2 Kgs 14:13-14; 2 Chr 25:23-24). This happened because Amaziah had become proud and rejected God by ignoring His warning. Second Chronicles 25:20 states, "But Amaziah would not listen, for it was from God, that He might deliver them into the hand of Joash because they had sought the gods of Edom."

Amaziah reigned about 15 more years with his son Uzziah after returning from a 10-year long captivity (2 Kgs 14:17; 2 Chr 25:25). He was then killed, like his father Joash, at the hands of his conspiring servants. The conspiracy had begun from the time that Amaziah turned away from following the Lord (2 Chr 25:27). Second Kings 14:19-20 states,

"They conspired against him in Jerusalem, and he fled to Lachish; but they sent after him to Lachish and killed him there. Then they brought him on horses and he was buried at Jerusalem with his fathers in the city of David." Amaziah fled all the way to Lachish, which was about 45 km (28 mi) southeast of Jerusalem, where he was killed.

The four kings (i.e., Ahaziah, Athaliah, Joash, and Amaziah) who were omitted from the second period of Jesus Christ's genealogy in Matthew 1 all ended their lives very miserably. Amaziah had witnessed his father Joash betraying God's grace in the latter part of his life and being killed wretchedly as a result. It is regretful that the son had to repeat the same mistake and walk the same path as the father. Joash and Amaziah both had names that mean "The LORD is mighty"; yet they challenged the mighty God, resulting in their murder by the conspiracy of their servants. Whoever stands against the mighty God will certainly be judged by God and end their lives miserably (Isa 3:1; Ezek 29:7). On the other hand, those who entrust their lives to God and totally depend on Him will be blessed. Then, God will take responsibilty for their lives by protecting them from beginning to end (Ps 28:7; 37:5; Prov 16:20).

לכל בר דעת דרך המסעות ארבעים שנה במדבר ... של ... ...

מדבר צין הוא קדש
עמלק

ים המלח

עיר כרמל

שבט

באר שבע

שמעון

שבט

ארץ פלשתם

מדבר סיני

מדברפארן

מדבר שור

ארבע גשן
פתם
שרה
צען
אלכסנדרי

לוח המסעות במדבר
אשר על פיהי סעו ועל פיהי חנו

שו׳ רתמה		א׳ רעמסם
טז׳ רמן פרץ		ב׳ סכת
יז׳ לבנה		ג׳ אתם
יח׳ רסה		ד׳ פיהחירת
יט׳ קהלתה		ה׳ מרה
כ׳ הרספר		ו׳ אילם
כא׳ חרדה		ז׳ ים סוף
כב׳ מקהלת		ח׳ מדבר סין
כג׳ תחת		ט׳ דפקה
כד׳ תרח		יו׳ אלוש
כה׳ מתקה		יא׳ רפידים
כו׳ חשמנה		יב׳ מדבר סיני
כז׳ מסרות		יג׳ קברת התאוה
כח׳ בני יעקן		יד׳ חצרות

רט׳ הרהגדגד
ל׳ ייטבתה
לא׳ עברנה
לב׳ עציןגבר
לג׳ מדבר צין
לד׳ הרההר
לה׳ צלמנה
לו׳ פונן
לז׳ אבת
לח׳ דיבן גד
לט׳ עלמן דבל
מ׳ הרי עברים
מא׳ ערבת מואב

PART FIVE

The History of the Kings of Israel, the Northern Kingdom

1 Jeroboam → 2 Nadab → 3 Baasha → 4 Elah

→ 5 Zimri → 6 Omri → 7 Ahab → 8 Ahaziah

→ 9 Joram (Jehoram) → 10 Jehu → 11 Jehoahaz

→ 12 Joash → 13 Jeroboam II → 14 Zechariah

→ 15 Shallum → 16 Menahem → 17 Pekahiah

→ 18 Pekah → 19 Hoshea

CHAPTER 22

The History of the Kings of Israel, the Northern Kingdom

After the death of King Solomon, the Davidic kingdom was divided into the southern kingdom of Judah and the northern kingdom of Israel as the prophet Ahijah had prophesied (1 Kgs 11:29-33). The immediate cause for the division of the kingdom was Solomon's idolatrous ways. Solomon had worshiped the idols brought in by foreign women and committed evil in the sight of the Lord; he was not wholly devoted to God (1 Kgs 11:1-8). Moreover, God had appeared to Solomon twice to warn him, and yet, he did not turn away from his sins (1 Kgs 11:9-13).

Just as God prophesied, the southern kingdom of Judah continued the dynasty of David's physical lineage. However, from its inception, the northern kingdom of Israel enthroned a king who was not of David's lineage. Nine dynasties would go on to repeat the vicious cycle of murder and retribution in their bloody efforts to seize the throne. The kingdom was driven into extreme chaos never once having attained true stability.

The subjects who clung to these wicked kings habitually committed adultery and were only looking to fulfill their own selfish desires and interests (Hos 4:12-14; 5:1-4). Even under the threat of Assyrian invasion, the people had lost their focus and stumbled because they were still deeply embroiled in adultery, extravagant indulgence, and idolatry—which is spiritual adultery (Hos 4:12; 5:4). The powerless and unenlightened people were mired in misery, forced to grieve and struggle with poverty and hunger (Amos 2:6-8). God lamented as He proclaimed judgment saying, "They have set up kings, but not by Me; they have appointed princes, but I did not know it. With their silver and gold they have made idols for themselves, that they might be cut off" (Hos 8:4).

However, God did not turn His back on the Israelites in the early days of the northern kingdom of Israel. He regarded them as the chosen people of the covenant. He said to their first king Jeroboam, "Then it will be, that if you listen to all that I command you and walk in My ways, and do what is right in My sight by observing My statutes and My commandments, as My servant David did, then I will be with you and build you an enduring house as I built for David, and I will give Israel to you" (1 Kgs 11:38). Just as He promised, God embraced the northern kingdom of Israel until the end. He led them with cords of love by sending prophets to them without ceasing (Hos 11:1-4). God never gave up on the Israelites. His absolute *agape* love toward them is shown through the heart of Hosea, who went out of his house to search for his wife even when she had returned to harlotry. It is further manifested through Hosea's act of reaching out his hand toward his defiled wife, signaling her to return home with him (Hos 3:1-3).

Nevertheless, the kings of the northern kingdom of Israel antagonized and betrayed the God of love who had continually reached out to them. They had forgotten His covenant (2 Kgs 17:15, 35-41; 18:12). Moreover, they oppressed powerless people and blocked off access to worship in Jerusalem in order to strengthen their own royal authority. These kings had made the entire nation forsake God (1 Kgs 12:28-33). The northern kingdom of Israel had infuriated God in extreme measure. Ultimately, in 722 BC, the nation was completely destroyed by the Assyrians and was obliterated from history (2 Kgs 17:1-18; 18:9-12).[46]

1. Jeroboam / ʼΙεροβοαμ / יָרָבְעָם

The people prosper, the people increase

– The first king overall in the northern kingdom of Israel; founder of Israel's first dynasty (1 Kgs 11:26-14:20; 2 Chr 9:31-10:19; 13:1-20)

Background
Father: Nebat (of the tribe of Ephraim; 1 Kgs 11:26)
Mother: Zeruah (1 Kgs 11:26)

Duration of reign
Reigned for 22 years (930–909 BC; 1 Kgs 14:20)
In the southern kingdom of Judah, Rehoboam acceded to the throne as the first king (930 BC).

Evaluation – extremely wicked king (1 Kgs 15:30)
Jeroboam set up golden calves at Bethel and Dan, built high places, and installed ordinary people as priests. He also changed the date of the Feast of Tabernacles from the 15th of the seventh month (Lev 23:34) to the 15th of the eighth month (1 Kgs 12:28-33).

Active prophets
① Ahijah: prophesied that Jeroboam would become king over the ten tribes as well as about the destruction of his house (1 Kgs 11:29-40; 14:1-18)
② Anonymous prophet of Judah: called the "man of God," prophesied that King Josiah would come later (about 300 years) and would burn the altar of golden calves and the bones on the altar (1 Kgs 13:1-32)

Historical sources – Chronicles of the Kings of Israel (1 Kgs 14:19)

Initially, Jeroboam was a valiant warrior. He was Solomon's servant who was made overseer of the forced labor when Solomon noticed his industriousness during the construction of the Millo and the repairing of the breach in the city of David (1 Kgs 11:26-28; Ref- 1 Kgs 9:23). In the latter years of Solomon's reign, the fortunes of the kingdom had fallen due to the many foreign women brought in by Solomon. At that time, Jeroboam heard the prophecy from Ahijah the prophet that he would become king (1 Kgs 11:29-31).

The prophet Ahijah tore the cloak that he had on into twelve pieces and told Jeroboam to take ten of those pieces (1 Kgs 11:30-31). This was a prophecy that Jeroboam would become a king ruling over the ten tribes. Jeroboam, who was now assured of a victory by hearing the prophecy of Ahijah, lifted his hand in rebellion to kill King Solomon (1 Kgs 11:26). In response, Solomon sought to kill Jeroboam; therefore, Jeroboam took refuge with Shishak king of Egypt until Solomon's death (1 Kgs 11:40).

Jeroboam (יָרָבְעָם) in Hebrew is a combination of the words רְבַב (*rābab*) and עַם (*'am*). Here, the word רְבַב means "to become numerous" (1 Sam 25:10) and "to multiply" (Gen 6:1), and עַם means "people." Therefore, the name *Jeroboam* means "the people increase or multiply."

After becoming king, Jeroboam took various measures to prevent the people from going down to the southern kingdom of Judah. His only interest was in seeing the increase and multiplication of the number of people. Jeroboam lived the remainder of his life trying to increase the number of his own subjects and was not interested in increasing the number of God's people. Consequently, he concluded his life in a very tragic and pitiful way.

1. Jeroboam held on to human thoughts instead of God's promise.

After Solomon's death, his son Rehoboam became king in his place (1 Kgs 11:43). The people requested that Rehoboam lighten the hard service and the heavy yoke of his father. Here, the word for *yoke* in Hebrew is עֹל (*'ōl*), which refers to wooden or iron bars put on beasts of burden to control them. This word exhibits the tremendous labor the kingdom had suffered during the reign of Solomon. But when Rehoboam refused the request of the people, ten tribes enthroned Jeroboam as their king and established the northern kingdom of Israel (1 Kgs 12:1-20). Thus, the kingdom was divided into the southern kingdom of Judah and the northern kingdom of Israel.

In 1 Kings 11:38, God spoke through the prophet Ahijah and promised to Jeroboam saying, "Then it will be, that if you listen to all that I command you and walk in My ways, and do what is right in My sight by observing My statutes and My commandments, as My servant David did, then I will be with you and build you an enduring house as I built for David, and I will give Israel to you."

After becoming king, however, Jeroboam built Shechem and Penuel to fortify his royal authority (1 Kgs 12:25). Moreover, he was caught up in human thoughts and made two golden calves, one in Bethel and the other in Dan, in order to prevent the people of Israel from going to Jerusalem to offer sacrifices (1 Kgs 12:26-29).

Jeroboam set up the golden calves as the new loci of faith in order to completely cut off the people from the southern kingdom of Judah and maintain his vested interests, whether in politics or religion. This was simply an act to satisfy his own greed and desires. Ultimately, this became a tremendous sin which would drag all of Israel down a tragic path.

Godly priests and Levites, who were opposed to such idolatrous policies of Jeroboam, left their pasture lands and property and moved to Jerusalem (2 Chr 11:13-16). In response, Jeroboam built high places and drove out the Levites. Then he appointed priests from among all the people who were not of the Levites (1 Kgs 12:31; 13:33; 2 Chr 13:9). This was a great sin that went against the Word of God which specified that the priesthood was to be given to the sons of Aaron (Exod 29:9). Jeroboam consecrated and appointed as priest anyone who would bring a young bull and seven rams (2 Chr 13:9). Moreover, Jeroboam moved the Feast of Tabernacles (Feast of Booths, Lev 23:34), which was normally held on the 15th day of the 7th month, to the 15th day of the 8th month according to his own desire (1 Kgs 12:32-33).

If Jeroboam had trusted in the promises of God and did what was right in His sight by observing His statutes and commandments, then God would have been with Him and built him an enduring house (1 Kgs 11:38). However, Jeroboam turned away from God and held on to fleshly thoughts; consequently, his life was completely ruined (Rom 8:5-8).

2. Jeroboam ignored the warning of the man of God.

Jeroboam had made a habit of ignoring God's covenants and committing treachery. He even went on to commit the great sin of burning incense—a task to be performed by the priests only (1 Kgs 13:1). God gave multiple warnings to Jeroboam in various forms.

First, God sent the anonymous man of God (1 Kgs 13:1-10).

The title "man of God" appears 16 times in 1 Kings chapter 13 (verses 1, 2, 4, 5, 6²ˣ, 7, 8, 11, 12, 14²ˣ, 21, 26, 29, 31). In verse 1 it says, "There came a man of God . . . by the word of the LORD" (1 Kgs 13:1). This statement emphasizes how God Himself came to him as the Word spoken through His servant in order to make King Jeroboam repent. The anonymous man of God risked his life and went up to Bethel, the epicenter of idolatry in the northern kingdom of Israel. Furthermore, he went directly to the sovereign of Israel, Jeroboam, and boldly proclaimed the Word of God that he would be ruined. When Jeroboam was beside the altar to burn incense upon it, the anonymous man of God cried out, "O altar, altar, thus says the LORD, 'Behold, a son shall be born to the house of David, Josiah by name; and on you he shall sacrifice the priests of the high places who burn incense on you, and human bones shall be burned on you'" (1 Kgs 13:2).

At the very moment when Jeroboam, in total disregard of the priesthood, was about to burn incense on the altar, the man of God from Judah appeared on the scene and proclaimed judgment (1 Kgs 13:1-3). A true prophet of God was not found in the northern kingdom of Israel—a prophet who would rebuke and correct Jeroboam's wicked religious policy, which encouraged idolatry, and proclaim the Word of God boldly.

Even after hearing the frightful words of impending judgment, Jeroboam vigorously stretched out his hand and shouted, "Seize him!" But at that moment, his hand dried up in midair and could not be retracted (1 Kgs 13:4). Moreover, the altar was split apart and the ashes were poured out from the altar in accordance to the sign given by the man of God (1 Kgs 13:5). Jeroboam finally came to his senses and sought the favor of the man of God. When he urgently pleaded, "Please entreat the LORD your God, and pray for me, that my hand may be restored to me" (1 Kgs 13:6), his shriveled hand was restored to its normal state.

Jeroboam had experienced a sufficiently shocking event in three stages and this could have served as an opportunity for him to repent of his ways; yet, the Bible records, "After this event Jeroboam did not return from his evil way" (1 Kgs 13:33a). He continued in his former ways and "again he made priests of the high places from among all the people; any who would, he ordained, to be priests of the high places" (1 Kgs 13:33b). Although he was warned, he completely ignored the Word of God and refused to turn from his wicked ways. Such iniquitous ways became "sin to the house of Jeroboam" which would be blotted out and destroyed from the face of the earth (1 Kgs 13:34). Baasha would go on to plot an insurrection against Jeroboam's dynasty in the second year of Nadab (Jeroboam's son; 1 Kgs 15:25-30). As a result, the entire house of Jeroboam was destroyed and not one person was left alive to Jeroboam's house (1 Kgs 15:29a).

Second, Jeroboam suffered a great loss in the battle against the southern kingdom of Judah (2 Chr 13:1-20).

In the 18th year of King Jeroboam, Abijah had become king over Judah and ruled three years in Jerusalem (2 Chr 13:1-2). Abijah of Judah had 400,000 valiant warriors while Jeroboam of Israel had twice that number, 800,000 soldiers in the battle (2 Chr 13:3). This was a great battle that mobilized the entire armed forces of both Judah and Israel. However, Jeroboam did not rely on God but solely on his armed forces in the battle. As a result, he suffered a great slaughter, losing about 500,000 men (2 Chr 13:17). In actuality, it was God who had routed Jeroboam and all Israel (2 Chr 13:5). After this battle, Jeroboam was never able to recover his power (2 Chr 13:20).

Third, Jeroboam's son Abijah was struck with an illness from God and died (1 Kgs 14:1-18).

Jeroboam did not turn from his evil ways even after his hand had been restored (1 Kgs 13:33). Therefore, God gave his final warning by striking Jeroboam's eldest son Abijah with an illness.

As Abijah became sick, King Jeroboam sent his wife in a disguise to the man of God Ahijah who was at Shiloh. This was the very prophet who had prophesied that Jeroboam would become king (1 Kgs 11:29-31).

At this point in time, Ahijah's eyes were dim because of his age (1 Kgs 14:4^b). As soon as Jeroboam's wife, who was in disguise, arrived at his door, Ahijah, as instructed by God, said, "Come in, wife of Jeroboam, why do you pretend to be another woman? For I am sent to you with a harsh message. Go, say to Jeroboam . . ." (1 Kgs 14:6-7).

The content of the prophet Ahijah's message to Jeroboam was as follows:

First, God tore the kingdom away from the house of David and gave it to Jeroboam, but he did not do what was right in God's sight (1 Kgs 14:8).

Second, Jeroboam has done more evil than all who were before him (1 Kgs 14:9).

Third, Jeroboam made molten images to provoke God to anger and cast Him behind his back (1 Kgs 14:9).

Fourth, every male person belonging to Jeroboam, whether bond or free, will be cut off (1 Kgs 14:10).

The prophet Ahijah's rebuke and prophecy did not end there. He went further by prophesying that God will strike the house of Jeroboam (entire dynasty and clan) and make a clean sweep of it as one sweeps away dung until it is all gone (1 Kgs 14:10). He also said, "Anyone belonging to Jeroboam who dies in the city the dogs will eat. And he who dies in the field the birds of the heavens will eat; for the LORD has spoken it" (1 Kgs 14:11). As such, Ahijah foretold of the great disgrace that Jeroboam's house will suffer even until the last moment of their destruction.

Indeed, as Ahijah had prophesied, when Jeroboam's wife had returned and was entering the threshold of the house, their eldest son Abijah died (1 Kgs 14:17-18). Then Jeroboam, according to God's disciplinary measures, died in the 22nd year of his reign (1 Kgs 14:20; 2 Chr 13:20). Moreover, his son Nadab, who had succeeded the throne after Jeroboam, died very soon thereafter (1 Kgs 15:25-28). In this way, Jeroboam's house was completely eradicated from the face of the earth only after two generations (1 Kgs 15:29; Ref 1 Kgs 13:34; 14:14).

Likewise, anyone who ignores God's warnings and remains unrepentant will perish tragically even if he may be a king. Jeroboam had received the great blessing of going from being Solomon's servant to becoming the king of the northern kingdom of Israel. Even when he had fallen deep into his sinful ways, God rebuked him twice through the prophet from Judah, hoping to turn him back to the way of life through repentance. However, Jeroboam ignored God's favor and blessings. In his continuing defiance of God, Jeroboam initiated and led the worship of idols, which led to the instantaneous destruction of his entire household.

Jeroboam not only sinned by himself but led his people to commit iniquities and thereby provoked the Lord God to His anger. First Kings 15:30 states, "And because of the sins of Jeroboam which he sinned, and which he made Israel sin, because of his provocation with which he provoked the LORD God of Israel to anger." The word *provoked* in Hebrew is the hiphil form of the verb כָּעַס (*kāʿas*) and means "to provoke to anger or distress." Anyone who provokes God to anger will end up in a tragic state like Jeroboam.

God gave Jeroboam many opportunities to repent. God is patient and does not desire any to perish and wishes for all to come to repentance (2 Pet 3:9). However, Jeroboam was hardened in his heart, refusing God's mercy. He continued in his sinful ways and led all of Israel into iniquity, thus becoming the epitome of the rebellious man. Therefore, the expression "way of Jeroboam" became an idiomatic phrase describing the way of someone who provokes God to anger and leads all of Israel to sin (1 Kgs 13:33; 15:26, 34; 16:2, 19, 26; 22:52; 2 Kgs 3:3; 15:9, 18, 24).

2. Nadab / Ναδαβ / נָדָב

Exaltation, generosity, liberality

– The second king of the first dynasty of the northern kingdom of Israel; second king overall (1 Kgs 15:25-32)

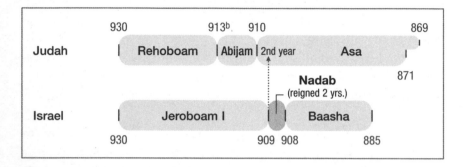

Background
Father: Jeroboam I (1 Kgs 15:25)

Duration of reign
Reigned for two years (909–908 BC; 1 Kgs 15:25)
He acceded to the throne in the "second year of Asa king of Judah" (1 Kgs 15:25). From the perspective of Judah following the accession year dating method, Nadab's accession in the "second year of Asa" is actually the first of Asa (approximately 909 BC).

Evaluation – wicked king (1 Kgs 15:26)
Nadab walked in the way of his father and in his sin which he made Israel sin.

Active prophet – Jehu
Since Jehu prophesied about the downfall of Baasha who became king after Nadab, we may conclude that Jehu was active during Nadab's time as well (1 Kgs 16:12).

Historical sources – Chronicles of the Kings of Israel (1 Kgs 15:31)

Nadab succeeded Jeroboam I to become king (1 Kgs 15:25). The name *Nadab* in Hebrew is נָדָב (*nādāb*), which means "generosity" or "liberality." Here, the word *liberality* means "the quality or state of being very generous and openhanded in giving." Moreover, נָדָב (*nādāb*) is derived from the Hebrew verb נָדַב (*nādab*), which means "to do willingly or voluntarily." The verb נָדַב (*nādab*) was used when speaking of giving a freewill offering to God (Exod 25:2; 35:21, 29) or devoting oneself to the work of God voluntarily (Judg 5:2, 9).

King David, in repenting of his adultery with Bathsheba, said, "Restore to me the joy of Your salvation and sustain me with a willing spirit" (Ps 51:12). The word *willing* in this passage is the feminine form of נָדִיב (*nādîb*), which means "willing," "noble," "generous," and "inclined."

Nadab may have been able to purge his household of the curse that had befallen Jeroboam and restore the clan if he had willingly devoted himself to doing good deeds as his name signifies. However, he was neither generous nor inclined toward good works. Rather, he followed in the way of his father Jeroboam. He did not cease to sin during his short tenure as regent and immersed himself into doing evil.

1. Nadab did evil in the sight of the Lord.

First Kings 15:26 comments, "He did evil in the sight of the LORD, and walked in the way of his father and in his sin which he made Israel sin." The phrase, "He did evil in the sight of the LORD," was an expression used in common for all the kings of Israel who had defied God (1 Kgs 15:34; 16:19, 25, 30; 21:20). On the other hand, the kings who had done what was right in His sight are David (1 Kgs 15:5), Asa (1 Kgs 15:11), and Jehoshaphat (1 Kgs 22:43).

The phrase "in the sight of the LORD" is expressed with the Hebrew word עַיִן (*'ayin*), combined with the preposition בְּ (*bě*) meaning "in." Thus it means "in the eyes." The eyes of the Lord are always open from the beginning to the end of the year (Deut 11:12). The eyes of the Lord move to and fro throughout the earth (2 Chr 16:9; Zech 4:10). The eyes of the Lord watch the evil and the good (Prov 15:3). And the eyes of the Lord are too pure to approve evil (Hab 1:13). There is no room for lies in the eyes of the Lord; therefore, a man cannot sin and deceive the eyes of the Lord.

2. Nadab walked in the way of Jeroboam his father.

First Kings 15:26 says regarding Nadab, "He did evil in the sight of the LORD, and walked in the way of his father and in his sin which he made Israel sin." Here the expression "way of his father" is speaking of the "way of Jeroboam." The word *walked* in Hebrew is הָלַךְ (*hālak*), meaning "to walk" and "to follow." Therefore, the passage is saying that Nadab followed exactly in the way of idolatry that his late father Jeroboam had walked.

Moreover, the phrase "in his sin" employs the word חַטָּאָה (*ḥaṭṭā'â*). This word is used in the sense of "a failure to respect the full rights and interests of another person." The word, then, exhibits Nadab's adherence to the way of Jeroboam by disobeying God and exploiting the people through his unrighteous ways.

Since Nadab could not forcibly repulse sin but was rather tolerant toward it, he was ultimately killed by Baasha the son of Ahijah of the house of Issachar. At the time, Nadab was in a battle against the Philistines at Gibbethon. He was unaware that there was a conspiracy against his life and was eventually killed by Baasha (1 Kgs 15:27-28).

In 1 Kings 15:27, the word *conspired* in Hebrew is קָשַׁר (*qāšar*), which means "to tie," "to plot or conspire," and "to be joined." There were many people who were opposed to Nadab's policies and these people united to assassinate Nadab. After killing Nadab and arising to the throne, Baasha struck down the house of Jeroboam, so that there was not a single person alive (1 Kgs 15:29). This took place exactly according to the prophecy of Ahijah the prophet (1 Kgs 14:14; 15:29).

Today, we must be zealous for good works (Eph 2:10; Titus 2:14), generous in heart, and yet we must not be tolerant toward sin. Those who commit evil must pay the price of sin, and they will meet a tragic conclusion to their lives. Nadab, who was completely depraved and took pleasure in sin, barely reigned for two years and died suddenly while his entire household was completely wiped out (1 Kgs 15:29).

3. Baasha / Βαασα / בַּעְשָׁא
Offensive, wickedness

– The first king of the second dynasty of the northern kingdom of Israel, third king overall (1 Kgs 15:28; 15:33 – 16:7; 2 Chr 16:1-6)

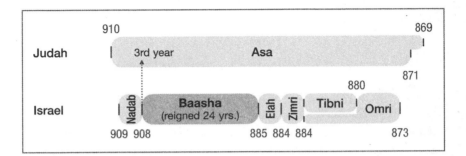

Background
Father: Ahijah (tribe of Issachar; 1 Kgs 15:27)

Duration of reign
Reigned for 24 years (908–885 BC; 1 Kgs 15:28, 33)
He acceded to the throne in the "third year of Asa king of Judah" (1 Kgs 15:28, 33). From the perspective of Judah following the accession year dating method, Baasha's accession in the "third year of Asa" is actually the second year of Asa (approximately 908 BC).

Evaluation – Wicked king (1 Kgs 16:7)
Baasha walked in the way of Jeroboam and in his sin which he made Israel sin (1 Kgs 15:34). Therefore, God declared that He will "consume Baasha and his house (1 Kgs 16:3).

Active prophet – Jehu
The prophet Jehu prophesied that Baasha will be tragically destroyed like the house of Jeroboam (1 Kgs 16:1-4, 11-13).

Historical sources – Chronicles of the Kings of Israel (1 Kgs 16:5)

Baasha killed Nadab and became the first king of the second dynasty of the northern kingdom of Israel. The name *Baasha* in Hebrew is בַּעְשָׁא (*ba'šā'*), which means "offensive" or "wickedness" and is derived from a root that means "to stink."

Baasha became king over all Israel at Tirzah (1 Kgs 15:33). Despite the fact that Baasha was used as an instrument of God to judge Nadab and the house of Jeroboam, who had walked in the way of Jeroboam, Baasha also walked in the way of Nadab and Jeroboam. First Kings 15:34 states, "He did evil in the sight of the LORD, and walked in the way of Jeroboam and in his sin which he made Israel sin." This passage is an exact repetition of the commentary regarding Nadab in 1 Kings 15:26. Indeed, Baasha, more than anyone else, lived a life that was offensive to God.

1. Baasha was exalted from the dust and became a leader of Israel.

The Word of the Lord came upon Jehu the son of Hanani against Baasha. First Kings 16:2 states, "Inasmuch as I exalted you from the dust and made you leader over My people Israel . . . ." Here, the word *dust* in Hebrew is עָפָר (*'āpār*), meaning "dry earth," "soil," and "dust." In referring to the status of a person, this word can denote a being that is as commonplace and worthless as dust (Ps 103:14-15). Through His sovereign workings, God enthroned Baasha, who otherwise could never have become king. However, Baasha, unmindful of the grace of God that had exalted a lowly being to the throne, worshiped idols and provoked God to anger. As his name indicates, Baasha was an ingrate who was offensive to God.

We, who are all as lowly as the dust of the earth, live on by the grace that God has bestowed upon us. Therefore, we must be grateful for His favor and hope to repay it someday. If we lose sight of the grace that God has bestowed upon us in the past, then our gratitude will dissipate and pride will sprout. When pride matures, destruction follows (2 Chr 32:25; Prov 16:18).

2. Baasha and his house were consumed because of his sins.

God declared that He would "utterly sweep away" Baasha and his house (1 Kgs 16:3-4; ESV). The expression *sweep away* in Hebrew is בָּעַר (*bāʿar*), which means "to burn" and "to consume." Especially since the participial form is used here, God is expressing His strong intention that He will continue to burn away until all is completely consumed.

There is something very unique about the record of Baasha's death. First Kings 16:5 states, "Now the rest of the acts of Baasha and what he did and his might, are they not written in the Book of the Chronicles of the Kings of Israel?"

The word *might* is usually not used in summing up the acts of kings (1 Kgs 14:29; 15:7, 31; 16:14); it is unique to Baasha. This word *might* in Hebrew is גְּבוּרָה (*gĕbûrâ*) which means "power," "might," and "strength." Its use leads us to deduce that Baasha possessed great authority and power which cannot be compared to any other king.

Many of the godly people of Israel could not endure the wicked reign of Baasha any longer. When these people heard that God was with King Asa of the southern kingdom of Judah, many of them defected southward to Judah (2 Chr 15:9). Then King Baasha planned the construction of Ramah in order to prevent the free travel of the people of Israel to and from King Asa of Judah (1 Kgs 15:17).

The name *Ramah* (רָמָה) means "height" or "high place." It is a strategic city located 6 km to the north of Jerusalem on the border of Judah and Israel (Josh 18:25; Judg 19:13). As Baasha fortified Ramah to use it as the base of operations for conquering the southern kingdom of Judah, Asa king of Judah took all the silver and gold from the treasuries of the house of the Lord and the treasuries of the king's house and sent them to Benhadad requesting reinforcement forces (1 Kgs 15:18-19). Then, Baasha was forced to cease fortifying Ramah (1 Kgs 15:20-21; 2 Chr 16:1-5).

Although Baasha ruled the kingdom with power and authority for 24 years, he committed evil in the sight of God and provoked Him to anger. Therefore, his entire house was destroyed instantly. Later, a man named Zimri killed Baasha's son Elah and became king. Zimri killed every male person of the house of Baasha and left none remaining (1 Kgs 16:11-13).

God used Baasha as His instrument to judge King Nadab. Baasha became God's instrument of judgment to strike down the wicked idolater Nadab. Baasha went on to completely annihilate the house of Jeroboam and became the third king of the northern kingdom of Israel. Despite all this, Baasha committed idolatry without any hesitation just like Nadab whom he had killed. In this way, he lived a life that was offensive to God, and ultimately brought God's judgment upon himself.

4. Elah / Ηλα / אֵלָה
Oak (terebinth)

— The second king of the second dynasty of the northern kingdom of Israel, fourth king overall (1 Kgs 16:6-14)

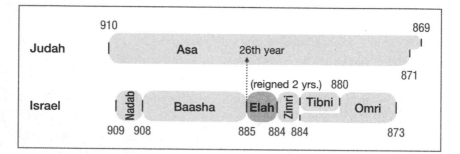

Background
Father: Baasha (1 Kgs 16:6)

Duration of reign
Reigned for two years (885–884 BC; 1 Kgs 16:8)
He acceded to the throne in the "twenty-sixth year of Asa king of Judah" (1 Kgs 16:8). From the perspective of Judah following the accession year dating method, Elah's accession in the "twenty-sixth year of Asa" is actually the 25th year of Asa (approximately 885 BC).

Evaluation – wicked king (1 Kgs 16:13)

Historical sources – Chronicles of the Kings of Israel (1 Kgs 16:14)

Elah is Baasha's son. He reigned two years after his father Baasha died. The name *Elah* is אֵלָה (*'ēlâ*) in Hebrew and means "terebinth." This name is derived from the Hebrew word אַיִל (*'ayil*), which means "mighty man," "pilaster" or "chief" (Exod 15:15; Ezek 17:13; 31:11). The terebinth or the oak tree symbolizes strength because it grows to about 10 to 13 meters high with thick, sturdy trunks that are appropriate to be used as metaphors for strength (Amos 2:9).

Elah's father Baasha was a powerful king whose "might" was especially denoted in the account of his 24-year reign (1 Kgs 16:5). It seems likely that Baasha named his son *Elah* because he wanted him to become a monarch as powerful and strong as an oak tree. Elah is also the name of a valley (1 Sam 17:2, 19) located near Gibbethon, where Baasha killed Nadab to establish his dynasty (1 Kgs 15:27-28). Elah was unable to gain fame for his strength and might as his name suggests because his life had ended after two short years of reign just as Jehu son of Hanani had prophesied.

1. While completely drunk, Elah was killed by Zimri.

When Zimri conspired against him, Elah was drinking himself drunk at the house of Arza, who was in charge of the household at Tirzah. First Kings 16:9 states, "His servant Zimri, commander of half his chariots, conspired against him. Now he was at Tirzah drinking himself drunk in the house of Arza, who was over the household at Tirzah." Here, the word translated as *drinking* in English is the Hebrew word שָׁתָה (šātâ), meaning "to drink or consume alcohol." This word is used in the participial form, indicating that Elah had been drinking continuously. Eventually, Elah was drunk to the point of losing consciousness when he was killed by Zimri (1 Kgs 16:9-10).

When a person gets drunk, he loses spiritual discernment and will fall into spiritual lethargy. Proverbs 23:21 states, "For the heavy drinker and the glutton will come to poverty, and drowsiness will clothe one with rags." Drunkenness is a desire of the Gentiles (1 Pet 4:3). Moreover, Galatians 5:21 states that drunkenness is one of the things done by those who will not inherit the kingdom of God (1 Cor 6:10). This is not simply referring to the consumption of alcoholic beverages, but a warning against getting drunk on worldly pleasures, interests, and delights (Eph 5:18). Our hearts will be inclined toward worldly interests if we are not filled with the Word of God and the Holy Spirit. Then, worldly concerns will seep into our thoughts and make our hearts dull, ultimately bringing great woes upon ourselves (Luke 21:34).

2. Elah was not faithful in his appointed duties.

During the time Elah was betrayed, his troops were in Gibbethon embroiled in a battle against the Philistines. Elah should have been leading the army in battle. However, he was back in Tirzah, the capital of the northern kingdom of Israel, getting drunk at a party, which he was hosting at his servant's house. Elah was not at all concerned with the lives of his people nor of the welfare of the kingdom. Although he possessed sufficient powers as king to battle the Philistines, Elah did not fulfill his duty as king because he was immersed in wanton pleasures.

James 5:5 states, "You have lived luxuriously on the earth and led a life of wanton pleasure; you have fattened your hearts in a day of slaughter." The New Living Translation renders the same verse as follows: "You have spent your years on earth in luxury, satisfying your every desire. You have fattened yourselves for the day of slaughter." The life of one living in wanton pleasure concludes in tragic destruction. Second Peter 2:12-13 states that those who "count it a pleasure to revel in the daytime" ("Their idea of pleasure is to carouse in broad daylight." NIV) will be destroyed in their revelry. Elah was completely unaware of his imminent destruction as he was reveling in wanton pleasure; and that is when he was tragically killed by Zimri.

The events did not stop with the sudden death of Elah the individual; they continued on to bring about the collapse of the dynasty. Zimri annihilated the entire household of Baasha; he did not leave a single male related to Baasha whether as kin or friend (1 Kgs 16:9-12). This happened in accordance with the words of reproach that the Lord spoke through the prophet Jehu regarding Baasha (1 Kgs 16:1-4, 12).

One of the main reasons for the complete destruction of Elah and his household is that he not only sinned against God but he also caused the entire nation to sin, thereby provoking the LORD God to anger (1 Kgs 16:13). The expression "provoke . . . to anger" in Hebrew is simply כָּעַס (kā'as), which means "to be vexed," "to be indignant," "to be angry," or "to be grieved." The expression indicates that all the sins of Baasha and his son Elah have reached their climax to provoke God so that there is no possibility of turning back His anger. Therefore, God did not delay any longer, but executed judgment that He had already prophesied to the house of Baasha through the prophet Jehu.

No matter how powerful an individual may be, he and his household cannot but instantly come to complete ruin if he gets drunk with the pleasures of this world to grieve God and provoke Him to anger.

5. Zimri / Ζαμβρι / זִמְרִי
Praising with songs, my song

— The first king of the third dynasty of the northern kingdom of Israel, fifth king overall (1 Kgs 16:8-20)

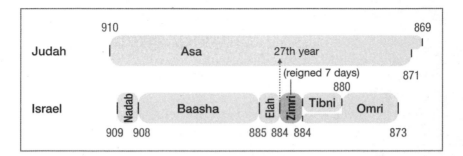

Background
As a commander in Elah's army, Zimri was in charge of half the chariots of the king (1 Kgs 16:9).

Duration of reign
Reigned for seven days (884 BC; 1 Kgs 16:9-10, 15)
He acceded to the throne in the "twenty-seventh year of Asa king of Judah" (1 Kgs 16:15). From the perspective of Judah following the accession year dating method, Zimri's accession in the "twenty-seventh year of Asa" is actually the 26th year of Asa (approximately 884 BC).

Evaluation – wicked king (1 Kgs 16:19)

Historical sources – Chronicles of the Kings of Israel (1 Kgs 16:20)

Zimri murdered Elah to become king; however, he only ruled for seven days and committed suicide (1 Kgs 16:18). The name *Zimri* is זִמְרִי (*zimrî*) in Hebrew, meaning "praising with songs" or "my song." This word is derived from the word זָמַר (*zāmar*), meaning "to praise" and "to sing." This word was used 45 times in the Old Testament with the majority of the usage being about praising the Lord (Exod 15:2; Judg 5:3; Ps 68:4, 32). Unlike his name, Zimri's life opposed the work of God; therefore, his life came to a tragic end.

1. Zimri was an extremely selfish and violent man.

Zimri was a commander over half the chariots of Israel (1 Kgs 16:9). However, when Israel was embroiled in a battle to the death against the Philistines at Gibbethon, Zimri did not participate in that battle and remained back at Tirzah, moving about independently. When the fate of the nation hung by a thread as the war raged on, Zimri was engrossed in his greed for power. He was an extremely selfish person who incited an insurrection and assassinated King Elah to usurp the throne.

Zimri was Elah's servant (1 Kgs 16:9). The word *servant* in Hebrew is עֶבֶד (*'ebed*), which means "slave" or "servant." Although Zimri should have given absolute obedience to his master, he committed mutiny by murdering the king.

After becoming king, Zimri did not hesitate to commit a large-scale massacre by killing "all the household of Baasha." "He did not leave a single male, neither of his relatives nor of his friends" (1 Kgs 16:11-12). In order to maintain his position as king, Zimri killed all the men who could possibly take revenge on him. He was indeed a brutal and violent person.

Zimri, who was so full of vigor and high-spirited, had the throne taken away from him in just seven days. Human beings may try to protect themselves using all the power and might of this world; however, they will vanish away like vapor if God is not behind them to uphold them with His power and might (Ps 127:1).

2. Zimri burned the king's house and killed himself.

The news that Zimri killed Elah and became king reached the Israelites, who were battling the Philistines at Gibbethon. The people did not acknowledge Zimri as king, but they took commander Omri as their king. Then, Omri led the soldiers, returned to Tirzah and took the city. Zimri saw that the city was taken and went into the citadel of the king's house. There he set the palace on fire and died in that fire (1 Kgs 16:16-18).

First Kings 16:19 explains that Zimri died like this "because of his sins which he sinned, doing evil in the sight of the LORD, walking in the way of Jeroboam, and in his sin which he did, making Israel sin." Zimri only ruled for seven days, and yet, why does the Bible state that he walked in the way of Jeroboam? The Bible is indicating to us that Zimri had been walking in the way of Jeroboam all his life, even including the time he was Elah's servant before becoming king.

Zimri was a meticulous person. When the army of Israel was battling the Philistines at Gibbethon, Zimri seized that opportunity to become king. No matter how flawlessly one may plot his schemes, it will fail instantly if the plan purposes to satiate his greed without regard to God's desires.

Later, the name *Zimri* was used to refer to someone who killed their master. In 2 Kings 9:31, we see Jezebel saying to Jehu, "Is it well, Zimri, your master's murderer?" The name *Zimri* originally had a positive meaning of "praising (God) with song." However, such a name had become synonymous with the shameful epithet, "master's murderer."

6. Omri / Αμβρι / עָמְרִי
Pile up sheaves, one who serves the Lord, servant of the Lord

— The first king of the fourth dynasty of the northern kingdom of Israel, sixth king overall (1 Kgs 16:15-28)

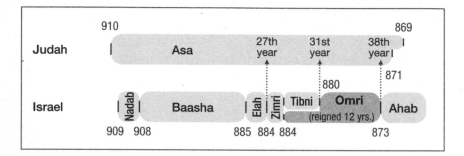

Background
There is no record of Omri's father in the Bible. He was a commander in Elah's army (1 Kgs 16:16).

Duration of reign
Reigned for 12 years (884–873 BC; 1 Kgs 16:23), his sole reign of eight years began after defeating Tibni in battle (1 Kgs 16:21-23)
He started his sole reign in the "thirty-first year of Asa king of Judah" (1 Kgs 16:23). From the perspective of Judah following the accession year dating method, Omri's sole reign actually started in the 30th year of Asa (approximately 880 BC) not in the "thirty-first year."

Evaluation – extremely wicked king (1 Kgs 16:25-26)
Omri was more wicked than all who came before him; he provoked God to anger.

Historical sources – Chronicles of the Kings of Israel (1 Kgs 16:27)

In the 27th year of King Asa of the southern kingdom of Judah (1 Kgs 16:15), Omri succeeded Zimri as king of Israel. However, since Israel was divided between those that followed him and those that followed Tibni, Omri only reigned over half the nation. Then, in the 31st year of King Asa of Judah, Omri completely defeated Tibni and became the bona fide king over all of Israel (1 Kgs 16:21-22). Omri became sole regent in the 31st year of King Asa (1 Kgs 16:23) and his son Ahab became king in the 38th year of King Asa (1 Kgs 16:29). Therefore, it seems that Omri had a sole reign of eight years after emerging victorious from a five-year battle against Tibni. Omri reigned in Tirzah for six years (1 Kgs 16:23).

The name Omri (עָמְרִי) in Hebrew means "to heap." This word is derived from the Hebrew word עָמַר ('āmar), which means "to heap" or "to bind sheaves." During his 12-year reign, Omri fought a bloody battle with Tibni for five years in order to bind up a sole reign.

1. Omri built a city on the hill of Samaria.

After Zimri's death, Israel was divided into two factions, one supporting Tibni and the other supporting Omri. Omri's factions triumphed and Tibni was killed. After firmly establishing his royal authority, he bought the hill of Samaria from Shemer for two talents of silver. There he built a city and named it Samaria after Shemer (1 Kgs 16:24). Two talents of silver is approximately 68 kg (1 talent = 34 kg). It is an amount of money that is too small to buy the hill of Samaria. Although the law forbids the sale of land (Lev 25:23), Omri used his power to practically take the hill of Samaria by forcing its sale.

Samaria is located approximately 56 km north of Jerusalem and approximately 33 km inland from the Mediterranean Sea at the heart of Palestine; geographically, it is a naturally formed fortress. The word *Samaria* in Hebrew is שֹׁמְרוֹן (šōmĕrôn), and appropriate to its geographical form, it means "watch-post" or "lookout."

Omri turned Samaria into an impregnable fortress. He then sought to establish a powerful monarchy by moving the capital of Israel from Tirzah to Samaria. However, Samaria would later become the hotbed of numerous national transgressions one of which was the establishment of the Baal and Asherah idols by Omri's son Ahab.

God disperses throughout the face of the earth all the people who build their own cities like the Tower of Babel (Gen 11:9). Today, we must not be focused on establishing our own lives but on establishing the glory of God (1 Cor 10:31).

2. Omri acted more wickedly than all the kings before him.

First Kings 16:25 states, "Omri did evil in the sight of the LORD, and acted more wickedly than all who were before him." The New Living Translation of the same verse says, "But Omri did what was evil in the

LORD's sight, even more than any of the kings before him." Therefore, absolute disregard for God, rebellion against God and the sin of idolatry were called the "statutes of Omri" (Mic 6:16).

First, Omri received recognition from the people of the world but not from God.

When Zimri murdered Elah and his family to usurp the throne, the people who were infuriated by such an act took Omri as their king (1 Kgs 16:8-16). Although Omri received recognition from the people, he committed more evil than any of the kings before him; therefore, he received no such recognition from God.

Second, Omri was famous for his show of might.

As was the case with Baasha, Omri's "might which he showed" were "written in the Book of the Chronicles of the Kings of Israel" (1 Kgs 16:27). Although Omri's acts of "might" are not clearly outlined in the Bible, we can still surmise about his show of might within politics, military affairs and in governance.

According to archaeological finds, a Moabite inscription from about 850 BC has "Omri King of Israel" inscribed on it. Moreover, in the records of Shalmaneser II king of Assyria, Israel is referred to as the "house of Omri" even after Omri's death. As such, Omri's name was well known even in far away regions. We can deduce that Omri was quite active in his diplomatic dealings with Gentile nations from the fact that his son Ahab was married to "Jezebel the daughter of Ethbaal king of the Sidonians" (1 Kgs 16:31).

The impregnable fortress of Samaria which Omri had built, his splendid diplomatic policies, which received recognition from historians, and his awesome display of military and political prowess all crumbled in 722 BC at the hands of Assyrians—merely 158 years after 880 BC. All things on earth that have been built up according to human desires will be destroyed in an instant (Isa 30:13; Lam 1:6). Only those things done by faith and the things stored up in heaven will remain for eternity.

7. Ahab / Αχααβ / אַחְאָב
Father's brother

— The second king of the fourth dynasty of the northern kingdom of Israel, seventh king overall (1 Kgs 16:28-22:40; 2 Chr 18:1-34)

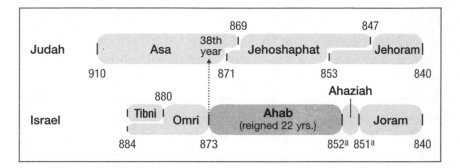

Background
Father: Omri (1 Kgs 16:28-29)

Duration of reign
Reigned for 22 years (873-852ª BC; 1 Kgs 16:29).
He acceded to the throne in the "thirty-eighth year of Asa king of Judah" (1 Kgs 16:29). From the perspective of Judah following the accession year dating method, Ahab actually acceded to the throne in the 37th year of Asa (approximately 873 BC) not in the "thirty-eighth year."

Evaluation – extremely wicked king
Ahab was married to Jezebel daughter of Ethbaal the king of the Sidonians. Ahab served and built Baal and Asherah idols (1 Kgs 16:31-33; 21:25).

Active prophets
Elijah (1 Kgs 17:1-2 Kgs 2:11)
Micaiah (1 Kgs 22:13-28)

Historical sources – Chronicles of the Kings of Israel (1 Kgs 22:39)

Ahab, who had reigned for 22 years as king, was Omri's son. The account of his life is voluminous, spanning from 1 Kings chapters 16 to 22. This fact reveals to us that Ahab's reign was the darkest time in the history of the northern kingdom of Israel. At the same time, it also shows us that the powerful illuminating work of God was still mightily at work, even during such a dark time, through the prophet Elijah.

The name *Ahab* in Hebrew is אַחְאָב ('ah'āb), which is formed by combining the words אָח ('āḥ: brother) and אָב ('āb: father); thus, the name means "father's brother."

1. Ahab married Jezebel and brought in idols.

Ahab married Jezebel daughter of Ethbaal king of the Sidonians. Then, he built shrines for Baal and there he set up images of Baal and Asherah, which he worshiped (1 Kgs 16:31-33). His father Omri had influenced Ahab into his iniquitous ways; however, his wife Jezebel was even more influential in this way. First Kings 21:25-26 explains that Jezebel incited Ahab to commit his abominable sins. The New Living Translation expresses this passage in the following way: "No one else so completely sold himself to what was evil in the LORD's sight as Ahab did under the influence of his wife Jezebel. His worst outrage was worshiping idols just as the Amorites had done—the people whom the LORD had driven out from the land ahead of the Israelites."

Jezebel is introduced as the "daughter of Ethbaal king of the Sidonians" (1 Kgs 16:31). The name *Ethbaal* is a combination of the words אֶת ('ēt: with) and בַּעַל (ba'al). Together, they mean "living with Baal."[47] When Omri took Jezebel as wife for his son Ahab, she brought along her Baal. She caused shrines to be erected for Baal (1 Kgs 16:32) and Asherah images to be made (1 Kgs 16:33). Because of that one woman Jezebel, "Ahab did more to provoke the LORD God of Israel than all the kings of Israel who were before him" (1 Kgs 16:33).

Jezebel even murdered the prophets of the Lord. First Kings 18:4 states, "for when Jezebel destroyed the prophets of the LORD…" And 1 Kings 19:10 and verse 14 also includes the phrase, "killed Your prophets with the sword." Due to that one woman Jezebel the daughter of Ethbaal, extreme cruelty and horrifying tyranny ran rampant in the northern kingdom of Israel so that lawlessness and disorder ruled the day.

As the northern kingdom of Israel worshiped Baal and Asherah, which had been brought in by Jezebel, people's reverence for God dissipated and the authority of the Word had hit rock bottom. The event that clearly epitomizes such a state of affairs is the construction of Jericho by Hiel of Bethel (1 Kgs 16:34). Hiel started to rebuild Jericho, the very city that had been prohibited for reconstruction by Joshua approximately 500 years ago. Just as Joshua had sworn by an oath (Josh 6:26), Hiel lost his eldest son Abiram when he laid the foundation and lost his younger son Segub when he set up its gates (1 Kgs 16:34). Hiel experienced a great ruin because he had ignored the Word of God.

2. Ahab contested against Elijah the prophet.

God declared through Elijah the prophet that there shall be no rain or dew for years to come (1 Kgs 17:1). A severe drought actually set in for three years and six months during Ahab's reign (1 Kgs 18:1-2; Jas 5:17). This was God's way of disciplining King Ahab and the people of his time who were worshiping Baal. The people of the generation believed that Baal was in control of the climate and agriculture.

After three long years of the drought had passed, God once again sent Elijah the prophet to King Ahab (1 Kgs 18:1). Ahab reproached Elijah by calling him the "troubler of Israel" (1 Kgs 18:17). Ahab believed that the cause of the drought in Israel was Elijah and not his own iniquities; he thereby passed all blame to the man of God.

In response, the prophet Elijah told Ahab to gather 450 prophets of Baal and 400 prophets of Asherah at Mount Carmel (1 Kgs 18:19). At Mount Carmel, God brought down fire upon the altar of Elijah and gave him victory. Then, Elijah seized the prophets of Baal, not allowing a single one to escape, and killed them all at the brook Kishon (1 Kgs 18:40).

Even after losing his battle against Elijah, Ahab did not repent but initiated with Jezebel an even more violent and oppressive religious policy. Under such oppression, even the prophet Elijah had to evade Jezebel and take refuge in Mount Horeb (1 Kgs 19:1-18).

Elijah's victory was in fact God's victory over the false gods Baal and Asherah. Despite the frantic rituals of their prophets, the Baal and Asherah did not reply with even a single word. They were indeed false gods, silent gods and slumbering gods (1 Kgs 18:27). The God of Elijah, on the other hand, is indeed the living God who answered Elijah's prayer by fire (1 Kgs 18:38).

3. Ahab battled against Ben-hadad II, king of Aram.

King Ben-hadad II of Aram besieged Samaria and exclaimed, "Your silver and your gold are mine; your most beautiful wives and children are also mine" (1 Kgs 20:1-3). God sent an anonymous prophet and prophesied of Israel's victory. He also gave instructions on how to prepare for the war (1 Kgs 20:13-15, 22). As God had prophesied, King Ahab was triumphant in the first and second battles against Aram; the victories were attained wholly through the help of the Lord (1 Kgs 20:16-21, 26-30). By defeating the kingdom of Aram, God was declaring that He is in control of history.

In the first war, King Ahab, with only 232 youth soldiers along with 7,000 men from the people, reaped a great victory against Ben-hadad who led a great army with the help of 32 kings. It was indeed a miraculous work of God (1 Kgs 20:15-21).

Even in the second war, King Ahab was leading a much inferior army. In regard to this situation, the Bible comments, "the sons of Israel camped before them like two little flocks of goats, but the Arameans filled the country" (1 Kgs 20:27). However, Ahab's army, which seemed like "two little flocks of goats," faced and defeated 100,000 enemy soldiers in one day by the intervention of God (1 Kgs 20:28-30).

Although Ahab and the people of Israel were deeply embroiled in idolatry, God desired for them to experience the power of God through the battle; and through such an experience, He hoped they would repent and return to him. This was truly an expression of God's wondrous love. Regarding this, 1 Kings 20:13 states, ". . . I will deliver them into your hand today, and you shall know that I am the Lord." First Kings 20:28 also states, "I will give all this great multitude into your hand, and you shall know that I am the Lord."

But King Ahab went against God's desire to punish King Ben-hadad. He arrogantly made a treaty with Ben-hadad and let him live. Therefore, Ahab is given the words of God's prophecy that he would die in place of Ben-hadad (1 Kgs 20:42). This prophecy is fulfilled approximately three years later in the third war against Ben-hadad the Aramean king. There, King Ahab dies a tragic death (1 Kgs 22:29-38).

4. Ahab took away Naboth's vineyard.

Ahab wanted to take Naboth's vineyard so that he could make a vegetable garden for himself (1 Kgs 21:1-2). Here, the word *vegetable* in Hebrew is יָרָק (*yārāq*), which means "greens," "garden herbs," and "plants for consumption." Therefore, it seems that Ahab desired to have a garden nearby his palace where he could relax.

The land of Canaan is the promised inheritance given by God; therefore, sale and purchase of this land was prohibited (Lev 25:23). However, Ahab was trying to gratify his personal desires by using his power. Naboth boldly replied, "The LORD forbid me that I should give you the inheritance of my fathers," (1 Kgs 21:3) and refused Ahab's offer. Naboth was a possessor of bold faith, who had an unwavering conviction to uphold the Word of God even in the face of such menacing and threatening display of power. This is quite a contrast from today's irresolute leaders who violate God's commands while submitting sycophantically to the powers that be.

When Naboth refused his offer, Ahab became "sullen and vexed"; he lay on his bed with his face turned away and ate no food (1 Kgs 21:4). When Jezebel found out the reason for Ahab's behavior, she sent letters to the elders and the nobles living in Naboth's city. In the letter she commanded, "Proclaim a fast and seat Naboth at the head of the people; and seat two worthless men before him, and let them testify against him, saying, 'You cursed God and the king.' Then take him out and stone him to death" (1 Kgs 21:9-10). As the letter commanded, Naboth was taken out of the city and stoned to death (1 Kgs 21:13-14).

While Ahab was on his way to take possession of Naboth's vineyard, God sent the prophet Elijah to prophesy, saying, "In the place where the dogs licked up the blood of Naboth the dogs will lick up your blood, even yours" (1 Kgs 21:19). God also had Elijah prophesy, saying, "The dogs will eat Jezebel in the district of Jezreel" (1 Kgs 21:23). Ahab heard these words, humbled himself, tore his clothes, put on sackcloth, and repented. Therefore, the wrath of God was postponed until his son's days; but Ahab's repentance was only temporary (1 Kgs 21:27-29).

Even amidst Ahab's numerous sins, God delayed the punishment that was coming to Ahab's house when He saw that Ahad had humbly repented, even if for just a moment (Ref Exod 34:6; Num 14:18; Ps 86:15; 103:8; 145:8).

Nevertheless, Ahab defied God's Word by using his God-given authority to gratify his selfish interests and desires. Ultimately, when Ahab died, dogs licked up his blood, thus concluding a wretched and dismal life (1 Kgs 22:38).

Ahab showed no fear of God; he abused his royal authority and behaved audaciously before God by his deceptions and murders. Ahab truly deserved to be recompensed for his wicked deeds through God's stern and just judgment. No covert actions remain concealed before God's eyes which are like flames of fire (Eccl 12:14; Rom 2:16; Rev 1:14; 2:18; 19:12).

5. Ahab was struck and killed by an arrow in a battle at Ramoth-gilead.

There had been a three-year period where no wars were fought between Aram and Israel. Then, King Ahab asked King Jehoshaphat to ally with him in attacking Ramoth-gilead (1 Kgs 22:1-4). Jehoshaphat requested that they inquire of God first. Four hundred false prophets replied, "Go up, for the LORD will give *it* into the hand of the king" (1 Kgs 22:6). Zedekiah, who was among the four hundred prophets, made horns of iron and prophesied falsely, saying, "Thus says the LORD, 'With these you will gore the Arameans until they are consumed" (1 Kgs 22:11).

On the other hand, the prophet Micaiah declared that God had put a lying spirit in the mouths of these prophets to tell the king to fight in this battle. He went on to prophesy that Ahab will die in battle and Israel will be scattered like sheep without a shepherd (1 Kgs 22:14-23). Zedekiah, the son of Chenaanah, struck Micaiah on the cheek when he heard these words. King Ahab ordered that the prophet Micaiah be imprisoned and be given meager rations of bread and water (1 Kgs 22:24, 27).

God had intended to destroy the house of Ahab; but when he tore his clothes and put on sackcloth and fasted, lying in sackcloth and going about despondently in repentance with humility (1 Kgs 21:27-29), God gave him a chance to be saved by giving wisdom and mercy through the prophet Micaiah. Nevertheless, King Ahab did not take hold of this opportunity and ignored God's prophecy and went into battle. He had put on armor along with a disguise as he went into battle. Ahab thought he would be safe if he were not targeted by the enemy. However, he was struck by an arrow that was shot at random. Ahab was bleeding as he continued on in battle, and his blood pooled at the bottom of his chariot (1 Kgs 22:34-35). King Ahab died and was buried in Samaria. His chariot was washed by the pool of Samaria where harlots bathed themselves, and dogs licked up his blood (1 Kgs 21:19; 22:37-40). This happened exactly as God had prophesied. Even though heaven and earth will pass away, God's Word will not fall to the ground but will all be fulfilled (Matt 5:18; 24:35; Luke 21:33). God always brings to fruition whatever He has spoken; He is not man that He should err or make mistakes (Ps 33:9;

Lam 2:17; Ezek 12:28). The arrow that was shot randomly did not have a target, but it was a necessary coincidence that was to fulfill what the Lord had spoken according to His sovereign providence (1 Kgs 21:19-21).

Despite having committed extremely wicked transgressions before God, Ahab received numerous chances to repent. As his name means "father's brother," Ahab received such chances to repent according to the abounding love of God the Father. Nevertheless, he continued to disregard the Word of God and did not think much about his sinful ways.

First Kings 16:31 states, "It came about, as though it had been a trivial thing for him to walk in the sins of Jeroboam the son of Nebat . . . ." Ultimately, trivializing sin is taking a disdainful attitude toward God. The Almighty recompenses each according to their deeds and repays them for their works (Job 34:11). When someone disdains God, due punishment will ensue (2 Pet 2:10). King Ahab, who disdained God, was, in turn, disdained by God (2 Sam 2:30), and wretched was the end of his days.

Heaven and earth may disappear, but not a single jot and tittle of God's Word will disappear; every word He speaks will come true (Matt 24:34-35). Therefore, we must revere God and become an obedient people of God who receive His Word by faith with fear and trembling.

8. Ahaziah / Οχοζιας / אֲחַזְיָה
The Lord has grasped, the Lord's possession

— The third king of the fourth dynasty of the northern kingdom of Israel, eighth king overall (1 Kgs 22:40, 51-53; 2 Kgs 1:1-18; 2 Chr 20:35-37)

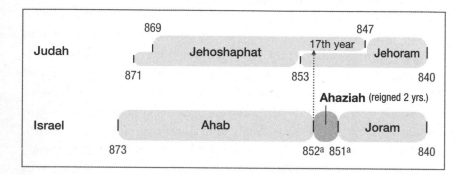

Background
Father: Ahab (1 Kgs 22:40, 51)

Duration of reign
Reigned for two years (852ᵃ–851ᵃ BC; 1 Kgs 22:51).
He acceded to the throne in the "seventeenth year of Jehoshaphat king of Judah" (1 Kgs 22:51). Jehoshaphat's "seventeenth year" does not include Jehoshaphat's entire reign but is counting from the beginning of his sole reign.

Evaluation – extremely wicked king (1 Kgs 22:52-53)

Active prophets
Elijah (2 Kgs 1:3-18)

Historical sources – Chronicles of the Kings of Israel (2 Kgs 1:18)

Ahaziah succeeded Israel's most wicked King Ahab and became the next monarch. The name *Ahaziah* is formed by combining the Hebrew words אָחַז (*'āḥaz*: to grasp, to take hold) and יָה (*yāh*: contracted form of the name of Jehovah). Together it means "the LORD has grasped." As the name signifies, God has taken a hold of Ahaziah on numerous occasions. But Ahaziah refused to listen to God's warnings and thus died only two years into his reign.

1. Ahaziah walked in the sinful ways of his parents.

Ahaziah knew all too well how his father Ahab had died a wretched death because he had committed idolatry and lived in defiance against God. Nevertheless, Ahaziah did not abandon the unbelieving ways of his parents; he followed in their footsteps by worshiping Baal and committing all kinds of sins (1 Kgs 22:52-53). First Kings 22:53 states, "So he served Baal and worshiped him and provoked the LORD God of Israel to anger, according to all that his father had done."

The word *worship*, which appears in 1 Kings 22:53, is שָׁחָה (*šāḥâ*) in Hebrew[48] and it means "to bow down," "to worship," or "to make obeisance." This verb appears in the hithpael form, indicating that Ahaziah voluntarily and proactively worshiped idols. Therefore, Ahaziah received the judgment of God not only because of his parents' influence, but also because of the sins that he committed on his own.

2. Ahaziah allied with Jehoshaphat to build ships.

King Ahaziah allied with the pious King Jehoshaphat to build ships at Ezion-geber in the Gulf of Aqaba to send to Tarshish. However, God had Eliezer son of Dodavahu of Mareshah prophesy to King Jehoshaphat, saying, "Because you have allied yourself with Ahaziah, the LORD has destroyed your works" (2 Chr 20:36-37). What was amazing was that the ships were broken and could not go to Tarshish as soon as God's prophecy was declared. The word *destroyed* here is פָּרַץ (*pāraṣ*) in Hebrew and means "to break down," "to destroy," or "to burst out." The ships were broken at the moment God uttered His prophecy. We must surely remember that no matter how great a ship we may build in our lives using our own money and power, it will be destroyed in an instant when God speaks.

God forbid Jehoshaphat from having an alliance with Ahaziah because Ahaziah was an extremely wicked person. Second Chronicles 20:35 states, "After this Jehoshaphat king of Judah allied himself with Ahaziah king of Israel. He acted wickedly in so doing." In this verse, the word *allied* in Hebrew is חָבַר (*ḥābar*), meaning "to unite," "to join," and "to bind." Since the hithpael form of the verb is used here, it indicates that Jehoshaphat voluntarily and proactively allied himself with Ahaziah. It is absolutely improper for devout people of God to proactively seek out alliances with those who commit wicked deeds.

3. Ahaziah fell through the lattice in his upper chamber and became ill.

Ahaziah experienced two major troubles in his life. Diplomatically, Moab revolted against Ahaziah. Personally, he fell through the lattice in his upper chamber in Samaria and became ill (2 Kgs 1:1-2). The "lattice"[49] was designed to prevent people from falling (Ref Deut 22:8). Ironically, Ahaziah fell through the lattice and became severely ill. When such a critical problem of life and death proportions occurs, Ahaziah should have known that it was a disciplinary intervention from God. Rather than inquiring of God regarding this illness, he sent messengers to inquire of Baal-zebub the god of Ekron (2 Kgs 1:2). The name *Baal-zebub* (בַעַל זְבוּב) means "lord of flies." In the New Testament, this was one of the exemplar names that was used to signify the devil (Matt 10:25; 12:24).

Infuriated by this, God sent the prophet Elijah to rebuke Ahaziah, saying, "Is it because there is no God in Israel that you are going to inquire of Baal-zebub, the god of Ekron?" Then He solemnly declared judgment by saying, "You shall not come down from the bed where you have gone up, but you shall surely die" (2 Kgs 1:3-4). Even upon hearing this message, Ahaziah was still stubborn and sent 50 soldiers to capture Elijah (2 Kgs 1:9). Even though God wanted to take a hold of Ahaziah, he continued to act in a defiant manner that rejected God's loving hand.

God sent fire from heaven and consumed the soldiers sent by Ahaziah. Undeterred, Ahaziah sent 50 more soldiers, and God once again consumed the soldiers sent by Ahaziah. He sent a group of 50 soldiers for the third time (2 Kgs 1:10-13). Fortunately, the captain of the third group of 50 humbly bowed down before Elijah and begged him, thus preserving his own life (2 Kgs 1:13-14).

The fire sent from heaven by God was a sure sign testifying of the following facts: that God of Israel exists, that Elijah was a true man of God, and that the Word of God spoken through the mouth of God's messenger is the true Word that will certainly be fulfilled.

When the third group of 50 soldiers came, Elijah heard the command of God saying, "Go down with him; do not be afraid of him" (2 Kgs 1:15). Therefore, he went down with them and stood before King Ahaziah. There, Elijah declared to him, "you shall not come down from the bed where you have gone up, but shall surely die" (2 Kgs 1:16).

God wanted to reach out to Ahaziah through his illness. However, he did not repent but continued to act in a defiant manner before God. Therefore, Ahaziah died at an early age without bearing a son—only two years after taking the throne (2 Kgs 1:17). Since Ahaziah died without a male heir, his brother Jehoram (Ahab's son, 2 Kgs 3:1) became king in his place.

The life of Ahaziah teaches us that a life that continues to dismiss God's warnings and acts defiantly toward Him will end in a most wretched way.

9. Joram (Jehoram) / Ἰωραμ / יוֹרָם (יְהוֹרָם)

The Lord is praised, the Lord is exalted

– The fourth king of the fourth dynasty of the northern kingdom of Israel, ninth king overall (2 Kgs 1:17; 3:1-9:29; 2 Chr 22:1-9)

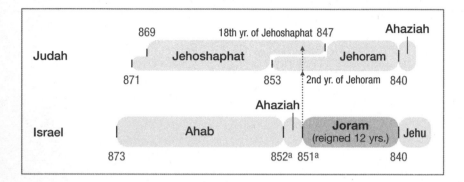

Background
Father: Ahab (2 Kgs 3:1; 2 Chr 22:5)
When elder brother Ahaziah died without a son, the younger brother Joram became king (2 Kgs 1:17).

Duration of reign
Reigned for 12 years (851a–840 BC; 2 Kgs 3:1).
He acceded to the throne in "the eighteenth year of Jehoshaphat king of Judah" (2 Kgs 3:1) and "the second year of Jehoram" (2 Kgs 1:17). Jehoshaphat's "eighteenth year" does not include Jehoshaphat's entire reign but is counting from the beginning of his sole reign (869 BC) and Jehoram's "second year" is based on the time he began his joint reign with Jehoshaphat.

Evaluation – wicked king (2 Kgs 3:2-3)
Joram "did evil in the sight of the LORD, though not like his father and his mother; for he put away the sacred pillar of Baal which his father had made. Nevertheless, he clung to the sins of Jeroboam the son of Nebat, which he made Israel sin; he did not depart from them."

Active prophets
Elijah, Elisha (1 Kgs 19:16-2 Kgs 13:21)
In the case of Elisha, he was active until the reign of Joash the twelfth king of the northern kingdom of Israel.

Historical sources – there is no record of Joram in the historical chronicles.

Joram is King Ahab's son who succeeded his brother King Ahaziah to become the next monarch. The name *Joram* is an abbreviated form of the name *Jehoram*. The name *Jehoram* is יְהוֹרָם (*yěhôrām*) in Hebrew, which is formed by combining the Hebrew words יְהוָה (*yhwh*: Jehovah) and רוּם (*rûm*: to be high, exalted). Therefore, יְהוֹרָם (*yěhôrām*) means, "the LORD is exalted," "the LORD is praised."

1. Joram became king in 851 BC, the year of Ahaziah's death.

The Bible has two seemingly conflicting accounts regarding the time of the accession of Joram (Jehoram) son of Ahab.

In 2 Kings 8:16, the Bible states that Jehoram son of Jehoshaphat became king in Judah in the fifth year of Joram, the son of King Ahab of Israel. The passage also comments, "Jehoshaphat being then the king of Judah." Here, it seems that Jehoram of the northern kingdom of Israel became king before Jehoram of the southern kingdom of Judah did.

However, in 2 Kings 1:17 the Bible states, "Jehoram became king in his place in the second year of Jehoram the son of Jehoshaphat, king of Judah." Here, in contrast to 2 Kings 8:16, it seems that Jehoram of the southern kingdom of Judah took the throne before Jehoram of the northern kingdom of Israel did.

How could this be?

Before King Jehoshaphat of Judah joined King Ahab of Israel in his battle to reclaim Ramoth-gilead, Jehoshaphat had already installed his son Jehoram as coregent. Thus, Jehoram and Jehoshaphat had been reigning jointly since 853 BC.

On the other hand, King Ahab's son Ahaziah took the throne (852 BC) when Ahab died in his battled attempt to reclaim Ramoth-gilead. Then, Ahaziah died only after two years of reign without leaving a male heir. Therefore, his brother Joram (Ahab's son) succeeds Ahaziah to become king of Israel (851 BC). By this time, Jehoram son of King Jehoshaphat of Judah had already been reigning as coregent for two years (2 Kgs 1:17).

After King Jehoshaphat returned alive from the battle at Ramoth-gilead, he reigned jointly with his son Jehoram. However, Jehoshaphat was the one who actually held the reins of Judah in his hands. When Jehoshaphat died in 847 BC, Jehoram of the southern kingdom of Judah finally became the sole regent of the kingdom. Hence in 2 Kings 8:16, when the Bible relates that Jehoram became king, it is talking about the beginning of his sole reign; and at this point in time, Jehoram of the northern kingdom of Israel had been reigning for five years.

2. Joram experienced the miracle of water on his way to punish Moab.

After King Ahab died, the King of Moab, who had been paying a tribute of 100,000 lambs and the wool of 100,000 rams, rebelled against Israel (2 Kgs 1:1; 3:4-5). In response, the first thing that Joram did was to muster all Israel (2 Kgs 3:6). Here, the word *muster* in Hebrew is פָּקַד (*pāqad*), which means "to count," "to take stock," or "to attend to." In order to punish Moab for rebelling against Israel, the first thing that Joram did was to take a count of the troops. Then, after forging an alliance with King Jehoshaphat of Judah and the king of Edom, he headed out to punish Moab (2 Kgs 3:7-12).

Seven days after the allied forces headed out to punish Moab, they arrived at the wilderness of Edom where there was no water to drink due to a severe drought. They had unexpectedly found themselves in a great crisis. They were facing absolute defeat in battle; a complete and utter annihilation awaited them. This was surely a punishment from God.

At that moment, Jehoram grumbled, displaying not even an inkling of faith, "Alas! For the LORD has called these three kings to give them into the hand of Moab" (2 Kgs 3:10). However, Jehoshaphat sought out God as he said, "Is there not a prophet of the LORD here, that we may inquire of the LORD by him?" (2 Kgs 3:11). Then, the prophet Elisha requested, "But now bring me a minstrel" (2 Kgs 3:15). When the minstrel played, the hand of the Lord came upon Elisha.

The phrase "the hand of the LORD came upon him" in 2 Kings 3:15 is וַתְּהִי עָלָיו יַד־יְהוָה (*wattĕhî 'ālāyw yd-yhwh*) in Hebrew. Here, the word *hand* (יָד, *yād*) expresses strength and power (Exod 9:3; Deut 8:17; 2 Chr 20:6; Ps 89:13, 21). Thus, it is indicating that the power of God had come upon Elisha. Likewise, the power of God came upon God's messenger when the minstrel played in obedience to Elisha's command. Then, Elisha was able to receive and deliver the Word of God (2 Kgs 3:16).

Elisha prophesied about three main things after being inspired by God. First, he commanded that they "make this valley full of trenches" (2 Kgs 3:16). Second, he said that they will not see wind nor rain, "yet that valley shall be filled with water" (2 Kgs 3:17). Third, he prophesied that the Moabites will be given into the hand of the Israelites so that they come out victorious (2 Kgs 3:18-19).

Next morning at the time of the sacrificial offering, when there was no wind or rain, water came by the way of Edom and filled the trenches in the valley just as Elisha had prophesied (2 Kgs 3:16-20). The sun shone on the water and the water seemed as red as blood to the Moabite army. They mistakenly thought that there had been an internal conflict within the Israelite camp. So, they invaded the Israelites with their guard down. The Israelites caught them off guard and attacked them; the Moabites were greatly slaughtered that day (2 Kgs 3:21-27).

The entire course of events transpired through God's miraculous intervention. God used both climate and geographic conditions providentially to bring victory for the Israelites, His people.

3. Joram tore his clothes in fear when Naaman, the captain of the Aramean army, came to him.

Naaman, the captain of the Aramean army, listened to the words of the servant girl who had been taken captive from Israel and took the letter written by the King of Aram to Israel in order to cure his leprosy. King Joram received the letter from the King of Aram saying, "And now as this letter comes to you, behold, I have sent Naaman my servant to you, that you may cure him of his leprosy" (2 Kgs 5:6). As he read this letter, Joram tore his clothes and said, "Am I God, to kill and to make alive, that this man is sending *word* to me to cure a man of his leprosy?" Joram was worried that this was a plot by the King of Aram to create a pretext for attacking Israel (2 Kgs 5:7).

When Elisha heard about this, he rebuked the king for tearing his clothes. Elisha also said that if Joram sends Naaman to Elisha, then he will come to know that there is a prophet in Israel (2 Kgs 5:8). This message is critically pointing out the attitude of faith that King Joram should have taken. This was also an implicit retort saying, "The work of God continues in Israel even now through the prophets, so why are you so afraid?"

Naaman, the captain of the Aramean army, was coming from a distant land simply based on hearsay. King Joram had directly experienced the miracles performed by Elisha on many occasions; nevertheless, he did not seek God or the man of God in times of crises. This revealed the wicked and unbelieving attitude of Joram, who disregarded and betrayed God's grace.

Naaman, the Aramean who had come a long distance, confessed, "Behold now, I know that there is no God in all the earth, but in Israel; so please take a present from your servant now" (2 Kgs 5:15). However, Joram, who had this great treasure in the man of God and prayer right by him at his disposal, proved himself to be foolish by tearing his clothes. He did this because he was fearful of what was immediately before his eyes, the possibility of an invasion by Aram. Naaman was cured of his leprosy by obeying the words of the prophet Elisha to dip his body in the Jordan seven times (2 Kgs 5:14).

4. Joram witnessed God blinding and opening the eyes of the Aramean soldiers during their first attack.

Wars continued on between Aram and Israel. However, Aram always lost because the prophet Elisha had foreknowledge of the plans of the King of Aram; thus, Israel was able to prepare for it beforehand (2 Kgs 6:8-13). No matter how great an army may be, it cannot overcome a devout man of God who communicates with the Almighty. Hence, the King of Aram mobilized a great army to besiege Dothan, where the prophet Elisha was dwelling.

God heard the prayers of the prophet Elisha and blinded all the Aramean soldiers in an instant. Since they could not see anything, they were led by Elisha from Dothan to the city of Samaria, which was 19 km away. Then, God opened their eyes once again, and they realized that they were in the middle of Samaria (2 Kgs 6:18-20). King Joram of Israel heeded the orders of Elisha and returned the Aramean troops well-fed (2 Kgs 6:21-23). Despite having had experienced such miraculous events, Joram neither fully believed nor trusted in the power of God to live a life that exalts God.

5. Joram witnessed the Aramean army suddenly leaving everything behind and fleeing on their second attack.

After the Aramean troops were treated to a generous feast by Israel, there was peace for some time. But the Aramean army broke that peace and attacked the northern kingdom of Israel again. The Arameans besieged Samaria and there was a great famine in Israel. Second Kings 6:25 states,

"Behold, they [Arameans] besieged it, until a donkey's head was sold for eighty *shekels* of silver, and a fourth of a kab of dove's dung for five *shekels* of silver."

Originally, donkeys are deemed unclean animals, and thus are not to be eaten (Lev 11:4). One shekel of silver is equal to four days worth of wages for a common laborer. Therefore, the fact that a donkey's head was sold for eighty shekels of silver shows how severe the shortage of food was in Samaria. Moreover, "dove's dung" is translated as "seed pods" in the NIV. Thus, it is signifying some type of beans or lentils that are shaped like dove's dung. The fact that a fourth of a kab (quarter of a cab: NIV) was sold for five shekels of silver also reveals how severe the famine was.[50] "Dove's dung" symbolizes the most unpleasant and wretched food.

The famine was so excruciating within the city of Samaria that women were eating their own babies and then quarreled with each other saying, "Give your son that we may eat him" (2 Kgs 6:28-29). King Joram tore his clothes and he had on sackcloth underneath his clothes next to his skin (2 Kgs 6:30). These things happened just as it was prophesied in Deuteronomy 28:53-57. Because King Joram and all of Israel did not trust in God, they were destroyed amidst hunger, thirst, nakedness, and complete deprivation (Deut 28:47-48; Ref Lev 26:26-29; Ezek 5:10; Lam 2:20; 4:10; Isa 9:20).

However, King Joram was enraged and put the blame on Elisha the man of God for all the horrors suffered by the people and sent his servant to cut off Elisha's head (2 Kgs 6:31). Joram believed that they were suffering the horrors because Elisha had not killed the Aramean soldiers when he had a chance but let them go free during their first invasion.

In the end, Joram not only sent men to kill Elisha, but he also followed behind them. Elisha was sitting at home, but he already knew that men were coming to take his life and also that Joram was following on their heels. Elisha remarked regarding Joram, "Do you see how this son of a murderer has sent to take away my head?" (2 Kgs 6:32). Then, he said, "Tomorrow about this time a measure of fine flour will be *sold* for a shekel, and two measures of barley for a shekel, in the gate of Samaria," thus declaring that the food shortage will be resolved (2 Kgs 7:1).

At that time one of King Joram's royal officers said doubtingly, "Behold, if the LORD should make windows in heaven, could this thing be?" Then, the prophet Elisha prophesied about the officer's death by saying, "Behold, you will see it with your own eyes, but you will not eat of it" (2 Kgs 7:2).

Because of the great famine, four lepers were sitting at the entrance of the gate. They could not enter into the city for they were lepers (Lev 13:45-46; Num 12:10, 15). Since there was no food inside the city anyway, the four lepers decided that they would rather surrender to the Aramean army. They had determined that dying of hunger was no better than dying at the hands of the Aramean soldiers.

When the lepers arose at twilight and went down to the camp of the Arameans, there was no one there (2 Kgs 7:5). It was because God had caused the Aramean army to hear sounds of chariots, horses and a great army when the four lepers rose up and walked down to their camp. When the Aramean troops heard the sound, they thought that the king of Israel had hired the Hittites and the Egyptians to attack them (2 Kgs 7:6). Therefore, the Aramean soldiers were stricken with fear, and they arose and fled in the twilight, leaving behind their tents, horses, and donkeys (2 Kgs 7:7).

They left in such a hurry that they left their tents, horses, donkeys, gold, silver, clothes and food behind (2 Kgs 7:7-8, 10). This happened because God, in His sovereign providence, put great fear into the hearts of the Aramean soldiers.

When the four lepers arrived at the camp of the Arameans, they were busy hiding the silver, gold, and clothes. But they later realized that what they were doing was not good, so they went to the king's house to deliver the good news (2 Kgs 7:8-15). The four lepers brought the joy of salvation to the city of Samaria, which was suffering from a severe famine. Today, we must also bring the joyous news of salvation and prosperity that comes through Jesus Christ to all the people who are suffering from a spiritual famine.

After hearing the news of salvation, the people went out to the camp of the Arameans and plundered it. Therefore, the Word of God was fulfilled as fine flour was sold for a shekel and two measures of barley for a shekel. However, the officer, who did not believe in Elisha's prophecy that the food shortage will be resolved by this time the next day, died while guarding the gate of the city; he was trampled by the people who were running out to gather food for themselves (2 Kgs 7:17-20).

Elisha's prophecy, which was to be fulfilled "tomorrow about this time . . ." (2 Kgs 7:1), was very hard to believe at the time. However, his prophecy was absolutely right on the mark.

2 Kings 7:16 ". . . according to the word of the LORD."

2 Kings 7:17 "he died just as the man of God had said"

2 Kings 7:20 "And that is exactly what happened to him" (NIV)

The Word of God cannot be broken (John 10:35). God is faithful for He keeps whatever He has promised (Matt 5:18; 24:34-35; Isa 55:11; Num 23:19).

One thing to be noted about the time of Joram's reign is that the people of the northern kingdom of Israel were suffering from poverty, hunger, and the hardships of life. It was a time when the number of those who were hungry and naked was increasing and the cries of the poor and the dejected were ringing throughout the heavens. It was to an extent when one of the sons of the prophets had died, his wife was about to lose her two sons into slavery because she was unable to pay off their debt (2 Kgs 4:1-7). However, there is no record whatsoever of Joram rescuing his people from their hunger.

In his latter years, Joram allied with his nephew Ahaziah king of Judah (Athaliah's son) and fought against Hazael king of Aram at Ramoth-gilead. There, he was wounded in battle and returned to Jezreel (2 Kgs 8:28-29). Later, Joram was struck and killed by the arrow shot by Jehu the leader of the revolt. Then, his body was thrown into Naboth's field (2 Kgs 9:23-26). This happened according to the word of prophecy given to King Ahab by the prophet Elijah (1 Kgs 21:24). Joram's life shows us clearly that those who do not exalt God and those who blame and try to kill the man of God will end their lives in a most tragic and miserable way.

10. Jehu / Ιου / יֵהוּא

He is the Lord, the Lord is He

— The first king of the fifth dynasty of the northern kingdom of Israel, tenth king overall (2 Kgs 9:1-10:36; 2 Chr 22:5-7)

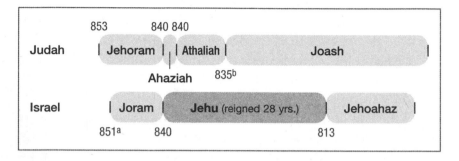

Background
Father: Nimshi (2 Kgs 3:1; 2 Chr 22:5)
The Bible also lists Jehu as Nimshi's grandson and son of Jehoshaphat (2 Kgs 9:2, 14). Jehu had escorted the king since the days of Ahab (2 Kgs 9:25).

Duration of reign
Reigned for 28 years (840–813 BC; 2 Kgs 10:36).
He acceded to the throne in the same year as Ahaziah king of the southern kingdom of Judah (840 BC; 2 Kgs 9:29).

Evaluation – wicked king
Jehu destroyed the sacred pillars of Baal and the house of Baal. He also destroyed the house of Ahab. Therefore, he was told in 2 Kgs 10:30, "Because you have done well in executing what is right in My eyes, and have done to the house of Ahab according to all that was in My heart, your sons of the fourth generation shall sit on the throne of Israel."
However, Jehu did not depart from the sins of Jeroboam which he made Israel sin—the sin of worshiping the golden calves at Bethel and Dan. He did not keep the law of God wholeheartedly (2 Kgs 10:28-31).

Active prophets
Elisha (1 Kgs 19:16; 2 Kgs 13:21)

Historical sources – Chronicles of the Kings of Israel (2 Kgs 10:34)

Although Jehu served the king since the days of Ahab, he killed King Joram and cut off the Omride Dynasty, thereby becoming the first king of a new dynasty. Before Jehu became king, God had Elisha call one of the sons of the prophets to go to Jehu and anoint him as the new king of the northern kingdom of Israel (2 Kgs 9:1-13). This was a fulfillment of the prophetic word spoken earlier by Elijah the prophet (1 Kgs 19:16).

The name *Jehu* (יֵהוּא) is a combination of the Hebrew words יְהֹוָה (*yhwh*) and הוּא (*hû'*). יְהֹוָה means Jehovah and הוּא means "he" or "she." Therefore, the name *Jehu* means "He is the LORD" or "the LORD is He." Jehu obeyed God's command and wiped out the house of Ahab. By doing this he revealed that the Lord is the One who fulfills what He has spoken; he also revealed that the One who judges in regard to sin is the Lord.

1. Jehu completely destroyed the house of Ahab.

When King Joram was injured during his battle against King Hazael of Aram at Ramoth-gilead, he returned to Jezreel to receive treatment. At that time, Jehu was guarding Ramoth-gilead. That is when Jehu received the word of prophecy from the messenger sent by Elisha that he would become king. He was anointed at that point and also received the command to destroy the house of Ahab (2 Kgs 9:6-10).

Jehu gave strict orders to keep the fact that he was anointed as king of Israel a secret. Then, he advanced toward Jezreel, killed Joram (Jehoram), and became king. Jehu remembered how the prophet Elijah had proclaimed the prophecy about the destruction of the house of Ahab (1 Kgs 21:17-26). Thus, he completely destroyed the house of Ahab according to the Word of God.

The following is a list of the people who belonged to the house of Ahab and were destroyed by Jehu.

(1) Joram, the ninth king of the northern kingdom of Israel (2 Kgs 9:21-26)

Joram was killed when he was pierced through the heart by the arrow that Jehu shot. His body was thrown into the field of Naboth the Jezreelite.

(2) Jezebel, the wife of King Ahab (2 Kgs 9:30-37)

Jezebel was thrown down from the king's house by the palace officials, and her blood splattered on the walls and the horses. Then, Jehu trampled on the gruesome body of Jezebel. Afterwards, Jehu finished eating, and then came to bury the body of Jezebel; however, the dogs had already eaten the body of Jezebel so that only her skull, feet and palms of her hands were found. This took place in accordance with the words of 1 Kings 21:23, which said, "Of Jezebel also has the LORD spoken, saying, 'The dogs will eat Jezebel in the district of Jezreel.'"

Jezebel also shows us the conclusion of the lives of idol-worshipers in the end times (Rev 2:20-23). Jezebel's wretched death gives solemn warning about the end of idolaters' lives (Ref Rev 20:12-14).

(3) Ahab's seventy sons, all his great men, his acquaintances, his priests and all who belonged to his house (2 Kgs 10:1-11)

Jehu sent letters to the rulers of Israel and confirmed their loyalty to him. Then, he sent a second letter ordering that they cut off the heads of Ahab's 70 sons. The rulers took the 70 princes and slaughtered them. Then, they put their heads in baskets and sent them to Jehu. Jehu put the heads in two heaps and put them at the entrance of the gate until the next morning (2 Kgs 10:7-8).

Jehu not only killed Ahab's 70 sons but he also killed all who belonged to Ahab including "all his great men and his acquaintances and his priests," so that none remained of the house of Ahab (2 Kgs 10:11). This took place in accordance with the prophecy of Elijah which stated, "Behold, I will bring evil upon you, and will utterly sweep you away, and will cut off from Ahab every male, both bond and free in Israel" (1 Kgs 21:21). Therefore, Jehu declared in 2 Kings 10:10, "Know then that there shall fall to the earth nothing of the word of the LORD, which the LORD spoke concerning the house of Ahab, for the LORD has done what He spoke through His servant Elijah."

(4) Ahaziah king of the southern kingdom of Judah (2 Kgs 9:27; 2 Chr 22:7-9), his 42 relatives and the princes of Judah (2 Kgs 10:12-14; 2 Chr 22:8)

Ahaziah had come to Jezreel to visit the injured King Joram. That is when Jehu struck down Ahaziah at the ascent of Gur but Ahaziah fled to Megiddo and died there (2 Kgs 9:27; 2 Chr 22:6-9). Then, Jehu killed all 42 relatives of Ahaziah who were on their way to Samaria to greet the members of the house of Ahab (2 Kgs 10:12-14). He killed them because they all belonged to Ahab. Second Chronicles 22:8 specifically mentions that "the princes of Judah and the sons of Ahaziah's brothers ministering to Ahaziah" were slain.

(5) Worshipers of Baal (2 Kgs 10:18-27)

Jehu gathered all the Baal worshipers at the house of Baal by saying that he also serves Baal, and he slaughtered all of them there. Jehu destroyed the sacred pillars of Baal and broke down the house of Baal and made it a latrine (2 Kgs 10:27). Seeing that 1 Kings 18:19 mentions 450 prophets (leaders) of Baal, it is most likely that the number of Baal worshipers (lay congregation) reached into the thousands. Indeed, Jehu's violent and bloody purge was so brutal and thorough that its equal would be hard to find in history.

Such a religious reformation in the northern kingdom of Israel was unique and singular in its attempt. It can truly be said that it resulted from Jehu's zeal for God (2 Kgs 10:16). Therefore, God said to Jehu, "Your sons of the fourth generation shall sit on the throne of Israel" (2 Kgs 10:30). In accordance with this Word, Jehu's dynasty continued on for four generations after Jehu with Jehoahaz, Joash, Jeroboam II and Zechariah.

Jehu's annihilation of the house of Ahab was indeed a fulfillment of the Word of God.

> **2 Kings 9:26**. . . says the Lord . . . says the Lord. Now then, take and cast him into the property, according to the word of the Lord.
>
> **2 Kings 9:36** And he [Jehu] said, "This is the word of the LORD, which He spoke by His servant Elijah the Tishbite . . . .
>
> **2 Kings 10:10** . . . the Lord has done what He spoke through His servant Elijah.
>
> **2 Kings 10:17** . . . according to the word of the Lord which He spoke to Elijah.

2. Jehu was unable to depart from the sinful ways of Jeroboam.

Jehu's religious reformation was very thorough in regard to Baal worship; however, it was not very thorough in regard to other religious aspects. He was commended by God for being faithful in his work in regard to the house of Ahab; however, he was rebuked for various other works that he had done.

First, Jehu did not depart from the sin of worshiping the golden calf at Bethel and Dan (2 Kgs 10:29).

Second, Jehu did not wholeheartedly keep the law of the Lord (2 Kgs 10:31).

Third, Jehu did not depart from the sins of Jeroboam which he made Israel commit (2 Kgs 10:31).

Therefore, the Bible says that the Lord began to cut off portions of Israel and Hazael defeated them throughout Israel "in those days" when Jehu did not depart from his sins (2 Kgs 10:32). Here, the expression *cut off* is קָצָה (*qāṣâ*) in Hebrew which means, "to trim off" or "to cut off." In the piel (intensive) form of the verb, it means that God will certainly cut off territory to reduce it. As a result, Jehu lost the most fertile land in the east to Hazael (2 Kgs 10:33).

Until now, Jehu had been used as a tool of judgment for the house of Ahab; however, now he had become the one being judged by God. Although a person may have been used as a tool of judgment by God, He will judge that person without exception if he departs from the Word of God and continues on the path of iniquity. The One who judged the house of Ahab and the One who judged Jehu are the one and the same, the Lord God Himself. Therefore, Jehu's dynasty received God's stern judgment as its last king Zechariah was murdered by Shallum (2 Kgs 15:10) and concluded its reign after four generations of Jehu's descendants.

11. Jehoahaz (Joahaz) / Ἰωαχαζ / יְהוֹאָחָז
The Lord has grasped, the Lord sustains

– The second king of the fifth dynasty of the northern kingdom of Israel, eleventh king overall (2 Kgs 13:1-9; 2 Chr 25:25)

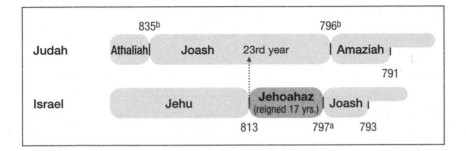

Background
Father: Jehu (2 Kgs 10:35; 13:1)

Duration of reign
Reigned for 17 years (813-797ª BC; 2 Kgs 13:1).
He acceded to the throne in the "twenty-third year of Joash" (2 Kgs 13:1) of the southern kingdom of Judah

Evaluation – wicked king (2 Kgs 13:2)
Jehoahaz did evil in the sight of the LORD and did not depart from the sins of Jeroboam son of Nebat which he made Israel sin.

Active prophets
Elisha (1 Kgs 19:16-2 Kgs 13:21)

Historical sources – Chronicles of the Kings of Israel (2 Kgs 13:8)

Jehoahaz succeeded Jehu to become the second king in Jehu's dynasty. The name *Jehoahaz* in Hebrew is יְהוֹאָחָז (yĕhōw'āḥāz) and in the Septuagint translation of 2 Chronicles 25:25, his name is listed as Ἰωαχαζ (*Iōachaz*: Joahaz). The Hebrew form of the name is a combination of the words יְהוָה (yhwh) and אָחַז ('āḥaz). יְהוָה means "Jehovah" and אָחַז means "to grasp," "to take hold," or "to take possession." Therefore, the name *Jehoahaz* means "the LORD has grasped." Second Kings 13:4 states, "Then Jehoahaz entreated the favor of the LORD, and the LORD listened to him; for He saw the oppression of Israel, how the king of Aram oppressed them." This passage reveals how God upheld Jehoahaz even in His wrath.

1. Jehoahaz did evil in the sight of the Lord and received God's wrath.

Jehoahaz did evil in the sight of the Lord by following in the sins of Jeroboam; he did not depart from those sins. Therefore, the anger of the Lord was kindled against Israel (2 Kgs 13:3). Here, the word *anger* in Hebrew is אַף ('ap), which means "nostril." The significance of the word "nostril" was magnified and expanded to mean "anger" because when someone gets angry, their nostrils flare up and their breathing gets rough. The word *kindle* is חָרָה (ḥārâ) in Hebrew and it means "to burn," "to be kindled," and "to get angry." Therefore, to say that God's anger was kindled actually means that He could no longer tolerate the sin and so His burning anger had exploded.

As such, the burning anger of God was displayed when He gave the northern kingdom of Israel over to King Hazael and his son Ben-hadad of Aram. Second Kings 13:3 states, "So the anger of the LORD was kindled against Israel, and He gave them continually into the hand of Hazael king of Aram, and into the hand of Ben-hadad the son of Hazael." In this passage, the word *continually* is כָּל־הַיָּמִים (kol-hayyāmîm), which literally means "all their days." In other words, during all the days of Jehoahaz's reign, God's anger allowed the oppression of the Arameans to continue. This state of affairs is described in 2 Kings 13:4 as "how the king of Aram oppressed them."

God used the neighboring kingdoms of Israel as a tool to judge Israel. Outwardly, these Gentile nations were attacking Israel, but inwardly this was God's providential way of disciplining Israel.

2. Jehoahaz entreated to God and was delivered from the hand of Aram.

Jehoahaz finally sought the help of God after trying so hard to endure the continuing oppression of the Arameans (2 Kgs 13:4). God heeded the prayers of Jehoahaz and sent a deliverer to Israel and allowed them to escape the hand of the Arameans (2 Kgs 13:5). Historically speaking, the deliverer mentioned here is Adad-nirari III (810–783 BC). He attacked

Damascus, the capital of Aram, in 803 BC and debilitated the kingdom of Aram. The northern kingdom of Israel was able to take this opportunity and escape the hand of the Arameans.

There are some implications in God rescuing Jehoahaz. First, it shows us that God will take a hold of us, even those who had been going down the way of sin, as long as we repent at that moment and earnestly seek His help. Second, God upheld Jehoahaz in order to fulfill the promise that He made to Jehu (the promise that up to 4 generations of Jehu's descendants will reign over Israel). Third, God protected the northern kingdom of Israel from Aram because of the covenant that he had established with Abraham, Isaac, and Jacob. Second Kings 13:23 states, "But the LORD was gracious to them and had compassion on them and turned to them because of His covenant with Abraham, Isaac, and Jacob, and would not destroy them or cast them from His presence until now."

The northern kingdom of Israel continued to serve idols and followed after the way of Jeroboam, thus provoking the Lord to anger. Despite all this, God protected Israel so that they would not be destroyed because He promised Abraham, "I will give to you and to your descendants after you, the land of your sojournings, all the land of Canaan, for an everlasting possession; and I will be their God." Even in His anger, God was compassionate and loving, and He helped Israel who did not deserve His mercy; this was entirely because of the covenant that He made with Abraham, Isaac and Jacob.

Such compassion notwithstanding, Jehoahaz forsook God's love and started to sin again. Second Kings 13:6 states, "Nevertheless they did not turn away from the sins of the house of Jeroboam, with which he made Israel sin, but walked in them; and the Asherah also remained standing in Samaria."

This was a true display of ingratitude, and thus, God once again sent the king of Aram to judge Jehoahaz. Second Kings 13:7 states, "For he left to Jehoahaz of the army not more than fifty horsemen and ten chariots and 10,000 footmen, for the king of Aram had destroyed them and made them like the dust at threshing."[51] The king of Aram had left behind only the minimum number of troops needed for domestic peace-keeping and destroyed the rest of the armed forces.

When Jehoahaz sought out God for relief from the oppression of the Arameans, God came and delivered him. However, when Jehoahaz forsook the loving hands of God and served the Asherah, God brought upon Jehoahaz even greater hardships than before. Therefore, if those who have repented before God sin again, then they will receive even greater sufferings (2 Pet 2:20).

We must not lose sight of the grace when God takes interest in us and upholds us. We must take a hold of that grace and cherish it until the end (2 Cor 6:1).

The Lord is strong, given by the Lord

– The third king of the fifth dynasty of the northern kingdom of Israel, twelfth king overall (2 Kgs 13:9-25; 14:8-16; 2 Chr 25:17-25)

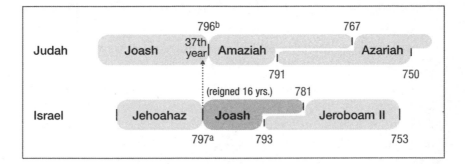

Background
Father: Jehoahaz (2 Kgs 13:9-10)

Duration of reign
Reigned for 16 years (797ᵃ–781 BC; 2 Kgs 13:10).
He acceded to the throne in the "thirty-seventh year of Joash" (2 Kgs 13:10) of the southern kingdom of Judah. From the time of Joash until their last king Hoshea, the northern kingdom of Israel used the accession year dating method just like Judah.

Evaluation – wicked king (2 Kgs 13:11)

Active prophets
Elisha (active until the time of Joash; 1 Kgs 19:16-2 Kgs 13:21)

Historical sources – Chronicles of the Kings of Israel (2 Kgs 13:12)

Joash succeeded Jehoahaz to take the throne as the king of the northern kingdom of Israel. The name *Joash* is יוֹאָשׁ (yô'āš) in Hebrew, but sometimes it is written as יְהוֹאָשׁ (yĕhô'āš) as well (2 Kgs 13:10). יְהוֹאָשׁ (yĕhô'āš) is formed by combining יְהוָה (yhwh: Jehovah) and אֵשׁ ('ēš: fire). Therefore, the name literally means "fiery Jehovah," and thus the meaning "the LORD is strong" was derived from there.

1. Joash visited Elisha, who was on his deathbed.

When Elisha was sick unto death, King Joash went down to Elisha and wept over him saying, "My father, my father, the chariots of Israel and its horsemen!" (2 Kgs 13:14). These tears that he shed were tears shed in concern for the future of the nation for they were about to lose Elisha who was their national defense.

Elisha told Joash to take up a bow and arrows. Then, he laid his hands on the hands of Joash and told him to open the windows toward the east and shoot the arrows. This was a symbolic act prophesying that the northern kingdom of Israel will strike and defeat Aram through the mighty power of God (2 Kgs 13:15-17).

The prophet Elisha said in 2 Kings 13:17, "The LORD's arrow of victory, even the arrow of victory over Aram; for you will defeat the Arameans at Aphek until you have destroyed *them*." Here, the phrase "until you have destroyed them" is עַד־כַּלֵּה ('ad-kallē) in Hebrew. This means "until it is completed," or "until it is finished." כַּלֵּה (kallē) is the piel infinitive absolute form of the verb כָּלָה (kālâ: to finish, to complete) thus signifying absolute victory. Therefore, God is stating that He will help them until they have completely defeated the Arameans in battle.

Furthermore, Elisha had the king take the arrows and strike the ground with them. The king should have continued to strike the ground until Elisha told him to stop. However, he stopped after three strikes. After seeing this, the prophet Elisha was greatly angered and said, "You should have struck five or six times, then you would have struck Aram until you would have destroyed *it*. But now you shall strike Aram *only* three times" (2 Kgs 13:19).

King Joash had just heard that the arrows signify God's help which delivers Israel from the hand of the Arameans. Naturally, then, Joash should have kept on striking the ground until Elisha said to stop. However, Joash was still caught up in his fleshly thoughts and guessed that about three times would be enough.

This indicates that King Joash lacked the earnest desire for victory over his enemies which comes with an aggressive battle mentality. If Joash was filled with this thirst for victory and the desire to wipe out the Arameans, then he would have kept on striking the ground with the arrows because this act symbolized the act of striking the Arameans. That is why the word "defeat" used in 2 Kings 13:17 where the Bible says, "for you will defeat the Arameans at Aphek until you have destroyed them" is the same Hebrew word used in the expression "strike the ground" which appears in 2 Kings 13:18. That Hebrew word is נָכָה (nākâ).

God is almighty, and He has given all things to us. Therefore, God will satisfy us with His complete and perfect victory when we trust in His mighty powers and strike the ground ten, twenty, nay a hundred times (Ref Ps 81:1).

2. Joash recovered the cities that his father Jehoahaz had lost.

In 798 BC, King Hazael died, and his son Ben-hadad III became king in Aram. Joash attacked Ben-hadad III three times and recovered the cities of Israel that his father Jehoahaz had lost. Second Kings 13:25 states, "Then Jehoash the son of Jehoahaz took again from the hand of Ben-hadad the son of Hazael the cities which he had taken in war from the hand of Jehoahaz his father. Three times Joash defeated him and recovered the cities of Israel."

The expression "three times Joash defeated him . . ." indicates how accurate Elisha's prophecy truly was. In 2 Kings 13:19 Elisha had prophesied, "But now you shall strike Aram *only* three times." Therefore, Joash was able to recover the lost territories from Ben-hadad III not because of his might and power; it was entirely because the all-powerful God helped King Joash and the northern kingdom of Israel. Through this event, Joash must have experienced how powerful God truly is.

3. Joash triumphed against King Amaziah of the southern kingdom of Judah.

Amaziah of the southern kingdom of Judah did right in the sight of the LORD after he became king in 796 BC. However, after his victory in the battle against Edom, he became proud (2 Kgs 14:10; 2 Chr 25:19) to the point of serving the idols of Edom (2 Chr 25:14).

Amaziah initiated the battle by making a declaration of war against Joash of the northern kingdom of Israel (2 Kgs 14:8-11; 2 Chr 25:17-21). Then, Joash rebuked Amaziah's arrogance and retorted saying, "The thorn bush which was in Lebanon sent to the cedar which was in Lebanon, saying, 'Give your daughter to my son in marriage.' But there passed by a wild beast that was in Lebanon, and trampled the thorn bush" (2 Kgs 14:9). Here, the thorn bush of Lebanon represents King Amaziah, and the Lebanon cedar represents King Joash. Getting trampled on by wild beasts symbolizes sudden destruction. The word *trample* in Hebrew is רָמַס (*rāmas*), and it means "to trample" or "tread upon." Therefore, this word expresses how horrible King Amaziah's defeat in battle will be. In accordance with this passage, Amaziah experienced a horrendous defeat in battle and he suffered the shame of being taken as a captive. Joash of Israel reaped a great victory that day (2 Kgs 14:12-14; 2 Chr 25:22-24).

Joash captured Amaziah, and demolished about 400 cubits (approx. 200 yd.) of the wall of Jerusalem from the Gate of Ephraim to the Corner Gate. Moreover, he took all the gold, silver and utensils from the house of the Lord, and brought back to Samaria the treasures of the king's house as well as some hostages (2 Kgs 14:13-14; 2 Chr 25:23-24). This victory was given free to King Joash of Israel in order to discipline Amaziah of the southern kingdom of Judah for seeking the gods of Edom (2 Chr 25:20).

Likewise, Joash received many blessings from the Almighty God. However, 2 Kings 13:11 testifies, "He did evil in the sight of the LORD; he did not turn away from all the sins of Jeroboam the son of Nebat, with which he made Israel sin, but he walked in them." Joash's life shows us how tragic the conclusion of one's life will be if he cannot depart from the way of sin even though the Almighty God has bestowed great blessings on them.

13. Jeroboam II / Ἰεροβοαμ / יָרָבְעָם

The people prosper, the people increase

— The fourth king of the fifth dynasty of the northern kingdom of Israel, thirteenth king overall (2 Kgs 14:16-29)

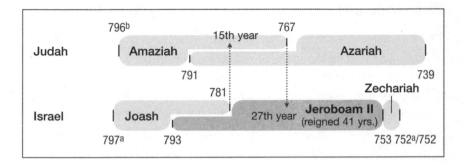

Background
Father: Joash (2 Kgs 14:23)

Duration of reign
Reigned for 41 years (793ᵃ–753 BC; 2 Kgs 14:23)
Azariah of the southern kingdom of Judah became sole regent in the "twenty-seventh year of Jeroboam II" (2 Kgs 15:1). That was the year that Azariah's father Amaziah died and it had been fifteen years since the death of Joash of the northern kingdom of Israel (2 Kgs 14:17-22; 2 Chr 25:25). That means Jeroboam II had been a coregent ruling with Joash twelve years before Joash's death. Then, in the fifteenth year of Amaziah of the southern kingdom of Judah, he took sole reign of the kingdom (2 Kgs 14:23).

Evaluation – wicked king (2 Kgs 14:24)
He did evil in the sight of the Lord and did not depart from the sins of Jeroboam son of Nebat by which he made Israel sin.

Active prophets
Hosea, Amos, Jonah (2 Kgs 14:25; Hos 1:1; Amos 1:1)

Historical sources – Chronicles of the Kings of Israel (2 Kgs 14:28)

The name *Jeroboam* (יָרָבְעָם) is formed by combining the Hebrew words רָבַב (*rābab*: to become many, increase) and עַם (*'am*: people). Therefore, the name *Jeroboam* means "the people increase and flourish." On the other hand, the name *Jeroboam* could be seen as the combination of the words רוּב (*rûb*: to strive, contend) and עַם (*'am*: people). In that case, the name *Jeroboam* means "the people will contend" or "the people will quarrel." Jeroboam II fought against and overcame many enemies so that his reign was the longest and most thriving out of all the kings of the northern kingdom of Israel.

1. Jeroboam II expanded Israel's territory to its largest.

The following was the geopolitical situation around Israel during the era of Jeroboam II: The kingdom of Aram, located in the Syrian region, had been harassing Israel. However, they were attacked by Assyria, the new rising imperial power of the region, and lost Damascus, their capital. Naturally, the Aramean army was debilitated, and Israel was able to break out from under the shadows of Aram and recovered much territory.

Second Kings 14:25 states that Jeroboam "restored the border of Israel from the entrance of Hamath as far as the Sea of the Arabah." Hamath is a city in the central part of Syria thus signifying the northernmost border of Israel. The Sea of Arabah is another name for the Dead Sea and thus signifies the southernmost border of Israel. This corresponds to the borders established during Solomon's reign which was the largest territory ever secured by Israel (2 Chr 8:4). Therefore, Jeroboam II was enjoying the height of his glory as he had restored the largest territorial outlines of Israel.

The prophet Amos, who was active during Jeroboam II's reign, also affirms that Israel had recovered the land from Hamath to the Arabah during Jeroboam II's reign by using the expression "from the entrance of Hamath to the brook of the Arabah" in Amos 6:14.

Also 2 Kings 14:28 neatly summarizes Jeroboam II's life, "Now the rest of the acts of Jeroboam and all that he did and his might, how he fought and how he recovered for Israel, Damascus and Hamath, which had belonged to Judah, are they not written in the Book of the Chronicles of the Kings of Israel?" Here, Damascus, just like Hamath, is a city that is located in Syria.

Therefore, the era of Jeroboam II was a time of prosperity since Israel had garnered much territory and much income was coming in from said territory.

2. The abundance that Jeroboam II enjoyed was entirely due to God's help.

The causes behind the prosperity during Jeroboam II's reign are as follows.

First, God saw the affliction of the Israelites.

> **2 Kings 14:26** For the Lord saw the affliction of Israel, which was very bitter; for there was neither bond nor free, nor was there any helper for Israel.

The phrase "the affliction of Israel, which was very bitter; for there was neither bond nor free" is translated in the NIV as "how bitterly everyone in Israel, whether slave or free, was suffering."

Moreover, the word *saw* in Hebrew is רָאָה (*rā'â*), and it means "to look," "examine," or "inspect." God understood the affliction that Israel was suffering and the fact that there was no one to help them. He, then, determined in His heart to save them. In the days of old, when the Israelites were suffering for 430 years in Egypt, God heard the outcry of the Israelites and took notice of them and rescued them from the oppression of the Egyptians (Exod 2:24; 3:7). If the merciful and compassionate God takes notice of our afflictions, then He will certainly deliver us from our afflictions.

Second, God remembered His covenant.

> **2 Kings 14:27** The Lord did not say that He would blot out the name of Israel from under heaven, but He saved them by the hand of Jeroboam the son of Joash.

Here, the phrase "The LORD did not say that He would blot out the name of Israel from under heaven" means that God remembered the covenant that He had made with the ancestors of Israel. Second Kings 13:23 also states, "But the LORD was gracious to them and had compassion on them and turned to them because of His covenant with Abraham, Isaac, and Jacob, and would not destroy them or cast them from His presence until now."

At that time, the northern kingdom of Israel was abounding in sin, and yet God saw their afflictions, remembered His past covenants, and determined to save them. Moreover, God struck down Aram because Elisha had prophesied that Israel would strike down Aram (2 Kgs 13:17-19). Therefore, the golden age of Jeroboam II came about because of the sovereign grace and love of God who is faithful to His covenants.

The prophet Hosea received the Word from God during the reign of Jeroboam II. Hosea 1:1 states, "The word of the LORD which came to Hosea the son of Beeri . . . during the days of Jeroboam the son of Joash, king of Israel." The prophet Amos was also active during Jeroboam II's time. Amos 1:1 states, "The words of Amos, who was among the sheepherders from Tekoa, which he envisioned in visions concerning Israel . . . in the days of Jeroboam son of Joash, king of Israel, two years before the earthquake." The prophet Jonah was also active during the days of Jeroboam II (2 Kgs 14:25).

As such, God granted the greatest amount of blessings and sent the most number of prophets during the time of Jeroboam II. Thus, He upheld the northern kingdom of Israel, which was in decline, and continued to give them chances to repent.

The prophet Hosea was active contemporaneously with the prophet Amos, who was active "in the days of Jeroboam son of Joash" (Hos 1:1; Amos 1:1). Through the words of Hosea we get a sense of the gravity of the depravity that was prevalent during the days of Jeroboam II in the northern kingdom of Israel. Outwardly, it seemed as though there was peace and prosperity during the days of Jeroboam II, but in actuality, it was only a small minority of the upper echelons who enjoyed those things.

The poor and the needy have been oppressed and exploited by the leaders who sell "the poor for a pair of shoes" and "pant after the dust of the earth on the head of the poor." Thus, the groaning of the poor has reached the heavens (Amos 2:6-7; 4:1; 8:4). The leadership had lived a life of extravagance and debauchery financed by the bribes they had received. They built winter houses, summer houses (vacation houses), houses of ivory, and great houses (Amos 3:15). They also reclined and sprawled on their beds of ivory, put on expensive fragrances and feasted with expensive wines (Amos 6:4-6).

Violence and oppression was rampant, anyone speaking with integrity was abhorred so that the prudent persons could not open their mouths (Amos 5:10, 13). Justice and righteousness had disappeared; only lawlessness flourished (Amos 5:7). There was no faithfulness, kindness or knowledge of God; there was only swearing, deception, murder, stealing and adultery. They were violent so that bloodshed follows bloodshed (slaughters and massacres abounded). The land and all who lived in it mourned along with the beasts of the field and the birds of the sky and even the fish of the sea disappear because of the depravity of the northern kingdom of Israel (Hos 4:1-3).

Moreover, they were sexually promiscuous so that a man and his son habitually frequented the same young woman (Amos 2:7). God rebuked the people because they were so intent on departing from God and walking in their adulterous ways (Hos 4:12-14).

The people transgressed and committed injustice to earn wealth and with that they offered sacrifices to God; therefore, how can God accept their offerings (Amos 4:4-5; Ref Hos 6:6; 8:13)? Finally, God lamented and told the people that they should not seek Bethel or Gilgal or even Beersheba to offer sacrifices (Amos 5:5).

During the 41-year reign of Jeroboam II, there was not a single place that was unscathed, but every place and person within the northern kingdom of Israel was corrupt, rotted and severely diseased.

Although God had been very patient and bestowed upon him boundless love and compassion, Jeroboam II continued as ever to walk down the path of treachery (2 Kgs 14:24). As a result, he died, and Jehu's dynasty was completely destroyed during the reign of his son Zechariah. In a word, the prosperity that was enjoyed during the days of Jeroboam II was in fact a "false prosperity." Outwardly, they had reached the height of prosperity in the history of the northern kingdom of Israel; but inwardly, debauchery, extravagance, injustice and obscenity prevailed at every street corner. Even today, we must meditate deeply upon our own souls to see if we are filled with concealed sins in our hearts while outwardly exuding a "false prosperity" for others to see. Are we not merely settling and finding satisfaction with this "false prosperity"?

14. Zechariah / Ζαχαρίας / זְכַרְיָה

The Lord remembered, the Lord remembers

— The fifth king of the fifth dynasty of the northern kingdom of Israel, fourteenth king overall (2 Kgs 14:29; 15:8-12)

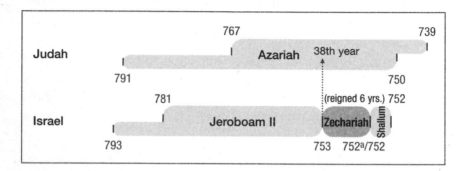

Background
Father: Jeroboam II (2 Kgs 14:29)

Duration of reign
Reigned for 6 months (753–752ª BC; 2 Kgs 15:8)
Zechariah acceded to the throne in the "thirty-eighth year of Azariah" (2 Kgs 15:8) of the southern kingdom of Judah. This was the year 753 BC when Jeroboam II ended his reign. The year 753 BC was reached by harmonizing the synchronism for the end of Amaziah's reign (also the beginning of the sole reign of Azariah of Judah) which was in the "twenty-seventh year of Jeroboam" (2 Kgs 15:1) and the synchronism for Zechariah which was the "thirty-eighth year of Azariah" (2 Kgs 15:8). With 753 BC as the starting point, we are enabled to calculate many of the regnal years for both Judah and Israel such as 791 BC, the accession year of Azariah as well as 793 BC when Jeroboam II acceded to the throne.

Evaluation – wicked king (2 Kgs 15:9)
The reason for the destruction of the Jehu Dynasty was that they did not depart from the sins of Jeroboam.

Active prophets – Hosea

Historical sources – Book of the Chronicles of the Kings of Israel (2 Kgs 15:11)

Zechariah succeeded Jeroboam II to become king of the northern kingdom of Israel. Zechariah was the last king in the Jehu Dynasty. The name *Zechariah* is זְכַרְיָה (*zĕkaryâ*) in Hebrew. This word is formed by combining the words זָכַר (*zākar*) and יָה (*yāh*). The word זָכַר (*zākar*) means "to remember" or "to bring to mind," and the word יָה (*yāh*) is the abbreviated form of "Jehovah" (Yahweh). Therefore, the name *Zechariah* means "the LORD remembered."

Due to limitations in the human memory, human beings can be mistaken about things at times or not even remember altogether. However, God is never mistaken and He never forgets.

1. Zechariah had the shortest reign in the house of Jehu.

After becoming king of the northern kingdom of Israel, Zechariah reigned for a very short duration of six months (2 Kgs 15:8). Zechariah was murdered by Shallum, son of Jabesh.

> **2 Kings 15:10** Then Shallum the son of Jabesh conspired against him and struck him before the people and killed him, and reigned in his place.

In the above passage, the word *struck* is נָכָה (*nākâ*) in Hebrew and means "to beat" or "to strike." However, since the hiphil (causative) form of the verb is used in the passage, it comes to mean "to slaughter" or "to kill." Also, the word *killed*, which appears later in the sentence is מוּת (*mût*) in Hebrew and means "to die." However, since the hiphil (causative) form of the verb is used here, it means "to slaughter." Therefore, when it says that Shallum "struck . . . and killed him," it means that he violently and brutally slaughtered Zechariah to death. Moreover, the Bible tells us that Zechariah was killed "before the people." This expression signifies that Zechariah was responsible for the affairs of the kingdom and was tragically killed in public. Seeing that Zechariah was publicly executed even though he had a very short reign goes to show us that he did not reign properly. When Shallum tried to kill Zechariah in front of the people, there was no one who tried to help Zechariah. King Zechariah's death was an obvious consequence of his own sins and incompetent administration.

2. The destruction of Zechariah occurred according to God's prophecy.

God unequivocally stated to Jehu, the man who destroyed the house of Ahab, ". . . your sons of the fourth generation shall sit on the throne of Israel" (2 Kgs 10:30). In accordance with this prophecy, the Jehu

Dynasty collapsed four generations of kings after Jehu himself, including Jehoahaz, Joash, Jeroboam II and Zechariah.

Second Kings 15:12 also states, "This is the word of the LORD which He spoke to Jehu, saying, 'Your sons to the fourth generation shall sit on the throne of Israel.' And so it was." God remembered this word of prophecy just as He had spoken it to Jehu and fulfilled it in the days of Zechariah. The Word of God will be accomplished without fail (Matt 5:18; 24:34-35; Josh 23:14). Even the prophecies of the Bible, which have not yet been fulfilled, will come to fruition exactly as God has stated.

Zechariah became king by succeeding Jeroboam II—in whose days the northern kingdom of Israel enjoyed the heights of her golden age. Wealth and power were guaranteed for him. However, he was murdered brutally because he committed evil in the sight of the Lord and did not depart from the sins of Jeroboam the son of Nebat (2 Kgs 15:9-10).

Our God is a God who remembers the covenant (Gen 9:15-16; Exod 2:24; 6:5; Ps 105:8; 106:45; 111:5; Jer 14:21; Ezek 16:60; Luke 1:72) and also all of our actions (Ezek 20:43). God knows our sitting down and rising up; He knows our thoughts, our paths and our lying down. He is intimately acquainted with all of our ways (Ps 139:2-4).

Although God told Jehu that his dynasty would end after four generations, Jehu's end would not have been so tragic if he had acted righteously before God. Today, we must also live a life that is remembered for its holiness and piety before our God who remembers all things.

The Jehu Dynasty had the longest reign out of the nine dynasties of the northern kingdom of Israel (89 years). Therefore, the fall of the Jehu Dynasty is tantamount to a forewarning of the fall of the northern kingdom of Israel. After the death of Zechariah and about 30 years after the disappearance of the Jehu Dynasty, the northern kingdom of Israel was completely smitten from history in 722 BC.

15. Shallum / Σελλουμ / שַׁלּוּם
Reward (retribution), peace

— The first king of the sixth dynasty of the northern kingdom of Israel, fifteenth king overall (2 Kgs 15:10-15)

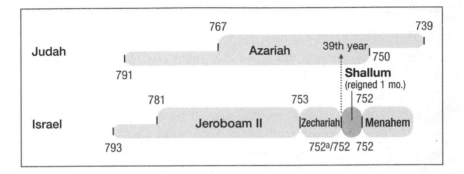

Background
Father: Jabesh (2 Kgs 15:13)

Duration of reign
Reigned for one month (752 BC; 2 Kgs 15:13)
After Jeroboam II ended his 41-year reign (2 Kgs 14:29), Zechariah acceded to the throne in "thirty-eighth year" of Azariah of the southern kingdom of Judah and reigned for six months (2 Kgs 15:8). Then, Shallum conspired against Zechariah and killed him in front of the people (2 Kgs 15:10). Thus, Shallum became king in the "thirty-ninth year" of Azariah of the southern kingdom of Judah and reigned for one month (2 Kgs 15:13). Considering that the regnal year of Judah's King Azariah changed from the 38th year to the 39th year somewhere in between the six-month reign of Zechariah and the one-month reign of Shallum, we may conjecture that the one-month reign of Shallum falls within the year 752 BC.

Evaluation – wicked king
There is no written evaluation regarding Shallum. However, his only accomplishment that is mentioned is "his conspiracy" (2 Kgs 15:15), therefore he is classified as a wicked king.

Active prophets – Hosea

Historical sources – Book of the Chronicles of the Kings of Israel (2 Kgs 15:15)

Shallum became king of the northern kingdom of Israel by killing Zechariah and bringing down the Jehu Dyansty. The name *Shallum*

(שָׁלוֹם) in Hebrew means "reward" and "peace." This word was derived from the word שָׁלַם (šālam), which means "to be complete," "peace," and "to repay." Shallum did not live a peaceful life as the meaning of his name indicates. Rather, he lived a life full of greed and murder; and regrettably, he was recompensed for his sins.

1. Shallum did not leave behind any accomplishments.

For all the kings of the northern kingdom of Israel, their accounts are concluded with the phrases "rest of the acts" followed closely by "and all that he did" (Ref 1 Kgs 15:31; 16:5, 14; 2 Kgs 10:34; 13:8, 12; 14:28; 15:21, 26, 31). However, in Shallum's case, the expression "and his conspiracy" appears in place of the phrase "and all that he did" (2 Kgs 15:15). This indicates that "his conspiracy" was the only thing that Shallum achieved as king. Thus, the scriptural account is emphasizing how Shallum was overcome by his lust for power so that he conspired and killed Zechariah. In this context, the word *conspire* meant to "scheme the overthrow of the king in order to usurp power."

Our God is the God who rewards our works. In Revelation 22:12, He declares, "Behold, I am coming quickly, and My reward is with Me, to render to every man according to what he has done." When we work for the will of God, a due reward will certainly follow (1 Cor 3:8; 2 Cor 5:10; Heb 11:6; Rev 2:23).

2. Shallum received rightful retribution for his murder.

Shallum, who overthrew Zechariah, was tragically killed by Menahem as well (2 Kgs 15:14). When Shallum killed Zechariah, the Bible explains that he "struck him before the people and killed him, and reigned in his place" (2 Kgs 15:10). As was explained above, to "strike and kill" someone is a very brutal mode of murder. Likewise, when Menahem killed Shallum, he also "struck Shallum . . . and killed him and became king in his place" (2 Kgs 15:14). In other words, Shallum was precisely recompensed for his murder of Zechariah.

God repays us according to our works. Job 34:11 states, "For He pays a man according to his work, and makes him find it according to his way." Matthew 16:27 also says, "For the Son of Man is going to come in the glory of His Father with His angels, and WILL THEN REPAY EVERY MAN AC-

CORDING TO HIS DEEDS." Hosea 4:9 remarks, "And it will be, like people, like priest; so I will punish them for their ways and repay them for their deeds." A person will always reap what he/she sows (Gal 6:7). Someone who sows murder is bound to reap murder. Jesus also commanded, "Put your sword back into its place; for all those who take up the sword shall perish by the sword" (Matt 26:52). Christians are to be peacemakers who reap the fruits of righteousness which was sown in peace (Jas 3:18).

16. Menahem / Μαναημ / מְנַחֵם
The consoler, the comforter

— The first king of the seventh dynasty of the northern kingdom of Israel, sixteenth king overall (2 Kgs 15:14-22)

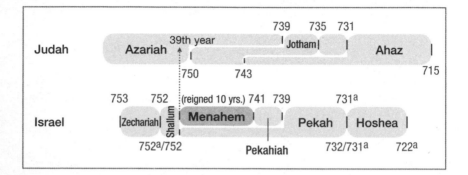

Background
Father: Gadi (2 Kgs 15:14)

Duration of reign
Menahem became king in 752 BC. He, then, reigned for ten years (751–741 BC; 2 Kgs 15:17) after the resistance by Tiphsah (2 Kgs 15:14-17).

He acceded to the throne in the "thirty-ninth year of Azariah" of the southern kingdom of Judah (2 Kgs 15:17). Subsequent to Shallum's one-month reign, Menahem became king in the "thirty ninth year of Azariah" King of Judah. Therefore, it seems that his accession year was 752 BC.

Evaluation – wicked king (2 Kgs 15:18)

Active prophets – Hosea

Historical sources – Book of the Chronicles of the Kings of Israel (2 Kgs 15:21)

Only one month after Shallum felled the Jehu dynasty to usurp the throne, Menahem killed Shallum and became king in his place. As more murders and bloody coups continued, the northern kingdom of Israel rushed headlong toward destruction.

The name *Menahem* is מְנַחֵם (*měnaḥēm*) in Hebrew which means "comforter." The name is derived from the Hebrew word נָחַם (*nāḥam*), which means "to be sorry" or "to console oneself." However, Menahem did not become a person that delivers the consolation of God to the world. Through brutal murders and a tyrannical reign, he became an oppressive king who was bemoaned by the people.

✳ Organized for the first time in history

1. In the Bible, there are two accounts of Menahem becoming king.

Menahem was a military leader who had control over Tirzah.[52] He came up to Samaria, the capital of the northern kingdom of Israel and "struck and killed" Shallum to become king (2 Kgs 15:14). Then, he came up from Tirzah and attacked Tiphsah. Second Kings 15:16 states, "Then Menahem struck Tiphsah and all who were in it and its borders from Tirzah . . . ." In this passage, the word *struck* (יַכֶּה: *yakke*) is in the hiphil (causative) imperfect form of the verb נָכָה (*nākâ*), which means "to be hit" or "to be struck down." In the hiphil form, it means "to strike," "to hit," "to beat," or "to strike dead." Therefore, the term signifies that Menahem struck Tiphsah, its people, and the surrounding areas; and his strikes were intense and continued for a time.

Such a persistent attack notwithstanding, the people of Tiphsah resisted tenaciously and did not open the gates of the city. Finally, after Menahem conquered Tiphsah, 2 Kings 15:16 relates that he "ripped up all its women who were with child." In that phrase, the word *ripped* is בָּקַע (*bāqaʿ*) in Hebrew and means "to split" or "to break open." Moreover, the passage employs the piel (intensive) form of the verb as well as the word כָּל (*kāl*: "all"). The passage conveys the fact that Menahem slashed to pieces every pregnant woman in that region. It is graphically depicting the extreme brutality of Menahem. Even as he was brutally ruling over the people, Menahem did not realize his wrongdoing. He had indeed been seared in his own conscience (1 Tim 4:2). Truly, the words of Proverbs 11:17, which states, "The merciful man does himself good, but the cruel man does himself harm," have been fulfilled.

Interestingly, the Bible records Menahem's accession twice, once in 2 Kings 15:14 and once more in 2 Kings 15:17. After Menahem became king (2 Kgs 15:14), there was resistance in Tiphsah by the people who did not acknowledge Menahem's usurpation of the throne (2 Kgs 15:16). Therefore, after he killed Shallum in 752 BC to become king, Menahem continued to fight the people of the region of Tiphsah. Afterwards, he completely conquered Tiphsah and its surrounding areas, thenceforth reigning officially for ten years from 751 BC to 741 BC (2 Kgs 15:17).

2. Menahem did not rely on God but on the king of Assyria.

In 2 Kings 15:19 the Bible states, "Pul, king of Assyria, came against the land, and Menahem gave Pul a thousand talents of silver so that his hand might be with him to strengthen the kingdom under his rule." Pul, the king of Assyria, mentioned in this passage is also known as Tigleth-pileser, whose name means "my trust is in the son of Esharra." He was a most powerful king who had elevated Assyria to the position of the greatest power in the world at the time (reigned over Assyria from 745–727 BC).

Menahem gave 1,000 talents of silver so that he may rely on the power of the Assyrian king to help him maintain his hold on the throne. One talent of silver is 6,000 drachmas; thus, 1,000 talents of silver equals 6 million drachmas. One drachma is one day's wage for a laborer. If one day's wage is estimated to $50, then 1,000 talents of silver would be equivalent to an enormous amount of $300 million!

In order to procure such an astounding amount of money, Menahem exacted fifty shekels of silver from all the mighty men of wealth. One shekel of silver is equivalent to four days' wages for a laborer; thus, fifty shekels of silver would amount to 200 days' wages for a laborer. Again, estimating one day's wage at $50, fifty shekels of silver would equal to $10,000. It was indeed a large sum of money. In order to maintain his hold on power, Menahem plundered his subjects for exorbitant amounts of money and put a backbreaking burden upon the people.

Menahem did not use his life to console the people. Instead, he became a fake shepherd (a hired hand: John 10:12) and a vicious tyrant. He did evil in the sight of the Lord and never departed from the sins of Jeroboam. Second Kings 15:18 states, "He did evil in the sight of the Lord; he did not depart all his days from the sins of Jeroboam the son of Nebat, which he made Israel sin." There is one thing different about this evaluation of Menahem from all the other evaluations of the Israelite kings; the words "all his days" have been added. This signifies that Menahem's evil was much more serious than all the other kings of the northern kingdom of Israel and that his wickedness continued throughout his ten-year royal tenure.

Ultimately, Menahem relied on Assyria to maintain his power; but ironically, the northern kingdom of Israel would incur the tragedy of being destroyed by Assyria. Although the prophet Hosea gave multiple warnings that reliance on Assyria will bring about tragic consequences (Hos 5:13; 7:11; 10:6), Menahem did not heed this warning. Therefore, Menahem's life teaches us the grave lesson that relying on worldly powers brings about tragic consequences (Ps 146:3-5).

17. Pekahiah / Φακεΐας / פְּקַחְיָה

The Lord has opened, the Lord has opened the eyes

— The second king of the seventh dynasty of the northern kingdom of Israel, seventeenth king overall (2 Kgs 15:14-22)

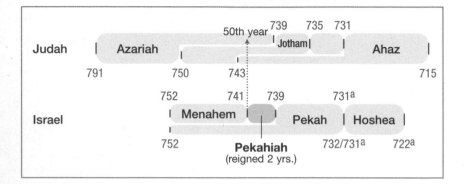

Background
Father: Menahem (2 Kgs 15:23)

Duration of reign
Reigned for two years (741–739 BC; 2 Kgs 15:23)
After Menahem ended his ten-year reign, Pekahiah took the throne in the 50th year of Azariah of the southern kingdom of Judah (2 Kgs 15:23).

Evaluation – wicked king (2 Kgs 15:24)

Active prophets – Hosea, Isaiah (Isa 1:1)

Historical sources – Book of the Chronicles of the Kings of Israel (2 Kgs 15:26)

Pekahiah, being the son of Menahem, succeeded his father to become the king of Israel. The name Pekahiah is פְּקַחְיָה (pĕqaḥyâ) in Hebrew, which is formed by combining the words פָּקַח (pāqaḥ) and יָה (yāh). The word פָּקַח means "to open (the eyes)" and יָה is the abbreviated form of Jehovah (YHWH). Therefore, the name *Pekahiah* means "the LORD has opened," "the LORD has opened the eyes."

1. Pekahiah built a citadel of the king's house.

Pekahiah built a "citadel of the king's house" (2 Kgs 15:25, ESV). A "citadel of the king's house" is a high fortress or a watchtower built to protect the king's house. Pekahiah built a place of refuge called the "citadel of the king's house" to protect his own life because he knew all too well about the continuing revolts and coup d'etats in the history of the northern kingdom of Israel. Moreover, he placed servants around him to protect himself. Their names were Argob and Arieh. But ironically, Pekahiah died with his servants who were supposed to protect him inside the "citadel of the king's house" that he built. Second Kings 15:25 states, "Then Pekah son of Remaliah, his officer, conspired against him and struck him in Samaria, in the castle of the king's house with Argob and Arieh; and with him were fifty men of the Gileadites, and he killed him and became king in his place." This incident shows us that man-made refuge and citadels are useless. God is our true refuge and fortress. Unless God guards the city, the watchman keeps awake in vain (Ps 127:1).

During the plague of the sixth seal in the book of Revelation, the king of the earth, the great men, the commanders, the rich, the strong, every slave and free man "hid themselves in the caves and among the rocks of the mountains; and they said to the mountains and to the rocks, 'Fall on us and hide us from the presence of Him who sits on the throne, and from the wrath of the Lamb'" (Rev 6:15-16). However, the mountains and the rocks can never become a place of refuge for men. No matter what the situation may be, blessed are those who take refuge in God (Ps 34:8). Take God as your eternal place of refuge and place your absolute trust and faith in Him alone (Ps 46:1; 61:3; 73:28; 91:2; 144:2). In the dead end alleyways of life, one may throw away or give up everything else, but one must never give up on God. If you seek out God, you will be rescued no matter what kind of crisis you may be in (Ps 7:1; 31:1; 143:9).

2. Pekahiah relied on man.

It was Pekah who killed Pekahiah. Second Kings 15:25 records that the killer was "Pekah son of Remaliah, his officer." Here, the word *officer* is שָׁלִישׁ (*šālîš*) in Hebrew. Originally, this word meant "third." However, when it is used in a military setting, it means "the third man in the war chariot" or "a high military officer serving as adjutant [military assistant] to the king."[53] We can surmise, from the fact that Pekah was able to enter into the citadel of the king's house, that Pekahiah had placed his trust in Pekah. As it turns out, Pekahiah was killed by his most trusted subordinate officer. Pekahiah must have installed Pekah as his military aide because Pekahiah, in his personal judgment, thought that Pekah would always protect him and never betray him.

The judgment that only takes into account the visible reality of things is uncertain. It is temporary and limited. Unless God opens our eyes, we will always be deceived. We must never judge with our imperfect eyes or rely on imperfect human beings (Isa 2:22). We must always entrust all of our judgments to God. In other words, we must wholly rely on God alone.

18. Pekah / Φακεε / פֶּקַח

Opened eyes, an opening

– The first king of the eighth dynasty of the northern kingdom of Israel, eighteenth king overall (2 Kgs 15:25-31; 2 Chr 28:5-8)

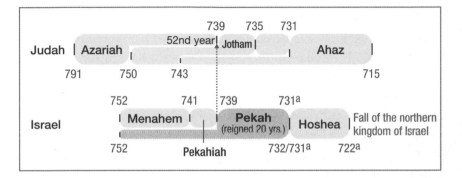

Background
Father: Remaliah (2 Kgs 15:25, 27)
Commander in Pekahiah's armed forces (2 Kgs 15:25)

Duration of reign
Reigned for 20 years (752–732/731a BC; 2 Kgs 15:27)
Pekah took sole control of the throne in the "fifty-second year of Azariah" (2 Kgs 15:27) king of Judah, and reigned for 8 years. The regnal data in 2 Kings 15:27 which states that Pekah reigned for 20 years may not seem correct. During Pekah's 20-year reign, the first part of the reign overlapped with the reign of his predecessor Pekahiah as well as with the reign of Pekahiah's predecessor Menahem. However, during those overlapping years, Pekah was a regional leader in his home region of Gilead. Therefore, Pekah only started to rule over all of the northern kingdom of Israel since 739 BC, which is after the reign of Pekahiah.

Evaluation – wicked king (2 Kgs 15:28)

Active prophets – Oded
Oded criticized the atrocities committed by the Israelites during the war between Israel and the southern kingdom of Judah. He then urged Israel to return the prisoners of Judah (2 Chr 28:8-11).

Historical sources – Book of the Chronicles of the Kings of Israel (2 Kgs 15:31)

Pekah was a trusted servant of Pekahiah. However, he killed Pekahiah in the citadel of the king's house and became the king of Israel. The name

Pekah is פֶּקַח (peqaḥ) in Hebrew, which is derived from the word פָּקַח (pāqaḥ). The word פָּקַח means "to open (the eyes)." Therefore, the name *Pekah* means "opened eyes" or "an opening."

1. Pekah's "eyes were open" toward the lust for power.

Pekah was one of the top servants who had access to Pekahiah's citadel of the king's house (2 Kgs 15:25). He was most likely much loved and trusted by Pekahiah. However, once Pekah had his "eyes opened"—a phrase meaning "to take an interest in"—toward his lust for power, he mobilized 50 Gileadites, who followed him, to brutally kill Pekahiah and became king of Israel (2 Kgs 15:25).

Later on, just as he had killed Pekahiah, Pekah was also brutally murdered by Hoshea (2 Kgs 15:30). Ultimately, Pekah reaped exactly the lust for power, which he had sown, and was killed tragically. He had indeed conceived lust and brought forth death (Jas 1:15).

2. Pekah's "eyes were opened" toward international politics.

During the days of Pekah's reign, Assyria was experiencing rapid growth. Pekah, king of Israel, allied with Rezin king of Aram to institute an anti-Assyrian policy in order to oppose Assyria (Isa 7:1-9). Pekah, in his own way, had his eyes opened to international politics and skillfully developed a diplomatic policy.

On the other hand, Ahaz king of Judah had adopted a pro-Assyrian policy. Therefore, Pekah king of Israel allied with Rezin king of Aram to attack the southern kingdom of Judah. Although he was not able to topple Jerusalem (2 Kgs 16:5), Pekah was able to kill 120,000 Judahite soldiers and brought back 200,000 prisoners including women to Samaria. For this, he was rebuked by the prophet Oded, who told him to "return the captives." At that time, "some of the heads of the sons of Ephraim"—Azariah, Berechiah, Jehizkiah, Amasa—arose against those coming back from battle and forced them to return the captives from the southern kingdom of Judah (2 Chr 28:6-15).

Superficially, it may seem as though Pekah's diplomatic policies had succeeded. However, King Ahaz of Judah, who was attacked by Pekah and Rezin, turned pale from astonishment and requested reinforcement troops from Assyria. Tiglath-pileser king of Assyria gladly obliged and attacked the northern kingdom of Israel. As a result, Israel lost all of the northern regions around Galilee and many of the people were taken captives (2 Kgs 15:29). Pekah received from Assyria exactly as he had dealt out toward Judah. At this, the prophet Isaiah rebuked him for his pride and delivered the message that the sins of Samaria will be judged (Isa 9:9-17).

Ultimately, King Pekah did not have his eyes opened toward God until the end. He continued his prideful ways and did not repent until the end when he was killed by his servant Hoshea.

19. Hoshea / Ωσηε / הוֹשֵׁעַ
Lord, save us

– The first king of the ninth dynasty of the northern kingdom of Israel, nineteenth king overall (2 Kgs 15:30; 17:1-41; 18:9-12)

Background
Father: Elah (2 Kgs 15:30)

Duration of reign
Reigned for nine years (731a–722a BC; 2 Kgs 17:1)
He acceded to the throne in the "twelfth year of Ahaz" king of Judah (2 Kgs 17:1), the "twentieth year of Jotham," king of Judah (731a BC, 2 Kgs 15:30).

Evaluation – wicked king (2 Kgs 17:2)
Although Hoshea was wicked, he lived a better life than the previous kings of the northern kingdom of Israel.

Active prophets – Hosea (Hos 1:1)
It is known that the prophet Hosea was alive at the time of the destruction of the northern kingdom of Israel in 722 BC.

Historical sources
Since Hoshea was the last king of Israel and since the kingdom was destroyed, there is no record of him in the book of the chronicles of the kings.

King Hoshea is the last king of the northern kingdom of Israel. He forged an alliance with Egypt and adopted an anti-Assyrian policy. As a result, the great misfortune of having the entire kingdom destroyed came upon Hoshea.

The name *Hoshea* הוֹשֵׁעַ (*hôšēaʻ*) means "salvation" and is derived from the Hebrew word יָשַׁע (*yāšaʻ*), which means "to save," "to deliver," and "to rescue." Contrary to the meaning of his name, King Hoshea was not able to save Israel from its crisis. Rather, it is quite unfortunate because he became the king who drove the nation into destruction, thereby completely uprooting any hope of salvation.

1. Hoshea betrayed Assyria and relied on Egypt.

Hoshea, originally part of the pro-Assyrian faction, killed Pekah, an anti-Assyrian king, in order to become king in his place (2 Kgs 15:30). At that time, King Tiglath-pileser III of Assyria helped Hoshea to become king.

In official documents discovered in Assyria, it is recorded that Tiglath-pileser intervened in the domestic affairs of Israel and killed Pekah to install Hoshea as their king. This signifies that Tiglath-pileser was actually controlling Hoshea to start a revolt and then he placed Hoshea on the throne.[54] When such historical factors are taken into consideration (2 Kgs 15:29-30), Hoshea's accession year is conjectured to be in 731 BC, one year after 732 BC when Assyria intervened in Israel's domestic affairs.[55]

After the death of Tiglath-pileser, Hoshea betrayed Assyria and adopted a pro-Egyptian policy. In response, King Shalmaneser V (son of Tiglath-pileser III) attacked Hoshea, forced his submission, and made him pay a tribute (2 Kgs 17:3). However, Hoshea again took on an anti-Assyrian policy after a while, trusting Egypt to support him (2 Kgs 17:4; Hos 7:11). But this was a misjudgment on Hoshea's part. At the time, King So of Egypt, whom Hoshea requested for help, was powerless (2 Kgs 17:4); and Egypt was mired in utter chaos as several lesser kings had taken their places throughout Egypt.

The king of Assyria took note of Hoshea's betrayal and attacked the northern kingdom of Israel. Indeed, it was a great diplomatic blunder to rely on Egypt rather than Assyria; however, it was an even greater mistake to rely on worldly powers rather than God (Hos 7:10). Our salvation comes only from God (Ps 3:8; Isa 12:2). It is a most foolish thing to seek help from man who is not even worthy to be counted (Isa 2:22). Man does not have any power to give help to others. The eternally living, Almighty God—He is the only one who can be our help and our trustworthy refuge (Ps 146:3-10).

2. Israel, the northern kingdom, perished completely during Hoshea's reign.

The Assyrian king who attacked Israel during the days of Hoshea was Shalmaneser V, the son of Tiglath-pileser III. He attacked the entire region of the northern kingdom of Israel and completely laid it to waste. In regard to this, 2 Kings 17:5 comments, "the king of Assyria invaded the whole land."

Shalmaneser V (727–722 BC) besieged Samaria in the seventh year of King Hoshea. Israel resisted fiercely for three years at Samaria. During the besiege of Samaria, Shalmaneser V died suddenly. However, Sargon II (722–705 BC) succeeded him and subsequently in the ninth year of King Hoshea, he completely destroyed the city of Samaria (2 Kgs 17:5-6; 18:9-12).

Samaria, the capital of the northern kingdom of Israel, was surrounded by a very strong and sturdy exterior wall. The palace and the fortress were surrounded by a natural rock barrier and also an inner wall. However, even such a sturdy fortress ultimately fell at the persistent attack of the Assyrians. Since the northern kingdom of Israel was filled with sin and did not repent, God did not save them anymore but gave them over to the hands of the Assyrians.

Assyria destroyed Israel and took many captives. According to the inscription of Sargon II, the son of Shalmaneser V, Assyria took 27,290 captives back to their land at this time.

Assyria forced foreign nations to migrate to northern Israel to live there. Therefore, in northern Israel, faith in Jehovah God was mixed with the faiths of various "regional gods" that were brought by these foreigners, so that true faith in God had gradually faded (2 Kgs 17:24-41). The faith and identity of the northern kingdom of Israel completely disappeared from the arena of history.

The only consequence from betraying our true Savior God and His covenants is utter destruction (Lev 26:14-20). Since he relied not on God but on the nations of this world, Hoshea was unable to save the nation that was rushing toward destruction. Instead, he found himself in the unfortunate position of being the king that led the nation to its complete destruction. Ultimately, the northern kingdom of Israel, which lasted for 208 years (930–722 BC) through nine dynasties and 19 kings, was destroyed by Assyria in 722 BC and disappeared completely into history.

Conclusion:

The administration of redemptive history as revealed in the history of Israel, the northern kingdom

After the death of Solomon, the kingdom was divided into two. Jeroboam took the ten tribes of the north to establish the northern kingdom of Israel. God said to Jeroboam in 1 Kings 11:38, "if you listen to all that I command you and walk in My ways, and do what is right in My sight by observing My statutes and My commandments, as My servant David did, then I will be with you and build you an enduring house as I built for David, and I will give Israel to you." This proclamation means that although the kingdom was divided into two, God has acknowledged the northern kingdom of Israel as His people based on the Davidic covenant. However, the northern kingdom of Israel, starting with its first king Jeroboam, made golden calves at Bethel and Dan, built high places, and worshiped the Baal and Asherah (1 Kgs 12:28-33).

God, through numerous prophets, gave continuous and sufficient warnings to Israel regarding her sins (2 Kgs 17:13; Jer 32:32-35). In considering the rebellions of Israel, God had reason enough to completely destroy them much earlier. Neverthless, God patiently waited for them to return to Him (Hos 5:15). As stated in 2 Kings 13:23, "But the LORD was gracious to them and had compassion on them and turned to them because of His covenant with Abraham, Isaac, and Jacob, and would not destroy them or cast them from His presence until now." God waited because of the covenants God made with their ancestors. That is why 2 Kings 14:27 says, "The LORD did not say that He would blot out the name of Israel from under heaven, but He saved them by the hand of Jeroboam the son of Joash."

God established His eternal covenant; and in order to fulfill that covenant, He continued his providential work within the history of the northern kingdom of Israel even though they were depraved and corrupt. However, this was tantamount to continuously pouring clean and fresh living waters into a polluted sewer. Nevertheless, the northern kingdom of Israel actually profaned God's patient compassion by walking after the way of Jeroboam. They continued to walk down the path of opposition and rebellion toward God so that eventually, they were destroyed by Assyria (2 Kgs 17:22-23).

The reasons for the inevitable destruction of the northern kingdom of Israel are as follows:

First, they burned incense and worshiped idols at every high place.

Second Kings 17:11-12 state, "and there they burned incense on all the high places as the nations did which the LORD had carried away to exile before them; and they did evil things provoking the LORD. They served idols, concerning which the LORD had said to them, 'You shall not do this thing.'"

In 2 Kings 17:9 the Bible says, "The sons of Israel did things secretly which were not right against the LORD their God. Moreover, they built for themselves high places in all their towns, from watchtower to fortified city." Here, a "watchtower" signifies a secluded place where there are not many people around. On the other hand, the "fortified city" signifies a place with a lot of people. Thus, the phrase "from watchtower to fortified city" is used in an idiomatic sense to mean the entire country. In other words, the entire northern kingdom of Israel, without exception, was filled with high places of idolatry. Therefore, the high place became the breeding ground of idolatry, the base from which all evils were produced. It was the very place which "provoked God to anger" (2 Chr 28:24-25; 2 Kgs 23:19; Ref Jer 7:31; 19:5; Ezek 16:16).

Second, they did not heed the prophets nor their warnings.

Second Kings 17:13-14 state, "Yet the LORD warned Israel and Judah through all His prophets and every seer, saying, 'Turn from your evil ways and keep My commandments, My statutes according to all the law which I commanded your fathers, and which I sent to you through My servants the prophets.' However, they did not listen, but stiffened their neck like their fathers, who did not believe in the LORD their God."

God never stopped sending numerous prophets to every king and gave them sufficient warnings (2 Kgs 17:13; Jer 32:32-35). This was God's gracious intent not to forsake His people; it revealed His compassionate desire to continuously protect and guide His people. However, the people of the northern kingdom of Israel got farther away from God the more the prophets called out to them. They even stoned the prophets to death (Hos 11:2; 1 Kgs 19:10, 14; Neh 9:26).

Third, they forsook the law, covenant, and the Word of God.

Second Kings 17:15 states, "They rejected His statutes and His covenant which He made with their fathers and His warnings with which He warned them." They did evil in the sight of the Lord to provoke Him to His anger (2 Kgs 17:17). In regard to the fall of Samaria and the destruction of the northern kingdom of Israel 2 Kings 18:12 remarks, "because they did not obey the voice of the LORD their God, but transgressed His covenant, even all that Moses the servant of the LORD commanded; they would neither listen nor do it."

God could no longer leave alone the heinous deeds of the Israelites, who continually broke their covenants with God and actually established new agreements with Gentile nations (Hos 12:1-2). As a result of their forsaking God's covenant, the lamp of the northern kingdom of Israel went out, and they became a pitch dark world. Darkness was prevalent throughout the 208-year history of Israel in which 19 kings from Jeroboam to Hoshea ruled. Finally, with the destruction of Israel, their lamp was completely snuffed out.

The destruction of the northern kingdom of Israel was not harsh punishment at all. It was a righteous judgment in which the justice of God burst forth (2 Kgs 17:22-23). For God had waited so long for them to repent; He called out to them saying, "Return, O Israel, to the LORD your God, for you have stumbled because of your iniquity. Take words with you and return to the LORD" (Hos 14:1-2).

Although God destroyed the northern kingdom of Israel, He did not immediately destroy Judah, who had been depraved just as much as their northern neighbor. God gave His warning through the destruction of the northern kingdom of Israel that if Judah does not repent, then the judgment of God will soon ensue (2 Kgs 17:19-20). Another opportunity for repentance had been given to the southern kingdom of Judah because of God's covenant that He had established with His faithfulness and oath. Moreover, it was also so that God's redemptive history would not be halted but proceed on through the people of Judah.

On one hand God disciplines His chosen people; but on the other, He watches over them until the end because of the covenant that He made with their ancestors. By so doing, God had continued the history of redemption without interruption. In actuality, God's mysterious and profound providence and love were poured forth through His administration of redemptive history within the history of the kings.

עמלק

מדבר צין הוא קדש

ים המלח

עמרה

עתר

מקדה

עיר כרמל

שבט

ענב

באר שבע

שבט שמעון

שבט

מדבר פארן

מדבר שור

מדבר סיני

ארץ פלשתים

גת

אשקלון

ארק גשן

פתם

רעמסס

אלכסנדרי

צען

לוח המסעות במדבר

אשר על פיהיסעו ועל פיהיחנו

כט' חרהגדגד	טו' רתמה	א' רעמסס
ל' יטבתה	טז' רמןפרץ	ב' סכת
לא' עברנה	יז' לבנה	ג' אתם
לב' עציןגבר	יח' רסה	ד' פיהחירת
לג' מדברצין	יט' קהלתה	ה' מרה
לד' הרההר	כ' הרספר	ו' אילם
לה' צלמנה	כא' חרדה	ז' ים סוף
לו' פונן	כב' מקהלת	ח' מדברסין
לז' אבת	כג' תחת	ט' דפקה
לח' דיבןגד	כד' תרח	יו' אלוש
לט' עלמןדבל'	כה' מתקה	יא' רפידם
מ' הרי עברים	כו' חשמנה	יב' מדברסיני
מא' ערבתמאב	כז' מסרות	יג' קברתהתאוה
	כח' בני יעקן	יד' חצרות

CONCLUSION

The Transmission of Faith and the Lamp of the Eternal Covenant

The genealogy of Jesus Christ is categorized into three periods (Matt 1:17). The first period consists of 14 generations from Abraham to David, the second period consists of 14 generations from David to the deportation to Babylon, and the third period consists of the 14 generations from the deportation to Babylon to Jesus Christ.

The third book in this series (i.e., The History of Redemption series), *The Unquenchable Lamp of the Covenant*, is about God's administration in redemptive history covered in the first period of Jesus Christ's genealogy. Now, this fourth book in the series, *God's Profound and Mysterious Providence*, continues to reveal God's administration in redemptive history as revealed in the second period of Jesus Christ's genealogy.

In concluding the study of God's redemptive administration in the second period, I would like to reiterate the importance of transmitting faith down to the following generations for it is a path through which the covenant of God continues. Also, I would like to reemphasize the unquenchable love of God, who does not forget His eternal covenant and the future prospect of the covenant.

1. The Transmission of Faith, a Channel for the Succession of the Covenant

The entire history of redemption continued according to God's mysterious and profound providence, in which God established and fulfilled His covenants. Satan's ceaseless attacks on God's work of providence continually tried to put an end to the lineage of faith that was to fulfill God's administration in the history of redemption. Satan's attacks were attempts to stop faith from being transmitted from one generation to the next. As we look back on the history of redemption, we can see the importance of transmitting faith, through which the covenant is passed down.

God's purpose in choosing Abraham was to fulfill His covenant with Abraham by teaching his children to obey God and do righteousness and justice.

> **Genesis 18:18-19** Since Abraham will surely become a great and mighty nation, and in him all the nations of the earth will be blessed? "For I have chosen him, so that he may command his children and his household after him to keep the way of the LORD by doing righteousness and justice, so that the LORD may bring upon Abraham what He has spoken about him."

After Abraham and Isaac, Jacob took his family of 70 into the land of Egypt. Then after 430 years of life in Egypt, the Israelites were led by Moses out of Egypt through God's work of power and authority. At Mt. Sinai, God gave them the Law through Moses and established their faith in Jehovah. Eventually after 40 years of the wilderness journey, the Israelites under the leadership of Joshua defeated the Canaanite tribes and received the Promised Land as an inheritance.

In order to remind the Israelites of the importance of transmitting the covenant, Moses commanded the Israelites, who were preparing to enter into Canaan, saying, "These words, which I am commanding you today, shall be on your heart. You shall teach them diligently to your sons and shall talk of them when you sit in your house and when you walk by the way and when you lie down and when you rise up" (Deut 6:6-7). He continues to command them regarding the transmission of faith repeatedly in Deuteronomy 4:9-10; 11:19; 32:27, 46.

However, the entire generation, who arose after Joshua and the elders of his generation had passed away, did not know the Lord nor the work which He had done for Israel (Judg 2:7-10). The sons of Israel forsook their God and did evil as they served Gentile gods (Judg 2:11). In the end, Israel entered into an age of darkness during the time of the judges when every man did what was right in his own eyes (Judg 17:6; 21:25). It was a result of not transmitting faith correctly as God had entreated them in the wilderness.

Later, there came a revival of faith through Samuel and David, and David's kingdom was established. Although David had committed adultery with Bathsheba, Uriah's wife, he repented thoroughly with tears of a broken heart and set Israel upon the rock of the covenant through his faith that obeyed and depended on God. On this foundation that David had set up, Israel enjoyed its golden days.

Nevertheless, even David's faith was not transmitted down to the kings of the following generations. Solomon, who succeeded David, married Gentile women and brought in abominable idols to the kingdom. As a result, Israel was divided into the northern kingdom of Israel and the southern kingdom of Judah (1 Kgs 11:1-13).

The northern kingdom followed the corrupt tradition of faith that Jeroboam had set up and was completely destroyed by Assyria in 722 BC. The southern kingdom of Judah did not learn from watching the northern kingdom and eventually forsook the covenant, persecuted and killed prophets, and rebelled against God. Then, the southern kingdom also was defeated and taken captive by Babylon in 586 BC.

Regarding the reason for the destruction of the southern kingdom of Judah, 2 Chronicles 36:16 explains, "But they continually mocked the messengers of God, despised His words and scoffed at His prophets, until the wrath of the LORD arose against His people, until there was no remedy." The word *remedy* means "healing" or "deliverance" and is used for the restoration of health, object, or situation. Therefore, to say that there was no remedy means that they had fallen to a point where it was difficult to re-establish. All these tragedies in history were results of letting the Law given through Moses and the way of upright faith established through David be cut off and not transmitted to the kings of the following generations.

When faith is not passed down properly, the nation will not only lose all the blessings that God had promised, but also end up in complete destruction. Despite the circumstances, God brought Judah back from Babylonian captivity in order to fulfill His promise with Abraham. By doing this, God protected the holy lineage of faith, through which Jesus would come, from being cut off. Then when the fullness of the time came, He sent the Messiah as the son of David (Gal 4:4).

Rather than receiving the Messiah, who came to His own land, as the King of all kings, the Israelites despised and persecuted the Lord of Salvation, crucifying the Lord of life and glory because of their hardened hearts (John 1:11; Acts 3:13-15; 4:10; 7:51-53; 1 Cor 2:8). This was the fearful and wretched result of the lapse in transmission of faith. They were so ignorant and irresponsible toward their descendants even to the point of saying, "His blood [the blood of Jesus Christ] shall be on us and on our children!" (Matt 27:25). Nevertheless, Jesus bore the cross and shed His precious blood to complete the work of salvation for His chosen people just as prophesied in the Bible. What a reason to give thanks!

Jesus foresaw God's judgment that would fall upon the people of Israel, who asked that the blame for the shedding of Jesus' blood be on them and their children, and the great tribulation that their descendants would receive. This great tribulation was the destruction of Jerusalem and the massacre of the Jews by the Roman general Titus in AD 70. According to the records of Josephus (AD 37–100), a Jewish historian, Roman soldiers pierced the belly of pregnant women, crushed the heads of nursing babes against rocks, and mothers with children who could not escape were killed cruelly. The tribulation was so severe and extreme that some were saying, "Blessed are the barren, and the wombs that never bore, and the breasts that never nursed" (Luke 23:29). Jerusalem was completely besieged by the Roman army that those inside the city could not come out and the food supply was cut off from the outside. The city was filled with dead bodies of children, women, and old people, but no one had the energy to bury them. The situation was so appalling; emotions and feelings were stifled so that no one would cry or lament. Hatred sprouted amongst brothers, spouses, parents and their children. Not only did they not see each other, but some parents even ate the flesh of their children. The prophecy in Deuteronomy 28:53-57 was fulfilled.

Seeing what would happen to the people of Israel, Jesus said to the women who were weeping as they followed Jesus up the hill of Golgotha, "Daughters of Jerusalem, stop weeping for Me, but weep for yourselves and for your children" (cf. Luke 13:34; 19:41-44).

> **Luke 23:27-28** And following Him was a large crowd of the people, and of women who were mourning and lamenting Him. But Jesus turning to them said, "Daughters of Jerusalem, stop weeping for Me, but weep for yourselves and for your children."

The word *weep* is κλαίετε (*klaiete*) which is in the second person, plural form, of the imperative voice of κλαίω (*klaiō*), thus meaning "cry out loud" or "weep and lament in a loud voice."

The command to "weep for yourselves" was a message for them to wail over their sins and repent with all their hearts in order to avoid the destruction that was to befall Jerusalem imminently. In other words, they needed to mourn and lament in repentance over their sins for they have rejected Jesus and forsook His grace, causing him to carry the predestined cross up the hill of Golgotha for the completion of salvation (John 1:11).

If those women had given their hearts to what Jesus told them and repented, teaching their children the Word of God throughout the nation, then Jerusalem would not have been destroyed 41 years later (AD 70) by Rome.

We must realize that this short message that Jesus proclaimed under the cross on His way up the hill of Golgotha is as weighty and crucial as the seven messages He gave on the cross (Matt 27:46; Luke 23:34, 43, 46; John 19:26-27, 28, 30); thus, we must engrave it deep in our hearts. The message was not only for "daughters of Jerusalem" nor was it simply about the judgment of Jerusalem. It also applies to all Christians today who believe and follow Jesus and it also applies to the great judgment of the end time.

We are called to pray sincerely for ourselves and our children before the coming of the day that is even more terrifying and wrathful than the time of Jerusalem's destruction (Rev 6:17).

Educating our children, who will lead the future, is not an easy thing to do. It requires persistence in nurturing them with God's Word along with tearful prayers like the prayers of Samuel's mother Hannah. Samuel's mother Hannah prayed sincerely for Samuel. Her tearful prayers for Samuel would enable him to rekindle the lamp of God and thereby put an end to the tragic period of Ichabod in which God's glory had departed from Israel. (1 Sam 3:3; 4:21). Likewise in the New Testament, Timothy was able to possess a pure heart, a good conscience, and a sincere faith because of his grandmother Lois and mother Eunice's nurturing and prayerful tears (2 Tim 1:5). He was the Apostle Paul's successor and true beloved son in the faith (1 Tim 1:2; 2 Tim 1:2).

Times are racing toward the end, the dusk of history. What we Christians need to do in order to fulfill God's redemptive history in times like this is to preach the Gospel with all our strength in season and out of season, so that the lost spiritual sons of Abraham can be found (Luke 19:9-10; Acts 20:22-24; 2 Tim 4:1-2).

Furthermore, we must enable the lineage of faith to continue without ceasing by teaching our children righteousness and justice. This is how we can transmit the faith in our families from generation to generation. The Bible repeatedly emphasizes the importance of transmitting faith.

> **Deut 6:6-7** These words, which I am commanding you today, shall be on your heart. You shall teach them diligently to your sons and shall talk of them when you sit in your house and when you walk by the way and when you lie down and when you rise up.

Joel 1:3 Tell your sons about it, and *let* your sons *tell* their sons, and their sons the next generation.

Psalm 78:5-8 For He established a testimony in Jacob and appointed a law in Israel, which He commanded our fathers that they should teach them to their children, that the generation to come might know, *even* the children *yet* to be born, *that* they may arise and tell *them* to their children, that they should put their confidence in God and not forget the works of God, but keep His commandments, and not be like their fathers, a stubborn and rebellious generation, a generation that did not prepare its heart and whose spirit was not faithful to God.

2 Timothy 1:5 For I am mindful of the sincere faith within you, which first dwelt in your grandmother Lois and your mother Eunice, and I am sure that it is in you as well.

From the time when God gave His covenant to Abraham, mankind was given the duty to teach their children to do righteousness and justice in order to fulfill the covenant (Gen 18:18-19). Through the transmission of faith, the covenant can be passed down to godly descendants generation after generation without interruption (Mal 2:15). This command to transmit the faith is a duty given not only to Abraham, but to all Christians today who seek and wait for the Lord's return.

It is our duty to teach our children and their children about all the works of God's administration in the history of redemption. We must do this so that they can discern the times and that God's covenant that we have inherited may not depart from "[our] mouth nor from the mouth of [our] offspring, nor from the mouth of [our] offspring's offspring" (Isa 59:21). Continuing the lineage of faith is our great mission in fulfilling God's administration in the history of redemption.

God rewards those who keep His covenant and His testimonies with lovingkindness and truth (Ps 25:10). When we are faithful in obeying God's Word and keeping the covenant, God will make us His own possession among the nations. God promises in Exodus 19:5, "Now then, if you will indeed obey My voice and keep My covenant, then you shall be My own possession among all the peoples, for all the earth is Mine." The word *possession* in the verse is סְגֻלָּה (*segullâ*), which also means "treasured possession" or "valued personal property." Therefore, God will have special affection and guard us in order to fulfill His administration in the history of redemption.

2. The Love of God Who Remembers the Covenant

The genealogy of Jesus Christ records not only the people of great faith, but contains many people who walked the path of disobedience and wickedness. It is evident that Satan is giving all his forces of evil to obstruct the way of Jesus Christ's coming. Satan ceaselessly tempted and tried the covenanted descendants, who were to continue the lineage of Jesus Christ, causing them to forsake God.

Although the lineage of faith seemed as though it was at the verge of getting cut off, it continued all the way to Jesus Christ because of the fervent love of God who remembered the eternal covenant. The love of God who remembers the covenant is the driving power that fulfills the administration of redemptive history and the unbreakable cord that holds together the lineage of faith. It is the love of God who remembers the covenant that saved the Israelites from the slavery in Egypt (Exod 2:24; 6:5). It is also the love of God who remembers the covenant that saved the Israelites from the sufferings of the Babylonian captivity. God said in Leviticus 26:42, "then I will remember My covenant with Jacob, and I will remember also My covenant with Isaac, and My covenant with Abraham as well, and I will remember the land." God does not completely obliterate His people because of the unbreakable covenant (Lev 26:44). Psalm 106:45-46 states, "And He remembered His covenant for their sake, and relented according to the greatness of His lovingkindness. He also made them *objects* of compassion in the presence of all the captors." In other words, God's work of saving us from Satan, our enemy, is accomplished through His love in remembering the eternal covenant (Luke 1:71-73).

Abraham and David stand at the center of God's covenantal love. That is why the genealogy of Jesus Christ begins with the statement, "The record of the genealogy of Jesus the Messiah, the son of David, the son of Abraham" (Matt 1:1).

God remembered the covenant He had established with Abraham and helped the Israelites. By remembering His covenant with Abraham, God took notice of the sons of Israel and led them out of Egypt (Exod 2:24-25). God gave the Israelites the land of Canaan for He remembered the covenant with Abraham—the word which He commanded to a thousand generations (Ps 105:8-11). Through the ten plagues, God brought the Israelites out of Egypt (Ps 105:26-38), led them by the pillars of cloud and fire, fed them with manna and quails, and made rivers with water from a rock (Ps 105:39-40). God performed all these miracles and works of His power for He "remembered His holy word with Abraham His servant" (Ps 105:42).

When Israel, after settling in Canaan, was divided into the southern kingdom of Judah and the northern kingdom of Israel and acted treacherously against God, He did not destroy them immediately. Rather, God restored Judah even after they were destroyed because He remembered His covenant that He would not put out the lamp forever.

God reminded His people three times of the promise that He would not let the lamp of David's house be put out. First, God made the promise as He prophesied the division of the kingdom after Solomon had sinned. In 1 Kings 11:36, God promised, "...that My servant David may have a lamp always before Me in Jerusalem."

Then, God mentioned the promise in the time of Abijam, king of Judah. Abijam had walked in all the sins of his father Rehoboam, and his heart was not wholly devoted to God like the heart of his father David. Therefore, he only reigned three years and died (1 Kgs 15:3). However, in 1 Kings 15:4, God said, "But for David's sake the LORD his God gave him a lamp in Jerusalem, to raise up his son after him and to establish Jerusalem."

Lastly, God reiterated the promise in the time of Jehoram, king of Judah. Jehoram was married to Ahab's daughter Athaliah and did evil in the sight of the Lord. Nevertheless, God did not destroy the house of David "since He had promised him to give a lamp to him through his sons always" (2 Kgs 8:19; 2 Chr 21:7). This took place not long after Jehoram had finished his joint reign with Jehoshaphat, which was about 155 years after God had established David as the lamp of the covenant in Israel (2 Sam 21:17). Although 155 years had passed, God remembered the covenant He made with David. This is a guarantee that God would never forget the covenant until it is completely fulfilled (Ps 132:17).

Every situation in which God reconfirmed to His people the promise that He would not let the lamp of David's house be put out was when their kings had sinned against God and did evil. No matter how much Satan interferes with evil schemes and people disobey God, God remembers the eternal covenant and keeps the lamp of the covenant burning ever brightly, so that God's administration in the history of redemption can continue to advance without ceasing.

We should always give thanks with all our hearts for God's love and His mysterious and profound providence for He ceaselessly moves forward in His administration of redemptive history until the realization of the Kingdom of God despite Satan's persistent attacks and fallen mankind's treacherousness.

3. The Eternally Unquenchable Lamp of God

Satan desperately tries every possible means to discontinue Jesus Christ's genealogy, and has caused people to fall and temporarily made the lamp of the covenant flicker. However, he cannot completely put out God's eternal lamp of the covenant. It is because God's mysterious and profound providence, which unfolds within the eternal covenant, will never be interrupted. God's administration in redemptive history has continued on toward its completion even in the midst of Satan's persistent attacks, and now the final day of completion will gloriously dawn in the appointed time.

We are called to be used as God's lamp of the covenant that fulfills the history of redemption through the mysterious and profound providence. The spirit of man is the Lord's lamp (Prov 20:27), and God's Word is our lamp (Prov 6:23; Ps 119:105).

Peter says in 2 Peter 1:19, "So we have the prophetic word *made* more sure, to which you do well to pay attention as to a lamp shining in a dark place, until the day dawns and the morning star arises in your hearts." There is a lamp for the people of God, a lamp shining in a dark place. That lamp is God's Word. When God's Word of the beginning, which eternally shines and illuminates our spirits, we can also become God's lamp (John 5:35).

God's Word is the Word of creation that created *ex nihilo* (out of nothing) in an instant (John 1:3, 10; Heb 11:3). God's Word is the Word of power that upholds all things in an instant (Heb 1:3). God's Word is the Word of judgment that burns up the old heavens and earth in an instant (2 Pet 3:7). God's Word is the Word of healing that delivers us from our destructions in an instant (Ps 107:20). God's Word is the Word that scolds death and raises the dead in an instant (John 11:43-44). God's Word is the Word of fullness that covers the entire world in an instant (Hab 2:14; Isa 11:9).

Therefore, when the lamp of the Word is kindled in one person, the fire of the lamp will spread through every tribe and nation. It will reach the ends of the vast universe which the human mind cannot even fathom.

The world has now fallen into the depth of darkness, where people are walking the path of lustfulness, disobedience, and rebelliousness as in the times of Sodom and Gomorrah. Mankind is groaning under the violent waves of sin. Souls are fainting away in the wind of sinfulness and their lamps are about to be put out.

God is the only One who can let the lamp of our spirit burn brighter (2 Sam 22:29; Ps 18:28). Only Jesus Christ, who is the Word of the beginning and the Light of men, can brighten the light of our lamp (John 1:1-4). By putting complete trust in God, our lamp can burn brightly again even if it had dwindled down to the point of being extinguished.

In order to guard His administration of redemptive history from Satan's strong interference, God established His lamp in every period. During the time when the theocracy of Israel was threatened because of its first king Saul's disobedience, God established David as His lamp (2 Sam 21:17).

John the Baptist was also God's lamp sent to testify of Jesus Christ, who came as the fulfiller of all covenants made in the Old Testament. John 5:35 states, "He was the lamp that was burning and was shining...."

The Apostle Paul was chosen as an instrument for the Gentiles (Acts 9:15), and he did not consider his life of any account as dear to himself in finishing his ministry of testifying of the gospel of God's grace (Acts 20:24). God's Word is the light and the lamp (Ps 119:105; Jer 23:29); and the Apostle Paul, who had given his life in testifying of God's Word, was God's lamp that shined brightly upon the world during his time.

The cross of Jesus Christ is God's lamp for it is the fulfillment and climax of all covenants for the salvation of God's people. Sin, death, and darkness have all been destroyed on the cross, and the lamp of perfect salvation and eternal life burns brightly. Therefore, the church that has the cross of Jesus Christ is the lamp of God that illuminates the time of darkness (Rev 1:12-13, 20; 2:1).

A lamp is surely raised up high. It needs to be placed on a high place in order to give light and fulfill its role. Matthew 5:15 states, "...nor does anyone light a lamp and put it under a basket, but on the lampstand, and it gives light to all who are in the house" (Luke 8:16; 11:33). As the end of time draws closer, the churches and Christians whose lamp of the cross and the Word shines brightly will be lifted up high and used by the sovereign hands of God.

The entire universe is getting darker and darker. It is a sign that tells us that God's judgment is drawing nearer. God's judgment will reveal the truth and falsehood of mankind and every man will be judged according to his deeds.

> **Romans 2:6-9** Who will render to each person according to his deeds: to those who by perseverance in doing good seek for glory and honor and immortality, eternal life; but to those who are selfishly ambitious and do not obey the truth, but obey unrighteousness, wrath and indignation. There will be tribulation and distress for every soul of man who does evil, of the Jew first and also of the Greek.

Revelation 20:12-15 warn us that everyone is judged according to his deeds, and those whose names are not found written in the book of life will be thrown into the lake of fire, the second death. Now, what sort of people ought we to be (2 Pet 3:11)?

First, we must become the people whom God knows.
First Corinthians 8:3 states, "…but if anyone loves God, he is known by Him," and 2 Timothy 2:19 states, "…the LORD knows those who are His" (cf. Num 16:5). The people whom God knows are God's sheep (John 10:14), and they hear His voice and follow Him (John 10:27). They take refuge in God (Nah 1:7), and they are the ones who have washed their robes and made them white in the blood of the Lamb (Rev 7:13-14).

However, Jesus declared that those regarding whom God says, "I tell you, I do not know where you are from," will be cast out of God's kingdom, and there will be weeping and gnashing of teeth (Luke 13:27-29). Also in Matthew 7:23, Jesus said that the lawless about whom God declares, "I never knew you," will be cast out from the presence of the Lord (Matt 7:23).

Second, we must become the people who put our hope in God only (Ps 146:5).
Those whose hope is in God certainly do not trust in mortal man. We human beings are not eternal beings for our breath of life is in our nostrils and we cannot be esteemed (Isa 2:22). Our days are like a lengthened shadow, and we wither away like grass (Ps 102:3, 11). Man is like a mere breath, and his days are like a passing shadow (Ps 144:4). The path of

human life passes like a shadow when it lengthens and is shaken off like the locust (Ps 109:23). There is no salvation in mortal man (Ps 146:3), and deliverance by man is in vain (Ps 60:11; 108:12; cf. 1 Sam 14:6). When God takes away the breath from man, he would return to dust and all his thoughts perish (Job 10:9; 34:14-15; Ps 104:29; 146:4; Eccl 12:7).

Therefore, we must not trust in mortal man for blessed are those who put their hope in God eternal (Ps 118:8-9). Those who trust in mankind, make flesh their strength, and whose heart turns from the Lord will surely be cursed (Jer 17:5).

Third, we must live in holy conduct and godliness, without any deceit (2 Pet 3:11-12).

Enoch, the seventh generation from Adam, prophesied that the Lord would come with many thousands of His holy ones to execute judgment and convict all the ungodly of all their ungodly deeds and ungodly things that sinners have spoken against Him (Jude 1:14-16). Therefore, we must refrain from ungodly lies.

It is regrettable to see some people, who claim to be experts in doctrines and heresies, make up lies and take words out of context to accuse faithful people and churches of sound doctrine as heretics, hunting down many innocent souls and killing them with their writings and rumors. Such act of slandering each other within the same denomination or group seldom happens in other religions.

We are living in a time of dusk in the history of salvation that requires us to have the heart of the Lord who is out to find one lost sheep. Thus, we must give our every effort and time to lead even one more person to the path of salvation (Matt 18:14; Luke 15:4; John 6:39). What would be the end of those who stumble and keep people from coming to God through lies and slander rather than leading them to God? There awaits great woes to those who do not enter in but shut off the kingdom of heaven from people (Matt 23:13). Revelation 21:8 states that all liars will take part in the lake that burns with fire and brimstone, which is the second death. Revelation 22:15 also sternly states that everyone who loves and practices lying will be outside the city.

We are sojourners in this world (1 Chr 29:15; 1 Pet 2:11). Life passes by like the silhouette of the setting sun and everyone inevitably has to stand before God's judgment throne once. There, the truth of their past life will all be revealed. Therefore, we must listen solely to God's Word and obey. We need to lay aside falsehood and ungodly deeds of darkness (Rom 13:12) and illumine our spirit and soul brightly with the light of God's Word as the five prudent virgins had prepared the oil and lit up their lamps (Matt 25:1-13; Prov 20:27; Ps 119:105). Then, the world will overflow with peace like a river and righteousness like the waves of the sea (Isa 48:17-18).

As God said, "…at evening time there will be light" (Zech 14:7), He will shine the powerful light of the Word brighter as the world becomes darker. And the day when the Lord returns as the lamp Himself (Rev 21:23), the darkness will disappear completely and only the glory of God will fill the world that He has created.

I sincerely hope that we may look forward to the glorious day that God will bring and fully dedicate all that we have to Jesus Christ, who is the true treasure in the entire universe (2 Cor 4:7; Col 2:2-3). Hallelujah!

עמלק

מדבר צין הוא קדש

ים המלח

עיר כרמל

שבט יהודה

שבט שמעון

שבט בנימין

מדבר סיני

מדבר פארן

מדבר שור

ארץ פלשתים

קדש ברנע

באר שבע

אשקלון

אלכסנדרי

ארץ נשן

פתם

רעמסס

בני יעקן

לוח המסעות במדבר
אשר על פי הסעו ועל פי חנו

כט' הר הגדגד	טו' רתמה	א' רעמסס
ל' יטבתה	טז' רמן פרץ	ב' סכת
לא' עברנה	יז' לבנה	ג' אתם
לב' עציון גבר	יח' רסה	ד' פי החירת
לג' מדבר צין	יט' קהלתה	ה' מרה
לד' הר ההר	כ' הר ספר	ו' אילם
לה' צלמנה	כא' חרדה	ז' ים סוף
לו' פונן	כב' מקהלת	ח' מדבר סין
לז' אבת	כג' תחת	ט' דפקה
לח' דיבן גד	כד' תרח	י' אלוש
לט' עלמן דבלתים	כה' מתקה	יא' רפידים
מ' הרי עברים	כו' חשמנה	יב' מדבר סיני
מא' מסרות	כז' מסרות	יג' קברת התאוה
מב' חצרת	כח' בני יעקן	יד' חצרת

Commentaries

Dr. Yong-kuk Wone

Professor Emeritus at Anyang University
Honorary Chairman of the Korean Archaeological Society

In 2009, which marks the 500th year of John Calvin's birth, the Protestant Churches worldwide (Korea included), started actively carrying out a movement toward purification and revival of the Protestant Church through commemoration ceremonies and studies on Calvinism.

The work of Calvin, who left the greatest legacy in church history, is regarded as follows: "Through Calvin, reformation in Geneva transcended time and space and became the propelling force that kindled spiritual revival throughout Europe, England, and America. From Luther and Augustine, he acquired a vision on God's grace that saves sinners with His absolute sovereignty. This vision stirred up not only pioneering missionaries, such as William Carey, but also great leaders like Richard Baxter, John Bunyan, George Whitefield, Jonathan Edwards, Charles Spurgeon, and Martin Lloyd-Jones into flame" (Jung-ho Oh, et al, *Calvin and Church in Korea*, Seoul: Life Book, 2009. 16-17). Being published in times like this, Rev. Abraham Park's History of Redemption series in the course of the Calvinistic tradition is carrying out a tremendous work of beaming forth a new blaze of spiritual revival across the world.

Rev. Abraham Park's fourth book, *God's Profound and Mysterious Providence*, together with the other volumes in the series, *The Genesis Genealogies, The Covenant of the Torch*, and *The Unquenchable Lamp of the Covenant*, unravels redemptive history, using only the Bible from the beginning to the end of the book. Such work is a remarkable accomplishment that would be impossible without a full grasp of the Old and New Testaments.

In past years, Rev. Abraham Park has lived through difficult years in Korea, during which he was afflicted beyond what any human strength could bear. Yet, he silently continued on with this amazing work of writing even during this time of agony. The author is now well beyond 80 years of age, and his work has finally reached its consummation through the History of Redemption series. Such splendid accomplishment is indeed a fruition of the author's precious and blessed life; it is a result of his willingness to bring a beautiful closure to his life. I believe that this book is the sweet rain of blessing given to the Korean Church, which is stricken by the famine of the Word.

The author's literary skills are superb, and his profound spiritual insight heightens the spiritual beauty of this book. I have personally authored over 40 books until now. Beginning with *Moses' Pentateuch*, I have authored *The Christology of the Pentateuch, The Dictionary of Biblical Archaeology, The Up-to-Date New Testament Archaeology, Commentary on Genesis,* and *Commentary on Psalms*. I have recently begun a commentary on the New Testament and published a commentary on the book of Jude.

However, as I read the author's book, I discovered that he was on a completely different level than I was. If my writing is a scholarly study, then the author's writing contained in this book is a profound spiritual study that penetrates through the entire Bible. He possesses this inexplicable ability to disclose the enriched treasures hidden in the Bible in light of Christology. And the power of his words is like the forceful spewing eruptions of an active volcano.

This fourth book unfolds the second period in the genealogy of Jesus Christ. The author uses Jesus Christ's genealogy to trace back and illumine the history of the Old Testament. Such undertaking originates from his spiritual insight that holds Jesus Christ's genealogy as the condensation of the entire Old Testament.

The most remarkable feature of this particular volume is the explanation about the omitted generations in the genealogy of Jesus Christ. As we read Matthew 1:4-5, which says, "Ram begot Amminadab, Amminadab begot Nahshon, and Nahshon begot Salmon. Salmon begot Boaz by Rahab. . .," we often thought that Ram's biological son was Amminadab and Salmon's biological son was Boaz. However, the author elucidates that there was a gap of hundreds of years in history among these figures and successfully presents the evidences from the Bible. Surely, this is an unprecedented achievement that no other theologian in the world has been able to undertake to this day. The author also clearly explains the omissions of the three kings between Joram and Uzziah.

What is the problem in Korea's pulpits and theological society today? It is that they are gradually drifting away from the Word of God. Numerous preachers are presenting their sermons in flowery words, charismatic humor and embellished speeches; but great indignation overwhelms us as we find sermons without Jesus Christ and preaching irrelevant to God's Word. At a time like this, Rev. Abraham Park's work clearly directs the churches and theological societies of this world to the path they must take.

This book by Rev. Abraham Park lifts up its voice that the only way of survival for Korea's church and theological society is "by scripture alone," or "by the Word of God alone (*Sola Scriptura*)," the very plea for which the Protestant Reformers have fought.

In today's spiritually dim generation, I heartily recommend Rev. Abraham Park's latest book for I am fully assured that it will light up the darkness as a torch of God's profound providence.

Yong-kuk Wone

Notes

1. Abraham Park, *The Unquenchable Lamp of the Covenant: The First Fourteen Generations in the Genealogy of Jesus Christ* (Singapore: Periplus, 2010), 35.

2. Ibid, 285-286.

3. D. J. Wiseman, *Chronicles of Chaldean Kings* (London: The Trustees of the British Museum, 1956), 33.

4. The Davidic kingdom used the accession year dating method. The Bible records the duration of David's reign in Hebron as "seven years" or "seven years and six months." Why are there two different accounts of the duration? First Kings 2:11 and 1 Chronicles 29:27 considered David's accession year separately and recorded "seven years," but 2 Samuel 5:5 and 1 Chronicles 3:4 included the time he reigned within the accession year and recorded, "seven years and six months." This is another proof that the accession year dating method was used during the time of David and a clue that the southern kingdom of Judah continued to follow David's reign and used the accession year dating method.

5. Edwin R. Thiele, *The Mysterious Numbers of the Hebrew Kings* (Grand Rapids: Kregel, 1983), 56-60.

6. Comparing the chronology and years of Israel with the history of the Assyrian king Shalmaneser III reveals that Ahab died in the 6th regnal year of Shalmaneser III, and it was in his 18th year that Jehu became king. Twelve years had passed since the death of Ahab until Jehu was enthroned, but the calculation of Ahaziah's 2-year reign and Joram's 12-year reign can fit in only when the non-accession year dating method is used. This is evidence that Israel used the non-accession year dating method even during the time of Jehu [J. I. Packer, M. C. Tenney, and W. White Jr., *The World of the Old Testament* (Nashville: Thomas Nelson Inc., 1982), 37)].

7. R. K. Harrison, *Introduction to the Old Testament* (Grand Rapids, MI: Hendrickson Publishers, Inc., 2004), 181.

8. From the month of Kislev (9th month, Neh 1:1) in Artaxerxes' 20th year four month had passed and it was the month of Nisan (1st month). However, Nehemiah does not call this point in time Artaxerxes' 21st year of reign but the 20th (Neh 2:1). This is because Nehemiah is following Judah's method of reckoning the regnal year from the month of Tishri (7th month). [F. Charles Fensham, *The Books of Ezra and Nehemiah* (Grand Rapids, MI: Eerdmans, 1983), 150.]

9. Edwin R. Thiele, 111.

10. Abraham Park, *The Unquenchable Lamp of the Covenant*, Excursus 4.

11. Ibid.

12. First Kings 4:26 indicates that Solomon possessed "40,000" stalls whereas 2 Chronicles 9:25 records the number at "4,000." However, seeing that the number of horsemen in his service were 12,000, it seems that 4,000 stalls as recorded by 2 Chronicles 9:25 is the more plausible figure because it is unlikely that there would be more stalls than horsemen. Furthermore, it is conjectured that the number "40,000" as recorded in 1 Kings 4:26 was an error committed in the transcription process.

13. Carl Friedrich Keil and Franz Delitzsch, *Commentary on the Old Testament, vol.3*, (Peabody, MA: Hendrickson, 2002), 40-41.

14. James Swanson, *Dictionary of Biblical Languages with Semantic Domains: Hebrew (Old Testament)* (electronic ed.; Oak Harbor: Logos Research Systems, Inc., 1997), DBLH 3215. Also, Warren Baker, *The Complete Word Study Dictionary: Old Testament* (Chattanooga, TN: AMG Publishers, 2003, c2002), 401.

15. First Kings 7:15 records the length as 18 cubits whereas 2 Chronicles 3:15 states it as 35 cubits. There are some opinions that this was an error on the transcriber who wrote "35" (לה) instead of "18" (יח), i.e., C. F. Keil & F. Delitzsch, *Commentary on the Old Testament, vol. 3* (Peabody, MA: Hendrickson, 2002), 70.

E. L. Curtis asserts that the Chronicler misread 1 Kings 7:15 which stated, "eighteen cubits was the height of one pillar, and a line of twelve cubits measured the circumference of both." Curtis posits that the Chronicler mistook 12 cubits to be the height, thus he interpreted the height to be 18+12=30 cubits. In that case, the capital on top of the pillar is 5 cubits high, making the combined height 35 cubits. E. L. Curtis & A. A. Madsen, *The Books of Chronicles, Critical and Exegetical Commentary* (Edinburgh: T & T Clark, 1976), 328-329.

16. Paul Lawrence, *The Lion Atlas of Bible History* (Oxford: Lion Hudson Plc., 2006), 75.

17. Paul R. House, *1, 2 Kings* (New American Commentary, vol. 8; Nashville: Broadman & Holman Publishers, 2001), 137.

18. James Strong, *The Exhaustive Concordance of the Bible: Showing Every Word of the Text of the Common English Version of the Canonical Books, and Every Occurrence of Each Word in Regular Order.*, electronic ed, H3320 (Ontario: Woodside Bible Fellowship, 1996).

19. The law stipulates requisite offerings which God had commanded for the ordination of the priests from the sons of Aaron of the tribe of Levi (Exod 29:1-37; Lev 8:1-36). However, Jeroboam totally disregarded such stipulations and gave away the priesthood to anyone who would bring a young bull and seven rams (2 Chr 13:9). The offering that God had stipulated are one young bull, two rams without blemish (Exod 29:1; Lev 8:2), unleavened bread made of fine wheat flour (Exod 29:2), unleavened cakes mixed with oil made of fine wheat flour (Exod 29:2), and unleavened wafers spread with oil also made of fine wheat flour (Exod 29:2). The young bull is to be offered as a sin offering (Lev 8:14-17). One of the two rams is to be offered as a burnt offering (Lev 8:18-21) whereas the other ram is the ram of ordination (Lev 8:22-29). Moreover, a bull was offered as a sin offering everyday during the 7-day ordination ceremony. Atonement was also made for the altar everyday and it was anointed and consecrated (Exod 29:35-37).

20. James Strong, H6817.

21. James Strong, H4322.

22. Stelman Smith and Judson Cornwall, *The Exhaustive Dictionary of Bible Names* (North Brunswick, NJ: Bridge-Logos, 1998), 174.

23. Abraham Park, *The Unquenchable Lamp of the Covenant*, Excursus 4.

24. James Strong, H4601.

25. The thirty fifth year of Asa's reign actually refers to his fifteenth regnal year (Please refer to endnote number 260). First Chronicles 15:19 states, "And there was no more war until the thirty-fifth year [*fifteenth year*] of Asa's reign." In other words, this passage is telling us that there had been no war until the fifteenth year of Asa's reign. However, in the sixteenth year, Baasha invaded the southern kingdom of Judah and fortified Ramah in order to prevent the people of the northern kingdom of Israel from travelling freely to and from Judah. Asa, who was threatened by all this, utilized human-centered methods to frustrate Baasha's plan.

26. The phrase "the thirty-sixth year of Asa's reign" is not an actual reference to Asa's regnal years. This is also the case for the phrase "the thirty-fifth year of Asa's reign." Baasha

became king in the third year of Asa's reign (1 Kgs 15:28, 33) and reigned for twenty four years and died. His son Elah succeeded him as king in Asa's twenty-sixth year (1 Kgs 16:8). Then it follows that Baasha would have already been dead in the thirty-sixth year of Asa's reign; therefore, it is impossible to say that Asa and Baasha fought a war against each other in that year.

Moreover, just from the literary context we can see that Baasha's invasion of Asa's kingdom follows on the heels of Asa's religious reformation in his fifteenth year (2 Chr 15:8-15). Therefore, contextual evidence shows that this incident took place in Asa's sixteenth year and not his thirty-sixth year. Baasha attacked King Asa because when Asa instituted a religious reformation, many people from the northern kingdom of Israel defected to Asa for they saw that God was with him (2 Chr 15:9). Thus, in order to prevent the people from the northern kingdom to have any further contact with King Asa, Baasha went up to strike Judah and built up Ramah (2 Chr 16:1).

The second half of 2 Chronicles 16:1 tells us that the specific purpose of this war was "to prevent anyone from going out or coming in to Asa king of Judah." Since the people of the northern kingdom of Israel started to travel to Judah right after Asa instituted the religious reformation in his fifteenth year, Baasha immediately went up to wage a war against Asa in his sixteenth year of reign.

There are two views asserting that Asa's thirty-sixth year is actually the sixteenth. The first view posits that the "thirty six years" is the time that has passed since the Unified Kingdom had divided (930 BC) and Rehoboam became king in the southern kingdom of Judah. Since Rehoboam reigned for seventeen years and his son Abijam for three, "the thirty-sixth year" would equate to King Asa's sixteenth year [36-(17+3)].

The second view maintains that the difference in the years was caused by errors that the Hebrew scribes committed in transcribing the text. In the Hebrew alphabet, the first letter of the word "thirty" is "lamed (l)" which looks similar to a "yodh (y)" which is the first letter of the word "ten." Due to the similarity of these letters, it is said that scribes had often interchanged the two letters by mistake. Therefore, it is possible that the numbers "thirty five" and "thirty six" can be mistakenly written out as "fifteen" and "sixteen."

As such, the above two views both agree that Asa's "thirty-fifth year" (2 Chr 15:19) is actually Asa's fifteenth year and Asa's "thirty-sixth year" (2 Chr 16:1) is actually his sixteenth. Thus, we can conclude that Baasha actually came to attack the southern kingdom of Judah in the sixteenth year of Asa's reign (1 Kgs 15:16-22; 2 Chr 16:1-10).

In the above mentioned battle against Baasha, King Asa did not rely on God but sought the help of King Ben-hadad of Aram. Asa brought out silver and gold from the treasuries of the house of the LORD and the king's house and sent them to the king of Aram who lived in Damascus (2 Chr 16:2-4). Because he did this, Asa was reproached by Hanani the seer who told him "from now on you will surely have wars" (2 Chr 16:7-9). There was war between Asa and Baasha "all their days" just as Hanani had prophesied (1 Kgs 15:16, 32). Wars between the two kingdoms continued for about ten years from Asa's sixteenth year of reign (accession year method) until the death of Baasha in the twenty-seventh year of Asa's reign (accession year method).

27. Wilhelm Gesenius and Samuel Prideaux Tregelles, *Gesenius' Hebrew and Chaldee Lexicon to the Old Testament Scriptures* (Translation of the author's Lexicon manuale Hebraicum et Chaldaicum in Veteris Testamenti libros, a Latin version of the work first published in 1810-1812 under title: Hebräisch-deutsches Handwörterbuch des Alten Testaments; Includes index; Bellingham, WA: Logos Research Systems, Inc, 2003), 640.

28. All of these definitions are taken from Enhanced Strong's Lexicon except for "Amasiah"

29. Young-yup Cho, *Ecclesiology* (Seoul: Mizpah Books, 2001), 270. (Korean)

30. James Strong, H2266.

31. James Strong, H6555.

32. James Strong, H995.

33. Accordingly, when a remarkable day was come, and a general festival was to be celebrated, he put on the holy garment, and went into the temple to offer incense to God upon the golden altar, (224) which he was prohibited to do by Azariah the high priest, who had fourscore priests with him, and who told him that it was not lawful for him to offer sacrifice, and that "none besides the posterity of Aaron were permitted so to do." And when they cried out, that he must go out of the temple, and not transgress against God, he was wroth at them, and threatened to kill them, unless they would hold their peace. (225) In the meantime, a great earthquake shook the ground,* and a rent was made in the temple, and the bright rays of the sun shone through it, and fell upon the king's face, insomuch that the leprosy seized upon him immediately; and before the city, at a place called Eroge, half the mountain broke off from the rest on the west, and rolled itself four furlongs, and stood still at the east mountain, till the roads, as well as the king's gardens, were spoiled by the obstruction. [Flavius Josephus and William Whiston, *The Works of Josephus : Complete and Unabridged* (Includes index.;Peabody: Hendrickson, 1996, c1987), Ant 9.223-225.]

*This account of an earthquake at Jerusalem, at the very same time when Uzziah usurped the priest's office, and went into the sanctuary to burn incense, and of the consequences of the earthquake, is entirely wanting in our other copies, though it be exceeding like to a prophecy of Jeremiah, now in Zech. 14:4–5; in which prophecy mention is made of "fleeing from that earthquake, as they fled from this earthquake in the days of Uzziah, king of Judah;" so that there seems to have been some considerable resemblance between these historical and prophetical earthquakes.

34. Assyria overcame a drawn out period of decline and extended their borders to the Mediterranean Sea. More specifically, Tiglath-pileser III (745-727 BC) went out on an expedition between 743-738 BC in order to take control of the nations that were wielding influence in the north and the west. As a result, many nations were annexed by the Assyrians. [Hershel Shanks, Ancient Israel…]. In this expedition, he proposed unprecedented financial terms and thus drove his vassal states into a state of terror. Consequently, many nations were annexed to the Assyrians. Moreover, the citizens of the conquered regions were banished to areas dictated by the Assyrian empire [Israel Finkenstein and Neil Asher Silberman, …].

35. James Strong, H270.

36. Israel Finkelstein & Neil Asher Silberman, …

37. Thomas V. Brisco, *Bible Atlas* (Nashville, Tenn.: Holman Reference, 1998), 133.

38. "…and the water flowed from the spring toward the reservoir for 1200 cubits, and the height of the rock above the heads of the quarrymen was 100 cubits" [Walter A. Elwell and Barry J. Beitzel, *Baker Encyclopedia of the Bible* (Map on lining papers.; Grand Rapids, MI: Baker Book House, 1988), 1964.]

39. Merriam-Webster Inc., *Merriam-Webster's Collegiate Dictionary*. (Includes index; Eleventh ed.; Springfield, MA: Merriam-Webster, Inc., 2003).

40. A world renowned biblical archaeologist, Dr. Yong-kuk Wone stated in his commentary, "Reverend Park has clearly revealed through biblical evidence that hundreds of years have been omitted from the genealogy. In fact, this could be called a world class achievement which no other theologian has been able to uncover until now."

41. Abraham Park, *The Unquenchable Lamp of the Covenant: The First Fourteen Generations in the Genealogy of Jesus Christ* (Singapore: Periplus, 2010), 71.

42. In the Hebrew text of Ruth 4:20 and 1 Chronicles 2:11, Salmon who married Rahab appears as Salma.

וְנַחְשׁוֹן הוֹלִיד אֶת־שַׁלְמָא וְשַׂלְמָא הוֹלִיד אֶת־בֹּעַז

The name *Salmon* (שַׂלְמוֹן) means "mantel" or "garment," and the name *Salma* (שַׂלְמָא) means "strength" or "firmness."

43. Abraham Park, *The Unquenchable Lamp of the Covenant*, 310.

44. When Jehoram father of Ahaziah died, he was 39 years old (2 Kgs 8:17). With 2 Kgs 8:26 and GL MT, forty-two years; Par, twenty; OL, sixteen. MT cannot be correct: Ahaziah would have been two years older than his father (21:5, 20). MT could be derived either from a conflation of G and 2 Kgs 8:26 (20 + 22 = 42) in an effort to preserve both traditions (Myers, 125), or a copyist could have been confused by ערבים at the end of a line in the preceding verse (Rudolph, 268), or a numerical notation could have been misread, perhaps a confusion of ך and ם to denote twenty and forty respectively. (Raymond B. Dillard, vol. 15, *Word Biblical Commentary: 2 Chronicles*, (Word Biblical Commentary; Dallas: Word, Incorporated, 2002], 171).

45. One talent of silver is equivalent to 6,000 drachmas. One drachma was one day's wage for a laborer. Considering one day's average wage is 50 USD today, one talent of silver would be equivalent to about 300,000 USD and 100 talents of silver would be equivalent to an enormous amount of about 30,000,000 USD.

46. Anson F. Rainey, R. Steven Notley, *Carta's New Century Handbook and Atlas of the Bible* (Jerusalem: Carta, 2007), 122.

47. Wilhelm Gesenius and Samuel Prideaux Tregelles, *Gesenius' Hebrew and Chaldee Lexicon to the Old Testament Scriptures*, 94 (Bellingham, WA: Logos Research Systems, Inc, 2003).

48. Due to recent discoveries in Ugaritic etymology, what has traditionally been considered a hithpael form of שָׁחָה (*šāḥâ*) is now being considered by some to be a modified form of the root חָוָה (*ḥāwâ*: to bow down, to worship). See Willem VanGemeren, vol. 2, *New International Dictionary of Old Testament Theology & Exegesis*, (Grand Rapids, MI: Zondervan Publishing House, 1998), 42.

49. M.G. Easton, *Easton's Bible Dictionary* (Oak Harbor, WA: Logos Research Systems, Inc., 1996). Easton's Bible Dictionary states, "Heb. sebakhah, the latticed balustrade before a window or balcony (2 Kings 1:2). The lattice window is frequently used in Eastern countries." It is clear that Easton views the "lattice" of 2 Kgs 1:2 as a "latticed balustrade."

50. Paul R. House, *1, 2 Kings*, (New American Commentary, vol. 8; Nashville: Broadman & Holman Publishers, 2001), 278.

Robert Jamieson, A. R. Fausset, A. R. Fausset et al., *A Commentary, Critical and Explanatory, on the Old and New Testaments*, 2 Kgs 6:25 (Oak Harbor, WA, 1997).

Matthew Henry, *Matthew Henry's Commentary on the Whole Bible: Complete and Unabridged in One Volume*, 2 Kgs 6:24–33 (Peabody: Hendrickson, 1996).

John F. Walvoord, Roy B. Zuck and Dallas Theological Seminary, *The Bible Knowledge Commentary: An Exposition of the Scriptures*, 2 Kgs 6:24–25 (Wheaton, IL: Victor Books, 1983).

51. The New Living Translation has translated this passage as follows: "Finally, Jehoahaz's army was reduced to 50 charioteers, 10 chariots, and 10,000 foot soldiers. The king of Aram had killed the others, trampling them like dust under his feet."

52. Tirzah is located about 7 km northeast of Shechem along an important trade route and is situated near a plentiful spring. It has been a central city in Israel for a long time. In Hebrew the name of the city is *tirṣâ* (הִצְרְתִּ) which means "a delight." Tirzah was Jeroboam's place of residence (1 Kgs 14:17) and Baasha "became king over all Israel at Tirzah" (1 Kgs 15:33). Baasha's son Elah was at Tirzah drinking himself drunk at the house of Arza who was over the king's household. It was here that Zimri assassinated him (1 Kgs 16:9-10). Then, Zimri also reigned seven days at Tirzah (1 Kgs 16:15). After having reigned at Tirzah for six years (1 Kgs 16:23), Omri moved the capital of the northern kingdom of Israel to Samaria (1 Kgs 16:24).

53. R. Laird Harris, Gleason Leonard Archer and Bruce K. Waltke, *Theological Wordbook of the Old Testament*, electronic ed., 933 (Chicago: Moody Press, 1999).

54. T. R. Hobbs, *Word Biblical Commentary: 2 Kings*, (Word Biblical Commentary, vol. 13; Dallas: Word, Incorporated, 2002), 203.

55. Anson F. Rainey & R. Steven Notley, *The Sacred Bridge* (Jerusalem: Carta, 2006), 232-233.

Index

order one's ways before God 161

pails 101, 103
palace 7, 73, 76, 87, 97, 105, 107, 109, 119, 122, 124, 149, 159, 169, 182, 194, 214, 256, 264, 281, 316
Passover 51, 56, 64, 75, 77, 176, 177, 178, 201, 347
Pekah 59, 60, 63, 74, 75, 152, 157, 162, 163, 164, 165, 166, 167, 168, 170, 235, 304, 308, 309, 310, 311-13
Pekahiah 60, 63, 152, 157, 163, 235, 308-10
period of the judges 210, 211
plan 22, 23, 27, 33, 93, 94, 95, 104, 111, 221, 257
plans 34, 93, 94, 95, 97, 104, 112, 121, 168, 276
porch 93, 98, 175
position as queen mother (Maacah's) 135
praise 35, 36, 37, 106, 145, 176, 223, 255
Preservation 33
pride 80, 122, 136, 155, 231, 250, 313
priesthood 85, 241, 242, 342
prophecy 73, 77, 85, 110, 141, 169, 181, 184, 189, 200, 218, 240, 244, 248, 264, 266, 269, 278, 279, 281, 282, 291, 299, 300, 326
providence 21, 27, 33-34, 36, 37, 49, 50, 61, 66, 97, 111, 142, 167, 170, 204, 208, 221, 267, 278, 319, 323, 331
Psalm 33:11, 34; 115:4-7, 199; 136 34, 35, 36

Ramah 135, 251, 342, 343, 350
Ramoth-gilead 141, 144, 218, 266, 273, 279, 281
rebuilding (of the House of God) 224
redemption 15, 21, 22, 23, 26, 33, 34, 35, 36, 45, 50,
61, 95, 96, 101, 176, 205, 208, 211, 215, 221, 319, 323, 328, 330, 331
redemptive history 15, 21-22, 24, 26-27, 30, 33, 46, 47, 48, 49, 95, 96, 98, 105, 111, 203, 204, 205, 213, 215, 317, 319, 323, 327, 329, 331, 332
regencies 50, 52, 57, 58
regnal chronology 6, 50, 51, 55, 60
Rehoboam 42, 45, 54, 57, 63, 71, 82, 110, 118-25, 135, 161, 239, 240, 246, 330
religious reformation 56, 77, 134, 135, 136, 140, 143, 144, 175, 178, 179, 197, 198, 283
remedy 325
remnants 204, 350
repent 45, 81, 136, 149, 150, 151, 172, 189, 190, 191, 192, 204, 214, 242, 243, 245, 263, 264, 267, 271, 287, 296, 313, 316, 319, 326
roots of sin 191

salvation 15, 21, 22, 23, 26, 29, 31, 33, 34, 36, 49, 66, 75, 96, 101, 111, 144, 169, 171, 184, 196, 247, 278, 315, 325, 326, 332, 334
Samaria 60, 164, 167, 168, 188, 218, 259, 260, 263, 266, 270, 276, 277, 278, 282, 287, 292, 305, 309, 312, 313, 316, 319
sea of cast metal 101, 102
seed 205, 221, 222, 277
Sennacherib 75, 174, 182, 183, 184
set their hearts 122
Shallum 42, 63, 152, 157, 168, 196, 200, 235, 301-303
Shalmaneser V 315, 316
Shemaiah 43, 71, 119, 120, 124
Shimei 85, 86, 179
shovels 101, 103
Sinai covenant 27
slaughter 243, 254, 299

So 31, 53, 66, 79, 88, 90, 91, 94, 103, 104, 105, 112, 121, 133, 134, 145, 161, 171, 172, 173, 178, 194, 269, 275, 286, 315, 331
Solomon 42, 45-46, 48, 51, 52, 56, 63, 70, 71, 73, 75, 78, 79, 80, 82-111, 146, 178, 199, 212, 225, 237, 239, 240, 244, 294, 317, 325, 330; Solomon's daily provision 87; Solomon's temple 45, 56, 91-107; Solomon's transgressions 45, 107-111; Excursus 7; Solomon's wisdom 89, 91
some measure of deliverance 119, 124
son of Tabeel 168
sons of Seir 214, 230
sound of God 97
sounds of men 97
sovereign covenant 27
spiritual discernment 141, 142, 253
stands of bronze 101, 102
stars 35, 199, 350
stewardship 22-25
Stewardship of God's grace 23, 25
strengthened 45, 120, 121, 122, 154, 168, 225, 230
strengthening 74, 121, 140, 159, 171
strengthening the national defense 8, 74, 140, 159
structure of Solomon's Temple 97-101
studying the chronology 6, 48

tables for the bread of the Presence 100
temple 43, 45, 56, 64, 70, 73, 74, 75, 76, 77, 80, 88, 90, 91, 92, 93, 94, 95, 96, 97, 98, 99, 100, 101, 102, 103, 104, 105, 106, 107, 109, 112, 113, 114, 115, 116, 119, 122, 123, 136, 155, 158, 159, 169, 172, 175, 176, 179, 187, 190, 191, 197, 198, 199, 200, 225